1984

LIVING ISSUES IN ETHICS

RICHARD T. NOLAN
Mattatuck Community College

FRANK G. KIRKPATRICK
Trinity College

with

HAROLD H. TITUS

and

MORRIS T. KEETON

Wadsworth Publishing Company
Belmont, California
A Division of Wadsworth, Inc.

ABOUT THE AUTHORS

Richard T. Nolan earned a B.A. from Trinity College (Conn.), M. Div. from The Hartford Seminary Foundation, M.A. from Yale University, and Ph.D. from New York University. Editor of *The Diaconate Now* and coauthor of the 7th edition of *Living Issues in Philosophy*, he is Professor of Philosophy and Social Sciences at Mattatuck Community College, Waterbury, Connecticut.

Frank G. Kirkpatrick received a B.A. from Trinity College (Conn.), M.A. from Union Theological Seminary-Columbia University, and Ph.D. from Brown University. Author of journal essays in process thought, he is Associate Professor of Religion and Chairman of the Department at Trinity College, Hartford.

Harold H. Titus earned a B.A. from Acadia University, B.D. and Th.M. at Colgate-Rochester Divinity School, and Ph.D. from the University of Chicago. The founding author of the five editions of *Ethics for Today* and seven editions of *Living Issues in Philosophy* (and other works), he is Professor of Philosophy *Emeritus* at Denison University.

Morris T. Keeton received a B.A. and M.A. from Southern Methodist University and an M.A. and Ph.D. from Harvard University. Author of *Values Men Live By* and *Experiential Learning* and coauthor of the 5th edition of *Ethics For Today* (and other works), he taught for several years at Antioch College; currently he is President of the Council for the Advancement of Experiential Learning, Columbia, Maryland.

Photographs—By permission of Black Star: photos by Werner Wolff on pages 2 and 152; photo by Jean Shapiro on page 78; by permission of Magnum Photos: photo by Burk Uzzle on page 226.

Philosophy Editor: Kenneth King

Printed in the United States of America

1 2 3 4 5 6 7 8 9 10—86 85 84 83 82

Library of Congress Cataloging in Publication Data

Nolan, Richard T.
  Living issues in ethics.

  Includes bibliographies and index.
  1. Ethics. I. Kirkpatrick, Frank G. II. Title.
BJ1012.N64   170   81-21869
ISBN 0-534-01140-3   AACR2

Contents

iii

Preface

"New Rules in American Life: Searching for Self-Fulfillment in a World Turned Upside Down"[1] expresses well some of the feelings of many individuals living in the 1980s. We are on a search in which we are reluctant to affirm either all the old moral rules or all the new alternatives. With the conviction that part of education involves facing reality, colleges and universities are recognizing the necessity of providing formal reflection on living issues. One such institution recently claimed:

> An educated person is expected to have some understanding of, and experience in thinking about, moral and ethical problems. It may well be that the most significant quality in educated persons is the informed judgment which enables them to make discriminating moral choices.[2]

Readers of *Living Issues in Ethics* are invited to share in the reflections of four persons who, along with all instructors and students, are confronted with moral decision making. We have provided a book designed to raise some fundamental questions of ethics including a multitude of unresolved issues; the field of ethics will be opened especially to those students who can take only one course in the subject. We hope that our readers' imaginations will be stimulated to understand that morality is an inescapable part of their lives and that points of view other than their own deserve thoughtful consideration. We have written with the intention that students realize that fundamental questions of right and wrong, of human rights and conflicting obligations, are raised by many technical, social, psychological, and political situations. We trust that they will come to respect the need for coherence, consistency, and clarity in thinking about moral matters. And we hope that they will begin to understand and appreciate the reasoned differences both in ethical theory and moral alternatives. In short, we invite readers to be provoked, at an introductory level, toward "some understanding of, and experience in thinking about, moral and ethical problems" so that they will be better enabled to make discriminating choices.

In Part 1 we are concerned with ingredients in the search for a moral philos-

[1]Daniel Yankelovich's extended essay in *Psychology Today* (April 1981).
[2]"Harvard's Report on the 'Core Curriculum,'" in *The Chronicle of Higher Education* (March 6, 1978), p. 15.

ophy: the recognition of choices forced by living situations, some issues of ethical theory, and the historical context out of which we carry on our search today.

In Part 2 we consider who we are as individuals and issues of quality in our relations with ourselves and with others especially close to us.

Part 3 focuses upon certain personal and biological aspects of our lives as individuals: moral dilemmas in health and medical care as well as sexual ethics.

Issues raised by living in a social order will be discussed in Part 4: issues of politics, economics, individual liberties, social and ecological obligations, and the threat of war.

We move, therefore, from the theoretical and historical foundations of ethics in Part 1 to applied ethics in our lives personally and socially for the remainder of the book.

We have attempted to keep our theoretical and applied reflections readable and nontechnical. The legitimate, technical problems of the professional philosopher engaged in ethics are not the problems of students exploring for the first time ethics and morality. We have avoided the seemingly endless qualifying of each idea so prevalent in technical discussions as well as complex academic surgery, hopeful that the book's purposes will be carried out effectively for an introductory adventure.

The chapter reviews are designed to help students recall the general thrust of the chapters but are not substitutes for reading, pondering, and learning ideas emphasized by instructors. The suggested readings include reference works as well as some important studies in each chapter's topics.

Another feature is the book's adaptability. In the art of teaching, each instructor can accomplish the book's purposes, as well as modify or expand its goals, by selecting an order of reading different from the book's sequence, by omitting some chapters, and/or by assigning additional materials. Appreciating flexibility, we encourage instructors to adapt the text to their own styles.

The authors have not worked in isolation! We have built on the foundations laid by the five editions of *Ethics For Today*, first published in 1936. Ernest L. Rothschild was a chief guide for those editions and for this new textbook, a companion to *Living Issues in Philosophy*. Elaine S. Krause edited our writing, and Rachel Hockett took responsibility for leading the manuscript to production. Typists included Nancy Stack and Ann Wilson, who meticulously produced the drafts and final manuscript. We are grateful to Robert C. Pingpank for his assistance with the proofreading.

A great deal of writing on morality is designed to inspire readers toward a particular moral viewpoint on all matters, to seek behavioral changes in readers, and to be entertaining and comforting. Our invitation does not include these designs. We invite readers instead to consider a wide range of theoretical and practical issues and the moral alternatives which they evoke. Students may feel on occasion some frustration at the variety and complexity of moral decision making. But the result, we hope, will be a greater awareness of and sensitivity toward their own responsibility to find and develop a reasoned morality of their own in a world filled with *Living Issues in Ethics*.

Richard T. Nolan
Frank G. Kirkpatrick
with
Harold H. Titus
and
Morris T. Keeton

LIVING ISSUES IN ETHICS

PART 1
THE SEARCH FOR A MORAL PHILOSOPHY

1

Morality
in Our Lives

Man is that creature who must have some criterion of the good. No man can wish to jump out of this situation without presupposing it; that is, without first judging that it would be "good" to do so. This means that the true realist is the man who acknowledges the distinction between good and evil.*

MORAL DECISIONS AND PERSONAL LIFE

Life Forces Choices

All of us face, directly and indirectly, problems that persons did not meet in the past—problems not covered in traditional codes of morality, problems on which we have had little time to reflect. Even members of today's senior generation were not confronted in their youth by such moral issues as:

heart and organ transplants: From whom should organs be taken and to whom given?

artificial insemination: Does this process violate or enhance human sexuality's emotional aspect? What constitutes parenthood?

biological engineering to control heredity: To what extent should we shape future generations? What qualities are desirable in planned offspring? Should such controls be limited to nonhuman animals and plants?

use and control of outer space: Who should own or control what?

energy: How do we determine environmentally sound sources and uses of energy?

Other moral issues faced throughout history by countless generations have acquired new dimensions, and many persons are torn between traditional understandings and new interpretations. Some of these dilemmas are:

*Edmond La B. Cherbonnier, Hardness of Heart (Garden City, N.Y.: Doubleday, 1955), p. 28.

5

the extent of personal responsibility: Who is my neighbor—individuals on my street or persons now reached by jet in a matter of hours?

human sexuality: Should genital relations be only for reproduction by married people or for pleasure between any consenting individuals?

interpersonal relationships: What is a family—the nuclear model of husband, wife, and offspring or other models such as a group bound by a written contract? How should men relate to women, and women to men, in homes, in jobs, as friends, and in social settings?

medical concerns: Is population control in the hands of God or of humanity? Should the onset of death be left to nature, or may human beings hasten or postpone it?

social justice: Should unrestricted competition or some form of socialism lead eventually to economic justice?

Other, more-or-less routine choices fill our lives. You have chosen to read the words on this page, either as your acceptance of an assignment or for your own enrichment. The choice involved your sense of what is right and what is wrong to do.

Some choices that come before us are entirely new, some add new dimensions to familiar problems. Other choices are so routine that we sometimes do not recognize them as choices. The act of living forces many choices on us.

A Unique Period of History

Reflective persons in each age have commented on their own respective crises. During the first century B.C., the Roman orator Cicero lamented "O the times! O the manners!" In the nineteenth century Charles Dickens began *A Tale of Two Cities* in this way:

> It was the best of times, it was the worst of times, it was the age of wisdom, it was the age of foolishness, it was the epoch of belief, it was the epoch of incredulity, it was the season of Light, it was the season of Darkness, it was the spring of hope, it was the winter of despair, we had everything before us, we had nothing before us, we were all going to heaven, we were all going direct the other way.

When we hear the inevitable cries of moral decay in our own day, should we be concerned? Is there anything really new since Cicero, or do thinkers in each age see their own period as uniquely awful, confronted with horrendous changes? Sociologist Peter Berger has observed that the modern age has a unique aspect: Humanity has moved from fate to choice. [1]

---

[1] Peter L. Berger, *The Heretical Imperative* (Garden City, N.Y.: Doubleday-Anchor, 1979).

For many persons, especially in the United States, a way of life is no longer determined in advance. Society as a whole does not uphold a single view of life. Individuals are not limited to the ideas and life styles of their own kind. Opportunities of easy travel and communication and exposure to mass media confront us with a plurality of viewpoints on reality, truth, and values as they are actually lived.

No longer destined to a single way of life, we must choose among possibilities that range from the conventional to the previously unthinkable. Finding that the most authoritative institutions differ within and among themselves as to what is worthwhile and right, we are forced more and more to rely on our own judgments.

More than in any other period of history, our personal lives demand choices from us today. What is right and what is wrong, generally and specifically, must be decided by more persons than ever before. Each reader of these pages must make such decisions. Whether one views this period of history as an exciting opportunity or as a prelude to the downfall of Western civilization (or even the entire globe) is itself a choice.

THE SEARCH FOR VALUES

Choices and Values

Valuing occurs whenever one thing—a physical object, a way of acting, an idea or an ideal, a person—is preferred or chosen over another. We rate things as better or worse and act on these decisions. The issue is not whether we will have loyalties and ideals around which our lives are organized, but what kind they will be.

VALUES: THE POLESTAR OF EDUCATION

Values, we have argued, are experiences that are at once satisfying and fulfilling. The purpose of education is to make us creators and centers of value. Technological education does that indirectly by supplying us tools for the exploiting of nature. Liberal education on its intellectual side provides the values of understanding, which makes us at home in our world. Liberal education on its appreciative side makes us responsive to the best that has been said and painted and built and sung. Liberal education on its practical side puts the wind of emulation in our sails and gives direction to our voyage. Values are the stars by which education may and should steer its course.

From Brand Blanshard, "Values: The Polestar of Education," in *The*

Goals of Higher Education, ed., Willis Weatherford (Cambridge, Mass.: Harvard Univ. Press, 1960), p. 96.

Brand Blanshard (b. 1892) has taught philosophy at a number of schools and was professor of philosophy at Yale University for nearly two decades. He has written many articles and books, the latter including The Nature of Thought, Reason and Goodness, *and* Reason and Analysis.

Because almost every traditional value is under scrutiny and because each of us must make choices and preferences, thinking people frequently find themselves searching for answers. This quest is not just a classroom exercise; it has reached the most practical ranges of daily experiences. For example, the *U.S. News and World Report* included a report on the search by American adults for more satisfying values and patterns of life. The popular magazine *Psychology Today* devoted much of an issue to similar themes.[2]

This is not to imply that all traditional values have been disregarded. Quite the contrary: Large numbers of people continue to rally around conservative values, especially as they are taught and reinforced by religious institutions. A Sunday morning spent surveying the ideals presented on most religious television programming will reveal this traditional perspective. Customary values of family life, the role of women, the purpose of sexuality, and others are restated emphatically, and these ideals are applied to new issues. The certainty and clarity these religious spokesmen project are attractive to many persons.

Others are not persuaded that traditional values have reached their full maturity or that all familiar values are still adequate. It is this large group whose search presents them most sharply with the problem of choice. Unconvinced by authoritative moral spokespersons (who often disagree among themselves), those on a quest for new or differently applied values join the ranks of philosophers ever open to new insights.

Philosophy and Real Life

Do we mean that philosophers never choose values but enjoy an ongoing intellectual search apart from ordinary folk? Is *philosophy*, which means the

---

[2]"America's Adults: In Search of What?" in *U.S. News and World Report* (Aug. 21, 1978); "The New Job Values," in *Psychology Today* (May 1978); Daniel Yankelovich, "New Rules in American Life: Searching for Fulfillment in a World Turned Upside Down," in *Psychology Today* (April 1981).

love of wisdom, removed from practical concerns? If by real life we mean attending to daily necessities (rest, food, shelter, and so on), clearly no one is exempt. Furthermore, no one—including the philosopher—is without choices to make. Even the person who accepts without much thought the values of the community has in a sense made a choice, however passively. In contrast, individuals who love wisdom consciously examine life. They will not be programmed; they will not passively accept what is given. At the very least, one might call oneself a philosopher if one reflects about living issues and practical concerns and makes choices required by daily involvements. "Wherever intelligence can be exercised—in practical affairs, in the mechanical arts, in business—there is room for *sophia*."[3]

When we reflect about **values,** we may be considering any of several practical areas of life. We may have clear preferences; that is, we may value particular artistic expressions, intellectual convictions, scientific developments, or economic goals. When we reflect on **morality**—what is right and what is wrong in human relations—we are doing **ethics.** In other words, ethics in philosophy is the study of morality—the good and bad, right and wrong in human conduct. My morality is my actual conduct; when I reflect upon or analyze my conduct I am engaged in ethics. In everyday conversation, however, ethics is used as a synonym for morality or morals or to designate a code of behavior (for example, Hindu ethics).

Ethics and Education

The search for practical moral values has taken its natural place within the general current search for values. Reflection on human conduct is regaining a central place in formal education. One university forcefully states its own commitment:

> An educated person is expected to have some understanding of, and experience in thinking about, moral and ethical problems. It may well be that the most significant quality in educated persons is the informed judgment which enables them to make discriminating moral choices.[4]

So pertinent is this search that on page 1 of *The New York Times* (Feb. 20, 1978) a major article appeared entitled "Ethics Courses Now Attracting Many More U.S. College Students." One might ponder whether a civilization on the brink of moral decay and chaos would devote so much public attention and concern to ethics and morality.

---

[3]John Passmore, "Philosophy," in *The Encyclopedia of Philosophy,* vol. 6 (New York: Macmillan and Free Press, 1967), p. 216. *Sophia* is the Greek word for wisdom.
[4]"Harvard's Report on the 'Core Curriculum,'" *The Chronicle of Higher Education* 16 (March 6, 1978), p. 15.

THE GROUNDING OF VALUES

If our lives inevitably involve moral decisions, if we must choose, passively or thoughtfully, values on which to base those moral decisions, what justifies any particular values? Are all values the momentary preferences of one or more individuals? Before the existence of humankind, were there any values? Or are there some values that are independent of human beings, values that are inherently preferable to others? Whether values are built into the very fabric of the universe or are the creations of human minds, how are they to be discovered?

Values as Subjective

One view is that matters of value are human opinion; this general view is termed **subjectivism.** Subjectivists make the following claims: Throughout history, individuals and groups have created preferences, measures of worth, in various ways. Philosophers have reached by reason what to them are desirable qualities. Inner ponderings, combined with folk wisdom, have led theologians to proclaim "God's will." Groups organized for cooperative living have selected by vote those moral values codified in their laws. Absolute monarchs have imposed their own values on societies. Subjectivists argue that such values may be thoughtful or emotional but that in every case they are imposed on a neutral universe by human beings.

Values as Objective

The term **objectivism** is frequently used to mean that particular values will be accepted by any rational person who reasons disinterestedly and has relevant information available. Another meaning of objectivism is that particular values are built in to the fabric of existence; such values exist without regard to human wishes and formulations. Thus, objectivists hold that there are preferable qualities in objects, behavior, ideas, persons, and so on; this is a fact of existence independent of human preference. Some objectivists hold that these values coincide with the evolving universe; for example, an anthropologist has written with regard to human behavioral values that

> the facts of man's biological nature, what *is*, determine the direction his development as a person must take. That is to say, that what *is* here clearly determines what *ought to be*; in short, that the biological facts give a biological validation to the principle of cooperation, or love, in human life. In other words, we can here demonstrate that there are certain values for human life which are not matters of opinion but which are biologically determined. If we do violence to those

in-built values, we disorder our lives, as persons, as groups, as nations, and as a world of human beings whose biological drives are directed toward love, toward cooperation.[5]

The declaration of God's will is an objectivist approach that assumes that values originate in the Creator's design of reality. The fundamental difference between Montagu's objectivism and a theologian's is that for the anthropologist values simply are, whereas the theologian believes the Creator deliberately has instilled certain values in His universe.

False values. Objectivists readily acknowledge that humanity chooses values inferior to or incompatible with the true values present in nature. The anthropologist can call false choices disorders and the like; the theologian labels them sin. To both kinds of objectivist, false choices lead us toward estrangement from true reality; we become out of alignment with what truly is and will be.

The Grounding and Selection of Moral Values

Moral values too may be regarded as either subjective (of human origin) or objective (independent of human beings). The debate over the subjectivity or objectivity of moral values is centuries old. Where does this uncertainty leave the person who is thoughtfully trying to choose moral values?

The problem becomes less monumental, though not easily solved, if we assume that what is at stake is human fulfillment. With human fulfillment as an assumed value, the question of whether values are subjective or objective is not crucial. What is important is the impact of various values on human life. The effect of available moral values is far more to the point than their alleged objectivity or subjectivity. For example, if a respected scholar proposes a subjective solution to a moral problem, or if a religious leader claims to know God's will on an issue objectively, and such claims, from either source, run counter to what you view as the long-range physical and emotional well-being of humankind, then both the subjective and the objective viewpoints will seem to you, as a thinking person, to be inadequate.

Thus we are left with the need for **principles** for selecting moral and other values. Admittedly, these principles are of human origin, but the reader is invited to consider them as a preliminary step in selecting values.

1. *Intrinsic values are preferable to extrinsic values.* Our everyday lives are filled with things that have **extrinsic** value; that is, they are good for something but not of value for just being there. Examples of things with extrinsic

[5]Ashley Montagu, *On Being Human* (New York: Hawthorn, 1966), p. 52.

value include most books, eyeglasses, pens, and cars. These objects are *good for something;* they are not of value for their own sakes. Something is **intrinsically** valuable when it is of value for its own sake and not for its ability to yield something else. For example, beauty, truth, love, friendship, and strength of character are considered intrinsic values by many persons.

Intrinsic and extrinsic values are not always either mutually exclusive or fixed. What is valued by one person for its own sake may be valued by another individual as a means to an end—for example, a beautiful vase can be valued as a work of art (intrinsic) or an attractive container for the display of flowers (extrinsic).

The danger of viewing values as exclusively extrinsic is that this leads to regarding everything and everyone as an instrument for yielding something else. In the moral sphere, human relations are reduced to the valuing of individuals for their productivity rather than for themselves.

2. *Long-term or permanent values are preferable to short-term or temporary values.* In a fast-paced society, we are likely to value what is instantaneous or offers desired results in the near future. Most readers of this book have adequate food, clothing, and shelter. However, we are as a people apt to value economic means that can provide us quickly with many luxury commodities. For example, many people are willing to incur debts so that they can acquire luxury items as early in life as possible. Resulting stress, which may damage health in future years, is given less consideration than immediate "success." Consider another example: Which is of greater value— the quickly written song designed to sell and die within a year or two or the music anguished over by composers for months and valued for centuries?

3. *Thoughtfully selected values are preferable to those passively accepted.* More than ever we are becoming conscious of deliberate as well as unintentional programing of human minds and hearts. As we study history, we are appalled at the readiness of masses of people to accept the values of decadent religion, ruthless government, bigoted families, and self-appointed moral spokespersons. Prepackaged values have been grasped eagerly by those who have not had the time and opportunity to reflect and choose, as well as by those who would rather have their thinking done for them. Also alarming is the fact that that large numbers of persons do not realize that they are being indoctrinated. For example, much contemporary advertising casually assumes values such as bigger is better, youth is optimum, more is necessary, adulthood means smoking and drinking, and buying such-and-such product will overcome your sense of negativity. These learning experiences subtly introduce and reinforce some values that have come to be taken for granted as "American."

The alternative to value brainwashing is deliberate reflection on other value proposals. Critical examination of values for their intrinsic or extrinsic character, for their durability, and for their probable practical implications may precede a conscious choice. Such reflection does not guarantee correct choices, but it enhances authenticity: The values selected will be *our* values. Our moral values will be grounded and reflected in the behavior of free human beings, not of robots or puppets.

MORAL RELATIVISM

Many responsible thinkers have been subjectivists in one way or another. To them, moral values are of human origin and have no basis apart from human ingenuity and customs. There are no universally applicable moral standards; their usefulness is dependent on historical, cultural, or other conditions. This general attitude is called **moral relativism.** Scholars vary in their accounts of moral relativism, and here we shall consider two fundamental types.

Descriptive Relativism

Social scientists such as sociologists and psychologists describe, among other things, the moral conduct of individuals and groups globally and throughout history. Reports of varying moral beliefs and practices tell us that in actual experience no moral standards are upheld everywhere as ideals or everywhere practiced. Any moral value, the social scientist states, can probably be found as a belief in some society at some period of history. **Descriptive relativism** is an acknowledgment of this moral variety among humankind.

Implications of descriptive relativism. Philosophers know that human moral variety exists; Plato and Aristotle drew from such observations the conclusion that many people do not know what is really good. From the variety of beliefs held by different people, they also concluded that many do not know right from wrong. This is no reason, they felt, to relax in the search for the good, the true, and the beautiful. Thinking or opinion alone does not make anything real, including moral values and right conduct. The attempt to justify or censure morality because of what is in fact is futile; what is does not imply what ought to be or what ought not to be. Descriptions provide insights about human behavior as it is, not as it ought to be. If we were to try to extract a moral principle from what has been and what is, we would be left with the idea that nothing is unacceptable.

Normative Relativism

Some philosophers have concluded that no statements about right and wrong can be judged true or false. There is no way to prove a value claim in any objective way. A statement such as "injury is wrong" is an expression of feeling or emotion; it is not a matter of truth or falsehood.

A CRITIQUE OF ETHICS

We find that ethical philosophy consists simply in saying that ethical concepts are pseudo-concepts and therefore unanalysable. The further task of describing the different feelings that the different ethical terms are used to express, and the different reactions that they customarily provoke, is a task for the psychologist. There cannot be such a thing as ethical science, if by ethical science one means the elaboration of a "true" system of morals. For we have seen that, as ethical judgments are mere expressions of feeling, there can be no way of determining the validity of any ethical system, and, indeed, no sense in asking whether any such system is true. All that one may legitimately inquire in this connection is, What are the moral habits of a given person or group of people, and what causes them to have precisely those habits and feelings? And this inquiry falls wholly within the scope of the existing social sciences.

From A. J. Ayer, *Language, Truth and Logic* (New York: Dover, 1952), p. 112.

Alfred Jules Ayer (b. 1910) taught philosophy at the University of Oxford, where he was educated. His writings include Language, Truth and Logic, The Problem of Knowledge, *and* The Concept of a Person.

If this theorizing is valid, then moral relativity follows as a standard. Moral relativity as the norm is the view that of the same action or situation X both "X is good" and "X is bad" may be asserted, because "good" is merely the feeling of the person making the statement. One person would judge an execution as good and another bad. Neither judgment is a matter of truth; neither can be proved or disproved. Both judgments are merely expressions of emotion. Thus moral values may legitimately vary and conflict among societies and individuals. The codes developed by groups so that they can live with some degree of security are arbitrary and not universally binding.

Implications of normative relativism. Moral relativism implies that there is no objectivity in matters of morality and there are no norms that apply to humanity as a whole. One moral position is as right as another. When we feel repelled by a particular moral outlook or practice, we are reacting emotionally but with no claim to a provable universal standard. What is right in New York City may be regarded as wrong in Salt Lake City, Utah. In either place human feelings, opinions, and customs determine what is morally right.

If one moral position is as right as another, then no choice or act can be justified or condemned by any universal standard. There can be no genuine dispute about morals; philosophically speaking, we can conclude that all value judgments, all moral statements, are of equal standing.

Many persons today are convinced that our search for moral values will result in some form of relativism, in spite of the theoretical and practical difficulties involved. We cannot dismiss such considerations without a fair hearing.

VALUES AND RIGHTS

In our discussion of morality in our lives we have considered moral decisions and personal life, the search for values, the grounding of values, and moral relativism. Another fundamental living ethical issue for us is the relation between values and rights.

A **right** is a claim to an achievable condition that both an individual and his or her society need for a better life. If there is something available and indispensable to a good life, it is an individual's right to have it. Whatever is valued as necessary for a good life is regarded as a right; if it is not readily available, the society ought to make it available. For example, two centuries ago a free education was not claimed as a right. The recognition of the **value** of education led people to argue that every child should be given an education. The right to public education at first included only elementary education, but later it was extended to secondary education. Now we are wrestling with the value and therefore the right of citizens to publicly supported higher education. Other values and rights under discussion today include medical care, private property, work, minimum financial security, and life itself. When a society ranks a condition as indispensable, it becomes a **right in theory;** when the condition is made available, it becomes a **right in fact.**

Natural Rights

For thousands of years individuals and groups have appealed to certain rights that they felt were theirs in a special sense. These rights, they have felt, are based on nature. The doctrine of **natural rights** goes back at least to the great thinkers of ancient Greece. The American colonies, in the Declaration of Independence, based their claim to independence on "certain inalienable rights," among which were "life, liberty, and the pursuit of happiness." The United States Bill of Rights assumes the same theory of natural rights.

Stripped of features that pertain only to particular times and places, the doctrine of natural rights expresses three claims: (1) persons have some rights that apply no matter what the circumstances or the culture; (2) these rights are due them whether or not their society or government recognizes them; and (3) these rights are inalienable—the person cannot surrender them nor can the society take them away for any cause. In the seventeenth and eighteenth centuries a typical advocate of natural rights based these claims on two further ideas: (4) all persons share the same essential nature and needs; and (5) by divine ordering, or simply by the nature of things, certain rights, such as those to life, liberty, and property, are implied by the very idea of treating persons according to their essential natures.

Today the debate continues as to whether any rights are imbedded in nature (an implication of objectivism). The question "Are there universal rights?" goes hand-in-hand with "Are there universal values?" Another debated question is "Do all rights entail obligations?" or "May I claim a condition necessary to a good life without any obligations on my part?"

VALUES AND FULFILLMENT

In recent years the ideal of personal fulfillment has found expression in popular literature and in so-called human potential movements. Any spokesperson with charm and a persuasive personality who can market a technique, religious or otherwise, that offers personal satisfaction and contentment is assured a following. If the results are quick, all the better.

Many, perhaps most, persons who legitimately seek a sense of being at ease with life by means of the varied available sources of fulfillment fail to consider the values assumed by these movements. Many, perhaps most, become disappointed with the weak effects of their so-called growth over the long term. Consider the following values and whether your own fulfillment is dependent on one or more of them:

personal independence	self-understanding
self-reliance	self-acceptance
oneness with a universal spirit	human fellowship
rationality	concernfulness
positive thinking	knowledge
emotional honesty	appropriateness
physical intimacy	purchasing power
salvation	self-control

Our present purpose is not to evaluate these preferences or qualities. We can simply recognize the fact that one or more of these values, as well as others not included here, are held as necessary to human fulfillment by competing movements or schools of thought. Each value or combination of values offers an implied interpretation of fulfillment; if a movement ranks personal independence and self-reliance high, its understanding of personal fulfillment will differ from that of a group preferring human fellowship. Thus, the offer of fulfillment by any movement or school of thought has values built into its concept of fulfillment. None is value free.

VALUES AND A CHANGING WORLD

We have begun our search for a moral philosophy with a consideration of the fact of morality in our lives. Moral decisions are an inevitable part of our personal lives. These decisions are based on our values, especially our moral values. When we examine our values, we find that some individuals regard them as human opinion whereas others look upon true values as rooted in nature. One's understanding of values as subjective or objective determines to a large extent whether moral values and rights are seen as relative or as imbedded in objective reality. As we strive for fulfillment in our lives, we are again involved with values, perhaps even competing and conflicting ones.

If we were to trace the history of morality through Western civilization, we would find a variety of value positions. Cultural change has been an ongoing process, and changing values have accompanied the evolution of civilized peoples. At any given moment, however, the range of moral choices has been narrow. Most individuals' options were fated by the restricted alternatives available to them.

Today we are confronted with not only a very broad range of values originating in Western civilization, but also the philosophies of the Orient and Third World (emerging nations, especially in Latin America and Africa). They provide us with new values to consider. Our values of time, prosperity, activity, and self-reliance are being challenged by the comprehensive world views of peoples who differ from us in their understandings of truth and reality.

Morality in our lives has moved from the traditional straight-and-narrow path of familiar values to a sometimes disconcerting range of choices. To yearn for the good old days when life was simpler is in a sense understandable; choosing is far more perplexing than simply doing what seems obviously right. For those willing to philosophize and choose, this new age of moral choice can be the best of times, an age of wisdom, the season of Light, the spring of hope with everything before us.

CHAPTER REVIEW

A. Moral decisions and personal life

1. Life itself forces choices upon us.
2. The choices that come before us are entirely new, familiar but with new dimensions, or so routine that we sometimes do not recognize them as choices.
3. The modern age has substituted choice for fate; the course of life for many individuals is not settled in advance.
4. Our choices now range from the conventional to the previously unthinkable.

B. The search for values

1. Valuing occurs whenever anything is preferred or chosen; we rate things as better or worse than other things and act on these decisions and ratings.
2. All values are being scrutinized today.
3. Some persons hold to traditional values and others to reconsidered values. Still others are searching for new or more genuine values.
4. Individuals are, in a sense, philosophers when they reflect about living issues and practical concerns and make choices required by daily involvements.
5. When we study or reflect on morality we are doing **ethics.** There is a nationwide, perhaps global, interest in ethics today.

C. The grounding of values

1. The discovery and justification of values are pertinent philosophical issues.
2. Subjectivists view values as created by human beings and imposed upon a neutral universe.
3. More than one kind of objectivism exists. Objectivists view values as objective when they are acceptable to any rational person who reasons disinterestedly and has available the relevant information, or when the values are built in to existence itself independent of humanity.
4. Some principles for selecting moral and other values are needed.

D. Moral relativism

1. Moral relativism claims that there are no universally applicable moral standards.
2. Descriptive relativism acknowledges the moral variety among humankind throughout history.

3. Normative relativism claims that no statements about right and wrong can be judged true or false; no norms apply to humanity as a whole.

E. Values and rights

1. A right is a claim to an achievable condition that the individual and his or her society need for a better life; whatever is valued as being necessary for a good life is regarded as a right.
2. A natural right is one that applies universally to men and women everywhere and at all times.

F. Values and fulfillment

1. One's interpretation of fulfillment depends on one's values.

SUGGESTED READINGS

DeGeorge, Richard T. *The Philosopher's Guide.* Lawrence: The Regents Press of Kansas, 1980.

> A guide to the general histories, basic bibliographies, and collections of readings in philosophy; the section on ethics within Part III, "Systematic Philosophy: Branches, Movements and Regions," lists dictionaries, bibliographies, histories, journals, and works on ethics in medicine and science, business and professional ethics, and social ethics.

Edwards, Paul, ed. *The Encyclopedia of Philosophy.* New York: Macmillan, Free Press, 1967.

> An eight-volume reference work containing such essays as "Value and Valuation," "Ends and Means," "Rights," and "Problems of Ethics." Each essay concludes with an excellent bibliography.

Lyons, David, ed. *Rights.* Belmont, Calif.: Wadsworth, 1979.

> A collection of essays that seek to understand what rights are, what rights we have, and why they are important.

Navia, Luis E., and Kelly, Eugene, eds. *Ethics and the Search for Values.* Buffalo, N.Y.: Prometheus, 1980.

> An anthology of some of the most important ethical writings of Western philosophy, including an informative introductory chapter, "The Search for Values."

2

Moral Wisdom
and Freedom

Philosophy does not begin out of nothing. It may, at best, be defined as a science with a minimum of presuppositions. It is, furthermore, involved in a specific way of thinking, in certain modes and categories of apprehension and evaluation.

How then is personal freedom possible? Its nature is a mystery, and the formidable array of cumulative evidence for determinism makes it very difficult for us to believe in freedom. And yet, without such a belief there is no meaning left to the moral life. Without taking freedom seriously, it is impossible to take humanity seriously.*

INGREDIENTS OF A MORAL PHILOSOPHY

A Sense of Frustration

We have acknowledged that life forces choices on us, that humanity has moved from fate to choice, and that values are inescapable for us all. In general, philosophers prefer that each of us reflect on the possible values in human relations; we should make discriminating moral choices rather than simplistically accept existing values prepackaged and delivered.

However, when we begin to do ethics, the apparent simplicity of the task rapidly fades. Our reflections lead to several questions: What justifies any values? Are values subjective or objective? Are there any universal moral standards? Are rights subjective or objective? Are certain values necessary to human fulfillment?

It is an understandable temptation to abandon these nagging questions. After all, hasn't the human race survived without each person being annoyed by such philosophizing? Why not just accept what is provided by existing moral authorities? Do we really have the time to think about all of these issues? Notice what happens: In thinking about the nagging questions, we philosophize about not philosophizing. We raise further ques-

*Abraham Joshua Heschel, *God in Search of Man* (New York: Farrar, Straus, 1955), pp. 14, 410.

tions of truth and of priorities. The real alternative to reflection is a thoughtless acceptance of someone else's moral convictions, prepackaged convincingly, delivered instantly, and consumed on the spot.

Socrates said, "The unexamined life is not worth living." No doubt this is an overstatement. The vast majority of human beings have not had and do not have the opportunity to examine and reflect. Most individuals have had the primary task of surviving or fulfilling obligations to families, work, and nation. Though we may be repelled by thoughtlessness and its consequences, we cannot justly censure the person who has had the opportunity only to gather randomly the sense and nonsense of limited moral resources. At the same time, we listen with awe to elderly people with little formal education who have a highly developed moral wisdom. The philosopher's preference for reflection, for the examined life, must be tempered by the reality of individual opportunity. Socrates would be pleased to know of increased opportunities for thought existing today in the United States. More individuals than ever before have the time and opportunity to reflect instead of merely to accept.

But the frustrations remain. The questions raised in the previous chapter are unanswered and more issues follow.

OBSTACLES TO CLEAR THINKING

As we consider any issue, large or small, our thoughts can become muddied by obstacles. Discussions seem to go nowhere, and we can't put our finger on what is holding us back. It could be that clear thinking is prevented by one or more of the following devices.[1]

Tradition.   "It's always been this way!" is an exaggerated response to a challenge or an attempt to validate a position by means of a claim of longevity. An appeal to habit or custom cannot support an argument for or against a claim.

Even when a religious person believes that God has guided the tradition of a faith, there are philosophical problems. Can the believer be sure that the formation of tradition is complete? Perhaps God is guiding the tradition to a fuller maturity in the distant future.

Common Sense.   "Use your common sense!" is a frequent plea. But whose common sense? Yours? Mine? That subculture's? This nation's? Another country's? This year's? Although it is an attractive way to end a conversation, an appeal to so-called common sense prevents deeper reflection.

[1]For a fuller exploration of the problem of knowledge, including obstacles to clear thinking, see Part 3, "Knowledge and Science," in Harold H. Titus, Marilyn S. Smith, and Richard T. Nolan, *Living Issues in Philosophy*, 7th ed. (New York: Van Nostrand, 1979).

Propaganda. "Our way is the only way!" proclaim spokespersons from many religious and political communities. Many such persons attempt to manipulate views with leaps of logic, emotional pitches, and offers of prepackaged solutions. Different from preaching (which proclaims a message with heart and mind, a free decision being left to the hearer), propaganda is a form of subtle mind control, a clear obstacle to thinking.

Authoritarianism. "Because I say so!" Although this impediment to thought is appropriate in a military command or a parent's order to a young child, it is unhelpful in philosophy. Not to be confused with the findings of a specialist—an expert, an authority on a topic who would welcome constructive criticism—the authoritarian style is tyrannical and dictatorial. No response or further inquiry is welcome.

Generalization. "They're all that way." To conclude that all (or even most) of anything is "that way" because one or some have been "that way" is no support for a claim. It is untrue that all the residents of a high-crime section of a town are immoral. It is equally unsupportable to claim moral approval for all persons living in a cultured residential area on the basis that one or some individuals are morally responsible people.

Universalization. "I've done it; therefore everyone else can and should." To universalize one's own experience or one's own group's experience is fallacious. For example, some converts can be so enthusiastic about their new lives that not only do they want to share them with others but also they prescribe their exact experience for everyone else. An accomplishment prized by one person, however, is not always desirable for all others. Persons who in their own opinion are making moral progress prevent thoughtfulness when they universalize their own experiences.

***Ad Hominem* Argument.** "You know *why* she believes that, don't you?" Notice what has happened. The issue has been set aside; what the person believes is not being debated. Instead, the speaker is getting personal. The why, the supposed motivations for a belief, is receiving the attention, not the belief itself. Another example might help: Ms. X states, "Abortion is moral." Mr. Y responds, "You're saying that because you've had several." Whether Ms. X has had none or several abortions has nothing to do with the merits of the statement "abortion is moral." Such an attack shifts from issues to personalities and fails to prove or disprove a point. Clear thinking about an issue is blocked by an *ad hominem* ("to the man") fallacy.

Prejudice. "My mind is made up!" If you've reached a conclusion without examining sufficient evidence on the matter, you have made a prejudgment, a prejudiced judgment. Although we frequently associate prejudice with issues of racial and ethnic heritage, it applies to any pre-judgment. Prejudicial conclusions can be made on the basis of thoughtless bias, no evidence, or partial data that confirms our existing feelings. Preju-dices help us to believe what we wish to believe, but they hinder clear thinking.

Impatience. "I've got to know right now." There are situations that call for an immediate intuitive decision; little time is available for reflection. On many issues, however, there are no instant answers, and an immediate decision may not be needed. There is often some time to suspend judg-ment or decision for the sake of thoughtfulness. Impatience can block sufficient reflection and clear choice.

"Knowledge" Via Fallacy

There are sincere, so-called moral authorities who use these obstacles, often unknowingly. These spokespersons rely on the fallacious arguments we've just listed and afterwards they proclaim their so-called knowledge as in-disputable certainty.

An observer of an often gullible public might become cynical about the possibility of the existence of educated persons, individuals who make discriminating moral choices. Persons who are aware of obstacles to clear thinking, however, are able to raise the sights of the victims of shoddy, inadequate thinking. Attention can be turned to issues and their merits. The obstacles can be exposed.

ETHICS AND PHILOSOPHY

We have considered some obstacles to clear thinking, but still we are faced with such questions as: How do we know anything for sure? How do we know whether values are subjective or objective? How do we know whether rights are of human origin or exist within nature itself? How can we know that our values are true or false?

True answers to these and other questions have been sought for cen-turies. Our desire to know for sure is understandable. Once the only true solution to a problem is discovered, our choices become easier: Select the truth and be confident in your rightness, or choose the obvious falsehood and be aware of your wrongness. With no uncertainties all rational people would have lives filled with clear decisions, loyalties, and knowledge.

The history of humanity shows us that in spite of sincere and honest attempts to answer life's questions, several answers to most questions are proposed. Let us now give our attention to the place of ethics in the human search for and love of wisdom.

Epistemology. The search for answers to philosophical questions is not unlike the search for truths in other areas of life. We use our powers of observation—in other words, our five senses; we examine evidence and we experiment. We also use our powers of reason, our minds, to reflect and to scrutinize views for their logical coherence. When adequate evidence is lacking or when logical inconsistencies are found, we can judge a claim as false or at least in need of further development and support. When the evidence is sufficient or when a view is logically developed, we may be ready to judge the position as true.

In philosophy the study of knowledge is called **epistemology,** from the Greek word *episteme,* "knowledge." This branch of philosophy raises three basic questions: (1) What are the *sources* of knowledge? Our five senses? Our minds? Intuition? Divine revelations? (2) What is the *nature* of knowledge? Subjective human opinion? Objective facts? (3) Is our knowledge *valid?* Are there proofs for our claims?

These questions are related to every area of human inquiry. Whenever we engage in **normative ethics,** that is, proposals of how people ought to behave, we are open to an epistemological challenge. "You ought to be faithful" is a normative ethical judgment. The epistemological challenge may be phrased in various ways: (1) Who said so? (Or, what is the source of your moral statement that I ought to be faithful?) (2) Is it an opinion or a fact that I ought to be faithful? (3) Prove it!

Metaphysics. Other related issues surface when we begin a thorough study of the sources, nature, and validity of knowledge. If we consider the role and reliability of our five senses in obtaining knowledge, we could ask such questions as: Do our senses perceive reality as it is or only as it appears through human senses? (Is the sky really blue or blue only to humans?) What do I mean by my "mind?" (Is my mind different from my brain?) Is nature morally neutral, or are there values built into nature? Is there a God who reveals His will? Is God's will revealed to my mind or can my senses detect it? These issues and many others are within an area of philosophy called **metaphysics,** the critical study of the nature of reality, its possible origins and essences.

What is Taken for Granted. Our study in ethics seems to grow more and more complicated. If making moral decisions is this complex, perhaps we should resort to intuition.

But we are not suggesting that for practical purposes an individual must first develop a formal, comprehensive epistemological and metaphysical system. We do suggest, however, that as we develop a moral philosophy and are engaged in the practical task of making moral decisions, we are assuming or implying many of our own beliefs about knowledge and reality. Consider this example: An individual who proposes a spiritually oriented moral decision (I ought to worship weekly) is expressing some sort of spiritual value, a spiritual source of knowledge about spiritual values, and a belief in some kind of spiritual reality. The philosophical details of these spiritual values, their sources, and their reality may never have been thought through, but they are assumed, however vaguely.

A goal at this point in our study of ethics is an increased sensitivity to the ramifications of the seemingly innocent question of how we know anything for sure, whether in ethics or other areas of life. Even after the obstacles to clear thinking have been cleared away, a whole range of issues remains. Our sensitivity can be sharpened with the realization that we enter every judgment process (every evaluation that a claim is true or false, every statement about reality, every occasion of valuing) with certain assumptions, postulates, or axioms. We do not enter any inquiry or come to any conclusions with indifferent objectivity. We all have certain beliefs we take for granted, and these so-called self-evident truths are the foundations upon which we build our philosophies.

Not only special disciplines or areas of study but also every society or civilization rests on a number of presuppositions about the world, human nature, knowledge, and values. Each person's interpretation of his or her observations and experiences depends on these convictions and value systems. At the foundation of every system of thought is what is taken for granted.

Reasons for Philosophical Disagreements. Throughout history sharp differences have existed on issues of reality, truth, and values. Many disagreements can be traced to one or more of the obstacles to clear thinking. But differences are not always caused by fallacious thinking. Instead, it may be a matter of building differing explanations upon differing, disputable assumptions.

Is there a method by which these differences can be resolved? Although any of us might be persuaded that one or more of our own axioms are somewhat inadequate to account for our experiences or those of others, some assumptions remain for which there is no agreed-upon method of evaluation. For example, there is no mutually agreed-upon method for the scientist to use that can disprove a mystic's idea that the world of time and space is only an appearance, not a fundamental reality. That mystic's assertion is, to the mystic, a self-evident truth, an axiom requiring no proof. By way of contrast, your axioms may include the assertion that the world of time and space is real, not an appearance. For you, this conviction is a self-evident truth, an axiom requiring no proof. Can you refute the mystic's position? With what methods?

If you try to disprove the claim that the world of time and space is only an appearance, you will use assumptions and methods unacceptable to the mystic. You may pound on the table or point to a rock, thereby (in your view) providing evidence against the mystic's claim. But you will not convince the mystic, in whose view all that you are doing is part of what merely seems to be; your pounding, the table itself, your act of pointing, and the rock are all aspects of this world, which the mystic asserts is only an appearance. Your views will never converge, because your assumptions are very different.

When a nation proclaims that certain truths are self-evident, it proclaims its assumptions, its beliefs. As philosophers think and write, they begin with presuppositions that differ from one to another.

Philosophical Pluralism. The inevitable result of our beginning with different postulates is the existence of more than one possible interpretation of issues. For example, a group of psychologists is asked to determine the reasons for certain behaviors and methods for changing them. Each responds according to the axioms of his or her school of thought—behaviorism, Freudian, Jungian, Gestalt, and so on. Each school has its own set of assumptions that provide the framework for interpreting the data.

A conference of physicists is assembled to explain the origins of the universe. With the same information available to all of them, they develop several different explanations. A meeting of mathematicians will also result in disagreements.[2]

By **philosophical pluralism** we mean the inevitable existence of different interpretations of reality, knowledge, and values. Setting aside systems of thought flawed by obstacles to clear thinking and exposed as inadequate or self-contradictory, we are convinced that thoughtful philosophical pluralism is here to stay.

Relativism Versus Tentativeness. Does philosophical pluralism imply that all views are equally true? Is there an unavoidable relativism among philosophers, economists, psychologists, physicists, mathematicians, and so on?

That each system is as true as its opposite makes no sense to us; we do not advocate relativism. We assert, however, that there is a certain degree of tentativeness to any school of thought, any interpretation, indeed any axiom. We propose that we human beings are limited in what we can know for sure, with finality, infallibly. Only God, if there is one, knows for sure, with finality, what is real, true, and of value. This is one of this book's axioms.

---

[2]See "Mathematics, Philosophy of," in Antony Flew, *A Dictionary of Philosophy* (New York: St. Martin's Press, 1979), the more advanced essay "Mathematics, Foundations of" in the *Encyclopedia of Philosophy* (New York: Macmillan, 1967), or Morris Kline, *Mathematics: The Loss of Certainty* (New York: Oxford Univ. Press, 1980).

So why think at all? This question takes us back to our first chapter's observation: Life forces choices.

Ethical Pluralism.   In some games, such as chess, there seems to be one correct solution. Think hard and long enough, and a player can find the right move. The right move, however, depends on the rules of the game. Human beings create the rules and the game itself. Even in chess one finds that all countries (outside the Orient) follow the laws of chess developed by the World Chess Federation.

Not all persons agree to the rules and goals of ethics, however. Human beings create the rules and the goals of ethics. We choose either (1) what we believe to be self-evident in nature, (2) what we believe to be revealed by God, or (3) what we believe to be a wise attitude. The initial choice of one of these three general positions reflects what we believe about reality, truth, and values.

By **ethical pluralism** we mean the inevitable existence of different views of what is taken for granted in moral matters. Human choice of different sources of ethical wisdom (nature, God, or insight), and different rules has resulted in the creation of many ethical systems throughout history. We are not suggesting that each position is as true as another; we propose that as human beings we are limited in what we can know in ethics with finality and infallibly. We hold that only God, if there is one, knows with finality and infallibly what is morally true. We proceed with ethics as with most human efforts as a thoughtful demanding art instead of a wholly objective, clear, obtainable body of truths.

We agree that once one agrees to some fundamental rules of scientific method, the truths of science are less difficult to discover than those of ethics. But even scientists choose their rules based on axioms, such as: The world is fundamentally real, not a seeming-to-be; nature is sufficiently uniform so that universal truths are discoverable; human perceptions and instruments are sufficiently reliable to perceive reality as it is.

In ethics there is more room for different sets of fundamental rules and axioms than in the physical sciences. A similar range of possibilities exists in the social sciences (economics, psychology, political science, sociology, and so on) for varied schools of thought.

Therefore, there will probably be more schools of thought in ethics than in the physical sciences. Ethicists disagree more than scientists about fundamentals—what is to be taken for granted, including what the rules of the game are. The extent of ethical pluralism will be more evident than scientific pluralism. How do we know anything for sure? To that haunting question more than one answer is possible; each answer will depend significantly on what is taken for granted by the person replying. Understanding the bases of pluralism, students of ethics are released from the frustrating search for the sole correct solution to moral dilemmas. Instead, they can come to grips with thoughtful moral options and their respective foundations.

PHILOSOPHICAL PLURALISM

Modern philosophizing recognizes no universals, no agreement as to facts, methods, or experiences. There are clearly many different views of facts, many proposed methods, many types of experiences to be found.

Philosophical fragmentation is the rule; hence attention has turned to the reasons for philosophical pluralism, and one of the reasons which has become increasingly obvious is the confessional character of metaphysical theories. Metaphysical theories differ because they are based upon different fundamental assumptions as to how the world goes, each one confessing its own version of what is the case. These assumptions may be held critically or uncritically and they may be changed through criticism and reflection, through the process of elaborating a consistent world view, or through harmonization of all the fragments of knowledge which seem well substantiated. However, at the end of the metaphysical quest the element of confession is still there. That it is still there is shown by the fact that competent philosophers disagree, after lifetimes of philosophical disputation.

Frank B. Dilley, *Metaphysics and Religious Language* (New York: Columbia Univ. Press, 1964), pp. 71–72.

Frank B. Dilley (b. 1931) has taught at Smith College and Milliken University, in Illinois. Since 1967 Dr. Dilley has been on the faculty of the University of Delaware as professor of philosophy. In addition to the aforementioned book, Dr. Dilley has written numerous articles for scholarly journals.

ARE WE FREE TO MAKE CHOICES?

A Crucial Ingredient of Moral Philosophy

We have commented frequently about choosing and choices. Not all philosophers believe that human beings are capable of making choices; the sense in which we have freedom to choose is crucial to ethics.

We usually assume that individuals can, at least at times, make things happen that would not happen otherwise, and that to some extent persons can deliberate, decide, and direct their own lives and the course of events. Some degree of freedom of action is assumed by nearly all people in the course of their daily lives. They praise and blame, make plans for the future, and hold themselves and other people responsible for their actions. Unless human beings are free to act on moral principles, it is absurd to talk about duty, or what we ought to do, or to pursue studies in the area of ethics and morality.

On the other hand, in the light of the numerous factors influencing conduct—physical, biological, psychological, and social—it is evident that conduct is determined at least to some extent and is not to be explained merely as the product of an isolated or unhindered free will. Numerous scientific studies, interpreted by means of the cause-and-effect postulates of scientific activity, make it clear that events of nonhuman nature are determined in some way by cause-and-effect sequences. We are naturally led, therefore, to ask to what extent human life is determined, how free we are. Some scholars, impressed with the reign of natural law, have claimed that humanity, like all objects in nature, is caught in the grip of cause-and-effect relationships and that our every act is rigidly determined so that we are not free to choose. This attitude arises when human nature is interpreted not only as self-conscious and reflective, but also as part of physical nature, exclusively conditioned by the external environment. Although this is a difficult question (because human behavior can be interpreted along a continuum from total freedom to rigid determinism), students of ethics need to clarify their thinking and to be able to meet critical questions when they arise.

Moral freedom, the subject of this discussion, means the capacity to choose and act on one's choice. It involves the power to choose between alternative courses of action and the power of the individual's deliberation to act as a causal agent in the process of behavior.

In the past, moral freedom has usually been called *freedom of the will.* Today the term "will" is less often used, because we do not think of will as a separate entity or faculty but as an interplay of volitional activity or motor tendencies of the organism. In a more restricted and personal sense, "will" refers to a person's ability to perform voluntary acts. The will is the person freely expressing him- or herself in action.

Extreme Schools of Thought

Moral freedom—freedom of choice or self-determinism—stands in contrast to two other positions, **determinism** and **indeterminism.**

Indeterminism. Indeterminism, the extreme view of freedom, is the idea that there are events in human mental and moral life that are uncaused, in the sense that the mind may work without any motivation. We may make choices, it is said, that are independent of our past actions, including our heredity and our environment.

Determinism.   In contrast to indeterminism, determinism as a postulate in scientific inquiry maintains the belief that the realm of nature, including humanity, is to be treated as an unbroken chain of cause and effect, so that human behavior is dependent on natural law and is determined exclusively by antecedent events and conditions. All events, including decisions of the human will, are explainable by preceding events. What is called the act of choice is determined either by external pressures or by desires and tendencies within the agent's character.

Determinism should be distinguished from both fatalism and predestination. **Fatalism** is the view that some, not all, events in life are determined independently of our own choices and acts, so that the future is removed from our personal control. It insists on the inevitable occurrence of an event at a specific time and insists that what is to be will be. Fatalism seems to have its origin or basis in human weakness or helplessness in the face of seeming evils, especially death. This outlook is most prevalent in places without advanced means of scientific and social control. It also allows people to blame outside forces for existing conditions, thus tending to trivialize human effort to improve these conditions.

Predestination, a theological determinism, is the view that the events of our lives, including our ultimate destiny, have been decreed by God. Based on a theological and a supernatural element, this doctrine, at least in its extreme form, has always aroused protests and opposition, because it seems to make God responsible for evil as well as good and to deny genuine human freedom.

Toward a Moderate Position

Let us begin our attempt to explain this seeming contradiction between a rigid determinism and a degree of freedom of choice by pointing out some different types of behavior that we observe in our everyday experience. Take, for example, the differences that exist among a stone, a tree, a dog, and a person. A stone stands in one place unless it is moved by some outside force. Although it is affected by weathering and certain slow changes that take place in its chemical or physical properties, it sets up no goals and exerts no effort. It has its existence in the realm of physical and chemical action and reaction. The tree, in contrast to the stone, is alive and growing. Its leaves and branches grow toward the sunlight, and its roots reach toward water and minerals in the soil. Although it is alive, it is anchored to the earth, however, and has little or no power of movement or choice.

The dog, in contrast to the stone and the tree, moves about, and can learn from experience and adapt to new conditions. Dogs are very much alive, with appetites and desires and sensitivities. They grow, reproduce, and develop senses to aid them in their activities. Yet although dogs can form precepts, their ability to grasp concepts or to live by their aid is quite limited.

When we come to human life, we find a wide range of new characteristics or powers. On the physical plane, humans have erect posture and large brains. On the cultural level, we develop complex symbols, inventions, and institutions. We have unique powers. Other animals are conscious; only humans are self-conscious. We are conscious of the fact that it is we who are conscious. The growth of self-consciousness, memory, and imagination makes possible a new creativeness and enables human beings, who are children of nature, to rise to some extent above nature. Through reflective thinking and abstract thought, we are able to carry on the trial-and-error process internally and to live in a new world of meanings. We can manipulate nature to some extent to satisfy our desires. In the light of what is, we say that such-and-such ought to be. Ethical discrimination and aesthetic appreciation open up a new world to us. As self-conscious beings, we formulate ideals and strive to attain them. To hereditary and environmental factors must now be added the human capacity for personal response.

The Problem.   Our problem is essentially this: On every side we seem to be surrounded by conditions that affect our lives and determine our conduct. From this point of view we are merely part of a chain of events. On the other hand, we are not like the objects of inanimate nature and not mere animal organisms. We have powers and characteristics that seem to set us apart and make us to some extent controllers of nature rather than things controlled. How is this seeming contradiction to be resolved?

We see, then, that we must reject the views of those who hold that there are only two clear-cut alternatives: You accept freedom of choice or you accept a rigid determinism, and there are no other positions. Freedom and determinism are a pair of incompatible presuppositions, and each point of view has been ably defended by outstanding thinkers. We cannot accept this rigid division; our position is not all on one side or the other.

How Free Are We?   With the development of self-awareness, understanding, and organization, there opens up for a person the possibility of self-control or self-determination that was not possible before. The important question is not "Are we free?" but "How free are we?" Some individuals have little freedom, whereas others apparently have a considerable amount. Moral freedom means that people are genuine sources of action and can bring about events that otherwise would not occur. In the universe there are definite causal sequences (mechanical causation), but we believe that there is also a significant capacity for personal response or personal causation. Freedom is in part the ability to make plans and then, within limits, to carry them out. We say that people are free when they are able to initiate action toward ends that they foresee. This position is called **self-determinism.** It provides for a sense of responsibility and moral accountability.

The Sense of Personal Responsibility.   Human beings distinguish between what is and what ought to be. At times we feel a sense of personal responsibility to exert ourselves on behalf of what ought to be. The development of this sense of moral obligation is quite meaningless apart from some power of choice. The consciousness of freedom expresses itself forcibly in the sense of what ought to be. This is central to the moral life. After some choices, we have a keen feeling of blame or even of guilt because of the way we acted.

Moral Judgments on the Conduct and Character of Others.   All judgments on conduct and character presuppose that persons are free moral agents. We hold children responsible for their acts in proportion to their age and experience. We do not hold very young children responsible, but as they come to an age of understanding and are able to grasp clearly the significance of an act and its rightfulness or wrongfulness, we do hold them accountable. In our courts we do not generally hold people fully responsible unless we think that they could have done otherwise than they did—that is, that their own deliberate acts made, or could have made, the difference. Our whole system of reward and punishment, praise and blame, approval and disapproval assumes a large degree of freedom and responsibility.

ETHICS AND PRESUPPOSITIONS

Every branch of knowledge assumes certain ultimate presuppositions. Moral philosophy as conceived in the West has its own presuppositions: (a) It assumes that men are free, autonomous beings capable of some choice. (b) It assumes that action proceeds from deliberation and a state of character. (c) Traditional practical ethics also holds that knowledge of moral principles has a role to play in life and that human beings may freely acquire and select standards, rules or precepts in making such choices. (d) And finally, it presupposes that individuals (and groups) are responsible for their decisions and actions.

Paul W. Kurtz and Blanchard W. Means, "A Reassessment: Does Ethics

Have Any Metaphysical Presuppositions?" *Philosophical Quarterly* 9 (January 1959), p. 8.

Paul W. Kurtz (b. 1925) has taught at several colleges including Trinity (Hartford, Connecticut), Vassar, and the New School for Social Research. He is currently on the faculty of the State University of New York at Buffalo. The author and editor of several books, including Moral Problems in Contemporary Society, *Dr. Kurtz was a colleague of the late Blanchard W. Means (1905–1973) Brownell professor of philosophy at Trinity when they coauthored this essay.*

A PAUSE IN THE SEARCH

At this point in our search for a moral philosophy, we have been acquainting ourselves with some metaethical issues; we have not been wrestling with moral problems. (**Metaethics** includes reflection on the meaning and justification of moral concepts and statements; see Chapter 4.) We have considered several issues that need to be thought about before problems of moral conduct are explored. Among our conclusions so far are the following:

1. Moral decision making is inescapable; life forces choices.
2. Our choices are based on our values.
3. Some people believe that values are subjective, whereas others are convinced that values are objective.
4. The selection of values can be based in part on some suggested principles.
5. Among human beings past and present there is a variety of values and implied moral outlooks.
6. Some persons believe that there ought to be this variety of values and implied moral outlooks; there should be no universal standards for humanity.
7. Whatever is regarded as necessary for a good life is a right; many persons assume that some values and some rights are objective or natural.
8. Whether rights are objective or subjective is an ongoing debate.
9. The frequently stated goal of human fulfillment means different things to different people, depending on the values implied in a particular use of the term "human fulfillment." No one can use these words without some implied values.
10. There are many philosophical issues to consider as a person de-

velops a moral philosophy; a sensitivity to these issues helps deepen one's reflections on morality.

11. There are many common obstacles to clear thinking that prevent thoughtfulness in moral matters.

12. What an individual takes for granted about knowledge, reality, and values is crucial to an understanding of his or her moral position.

13. Even professional scholars often differ among themselves because of their different assumptions.

14. Differences in interpretations are inevitable, frequently because people begin their thinking with different convictions taken for granted.

15. Pluralism is the position that more than one thoughtful interpretation of most matters will exist, but pluralism does not imply that all of these positions are equally true. Instead, it is an admission of the limitation of human ability to arrive at certainty about most issues.

16. The philosophical issue of freedom is crucial to a moral philosophy. A concept of self-determinism is proposed, which seeks to balance the extremes of indeterminism and determinism. Thereby a reasonable degree of moral responsibility is supported.

The Search Continues

The background provided by the first two chapters will help you as you proceed to learn of the experiences of others who for centuries have been wrestling with the goals of moral conduct, the sources of moral wisdom, and standards by which conduct can be evaluated. The search continues with a look at the great ethical theories of the past and present.

CHAPTER REVIEW

A. Ingredients of a moral philosophy

1. Discriminating moral choices rather than passively accepted morality are generally preferred by philosophers.
2. In doing ethics we are faced with several questions of a philosophical nature.
3. More individuals than ever before have the time and opportunity to reflect on philosophical issues, instead of merely accepting prepackaged answers.

B. Obstacles to clear thinking

1. Clear thinking is often prevented by one or more of the following devices: tradition, common sense, propaganda, authoritarianism,

generalization, universalization, *ad hominem* argument, prejudice, and impatience.
2. Sincere moral authorities frequently use these devices to assist with their public proclamations of their ideas.

C. Ethics and philosophy

1. An important philosophical question is, "How do we know anything for sure?"
2. Epistemology is the area of philosophy concerned directly with our sources of knowledge, the nature of knowledge, and the validity of knowledge; these topics are directly related to issues of normative ethics.
3. Another important philosophical question is, "What is reality?"
4. Reality issues are within another area of philosophy, metaphysics. Questions that exemplify the relation between metaphysics and ethics are, "Is there a God who reveals His will?," "Are values built into nature?"
5. Human philosophies are built on the beliefs we take for granted.
6. Philosophical disagreements have existed throughout history and will continue to exist, in part because in all fields of study thinkers start with different assumptions.
7. We propose that we human beings are limited in what we can know for sure, and we hold that God, if there is one, knows with finality what is real, true, and of value.
8. Ethical pluralism proposes that the existence of different interpretations of what is taken for granted in matters of morality is inevitable.

D. Are we free to make choices?

1. The sense in which human beings are capable of making choices is crucial to ethics.
2. Indeterminism, determinism, fatalism, predestination, and self-determinism view human freedom and moral responsibility in different ways.

SUGGESTED READINGS

Berofsky, Bernard, ed. *Free Will and Determinism.* New York: Harper, 1966.

Many classic discussions of the current century illustrate extreme and moderate views.

Davis, Lawrence. *Theory of Action.* Englewood Cliffs, N.J.: Prentice-Hall, 1979.

Beginning with an insight into the difference between human action and bodily motion, the text utilizes this insight in an attempt to resolve the perennial problem of human freedom.

Engelhardt, H. Tristram, Jr., and Callahan, Daniel, eds. *Knowing and Valuing: The Search for Common Roots.* Hastings-on-Hudson, N.Y.: Hastings Center, 1980.

A contemporary collection of essays concerned with the foundations of ethics and the impact of science on conceptions of the foundations of ethics and vice versa.

Frankena, William. *Ethics.* 2nd ed. Englewood Cliffs, N.J.: Prentice-Hall, 1973.

A careful presentation of the main types of ethical theory in modern philosophy.

Freeman, Eugene, ed. *The Monist* vol. 62, no. 4 (October 1979).

The general topic is "Objectivity in Knowledge and Valuation."

Nozick, Robert. *Philosophical Explanations.* Cambridge, Mass.: The Belknap Press of Harvard Univ. Press, 1981.

For the advanced general reader, Harvard Professor Nozick seeks to replace the ideal of proof with the notion of explanation. Philosophical pluralism is included in the "Introduction," followed by provocative sections on metaphysics, epistemology, and value.

Rachels, James. "Can Ethics Provide Answers?" in *The Hastings Center Report,* vol. 10, no. 3 (June 1980).

A discussion of whether ethics can in fact provide answers; preliminary remarks about the relation between ethics and ethical theory.

3

Western Ethics to the Modern Age

These are the main features of Aristotle's Man of Justifiable Pride . . . the Man of Perfected Self-Righteousness: he who is . . . so assured of his own perfect virtue and so secure in it, that he can . . . justly demand the highest honour in recognition of his perfect virtue . . . Having no sense of his own radical imperfection, he knows no humility and no gratitude. Having no fear of doing wrong, he never has need of forgiveness, or of repentance and expiation; . . . and in his perfect self-sufficiency is accountable neither to other men, nor to the God whom Aristotle occasionally mentions.*

From the moment, then, when "by one man sin entered into the world, and death by sin, and so death passed upon all men, because all men sinned," the entire mass of our nature was ruined beyond doubt, and fell into the possession of its destroyer. And from him no one—no, not one—has been delivered, or is being delivered, or ever will be delivered, except by the grace of the redeemer.**

THREE BASIC QUESTIONS

The history of moral philosophy is the history of how our thinking about moral issues has been shaped by the wisdom of the past. All moral theories attempt to answer the following questions: (1) what is the intended goal of my moral action; (2) what is the source of or authority for my moral action; and (3) how do I evaluate my moral action?

All action, including moral action, is intended for some end. Moral theories differ about the ends they propose for moral behavior. Most suggest happiness, but happiness can be understood as sensual pleasure, serving others, intellectual contemplation, or in other ways. All moral

---

*Dorothea Krook, *Three Traditions of Moral Thought* (Cambridge: Univ. of Cambridge Press, 1959), p. 73.
**St. Augustine, "The Grace of Christ and Original Sin," in *An Augustine Reader,* ed. John J. O'Meara (Garden City, N.Y.: Doubleday, 1973), p. 476.

schemes rely upon some authority for knowing what to do: Reason, the will of God, intuition, and inclination are among the various sources of moral wisdom. The evaluation of moral action is as diverse as its various ends and sources. Some theories judge an act by its intention, others by its consequences.

In our survey of the major moral philosophies of the West, we shall be concerned with the significant answers they have provided to the three questions above. Those moral philosophies that demand our attention today have contributed in some lasting way to our self-understanding as moral persons. Each has offered us an insight into some aspect of moral reflection, which we can neglect only at our peril.

We will not, therefore, be attempting an exhaustive analysis of each moral philosopher. We will try to identify those elements in the history of moral thinking that have made a permanent impact upon the discussion of morality in our own time.

THE JEWISH AND CHRISTIAN FRAMEWORK OF WESTERN ETHICS

Although most major moral philosophers and most of those who analyze moral thinking today are not working out of a self-consciously chosen Christian or Jewish framework, it is a fact that most people in the Western world who make moral decisions do so within one of these two frameworks. Whether their choices are as carefully thought through or understood as are those of philosophers of moral theory is another matter. But if we were to allocate space in our historical review of moral theory according to the degree of influence moral theories have had, our study might be almost exclusively confined to the Judeo-Christian tradition. Regardless of our opinion of the harm or benefit of their moral teachings, the traditions of Judaism and Christianity influence the decision making of far more people than those who will ever read the moral thought of most of those philosophers examined in this study.

Morality and Religion

The influence of the Judeo-Christian tradition has been so deep and pervasive that many people equate morality with religion and religion with this Bible-inspired tradition. Both equations are misleading. It is possible for a moral philosophy to develop without conscious reference to a supreme being or to the traditional notion of God. Some philosophers (such as Paul Tillich) have argued that every philosophy presupposes some notion of an ultimate reality and thus has within it a notion of God, however different that notion might be from the view of God held by the orthodox theologies of the biblical religions. Religion itself is a broad phenomenon that encompasses a variety of beliefs and expressions, of which Christianity and Judaism are only two. Religion, one writer has argued, "is constituted by the most ultimate, least easily surrendered, most comprehensive choices a person or a society acts out. It is the living out of an intention, an option, a selection among life's possibilities."[1]

This accent on the element of moral choice essential to religion is echoed by Ronald Cavanagh when he refers to religion as the "varied, symbolic expression of, and appropriate response to, that which people deliberately affirm as being of unrestricted value for them."[2] Religion involves moral choice, and all fundamental affirmations of value entail some form of religion, no matter how different those forms are from the ones prevailing in Western culture.

RELIGION AS ULTIMATE CONCERN

Man, like every living being, is concerned about many things, above all about those which condition his very existence, such as food and shelter. But man, in contrast to other living beings, has spiritual concerns—cognitive, aesthetic, social, political. Some of them are urgent, often extremely urgent, and each of them as well as the vital concerns can claim ultimacy for a human life or the life of a social group. If it claims ultimacy it demands the total surrender of him who accepts this claim, and it promises total fulfillment even if all other claims have to be subjected to it or rejected in its name.

Modern humanist faith is a state of ultimate concern. This gives it its tremendous power for good and evil. In view of this analysis of humanist faith, it is almost ridiculous to speak of the loss of faith in the Western secular world. It has a secular faith, and this has pushed the different forms of religion into a defensive position; but it is faith and not "unbelief." It is a state of ultimate concern and total devotion to this concern.

Paul Tillich, *Dynamics of Faith* (New York: Harper, 1957), pp. 1, 68–69.

Paul Tillich (1886–1965) was one of the twentieth century's most prominent Christian theologians. He taught at Union Theological

---

[1]Michael Novak, *Ascent of the Mountain, Flight of the Dove* (New York: Harper, 1971), p. 2.
[2]Ronald Cavanagh, "The Term *Religion*," in *Introduction to the Study of Religion*, ed. T. William Hall (New York: Harper, 1978), p. 19.

Seminary, Harvard, and the University of Chicago. He was the author of a three-volume Systematic Theology *and numerous popular works on theology in relation to culture, science, art, and philosophy.*

THE ETHICS OF JUDAISM

The first of the biblical religions was Judaism. It emerged over 6,000 years ago as different tribes of people were brought together through the power of a unifying belief in a single God. In their scripture the Jews recorded their memory of the events that had brought their nation of Israel into being. In the recital of these events the foundation of their morality was laid. God, or Yahweh, had liberated them from slavery, granted them a set of laws (Torah), bound them in a covenant relationship with Him, and brought them to a land in which they were commanded to live out the moral laws He had given them. Judaism is a God-centered religion; consequently, the values its people are expected to adopt must ultimately have divine sanction. The living out of these values often involves following a complicated set of laws, such as dietary laws. Behind these beliefs is the claim that in God's covenant Jews (and potentially all persons) have found the source of their fulfillment. The token of that covenant is the law with which He binds the people to Him. Therefore, the law to Jews is not a burden but a gift.

Justice and Love

It is misleading to overemphasize the strict detail of Jewish ceremonial law as if it were the essence of Jewish morality. Although following the law is important, it does not replace the centrality of justice and love. The prophets are particularly emphatic about the need to restore justice, or righteousness, to its central place in Jewish ethics. Hebrew morality is as much concerned with the fulfillment of the community as it is with the fulfillment of the individual. The Hebrew Bible refuses to draw the kind of distinction between individuals and communities so often drawn by some contemporary moral philosophies. As a result, there is little or no difference between personal morality and the morality that "ties together" (*re-ligio*) all dimensions of social life. The goal of moral action—individual fulfillment—can be reached only if the individual is in relation to God and through Him to other persons in community. Moral action is evaluated chiefly by its effect upon and enhancement of community through love and justice. One finds few, if any, characters in the Hebrew Bible agonizing over the moral purity of their own souls. Rather, they feel real agony over what their deeds have done to obstruct the establishment of a just and loving community.

One consequence of this emphasis upon social morality is a developed concern for the material, economic needs of others. By taking the doctrine of Creation seriously, in which God is declared to have created the material world and called it good, Hebraic morality believes very strongly in the importance of sharing and enjoying the material goods of creation. Thus, its prophetic voices call for attention to the political and economic systems by which such sharing and enjoyment are enhanced or retarded. Because of its belief in a God who has created and maintains dominion over the material world, Jewish ethics harmonizes its grounding in God with its concern for the material well-being of persons.

Because the created order is considered essentially good, Hebraic morality places a high value upon the essentially human part of that creation: the mind. Thus, while emphasizing that complete fulfillment involves the whole person living in community, this morality encourages the individual to make free, reasoned choices about the course of his or her life. Human reason and freedom are part of creation. Their intelligent exercise is part of the way persons demonstrate their gratitude for the gift of creation. This does not mean that a revelation from God is not on occasion necessary to provide insight into His laws and purposes. But divine revelations are not treated as incomprehensible, irrational absurdities that must be accepted on blind faith. They are seen as the kind of revelations persons provide each other in an interpersonal relationship. They reveal God's intentions and character and thus provide the basis for an intelligent response to Him. God's intentions, for Hebraic thinking, are the ultimate reasons for the existence of the universe. Knowledge of God's purposes, therefore, is based upon His revelations through His deeds and is the source of moral wisdom.

THE MORALITY OF JESUS

It is now a commonplace that Christianity, the other biblical religion, arose from the soil of Judaism. But some people believe that Christianity departs from Judaism over the question of how moral acts are to be evaluated. Some claim that Jesus was much more interested in the effect of a moral act upon the soul of the moral agent than in its effect upon other persons and social structures.

It is true that Jesus did not fulfill any of the political expectations some people had for a Messiah. But a major debate is still going on over whether Jesus' primary moral concern was the individual salvation of the soul or the enhancement of the Kingdom as a social and political reality.

As a rabbi, Jesus certainly endorsed the first two Hebraic answers to our basic questions. The goal of moral action was to live in fulfillment with God and, through Him, with others. The source of moral wisdom was God's will made known through His revelations. One important interpretation of Christianity is that it differs from Judaism only in its insistence that in Jesus' life one sees the most decisive, clearest, and final revelation by God of what the fulfilled human life looks like. The validation of this revelation is held to be the resurrection of Jesus.

Whether Jesus understood the morality implicit in conforming to God's will in a way different from his Hebraic tradition depends on how one interprets his understanding of the Kingdom of God. He proclaimed its imminent coming and the necessity for repentance. At the heart of the Kingdom was reconciliation among human beings and between human beings and God. This reconciliation involved an inward renewal of the person in addition to an alteration in outward behavior. Jesus' lack of a developed social ethic is sometimes traced to his emphasis upon this inward renewal coupled with his belief that the Kingdom would come so soon that it would itself bring the appropriate transformations in outer social relations.

Love or Justice?

The heart of the morality taught by Jesus is the need for the healing gifts of forgiveness, understanding, and love. He embodied his teaching by reaching out to persons and making them whole, capable of turning in love to God and to others. He tried to touch the hearts and wills of individuals. Some have claimed that Jesus' concern for the subjectivity of the individual set off his moral position from Judaism. But no Hebraic morality would have denied the importance of the interior dimension of the individual. The crucial question in determining whether Jesus broke from his Hebraic tradition is deciding if the consequences of inspiring the heart and soul are essentially social or individual. If love is understood primarily as an emotional stance of forgiveness and acceptance of other persons, a Hebraic understanding would want to add immediately that this love must be coupled with justice. Justice would seek to extend to another person, in his or her political, social, and economic setting, the enjoyment and use of the created order. To put the question simply but starkly: Does Jesus' understanding of love involve nothing more than the ability of slaveowners to love their slaves as fellow children of God or does it also require them to abolish the conditions of slavery that keep slaves from enjoying the same political, economic, and social freedoms slaveowners enjoy?

Although Jesus himself regarded God as the ultimate source of moral wisdom, there have been varying interpretations of how Jesus is to be understood in relation to God. Is he primarily an authoritative teacher who explains the essence of morality, is he primarily one who embodies that morality in his life and thus serves as a moral exemplar, or is he someone to be worshipped as an ongoing bestower of moral wisdom after his death and resurrection? Each of these alternatives has been chosen by one or more Christian groups. But because each regards Jesus as in some sense a revealer of God's love, each grounds moral wisdom in divine revelation, as the Hebraic view does.

Finally, it should be noted that in both Jewish and Christian ethics the whole person is affected by moral action. Unlike later moral theories, which distinguished between moral behavior and other kinds of action, the biblical view of morality insists that all action, mental and physical, is ultimately moral. This insistence is grounded on the assumption that all of life should be a response to the God who created it and that His intention is for all of creation to be fulfilled. What one thinks, how one feels, and how one acts in relation to others are all part of what a full response to God entails.

BIBLICAL VIEWS ON JUSTICE AND LOVE

Seek good, and not evil, that you may live . . .
Hate evil, and love good, and establish justice in the gate . . .
Take away from me the noise of your songs; to the melody of
　your harps I will not listen.
But let justice roll down like waters, and righteousness like an
　ever-flowing stream.

Amos 5:14–15, 23–24

[Jesus] opened the book and found the place where it was written, "The Spirit of the Lord is upon me, because he has anointed me to preach good news to the poor. He has sent me to proclaim release to the captives and recovering of sight to the blind, to set at liberty those who are oppressed, to proclaim the acceptable year of the Lord." . . . And he began to say to them, "Today this scripture has been fulfilled in your hearing."

Luke 4:17–19, 21

But Judas Iscariot . . . said, "Why was this ointment not sold for three hundred denarii and given to the poor?" . . . Jesus said, "Let her alone, let her keep it for the day of my burial. The poor you always have with you, but you do not always have me."

John 12:4–5, 7–8

Pauline Ethics

One of the most important early interpreters of Jesus' meaning was the apostle Paul. He articulated the meaning of Jesus' teaching, death, and resurrection for the emerging Christian community. His ethical views have had a profound effect through the centuries on how Christians understand their moral obligations. Paul, a converted Jew, emphasized the need for divine grace in the fulfillment (salvation) of the individual. He believed that a person was not able by his or her own effort to obey God's revealed law and be saved. The only hope for a whole life was to accept, in faith, as a gift, the love of God, which forgave sinfulness and which had been incarnated in Jesus. The doctrine of sin, which played a large role in Paul's thought, was understood to refer to an originally free refusal to conform to God's will that had become so much a part of human nature that no one possessed the freedom to return to God on his or her own. Paul proclaimed that God had freely chosen to forgive and accept persons despite their being unworthy of forgiveness and acceptance. God's decision was spontaneous and uncoerced. Paul called it **agapaic love.** Unlike **erotic love,** which embraces another because the other can satisfy the lover's desires, agapaic love embraces another for the sake of the other. The ethical implications of God's agapaic love were at the heart of Paul's moral theology. Christians were now free to love others in the way God had first loved them. Paul put great emphasis upon the Christian fellowship, in which agapaic love flourished. The love of the Christian community was, in the famous words of his letter to the church at Corinth: "patient and kind; love is not jealous or boastful; it is not arrogant or rude. Love does not insist on its own way; it is not irritable or resentful; it does not rejoice at wrong, but rejoices in the right. Love bears all things, believes all things, hopes all things, endures all things" (I Cor. 13:4–7).

Paul's own understanding of the implications of love within the fellowship of believers and between believers and "outsiders" was complicated by the social values of his time, his expectation that the world was coming to an end in the near future, and by his own psychological character. On the one hand, his view of agapaic love as concerned only for the needs of others led him to proclaim that within the Christian community all the social and economic distinctions of the larger society had no place. "In Christ, there is neither Jew nor Greek, there is neither slave nor free, there is neither male nor female" (Gal. 3:28). On the other hand, Paul set forth, almost as rules for Christian conduct, proscriptions on the role of women in worship and advice on sexual relations which betray strong antifeminist and antisexual biases.

It has been difficult for Paul's interpreters to sort out in his teaching the values implicit in the ministry of Jesus, the values Paul developed from his reading of Jesus' teaching, and Paul's personal beliefs that are not an essential part of his Christian faith. This mix of views was handed on from

Pauline Christianity to the larger Roman and Greek world into which the Christian faith was spreading.

CHRISTIAN ETHICS ENCOUNTERS GREEK PHILOSOPHY

Socrates

As Christianity came into contact with other religions and philosophies, it was the teaching of Paul that proved the most influential in shaping Christian morality from the first centuries B.C.E. (common era) down through the Renaissance and beyond. It is impossible to overestimate the importance of the encounter between the developing Christian religion and the philosophies emerging from Greece, especially those that had been influenced by the Greek philosophers Socrates, Plato, and Aristotle. The encounter was so influential that many people even today have trouble distinguishing the ethic of Jesus from the ethic of Socrates. The Greek philosophers brought the importance of rational reflection and the alignment of morality with truth to the forefront of moral thinking. Their voice of reason, which tended to call persons beyond the tyranny of passion and liberate them from enslavement to their own narrow biases, has been heard from their time to our own.

Interest in leading a life of reasoned conduct was not new with Socrates (470–399 B.C.E.). But he brought reflection on what a good life is to new heights and sophistication. Proceeding on the assumption that "the unexamined life is not worth living," Socrates explored by sympathetic but critical questioning the tacit assumptions people rely upon in their beliefs and actions. By employing what has become known as the Socratic method, Socrates asked questions of his followers about the implications of certain assumptions. If the implications, logically derived, conflicted with the original assumption, the believer would be obliged to go back and straighten out his thinking. Implicit in this Socratic questioning is the conviction that a living grasp of knowledge or Truth is not only a goal of life but also a source of happiness and a liberation from bias and prejudice.

While Socrates retained to the end of his life a healthy scepticism regarding his having attained absolute Truth, he imparted to his successors the belief that if Truth could be secured, it would reveal the nature of the Good. We would then be obliged by our own inner nature to live according to it. One of the most appealing acts of Socrates was the manner in which he chose to accept his own death according to his principle that truthfulness is virtue. Condemned to die on the charge that he had corrupted the youth of Athens because of his teaching that no claim to truth or right go unquestioned, he accepted death calmly, freely downing the fatal cup of hemlock.

THE PHILOSOPHER'S MISSION: SOCRATES' FINAL DISCOURSE

Men of Athens, I honour and love you; but I shall obey God rather than you and while I have life and strength I shall never cease from the practice and teaching of philosophy, exhorting any one whom I meet and saying to him after my manner: You, my friend,—a citizen of the great and mighty and wise city of Athens,—are you not ashamed of heaping up the greatest amount of money and honour and reputation, and caring so little about wisdom and truth and the greatest improvement of the soul, which you never regard or heed at all? And if the person with whom I am arguing, says: Yes, but I do care; then I do not leave him or let him go at once; but I proceed to interrogate and examine and cross-examine him, and if I think that he has no virtue in him, but only says that he has, I reproach him with undervaluing the greater, and overvaluing the less. And I shall repeat the same words to every one whom I meet, young and old, citizen and alien, but especially to the citizens, inasmuch as they are my brethren. For know that this is the command of God; and . . . Wherefore, O men of Athens, I say to you, . . . either acquit me or not; but whichever you do, understand that I shall never alter my ways, not even if I have to die many times.

Plato, *The Apology,* in *Works of Plato,* selected and ed. Irwin Edman. Jowett trans. (New York: Modern Library, 1928), pp. 74–75.

Plato

The philosopher who compiled the Socratic teachings was Plato (c. 427–347 B.C.E.). Like Socrates he was committed to the use of reason as the source of moral wisdom. Plato believed that the good of each thing in the universe was related to the Good of the universe as a whole. Therefore, if each thing follows what is good for it, it will be virtuous. For the human being, contemplation or knowledge of the Truth was good and therefore virtuous, according to Plato. But knowledge was not the sole good of the wise person. A balance or harmony between contemplation and enjoyment in moderation was necessary for complete well-being. The soul strives to know the Forms, or Ideas that transcend the changes of the empirical world, but it also seeks to control or harmonize two other parts of itself: a feeling part that is the origin of sensation, and a desiring part that is the source of unbridled passion. The good life will consist in the proper harmony of these dimensions of the human person under the guidance of wisdom or reason.

One very important implication of Plato's view was that a person who knew the Truth would necessarily act according to it. The true philosopher, the one who has correctly reflected, will necessarily choose what is best in any given situation. It follows that evil acts are done not by choice but by ignorance of what is good. The evaluation of moral action, therefore, is its success in following rational knowledge of the Good and in maintaining within the self and the state a harmony between passions and desires. The importance of this view is that it conflicts explicitly with the claim made by many Christian moralists that evil resides in the will, in deliberate choice, rather than in ignorance, which is normally not willed.

Aristotle

Aristotle (c. 384–348 B.C.E.) was a disciple of Plato. Like Plato he held that human happiness means well-being and that it will be achieved by well-doing. If people do best what they are suited to do best, then they will be happy. Although the intellectual activity is the highest one, persons will find happiness in the exercise of their other faculties as well. The development of such faculties, including the moral ones, is the development of virtue. A virtue is a mean between two extremes and is based on a disposition or tendency within the individual to choose such a mean. Virtue is relative, however, to the end to which a thing is oriented. The virtue of a hoe is to dig, the virtue of a mind to think. Virtuous human beings are those who have harmonized all the different functions of which they are comprised. The source or model of moral wisdom is the perfectly virtuous person—the one who has achieved the perfect balance and ordering of all functions. This is equivalent to being the perfectly realized moral individual: the one who has achieved moral self-sufficiency. Notice how different this view is from that of the biblical notion that morality is the way to achieve not self-sufficiency but the fulfillment that comes from dependence upon a divine creator.

In a sense, the moral goal of Aristotle is the individual's feeling of intrinsic satisfaction at having brought all faculties under the control of reason and moderation. We learn how to achieve this satisfaction by observing and then emulating the rules for virtuous action that wise persons follow. The virtues are acquired by practicing them.

This practice involves primarily the attempt to live by the golden mean, or moderation, a balanced course between too much and too little. For example, courage is the middle position between rashness and cowardice;

self-control is the mean between overindulgence and repression. The finding of the mean is a result of the application of practical wisdom, the ability to see, in the actual circumstances of life, what is the appropriate thing to do. In this sense, Aristotle was much more attuned to the nonspeculative parts of human life, much more commonsensical, than was Plato. He did not rely upon strict mathematical rules for determining what a mean is: He says it should be determined "relative to us" by a rational principle, by that "principle as would take shape in the mind of a man of sense or practical wisdom."[3]

Part of Aristotle's commonsense approach led him to assert that no individual can be truly happy apart from social relations with others. He called the ordered relations among persons the **state.** He declared that "it is evident that the state is a creation of nature, and that man is by nature a political animal. And he who by nature and not by mere accident is without a state, is either a bad man or above humanity."[4]

The Epicureans and Stoics

In addition to the schools of Plato and Aristotle, the moral philosophies of the Epicureans and Stoics, particularly the latter, were decisive in influencing Western morality. Distressed by what they regarded as the suffering that comes from overindulgence of the appetites and too much attachment to aspects of this changeable, frustrating world, both schools developed a philosophy and ethic that was intended to free the individual from distress. Like Plato and Aristotle, the Epicureans and Stoics saw morality as a way of liberating the self from the uncertainty and pain of emotional attachment to the transitory things of the world. They sought a moral stance that would lift them above the prison of worldly concern. Epicurus (b. 342 B.C.E) was concerned with relieving people from worry about death, calamity, and misfortune. He found that belief in the determinism of all things made it possible to avoid the worrisome sense of responsibility for pleasing the gods or for avoiding evil. All people pursue pleasure as the goal of life, but Epicurus considered the best pleasure to be that which avoided pain and emphasized intellectual pursuits. Epicurus was not crass or sensual: He believed that real pleasure came from a calm detachment from the pleasures of the moment. The way to achieve this state of tranquility was to eliminate as many needs as possible, because unfulfilled needs produce frustration and pain. Self-control and a moderate asceticism were recommended. The source of moral wisdom is the individual's rational assess-

[3]Aristotle, *Nicomachean Ethics*, book 2, ch. 6, trans. J. A. K. Thomson (Baltimore: Penguin, 1953), p. 66.
[4]Aristotle, "Politics," 1253a 1–4 in *Selections*, ed. W. D. Ross (New York: Scribners, 1927), p. 287.

ment of what will produce the greatest long-term avoidance of pain. One then judges one's actions by one's success at avoiding pain.

The Stoics were similar to the Epicureans in that they regarded the overcoming of pain as the goal of moral life. They believed that they could achieve this by living in accord with rather than in conflict with the laws of nature. Like Socrates, Plato, and Aristotle, they believed that the most important laws for man to follow were those of reason. Reason will enable us to know what the laws of nature are, and if we live in harmony with them we will not desire those things that cannot be ultimately satisfying. The laws of nature are so powerful that we would merely be frustrating ourselves if we tried to act against them. The virtue of a person is that by reason he or she can know these laws and willingly conform to them. The most troublesome part of the human character is the passions, which irrationally attach themselves to things which are unstable and transitory. The passions of pleasure, sorrow, desire, and fear are unnatural. If we can avoid being motivated by them we will experience a painless detachment from worldly struggle. As long as we are indifferent to events we cannot control, we cannot be hurt by the lack of material goods or an excess of physical illness. The wise person is the one who knows that goodness rests with the intrinsic satisfaction of the soul, not the extrinsic pleasure that comes from having the passions satisfied by worldly objects. Like Aristotle, the Stoics looked on self-sufficient individuals as moral exemplars. It was they who had achieved complete indifference toward all external objects and thus had removed from their concern things that could hurt them without their consent.

Summary

In summary, it can be said that all the Greek moral philosophers understood morality as the way by which individuals can bring themselves to happiness or self-realization. The essential meaning of happiness was a development of character that was sufficient in virtue unto itself. That is, it was intrinsically worthwhile and personally satisfying to reach that state in which one chose by rational contemplation those habits of mind, attitude, and action that were least dependent upon external objects for their fulfillment. This did not mean that the virtuous were oblivious to external objects or to other persons. But true virtue consisted in the ability to control one's acts and desires in accordance with the rational faculty. The perfectly self-controlled person, whose emotions are under the tight rein of reason, the person who knows that externally determined pleasure is not ultimately satisfying, is the perfectly autonomous moral being. Evil or vice are brought about by ignorance or by permitting the passions to dominate reason. But there is no inherent defect in the person that makes the overcoming of vice impossible. Individuals, therefore, have the power through reason to achieve moral self-sufficiency, and thus the happiness that their nature makes possible.

Although persons might not share in the optimism of the Greek philosophers regarding the power of reason, few would ignore their valuable stress upon critical reflection. The need to base moral action on objective grounds and not be swayed by desire for private gain became part of all subsequent moral thinking. In addition, the notions of moderation and harmony among the human faculties reveal a wisdom even alternative moral systems would respect.

THE CHRISTIANIZING OF GREEK PHILOSOPHY

Augustine

As these Greek moral philosophies came into contact with Christian moral philosophy from the third century of our common era, they found themselves becoming Christianized and the Christian outlook influenced by Greek thought. For example, it was easy for some to equate the Christian distrust of this world with stoic detachment from all external objects. Others equated Plato's idea of the Good with the Christian God. Still others gave Socrates' noble death a moral importance equal to that of Jesus' crucifixion. But it was essentially the apparently similar attempt to develop a moral stance superior to that which accepted the common ways of the political and commercial world or that based itself upon a hedonistic desire to satisfy the sensual passions that caused Greek moral philosophy to have such an impact on Christian ethics. The joining of these views profoundly affected the morality of the West from the fourth to the seventeenth century.

But the influence of Greek thought on Christian belief encountered stiff resistance at a number of crucial points. We see this most clearly in the thought of the enormously influential Christian bishop and theologian Augustine of Hippo (354–430). While clearly a Christian, Augustine was in some respects also a neo-Platonist. He had accepted from this school of thought that developed after Plato the belief that the true, the good, and the right had to have a supernatural origin. Nothing that was subject to change, time, space, or materiality could serve as the basis of truth. Therefore, God must be beyond all earthly conditions. Fulfillment could be found only with God. But Augustine's Christian convictions about the nature of sin prohibited him from accepting the hellenistic claim that human beings possessed the power to rectify their own moral inadequacies. He insisted that human creatures had so alienated themselves from God that they were unable to achieve happiness by their own efforts. Augustine declared that only an unmerited, agapastic decision by God to save the fallen human creature could accomplish salvation. Augustine knew from his own experiences how difficult it was simply to decide that one is too attached to the things of this world. As a result he concluded that it could only be by God's grace that the will could attach itself to God. He thus broke with the hellenistic assumption that fulfillment could come about through the achievement of moral self-sufficiency.

Augustine also rejected the hellenistic notion that evil was due to ignorance and that the source of goodness rested in the reason. He knew too deeply the pernicious power of the will, and consequently he made it the source of evil. It was by wrong choices, determined by their passions or will, that people fell into sin. Perhaps Augustine's major contribution to moral theory was his insistence that self-determined morality was not a possibility for rational man. It was possible only by the grace of God breaking into the corrupt human condition from the outside.

The State

One important social effect of Augustine's views, which was to shape the attitude of the medieval period toward the social order, was his claim that because persons are corrupt, they need the order and restraint of law. The state exists primarily to serve this function. Social structures do not exist essentially to enrich and deepen our social nature: They serve to keep sin's manifestations within bounds and are therefore a gift of God to his fallen creation. The state exists primarily because of sin, and the ruler of the state is appointed by God as a punisher and controller of the external manifestations of sin.

This view of the social order as established, at least in part, to curb the excesses of sinful behavior justified (for later generations influenced by Augustine) restraint and coercion by the state. It also contributed to the view that efforts to redeem social corruption are naïve in underestimating the power of human pride and greed.

In the area of moral theory, Augustine's greatest contribution was to deny the efficacy of free will for salvation. In his famous debate with the monk Pelagius, Augustine declared heretical the notion that human beings can choose to cooperate with divine grace or to avoid sinning. He does not deny that the original man, Adam, had free choice to obey God, but following his fall a moral incapacity (original sin) has been transmitted biologically to all Adam's descendants.

Augustine's pessimism regarding moral ability apart from God's grace is a legacy bequeathed to the leaders of the Reformation and, through diverse and complicated channels, to many religious moralities in the modern age. It represents, perhaps in an extreme form, an understanding of God's role in the formation of morality that according to its defenders has been dangerously diminished in secular moral thought.

Aquinas and Thomistic Ethics

Augustine's almost total reliance upon God's grace and denial of human contributions to salvation was qualified in significant ways by later Christian thinkers of the middle ages. The most important of these was St. Thomas Aquinas (1224–1274).

Aquinas was more concerned than Augustine to harmonize Christian faith with the best of philosophical thinking. Although he did not deny the priority and supremacy of revealed truth, Aquinas believed that the human intellect, created by God, had the capacity to understand the world of nature and to refute any rational attempts to deny the truth of revelation. The philosophy that he found most congenial to his Christian faith and to a rational understanding of the natural world was that of Aristotle. It is sometimes said that Aquinas Christianized the philosophy of Aristotle or that he Aristotelianized the Christian faith. Whichever view is more accurate, it is true that Aquinas accorded human reason much more worth than Augustine had.

We see this particularly in his moral theory. It is hard to overestimate Thomas's influence on vast segments of the Christian community down through the centuries. His thought has been virtually canonized by the Roman Catholic church and forms the basis of many other moral philosophies. Sometimes known simply as the natural law theory, the moral philosophy of Aquinas (the basis of Thomism) assumes a fundamental correspondence between the rational faculty of the human mind and the structures and laws of the natural world. Morality consists in acting in accordance with these laws as they are discerned by the rational mind.

As a Christian, Aquinas assumes that all persons have an ultimate end: the knowledge and love of God. Although he allows room for the love of God in humanity's final state of blessedness (happiness), the emphasis is clearly upon a rational contemplation of divine things. In this respect, Aquinas reveals his indebtedness to Greek philosophy and in particular to Aristotle. Unlike Aristotle, however, Aquinas holds that sin makes it impossible for human beings to achieve ultimate happiness by their own efforts. This is his debt to Augustine. God's grace is necessary, and it is to be found in the teachings, sacraments, and discipline of the church, which is the custodian of God's revelation.

Because Aquinas assumes God's supernatural status, he regards human beings as having a two-fold aim: supernatural happiness (to be achieved by faith and grace, and natural happiness (to be achieved by reason and the use of natural faculties). The two levels of happiness, although clearly distinct from one another, harmonize with each other in the sense that the natural world is ordained by the supernatural. This means that no natural end or desire of human beings is contrary to their supernatural end or desire (God), even though ultimate happiness requires the perfection of the natural world by supernatural grace.

In the moral world this means that persons are virtuous to the degree that they employ reason in understanding the natural laws that govern the created order and to the degree that their behavior conforms to those laws. The natural law is morally binding because its source is the divine law and because it is rational, that is, reflective of God's ordering principles:

> In voluntary activity the proximate measure is the human reason, the supreme measure the eternal law. When a human act goes to its end in harmony with the order of reason and eternal law then the act is right; when it turns away from that rightness it is termed sin. To disparage the dictate of reason is equivalent to condemning the command of God.
>
> To crown his natural appetites man is given a directive for his personal acts, and this we call law. Law is the reason and rule of activity, and therefore is reserved to those who can know the reason of what they do . . . Rational creatures share in the eternal reason and this communication of the eternal law to rational creatures is called the natural law. The natural light of the reason, by which we discern what is right and wrong, is aught else but the impression on us of divine light.[5]

We know that we are dealing with a natural moral law when it is discoverable to our minds that it is universal for all persons, unchangeable under all conditions, and ineradicable from rational insight. It is a law of nature, for example, that the organs of reproduction seek to fulfill their end. Thus it is a moral law that human beings should not artifically obstruct the primary end of their reproductive organs through contraception. To do so is to obstruct that which God intended through his creation of the natural order. There are other teachings of the Roman Catholic church on such topics as abortion and euthanasia, among others, that are drawn from the moral philosophy of Thomas Aquinas.

Although we will take up these issues later, in our consideration of contemporary moral problems, it is important to understand the underlying strength of the Thomist position as its proponents interpret it. It has clear answers to our three basic moral questions: Happiness, consisting in the harmony of the will and intellect loving and contemplating God, is the end of moral action. Moral wisdom is provided ultimately by God but proximately by our own human reason, which is a creation of God and, as such, is in conformity with the natural end of human beings and the created order as a whole. Therefore, there need be no inherent conflict in our moral determinations as long as we follow our own rational insights. Finally, we can evaluate our moral acts by the degree to which they conform to our rational understanding of the natural law. In all our moral deliberations, we are supported by the knowledge that what is truly natural is what is

---

[5]Saint Thomas Aquinas, *Philosophical Texts,* selected and trans. Thomas Gilby (New York: Oxford Univ. Press, 1960), pp. 284, 356–358.

moral and just because God has willed it this way in accord with his reason. Thomistic morality proceeds in a tight circle, but one that is large enough not to exclude anything significantly human or natural and that ties the human to the divine without contradiction or paradox.

The significance of this circle is that it links our moral choices directly to the reality of God through the divinely sanctioned medium of reason, to which, by virtue of being human, we have priviledged access. Although specific applications of moral law in concrete situations can be tricky and less than certain, the knowledge that we will be moral as long as we proceed rationally and in accord with the intent to conform to the natural law is spiritually and psychologically comforting. Although infused grace may be necessary for supernatural beatitude, the use of our natural faculties will suffice for determining our moral obligations in our natural state of existence.

Given Aquinas's stress upon the natural ends of man in this world, it is not surprising that the moral virtues he advocates are very similar to those of Aristotle. There are four cardinal moral virtues in his theory: prudence, temperance, fortitude, and justice. (These are perfected or complemented by the theological virtues, infused into humans by God alone, which direct them toward God: faith, hope, and love). Like the Greeks, although in a Christian framework, Aquinas leaned toward the view that the morally upright persons were the individuals of virtue, whose good habits had perfected their rational powers toward their right use.

Although Aquinas's confidence that the natural and supernatural realms could be harmoniously related without either paradox or recourse to the irrational was modified in the centuries after his death, his lasting contribution to moral theory was his view that reason, natural laws, human desire, and divine sanction must complement each other. As long as human reason, penetrating the order of nature, is able to discern laws and regularities, human moral choice will have a solid foundation. To violate the rationality and orderliness of the natural world in the name of a private or singular end is to violate the very basis of morality. Although the divine complement and supernatural perfection of the natural order was to be slowly and subtly removed by later, more secular thinkers, the rational core of Thomas's thought would be a lasting legacy to all later moral thought.

REFORMATION ETHICS

Before religion began to lose its exclusive hold upon moral thinking, however, one last contribution to the moral consciousness of the West was to come from religious thought. The dissolution of the medieval synthesis of reason and faith, church and state in the events of the Reformation was to have as one of its offshoots a loosening of the bonds between reason and morality. In their anxiety to remove the absolute legitimacy of human intermediaries between the individual and God, the reformers, especially Martin Luther and John Calvin, tended to undermine the absolute authority of human institutions. Afraid lest men rely upon these institutions to earn the love of God (which they insisted God dispensed freely, without human merit, and despite human corruption), these reformers undercut the authority of human reason, as the primary determinant of morality.

Although they insisted upon the necessity of a moral life (still equated with the Christian life), the origin of that morality and its evaluation had to come from God's grace alone. Thus they almost buried the natural, rational half of the Thomistic synthesis. Human reason and will were too corrupt to be trusted either to discern the natural laws or to follow them. In many respects, the reformers returned to the moral thinking of Augustine and even Paul. While trusting the indwelling of the Holy Spirit to guide moral action within the Christian community itself, the reformers held, like Augustine, that in public, social settings, like the state, human sinfulness needed to be checked by the coercive powers of law, threat, and punishment. As a result of these views, dualism slowly developed between the morality sanctioned within the church and that which prevailed in the world beyond its walls. The state and its institutions were given the power of the sword to restrain and punish the inevitable outbursts of sinful inclination. The morality incumbent upon Christians in their relation with one another was not to substitute itself for the orderly running of the social and political life of the society at large.

Social Versus Private Morality

Although the views of the reformers were to be swept aside by the tide of rationalistic and secular thought in the modern age, they continued to have a powerful effect on the lives of millions of people within one half of the now divided Christian church, most of whom would never read the works of secular theorists such as Kant, Hobbes, or Bentham. Perhaps the most important long-term consequence of these Reformation moral assumptions was the division of morality into private and social realms. It became axiomatic for many Protestants that if God's grace was necessary for the enactment of any good deed, then it would be found most likely in the personal deeds of individuals and not in the impersonal acts of institutions and the state. It might be wrong for an individual to strike another, but no such prohibition should be placed upon the acts of the state when defending its territory or laws. The office of the person entrusted with social or political power should be morally distinguished from the person holding such office. Whereas a ruler might be severely judged by God for hardening his heart to his wife, he would be expected to uphold his moral duty by condemning to death someone convicted of stealing.

It is instructive to note the difference between this Reformation view and that of the Thomistic moral philosophy. Because Thomas had insisted that all natural law conformed to the dictates of reason, he was justified in excluding no part of the natural order from rational, and hence moral, consideration. For example, the economic transactions of society were as much a matter of moral judgment as the relations within a family. Thus it was not unusual to find moral laws, sanctioned by the church, expressly forbidding certain economic practices, such as usury (money lending). But with the reformers we find a striking change of outlook. Although they were equally hostile to usury, they condemned it essentially for the sake of the individual soul. The attempt to prohibit it by social legislation they considered an improper intrusion of private morality into public concerns. In the words of R. H. Tawney, speaking of Luther's views on economic injustice, "the prophet who scourged with whips the cupidity of the individual chastised with scorpions the restrictions imposed upon it by society . . . He preaches a selfless charity, but he recoils with horror from every institution by which an attempt had been made to give it a concrete expression." The result, according to Tawney, was that the views of Luther "riveted on the social thought of Protestantism a dualism which, as its implications were developed, emptied religion of its social content, and society of its soul."[6]

In many respects the Reformation signalled the end of the religious unity that had prevailed in the West since the early days of the Christian church. Although it continued to influence the lives of millions of people, Christianity, now split in two, no longer dominated the mainstream of intellectual and moral thought. Modern moral philosophy began when thinkers no longer felt obliged to consult a theological system or to direct their thought by a sense of divine revelation or judgment.

Until the modern age, most theologians and moral philosophers tried to take seriously both the demands of reason and the reality (as they understood it) of sin. Reason required faithfulness to intellectual integrity and an acknowledgment of the human ability to participate in the creation of moral consciousness and behavior. Sin demanded an awareness of the need to rely upon a nonhuman power to overcome the corruption and blindness of moral action apart from God. As the modern age dawned, the consciousness of sin diminished and the attention of the moral philosopher turned more and more to the pragmatic need to provide guidance to self-motivated individuals struggling to realize their autonomy but living in sometimes conflicting and ambiguous relation with other individuals.

[6]R. H. Tawney, *Religion and the Rise of Capitalism* (New York: Harcourt, 1926), pp. 86, 90.

CHAPTER REVIEW

A. Three basic questions

1. All moral theories attempt to answer three basic questions: What is the goal of moral action? What is source of or authority for moral action? How is moral action evaluated?

B. The Jewish and Christian framework of Western ethics

1. Judaism and Christianity influence moral decision making for millions of people.
2. A moral philosophy need not have a religious foundation in the traditional sense, but all religions involve moral choice and all moral choice presupposes some ultimate values.

C. The ethics of Judasim

1. Judaism is based upon a belief that morality arises out of a covenant relation with God.
2. Its morality is concerned primarily with the community and with the establishment of justice among its members.

D. The morality of Jesus

1. There is debate over whether Jesus' ethics are essentially inward or whether they have an equally important social dimension.
2. Paul formulated the ethic of Jesus for the emerging Christian community. He emphasized unmerited love, *agape,* within the Christian fellowship.

E. Christian ethics encounters Greek philosophy

1. Socrates contributed the notion of the examined life to moral thinking.
2. Plato emphasized the notion that to know the good is to do it.
3. Aristotle provided a portrait of the virtuous person who lives by the golden mean.
4. The Epicureans and Stoics developed an ethic of indifference to transitory pleasure and the overcoming of pain through reason.

F. The Christianizing of Greek philosophy

1. Augustine challenged the Greek philosophers' assumption that virtue could be achieved by reason alone. He stressed human dependence upon God for moral wisdom.

2. One implication of Augustine's view was his notion of the state as an ordering and restraining power.
3. Thomas Aquinas developed a moral philosophy that gave prominence to the notion of natural law and the role of reason in discerning it.

G. Reformation ethics

1. Luther and Calvin challenged the medieval reliance upon reason in the formation of morality and returned to some of Augustine's concerns.
2. The reformers helped to create a dualism between private and social morality.

SUGGESTED READINGS

D'Entreves, A. P. *Natural Law: An Historical Survey.* New York: Harper, 1965.

A study of the development of the relation between morality, nature, and law.

Gardner, E. Clinton. *Biblical Faith and Social Ethics.* New York: Harper, 1960.

Especially good for its short summary of the development of Jewish and Christian ethics.

Krook, Dorothea. *Three Traditions of Moral Thought.* Cambridge: Cambridge Univ. Press, 1959.

The first part is a stimulating discussion of the relation between the moral philosophies of Plato, Aristotle, and Paul.

Manson, T. W. *Ethics and the Gospel.* New York: Scribners, 1960.

The development of Christian ethics from their origins in Judaism to the time of the earliest Christian communities.

Sidgwick, Henry. *Outlines of the History of Ethics.* New York: St. Martin's, 1967, pp. 1–162.

A classic, short survey.

Troeltsch, Ernst. *The Social Teachings of the Christian Churches.* 2 vols. Trans. Olive Wyon. New York: Harper, 1960.

A comprehensive history and analysis of the moral teachings of the Christian churches, including the various Protestant branches.

4

Moral Philosophy
in the Modern Age

*Our age is essentially one of understanding and reflection, without passion,
momentarily bursting into enthusiasm, and shrewdly relapsing into repose.*

*Morality is character, character is that which is engraved; but the sand and the sea
have no character and neither has abstract intelligence, for character is really inward-
ness. Immorality, as energy, is also character, but to be neither moral nor immoral is
merely ambiguous, and ambiguity enters into life when the qualitative distinctions are
weakened by a gnawing reflection.**

THE INDIVIDUAL IN SOCIETY

Since the Reformation, with some notable exceptions, moral philosophy
has concerned itself primarily with the development of principles of conduct for rational individuals living in a social order. Social orders require
that their subjects obey the laws that knit the social fabric together. The
moral philosophers of the modern age have tried to provide a justification
for such obedience.

Thomas Hobbes

One of the first to do so was the Englishman Thomas Hobbes (1588–1679).
He begins with the conviction that persons do need some rules for their
relations with each other and that they are basically opposed to each other's interests. People are, by nature, in a state of war, each one driven by
the desire for self-preservation and egoistic pleasure. Other persons are
obstacles to both goals and must therefore be guarded against or dominated. Individuals in this state of war are dependent solely upon their own

*Søren Kierkegaard, *The Present Age*, trans. Alexander Dru (New York: Harper, 1962), pp. 33,
43.

wits and power. In such a state no morality exists. It is a time of "continual fear and danger of violent death, and the life of man, solitary, poor, nasty, brutish, and short."[1] In this state "the notions of right and wrong... have no place... that to be every man's, that he can get: and for so long as he can keep it."[2]

The state of war is inimical to each person's own self-interest. Therefore, by reason and desire, persons come together out of self-interest to form social groups in order to avoid the worst consequences of continual warfare. Reason helps them to see that if they draw up agreements about their relations with each other, all will benefit. These agreements Hobbes calls laws of nature: They are precepts, or general rules, "found out by reason, by which a man is forbidden to do that which is destructive of his life or taketh away the means of preserving the same; and to omit that by which he thinketh it may be best preserved."[3] Notice here how the notion of the law of nature has been transformed from Aquinas's view that it is a structure of reality ordained by God to Hobbes's view that it is a creation of human self-interest. The formation of these laws permits the building of societies, or commonwealths, in which each person's desire for preservation and security is reasonably well satisfied. Hobbes lists in his *Leviathan* a number of these natural laws, foremost among which are those that state that everyone should seek peace if possible but if that is not feasible, all the advantages of war may be used; that persons should grant to others just the same amount of liberty they want for themselves; and that promises or covenants should be kept. Failure to abide by covenants will abolish any hope of justice. All the laws of nature depend upon the state's power to enforce them against transgressors. "Covenants without the sword are but word." The Leviathan (monster) referred to by Hobbes is the commonwealth. It chooses a sovereign, in the form of an assembly or a single ruler, who is granted the power to enact sanctions against the breaking of the social laws. The members of the commonwealth do so for their own sake as a pragmatic means of ensuring their own safety and pleasure.

COMPETITION OR UNITY: A CRITIQUE OF HOBBES

Though Hobbesism has been violently and triumphantly exposed and disproved by most modern social theorists, it seems to possess a vitality which refuses to succumb. The reason is that it dares to provide a rational defence of the practice of a compe-

---

[1] Thomas Hobbes, *Leviathan,* in *English Works of Thomas Hobbes*, vol. 3, ed. William Molesworth (London: John Bohn, 1936), p. 113.
[2] Hobbes, p. 115.
[3] Hobbes, p. 116–117.

titive society which in theory we find it emotionally necessary to disown.

The criticism [of Hobbes] may be put most stringently by saying that Hobbes is wrong in thinking that there is nothing in human nature to act as a bond of unity between man and man . . . Hobbes takes too low a view of human motives and too high a view of human reason. Because his conception of human motives is completely negative and egocentric, he is compelled to throw on human reason a task which it is too weak to undertake. Unless the natural tendencies of human behaviour themselves provided a bond of society, reason itself could never construct the State. Consequently, one has only to show that man's animal nature provides already a bond of unity between man and man to refute Hobbesism.

John Macmurray, *Persons in Relation* (New York: Harper, 1961), pp. 136, 138.

---

*John Macmurray (1891–1976) was a Scottish philosopher who wrote extensively on morality, religion, and the nature of persons in relation to one another. His best-known works come from his Gifford Lectures in 1954—*The Self as Agent *and* Persons in Relation. *He was professor of moral philosophy at Edinburgh from 1944 to 1958.*

In a sense Hobbes provides a secularized version of the Augustinian-Reformation understanding of human nature and its need for social restraint and coercion. No God ordains the power of the secular ruler; rather, it is justified for pragmatic reasons. In this respect Hobbes marks clearly his departure from the long-dominant Christian moral outlook and at the same time implicitly acknowledges his debt to its attempt to deal with one of the most persistent of all moral problems—the lack of perfect love in the relations of persons with each other.

Although he was not a Utilitarian in the technical sense, Hobbes did look forward to that moral philosophy, which was to continue the movement from the idea of divinely sanctioned behavior to action with natural, human justification. To Hobbes, the goal of the moral life was not a relationship with any supreme being or state of supernatural bliss: It was straightforward self-preservation and the pleasurable exercise of power. The source of moral wisdom was neither divine revelation nor natural law embedded in reality and discoverable to human reason: It was an explicit, rational consideration of one's own self-interest, and the evaluation of moral behavior was based simply on its success in achieving the goal of moral action.

Perhaps the most controversial aspect of Hobbes's position was his claim that persons have no natural affection for each other: that their passions have to be regulated by the rational power of restraint if they are to have amiable social relations. Morality, on this view, is not intrinsic to human beings but arises as the result of the practical necessity of having to get along with each other.

John Locke

These consequences of Hobbes's view were challenged in part by later British philosophers whose own moral theories have had great impact on ethical thinking since their time. John Locke (1632–1704), for example, whose political views were influential on the founding fathers of the American government, challenged Hobbes at a number of important points while agreeing with him at others. While accepting Hobbes's assumption that good must be that which causes pleasure and evil that which causes pain, Locke refused to identify moral good simply with pragmatic selfish interests. There is, he was convinced, a divine law accessible to human reason built into nature. Moral rules are as self-evident to the rational quest as are mathematical truths.

This fact leads Locke to a different emphasis from Hobbes when discussing social relationships in the state. Like Hobbes, Locke begins his reflections on persons in a state of nature. In this state persons live according to their inborn reason, which tells them not to harm each other with respect to life, health, liberty, or possessions. It is the right to property that Locke then develops further. Although he does not deny that people have a natural inclination for one another's company, Locke did recall Hobbes when he suggested that one of the most powerful reasons for coming together in society was the pragmatic regard of each person for the most practical way of preserving his or her rights and liberties. Chief among these rights and therefore primary in human motives for forming a society "is the preservation of their property."[4] Naturally, persons give up some of their individual liberty in order to get the benefits of society. They authorize a legislative assembly to make such laws as are necessary for the common good, and they agree, in this **social compact,** to submit their behavior to the will of the majority. All of these acts are self-evidently rational and therefore conform to the moral law that is intrinsic to reason.

[4]John Locke, *Of Civil Government, Second Essay* (Chicago: Regnery, 1948), p. 76.

Spinoza

On the continent of Europe, another moral philosopher, born in the same year as Locke, was also formulating a theory of morality that relied upon the power of reason to discern what was in the self-interest of the individual. Although he did not base his reflections upon experience, Benedict Spinoza (1632–1677) accepted the premise that persons primarily seek their own welfare. He then proceeded in a thoroughly rationalistic manner to deduce the necessary laws by which their behavior is governed. The most basic such law is that which necessitates each thing to preserve and perfect its own being. The fundamental emotions felt by each being are pain and pleasure. Love and hate are directed respectively to those things that cause pleasure and pain. Morally, we value things insofar as we judge them to be causes of pleasure or pain. Thus our emotions are determined by what affects us, and our moral judgements, following our emotions, are similarly conditioned. We are not free to feel as we like and thus to make moral judgments as we might like. The true goal of the moral life is, consequently, to free oneself from bondage to emotional valuation by seeking mental or intellectual transcendence. This transcendence will consist primarily in our knowledge that we are determined emotionally, but this knowledge is liberating because it is ultimately the knowledge of God. "In so far as we understand the causes of pain, it ceases to be a passion, that is, it ceases to be a pain, and therefore in so far as we understand God to be the cause of pain we rejoice."[5] Like the Stoics, Spinoza counsels us to rise above the feelings that are caused in us by things over which we have no ultimate control. Spinoza also accepts the complete determinism of all behavior. The only room that remains in his theory for morality is that which the mind makes by its reflection on the imprisonment of the body and its feelings. Whether determinism is compatible with the exhortation to act in such a way as to escape the worst emotional effects of determinism is problematic. But it is clear that Spinoza, like many other moralists of his time and later, saw in reason the only foundation for any moral theory worthy of human acceptance.

PHILOSOPHERS OF MORAL FEELING

There were moral philosophers, of course, who were sceptical of the power of reason in determining morality. These thinkers took much more seriously, but less negatively than Hobbes, the importance of feeling in our formation of moral judgments. Chief among such philosophers were two

---

[5]Benedict Spinoza, *The Ethics*, trans. R. H. M. Elwes, n. (New York: Dover, 1951), part 5, prop. 18, p. 256.

Scotsmen, Francis Hutcheson and David Hume. Without rejecting entirely the role of reason, these men looked to an innate moral sense as the seat of moral feeling and judgment. Hutcheson (1694–1746) argued for an inborn "faculty of perceiving moral excellence and its supreme objects."[6] These "objects" are primarily the affections of disinterested benevolence or a selfless concern for the welfare of others. (Note the striking difference between this view and that of Hobbes.) Morality then becomes the carrying out of these affections.

Hutcheson's countryman, and much more influential philosopher, David Hume (1711–1776) carried forward this view of the moral sense. He held that reason alone cannot produce moral blame or praise. This can be produced by feeling or sentiment alone. If we call something good it must be because we feel approval for it. We also know that what propels us into acting is not reason but emotion. Reason may help us determine matters of fact, but only passion (emotion) can make us take up an attitude toward matters of fact. These passions will arise in us according to whether the action contemplated leads to pleasure or pain. Virtue is defined by Hume as "whatever mental action or quality gives to a spectator the pleasing sentiment of approbation; and vice the contrary."[7] Hume felt that most people share the same general moral sentiments, chief among which he, like Hutcheson, felt was benevolence towards others. (Hume suggests in passing and in anticipation of the Utilitarians that whereas benevolence is not approved only because of its utility in making social relations possible, its usefulness is not a negligible factor in our approval.)

THE UTILITARIANS

The successors of the philosophers of the moral sentiment, the Utilitarians, extended the emphasis on the usefulness of moral feeling. Utilitarianism as an orientation within moral thinking has had a profound effect on contemporary ethics. It has clearly grown beyond the specific philosophies of the two Englishmen credited with its original expression, Jeremy Bentham (1748–1832) and John Stuart Mill (1806–1873). Like his predecessors, Bentham believed that persons are guided in their behavior by the desire for pleasure and an aversion to pain. He attached moral value to whatever brings pleasure and called evil whatever brings pain. Therefore, the goal of moral action is a form of hedonism: to maximize one's own happiness. But Bentham was very much aware of man's social relations, and so he in-

---

[6]Francis Hutcheson, *A System of Moral Philosophy*, vol. 1, ch. 4, sect. 1, in *Collected Works of Francis Hutcheson*, prepared by Bernhard Fabian (Hildesheim: G. Olms, 1969–1971), p. 53.
[7]*Enquiries Concerning the Human Understanding and Concerning the Principles of Morals*, ed. L. A. Selby-Bigge (Oxford: Clarendon, 1927, reprint of 2nd ed., 1902), appendix 1, 239, pp. 288–289.

cluded in his evaluation of moral acts their effect not just on the individual but also on his community. The major contribution of Utilitarianism to moral thinking was its conception of the way moral deeds should be evaluated. Accepting the principle that moral insight comes from rational analysis of one's own desires and an understanding of the natural world in which they have to be fulfilled, the Utilitarians stressed the importance of calculating what the probable effects of any intended course of action would be. The proper ethical attitude is to calculate carefully the amount of pleasure and the amount of pain any act will bring, then to subtract the pain from the pleasure and find the balance. If there is a balance in favor of pleasure, the act is a good act.

Writing in an age that saw the importance of quantitative mathematics in the great advances in science then taking place, Bentham not surprisingly developed a rather quantitative calculus, called the hedonistic calculus, to determine the dimensions of value in pleasure. Pleasures will be valued by their (1) intensity, (2) duration, (3) certainty (the probability that they will occur), (4) nearness in time, (5) productivity (the likelihood of producing or being associated with more of the same kind of pleasure), (6) purity (the likelihood of their not being followed by or mixed with pain), and (7) extent (the number of people they will affect). Bentham summarized his utilitarian creed as "the greatest happiness of the greatest number."

John Stuart Mill, a disciple of Bentham, refined the definition of utilitarianism as "the creed which accepts as the foundation of morals, Utility, or the Greatest Happiness Principle, [and] holds that actions are right in proportion as they tend to promote happiness, wrong as they tend to produce the reverse of happiness. By happiness is intended pleasure and the absence of pain."[8] Although he accepted Bentham's assumption that personal happiness corresponds to the happiness of the community as a whole, Mill modified Bentham's strictly quantitative understanding of pleasure. He insisted that some pleasures are qualitatively superior to others, such as the mental to the sensual.

Utilitarianism fit comfortably into the emerging commercial, capitalist middle-class world that, for a time, Britain led. It not only evaluated behavior by a standard familiar to any commercial agent (the calculation of the quantitative effect of the intended act), it also shared a common set of assumptions about human beings. Chief among these were the idea that persons sought their own pleasure primarily and that somehow the pleasure seeking of each person would complement that of every other person. A deeper, equally important assumption was that persons act according to their most powerful desires and that morality must adjust to this fact.

[8]John Stuart Mill, *Utilitarianism* (New York: Dutton, 1951), p. 8.

IMMANUEL KANT

A very different and extremely influential moral philosophy that challenged many of the Utilitarian assumptions arose outside England. The
philosophy of Immanuel Kant (1724–1804) is famous not only for its ethical
component but also for its theory of knowledge. Kant believed that our
knowledge of the world was conditioned by certain a priori laws or rules
for thinking. For example, we cannot know an event unless we think of it
as conforming to laws of causal connection. This means that we know the
world as necessarily subject to natural laws. But if causal necessity applied
to all occurrences, the basis of morality would be threatened, since moral
acts must be free. Kant believed that as long as our acts were determined
by forces outside our will they would not be free and thus could not be
moral acts. The freedom of the moral agent depends upon freedom from
the forces of passion, desire, and external control. Kant located the freedom of the moral agent in a moral law within the individual. Through this
moral law the agent was morally autonomous and rational, thus transcending the constraints of nonrational forces. The moral law known by each
moral agent is **categorical.** It does not admit of adjustment to meet different
empirical conditions. If it did, Kant believed, morality would become subject to the contingencies of changing circumstances and thus would become aribitrary or capricious. The **categorical imperative** provides a principle by which the agent can test whether an action is truly moral. "Act only
on that maxim whereby thou canst at the same time will that it should
become a universal law."[9] That is, only those rules are moral that we, as
their agents, are willing to make applicable to all persons, including ourselves, in all circumstances. For example, if I am tempted to steal some
bread, am I willing to make the rule "steal when tempted" universal? If
not, then it is clearly immoral for me to steal.

What we must avoid is doing an act for the sake of the pleasure it brings
us or in order to fulfill a desire or inclination. Kant assumes that we will
accord the greatest moral worth to the individual who acts out of a sense of
duty even when it conflicts with the person's own psychological desire
(such as the person who refuses to lie even though telling the truth will
bring great financial or physical harm). If we act according to a strict Utilitarian ethic, then we have no way of avoiding acting primarily out of desires
or temptations that do not do us justice as rational beings who are more
than the sum of our inclinations. The gap between the Utilitarians and
Kant is very wide on this issue.

Of course, Kant's ethical theory does not neglect the importance of the
welfare of other persons. But it assumes that because all persons are essentially moral, they all have a rational faculty. Therefore, Kant contends, no

---

[9]Immanuel Kant, *Fundamental Principles of the Metaphysic of Morals,* trans. T. K. Abbott (Indianapolis: Bobbs-Merrill, 1949), p. 38.

person shall be treated simply as a thing or as a means to an end. One of his most famous moral statements enjoins us always to act so as "to treat humanity, whether in thine own person or in that of any other, in every case as an end withal, never as means only."[10] This is the basis of human dignity and self-respect: that all persons are ends in themselves because they share in the capacity for moral—that is rational—self-determination.

The effect of Kant's moral position is that the evaluation of moral acts is concentrated not upon their effects but upon their motives. Kant knew that we cannot completely control the consequences of our acts. Insisting upon the importance of the autonomy of moral agents, their freedom from external determination, Kant consistently concluded that we must judge agents only by reference to those things under their control. What is under their control is their willingness to have their will determined by the rational moral law within them. Thus, as long as individuals act according to the categorical imperative, out of a sense of duty, and according to the maxim that the rule by which they are acting should be universalized, then they can rest assured that they have acted morally, even though the actual consequences of their acts are other than they had hoped. According to Kant, "nothing can possibly be conceived in the world, or even out of it, which can be called good without qualification, except a Good Will."[11]

The rigor and formalism of Kant's ethics will probably never be surpassed. He developed in detail the consequences of viewing morality solely from the point of view of the rational moral agent. He illustrated the implications of holding moral agents solely responsible for the determination of their own acts by reference to an unconditional, absolutely objective rationality which alone can keep individuals from being buffeted by passions over which they have no control.

For Kant the goal of moral action is the fulfillment of the rational, moral faculty that is the person's distinguishing characteristic. To act morally is an end in itself, because the fulfillment of the individual is an end in itself. The source of moral action is the moral law within the agent revealed through objective reason. And the evaluation of moral action is its faithfulness to the categorical imperative and the moral maxim of universalization. By virtually excluding any dependence upon the external world, either in the formation of morality or its assessment, Kant provided an almost entirely self-enclosed system of morality.

THE DEVELOPMENT OF NATURAL ETHICS: DEONTOLOGY

The part of Kant's moral philosophy that has the most abiding influence on later ethicists is his insistence that persons are morally autonomous, capa-

[10]Kant, p. 46.
[11]Kant, p. 11.

ble of reaching moral decisions by appeal to their own rational, moral nature. Although Kant did not believe that this fact ruled out the existence of God, it left nothing for God to do insofar as the determination of morality was concerned. The rational essence of morality, so thoroughly explicated by Kant, marked clearly the secular triumph of autonomous moral thinking over religiously grounded morality at the beginning of the nineteenth century. For those professional philosophers who followed in the footsteps of Kant, even when they disagreed with him on numerous issues, there was no turning back to an ethic that relied upon divine revelation for its insights and energy.

The history of moral theory since Kant has largely been a history of debate between those who, continuing Kant's line of inquiry, stressed the importance of appealing to a universal sense of right and wrong that is not intrinsically wedded to the actual consequences of one's acts and those who appealed either to an individualistic judgment of rightness or to the consequences of one's acts for a natural, social end. Sometimes called **deontologists** or **nonnaturalists,** thinkers such as W. D. Ross (1877–1973) and G. E. Moore (1873–1958) argued that morality must be based upon an appeal to something seen as intrinsically or a priori good in itself. Ross held that certain acts are "self-evidently" good and impose upon us certain obvious duties, such as keeping promises, doing justice, not injuring others, and acting beneficently. These things are right not because they can be justified by an appeal to their consequences but because we see that they are right. A person of insight immediately senses, by intuition, what is the appropriate action for the occasion. G. E. Moore contended that the Good could not be defined. It is a simple, unanalyzable, nonnatural characteristic that we are either aware of or not.

The self-evident character of our moral duties, which is the key to this kind of deontological intuitionism, has been challenged most often by those who fail to see the allegedly self-evident moral rules or who observe that even if such rules are apparent they often conflict with each other in particular cases (for example, the duty to preserve life and the duty to tell the truth when the agent is confronted with a mad killer who asks where the rest of the family is).

CONTEMPORARY ETHICAL THEORIES

Existentialist Ethics

Perhaps the closest to the moral intuitionists are those philosophers called **existentialists.** They share with the intuitionists the assumption that what is good must be discerned without lengthy argumentation or evidence derived from the natural world. They disagree with the intuitionists, however, that what is intuited as right is objective, rational, and the same for all persons. Deriving their name from their emphasis upon the unique moments of existence each person experiences, the existentialists insist that meaning and worth are given to the moments of life by each individual alone. They distrust the power of reason to discern meaning in or through an ideal objective reality that determines what beliefs and values the self must hold. Some existentialists who have had enormous impact on contemporary ethics, like Søren Kierkegaard (1813–1855), do believe in an objective God who alone knows in what fulfillment consists. But even these religious existentialists hold that God provides moral guidance only through direct commands to single individuals that have validity only in the particular situation in which they are given. One can grasp what God commands only by a leap of faith beyond reason and even beyond traditional ethics. Kierkegaard's classic example is the command to the Hebrew patriarch Abraham to kill his only son, Isaac. To obey this command was clearly not rational, nor was it even ethical by traditional standards. Only by a leap of faith at that moment in that situation could Abraham grasp the right thing to do—to obey God in this singular deed.

Nonreligious existentialists, of course, eliminate any reference to the divine. Like Kierkegaard, Jean-Paul Sartre (1905–1980) stresses the importance of human freedom in choosing what to do in any given situation. Unlike Kierkegaard, Sartre rejects any assumption that there is an objective reality to which moral choices are a response. The only reality, for Sartre, is each individual person with his or her own absurdly chosen project or intention. There is no meaning or purpose other than that which individuals determine for themselves. Morality, a human creation, is judged by its conformity to and enhancement of the individual's sense of freedom and dignity in using that freedom creatively and authentically.

Nietzsche

Sartre's words echo those of perhaps the most infamous of all existentialist thinkers, Friedrich Nietzsche (1844–1900). Writing in reaction to what he regarded as the pretentions and strength-sapping morality of Christian philosophers, Nietzsche argued that the only reality was that which arose through the conflict between beings struggling for power. Each being, filled with the will to power, constructed philosophies and moralities as tools in the advancement of its exercise of power and mastery over others. Strength, vitality, creativity, and conquest were the goals of each authentic being. Christianity, early finding itself relatively powerless and resentful of this position, managed to get the powerful to accept its negative values of powerlessness, love, suffering, sacrifice, and hatred of the natural world and its enjoyments. Nietzsche wants to expose this baneful influence of Christianity and to restore a healthy love of the body and its power drives, and he insists that what specific morality is adopted by any person or culture is relative to its own self-interests. Thus, with God and all absolutes dead, we are truly beyond good and evil and thus required to develop our ethics for ourselves out of our own power and desires.

Biological Ethics

Nietzsche's and Sartre's ethics, although they reject any absolute standard outside of human decision, do seem to be related to the unique needs of each person. The existentialists view these needs individually, not as set by a universal human nature. Gaining greater influence in the field of ethics, however, are those who believe that morality is the discovery of behavior that will enable persons to adapt to a given way of being which belongs to them by virtue of the structure of nature or what nature is evolving toward. These thinkers emphasize the social or biological ties persons have to the structure of nature, of which they are an organic part and to which they must conform if they are to achieve the fulfillment nature has made possible. In its crudest form, this kind of biological or evolutionary ethics, associated originally with the work of Darwin, led to the idea that humans should adopt the ethic of survival: Adapt or die. The doctrine of the "survival of the fittest" was used by many so-called social Darwinians to justify a social and economic system in which the wealthy thrived at the expense of the poor because they were obviously fitter.

Most advocates of evolutionary, naturalistic ethics, however, stress the importance, equally grounded in nature and equally conducive to survival, of cooperation with other persons and other parts of the natural environment. We will see the effects of such a view in more detail when we examine the moral issue of ecology and the preservation of natural resources (Chapter 16). The importance of the evolutionary approach to ethics is that it explicitly grounds moral obligation on the laws of nature, which are necessary and immutable. The greatest good, therefore, is the continuous adjustment or adaptation of the person to the environment.

One of the foremost proponents of naturalist ethics is B. F. Skinner, the famous behavioral psychologist whose work is widely read in many schools today. He has argued that with the proper conditioning people can be made to do what they really want to do. As a result they will feel content, because their motives will have been brought into harmony with their environmental conditions. In such a system, the notion of the free moral agent is no longer relevant. "As a science of behavior adopts the strategy of physics and biology, the autonomous agent to which behavior has traditionally been attributed is replaced by the environment—the environment in which the species evolved and in which the behavior of the individual is shaped and maintained."[12]

---

[12]B. F. Skinner, *Beyond Freedom and Dignity* (New York: Knopf, 1972), p. 185.

Marxist Ethics

Of potentially more influence worldwide than any of the moral positions examined so far is one that shares many assumptions with the naturalist or biological ethic. Marxism has had and continues to have a profound effect on many peoples around the world. Part of that effect stems from Marx's moral views. There is much debate among scholars of Marxism over whether the ethics of Marxism are those of Marx himself (and if so, which Marx—the early, allegedly more humanistic one, or the later, more deterministic one).

Although Karl Marx (1818–1883) certainly changed the emphasis in his writings, a strong case can be made that his moral position remained virtually unchanged throughout his intellectual development. That position has been described both as atheistic and as a secular equivalent of the moral vision of the Hebrew prophets. That it is atheistic is due to Marx's belief that religion is essentially oriented to the supernatural and consequently has little to contribute to the practical alleviation of suffering and injustice on earth.

Believing that human beings could achieve fulfillment only through creative work and mutuality with others, Marx located the sources of non-fulfillment (alienation) in the processes of the production of the goods that are intended to satisfy man's material needs. These processes have been appropriated by the capitalist economic class, which uses them to its profit and to the dehumanization of those it employs as productive tools. The result is a triple alienation: Workers become alienated from other persons, from the material world upon which they expend their labor (because they enjoy no creative relation with their work, merely the relation of a tool to an object), and from themselves (because as laborers in the hire of others they are not free to exercise their creative powers as they choose). The ethical imperative of Marx then becomes quite clear: One must work to overthrow the conditions of alienation as a means toward the good, which in this case is the practical, human experience of cooperation, mutuality, and fulfillment of the whole person in communism.

Marx's attitude toward religion is crucial here. Only if people can turn from supernatural concerns to worldly concerns can the ethical task be carried forward. Religion is an illusion. Therefore, for those still caught by religion, "the call to abandon their illusions about their condition is a call to abandon a condition which requires illusions... The criticism of religion disillusions man so that he will think, act, and fashion his reality as a man who has lost his illusions and regained his reason; so that he will revolve about himself as his own true sun... Man is the supreme being for man."[13] Once we know that we are the ultimate reality and that our

---

[13]Karl Marx, "Contribution to the Critique of Hegel's Philosophy of Right," quoted in *Religion for a New Generation*, eds. Jacob Needleman et al. (New York: Macmillan, 1977), p. 60.

fulfillment is the goal of moral action, then we can accept Marx's version of Kant's categorical imperative: "to overthrow all those conditions in which man is an abased, enslaved, abandoned, contemptible being."[14]

Believing that all the institutions, political processes, and values of a culture are a reflection of its economic modes of production, Marx regarded no prior historical moral values as absolute. This fact has been regarded by later Marxists, especially those who gained power in the Soviet Union, to justify almost any actions (including terrorism, inquisition, and brutality) as justified so long as they were directed toward the establishment or furtherance of communism. There are many Marxists who do not approve of the way in which Marx's views have been realized in the Soviet experiment. Consequently, they are not committed to the view that any means are justified by the end, which they share with Marx, of a just, sharing, free, fulfilling community. They do feel, however, that the moral standards of any culture must be judged ultimately by their approximation to or enhancement of the goal of all moral action. They also believe that human nature (our *species being*, as Marx called it) is such that, although not fixed or immutable, it is naturally oriented toward certain values rather than others, values appropriate to the kind of community of nonalienation that they anticipate the workings of nature and human effort will bring into being. Marx's attempts to ground his understanding of human beings upon a scientific, natural basis should not obscure the prophetic nature of his vision of humanity's end or his impassioned moral fervor in advocating the specific steps that would advance that goal.

Metaethics

The naturalism of Marx and his belief that no moral views could be absolute since they were the product of a particular culture and historical epoch were shared by many moral philosophers of the twentieth century who did not share Marx's social views. In this century, much of moral thinking has turned from a consideration of what people ought to do to a reflection on what they do when they consider what they ought to do. This kind of reflection has been called **metaethics.** Like metaphysics, which reflects on the meaning and justification of statements made about the world, metaethics reflects on the meaning and justification of moral statements. A metaethicist might ask what the meaning of the concept "Good" is, or what the difference between "moral" and "immoral" is, or how a moral judgment differs from a factual judgment, or what processes of reasoning are appropriate to moral thinking that might not be appropriate to aesthetic, scientific or religious thinking, and finally, how, if at all, moral judgments are proved, verified, or justified? Do we appeal to a set of objective

---

[14]Marx, p. 61.

facts for justification? If not, to what do we appeal? It is one thing to say that an act injures a fellow human being; it is something else to say that the act is wrong. Much debate swirls around the question of whether one can move logically from a statement of what is (this act hurts another) to a statement of what ought to be (we should not perform such acts).

One of the most radical positions taken up within metaethics by some moral philosophers is that which holds that no moral evaluations are ever objectively justified. In its extreme form—in the work of A. J. Ayer (b. 1910), for instance—this **emotive theory of ethics** holds that basic moral judgments are simply expressions of emotions. Because he assumes that emotions are neither true nor false, it follows that for Ayer moral views are neither true nor false. When we utter a moral opinion we are simply telling others in a roundabout way what we approve or disapprove. If I say that lying is wrong, what I am really saying is, "I don't like lying, that is my feeling." Ayer seems to hold that unless ethical beliefs are self-evident or unless they can be demonstrated to be true in the same way we demonstrate the truth of a scientific hypothesis (and he rejects both these options), then all ethical judgment is arbitrary and emotive.

Other thinkers who fall within the boundaries of this theory are less extreme than Ayer. One of the most influential, C. L. Stevenson (b. 1908), has modified Ayer's position to admit the role of reason in the consideration of some aspects of moral thinking. Although he acknowledges that a moral judgment does depend at a fundamental level upon a feeling of approval or disapproval that is not itself a direct effect of a factual observation, Stevenson points out that some factual information can alter a moral feeling. If I say that I approve of capital punishment because it keeps potential murderers from committing murder, you might convince me by factual information that capital punishment does not have this consequence. As a result, I might (but am not logically coerced to) change my mind. Later metaethicists have tried to enlarge the role of rational argument within ethical discussion and have examined moral judgments for some larger sense of justification than that used by the empirical scientist.

UNCOVERING OUR MORAL COMMITMENTS

I believe that Socrates . . . understood what contribution philosophical reflection may make to our self-knowledge and self-culture. That contribution is essentially the logical (or dialectical) analysis of the golden concepts, such as justice, truth, God, through which we focus the ideals by which we live. In a spiritual sense, we *are* our commitments. Therefore, if these concepts provide the terms through which alone our commitments are made manifest to ourselves and others, then their careful study must provide a revelation of what we are, both to

ourselves and to one another . . . We have been made to think
both by the existentialists and by the positivists that our basic
commitments and ends are fundamentally a matter of decision
or choice. Nothing could be further from the truth. I do not
choose what I mean, or intend, by truth or by justice; nor do I
decide what principles of knowledge or of justice I will live by. I
find myself talking and thinking in a certain way just as I find,
sometimes with great difficulty, those ideals and procedures by
which I live.

Henry David Aiken, *Reason and Conduct: New Bearings in Moral Philoso-*
phy (New York: Knopf, 1962), p. 368.

Henry David Aiken is professor of philosophy at Harvard. He is a
well-known moral philosopher and the author of Value: A Cooperative Inquiry *and* The Age of Ideology, *among other books and*
numerous articles.

Because of the influence of linguistic and logical analysis upon the education of professional philosophers, and because moral thinking is seen by
many as a professional philosophical enterprise, the technical work in
ethics is often done today by metaethicists. It should be remembered,
however, as our history of ethical thought reminds us, that moral thinking
arises out of a living situation in which reflection is a means toward the
living of a fuller, more wholesome life. Such reflection is more likely to
occur when people perceive threats to their sense of wholeness or integrity, especially threats against the successful enactment of values long
cherished. In our time, with the direct and tangible challenges thrown at us
by demands for justice by oppressed groups, for conservation of dwindling
resources, for an end to war, and even for a return to personal values
perceived to be under attack by social change, a great deal of moral thinking is done not by professional metaethicists but by people caught in the
midst of real moral turmoil. Although they are aided in many cases by the
clarifications of metaethics, most people are looking for a set of actual
moral judgments they can live by, not just for an understanding of how
moral judgments are made in general. The kind of moral response they
seek comes out of concrete, particular moral positions, including those,
such as the traditional religious ones, that are often overlooked by the
abstractions of metaethics.

THE LEGACY OF VARIETY

In this brief survey of the major ethical theories of the West, we have seen a variety of moral positions. We have looked at the history of ethical thought primarily through the perspective of three basic questions: What is the goal of moral action, where does moral guidance come from, and how is moral action evaluated? Although all moral philosophies stress the goal of happiness or fulfillment, there are many different views of what that comprises. The religious ethics of the West insist upon a relationship with a divine being for complete wholeness. Other positions look to the individual's adaptation to natural laws, to the exercise of reason, to the absurd exercise of radical freedom, to the deployment of power, to sensual pleasure, or to the well-rounded use of all natural faculties. One of the major criteria in categorizing the different goals of moral action has been that between goals sufficient for the individual alone and goals that require fulfillment in and through other persons. This is the difference between an individualistic and a social ethic.

There are many different sources of moral insight affirmed by these different theories. Some look to reason and others to intuition, innate affections or feelings, God, or radical freedom. Some seek a balance between several of these issues. Some claim that the source of moral wisdom is absolute, unchanging, accessible to all persons in the same way at all times and places; others claim that moral wisdom is relative and contingent upon personal needs and situations or upon the development of nature at a particular stage. Some look inside the individual for a subjective source of guidance, others look outside for an objective source.

In the area of evaluation, the field is split between those who look primarily to the consequences of their acts as they affect an end to be reached by moral behavior and those who look to the conformity of the act or its motive, regardless of consequences, to a moral law, or to an intrinsic sense of what is good.

The differences between the various moral philosophies outlined in this chapter are more clear-cut in the abstract than they are in actual practice in everyday life. The goals of moral action in a single theory may be a harmony among personal pleasure, relationship to God, and service to others. Some theories account for moral guidance by means of combining reason, feeling, and an understanding of God's will. Some claim that whereas the goal of moral action is absolute, the means to achieve it may be relative. There are teleological theories that are egoistic and others that are communal. There are deontologists who insist that what is right is essentially objective, universal, and rational and others who claim that it is subjective, particular, and irrational.

Although it is impossible to apply each one of the ethical theories examined in this history to each of the contemporary moral problems to be discussed in this book, it is useful to know something about the moral philosophies that have influenced Western thinking. We will have occasion in the remainder of the book to see how selected individual approaches represented in this survey can deal with specific moral issues. As we do so, however, we will need to remind ourselves of the variety of aspects that make up a moral theory, many of which will remain implicit in our discussion. We have tried in this survey to provide a sense of that variety as it has developed historically through the work of individual moral philosophers.

CHAPTER REVIEW

A. The individual in society

1. Thomas Hobbes developed a philosophy to justify the existence of the state as a necessary evil designed to safeguard individual interests.
2. John Locke emphasized the importance of individual rights, especially the right to property, which the social order must protect.
3. Spinoza recalled the rational detachment of the Stoics in his 17th-century moral philosophy.

B. Philosophers of moral feeling

1. Francis Hutcheson and David Hume located the source of morality in an innate faculty of perceiving moral excellence.

C. The Utilitarians

1. Jeremy Bentham and J. S. Mill contributed to moral philosophy a method of evaluation that judges the worth of a moral act by the greatest happiness principle.

D. Immanuel Kant

1. Kant wished to avoid evaluating moral deeds by their consequences or having them determined by factors beyond the control of the rational agent.
2. He contributed, therefore, the notions of the moral law within and the categorical imperative as a maxim for determining the morality of an action.

E. The development of natural ethics

1. Deontology argues that morality is based upon that which is seen as intrinsically good in itself.

F. Contemporary moral philosophy

1. The existentialists believe that morality must arise individually from each person's unique existential situation.
2. Nietzsche criticized all prevailing moralities for not suffiently understanding that moral values arise out of each individual's will to power. There are no moral absolutes.
3. Naturalist or biological ethics stress the need for behavior to conform to environmental conditions in order to ensure fulfillment.
4. Marxist ethics criticize the alienating conditions of capitalism and encourage the building of a community in which our social nature will be satisfied.
5. Metaethics is a study of the kinds of reasoning that go on in moral theories. It considers the question of the justification of moral values.

G. The legacy of variety

1. There are many different answers to the three basic moral questions. In the daily practice of morality the distinctions between the moral theories elaborated in the West are blurred, but understanding each theory helps us to see how our own moral thinking has been shaped by the past.

SUGGESTED READINGS

Historical Surveys

MacIntyre, Alasdair. *A Short History of Ethics.* New York: Macmillan, 1966.
Sidgwick, Henry. *Outlines of the History of Ethics.* New York: St. Martin's, 1967, pp. 163–337.
Warnock, Mary. *Ethics Since 1900.* New York: Oxford Univ. Press, 1960.

Issues in Moral Philosophy

Frankena, William K. *Ethics.* 2nd ed. Englewood Cliffs, N.J.: Prentice-Hall, 1973.

A short but excellent overview of major moral theories and principles.

Hare, R. M. *The Language of Morals.* Oxford: Clarendon, 1961.

A good example of metaethics.

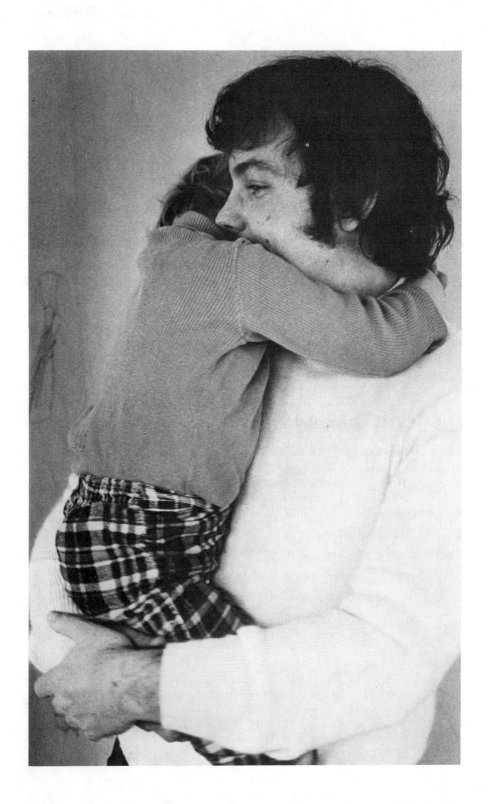

PART 2

PERSONAL IDENTITY AND FULFILLMENT

5

Who Am I?

*How can we discover the true person when we see only distorted and varied images . . . [especially] when these images derive their origin not only from the man himself, but also from ourselves, and from the whole environment to which he belongs? It is no use trying to arrive at an exact picture by adding all the many false images together. That would be like trying to get a complete picture of an individual by superimposing hundreds of different negatives of him on one photographic print.**

IDENTITY, VALUES, AND MORALITY

"Who am I?" can be a cry of despair from someone having an identity crisis and in search of a significant meaning to life. It can express the agony of young adults suddenly on their own, of the housewife whose sense of identity, worth, and purpose has vanished, or of the retiree who no longer holds a job and title.

Even with no crisis in one's life, the question is real. For some men and women the issue never becomes a problem. Throughout their lives they accept their apparent places in life and get on with the business of living: they roll with the punches, and the question never arises. They have, nevertheless, taken an answer for granted; and as long as that answer, perhaps never consciously formulated, feels satisfactory to them, there is no crisis. Ask such individuals "Who are you?" and they may respond, "Well, I've never had to think about that." If they choose to respond further, they will most likely recite a list of things they do. They may go to their graves apparently satisfied and without an identity crisis.

Philosophy and Identity

A customary philosophic approach to the identity issue is to raise such questions as: Am I more than my body? Am I my mind? What is mind? Am

*Paul Tournier, *The Meaning of Persons* (New York: Harper, 1957), p. 21.

I my soul? What is a soul? How is my mind related to my body? How are my soul and mind related to each other? Are there any reasons for supposing that "I" will survive the changes and decay of my body? These are legitimate philosophic problems, but they are not our focus here.[1] The person in an identity crisis does not seek answers to these questions. Perhaps some philosophers are convinced these issues ought to be foremost, but philosophers do not set the priorities and agendas in all human dilemmas. We rarely begin a pursuit of personal, philosophic matters with the professional philosopher's view; however, if we want to conclude the search for identity with philosophic depth, we must eventually deal with issues of mind, body, and soul.

Our philosophic focus here is on the day-to-day issue of identity, the images we have of ourselves as we live out who we are. Am I what I see in the mirror? Am I what I do? Though related to the issues of mind, soul, and body, our philosophic questions begin the search for identity differently. We begin with identity and values.

Am I as I value myself? My self-image, my own answer to "Who am I?" and its value to me determine how highly I regard myself. In my own eyes I might have the identity of "the white, Yankee, Protestant male named Cedric" or "president of Texas Enterprises." If one of these identities is mine and I highly value that image, my self-regard will be high; I know that I am worthwhile because of who I am. If one of these identities is mine and I attach a low value to it, my self-esteem will be low; I know that I am of little worth because of who I am.

Am I as I am valued by others? Regardless of how I see myself, others come to their own conclusions. Cedric might have a high regard for who he is; he thinks he's special because he's Cedric. Others who have values similar to his will also regard him highly. However, those having contempt for Cedric's image will hold him in low esteem.

Am I as I value others? Knowing that I am president of Texas Enterprises, I value other chief executives as highly as I regard myself. Others with lesser jobs are, I believe, of less value because they are less successful. I am important because I believe most people are unimportant and less valuable.

In addition, our search for identity incorporates a factor philosophers do not consider—morality. I am likely to treat myself as I value myself.

If I think highly of myself as Cedric, I could become my one and only friend! My primary moral obligation is to myself; I am at the center of the

---

[1]For an introductory discussion of the traditional problems of identity, see the chapters on human nature, the self, and the mind in *Living Issues in Philosophy* (New York: Van Nostrand, 1979).

universe, and others ought to subordinate their desires and needs to mine. My senses of identity and morality are self-centered.

If I think poorly of myself as Cedric, I could dislike myself and be filled with self-contempt. I am worthless. My primary moral obligation might be to serve others without regard for my own desires and needs.

Of course these are two extremes, and many other approaches to self-assessment and moral obligation are possible in between. Our contention is this: an individual's identity as valued by himself and by others *and* the value the individual places on the images he or she perceives of others are crucial to the individual's relations with other human beings. My sense of morality toward myself and others depends to a large extent on my self-regard and on my value of others' identities. A moral standard for an individual's behavior is linked inescapably to his or her answer to "Who am I?" and the identity's apparent worth.

IDENTITY IS LEARNED

Trees and goldfish have no identity problems. They have few (if any) choices to make and never suffer the agony of wondering who they are. They are, for the most part, programmed by nature and complete their lives rather simply.

Human beings are, perhaps, programmed by nature to some extent with genetically acquired tendencies, but we are definitely strongly influenced by persons close to us as well as by school, the media, religious institutions, and so on. If some particular identity is rooted in our very beings, it does not announce itself with any compelling force. Because we are influenced by persons and institutions, we human beings have many decisions and choices to make. Among them, if we care to make it, is the choice of an answer to "Who am I?"

Not many individuals have been formally warned "The time is coming soon when you must decide who you are." Instead we absorb a sense of who we are from our relationships. The infant's relationship to mother, then to others near and far as the early years pass, communicates an influential message. The message varies from culture to culture—a given family might have one, clear statement to its members; another family, along with the influences of school, the media, and religious institutions, might provide varied and conflicting identity signs. In contemporary Western civilization, the messages are varied and conflicting; there is no way to exclude outside influences. Even groups that insulate themselves extensively from these influences find increasingly that their members will at least hear of alternatives. In past years, Cedric's identity would be ingrained because he would have been exposed only "to his own kind." His

identity was a matter of social definition, not of choice, and it was unquestioned.

Even with greater exposure at early ages to competing identities, those
of us in Western civilization still learn from birth from our immediate
families an initial sense of "who we are." We may thereafter (1) be nurtured in our initial identities such that alternatives have no significant
impact, (2) be nurtured in our initial identities with options intruding and
conflicting significantly or inconsequentially for our entire lives, or (3) be
nurtured in our initial identities, reflect on those competing, and choose an
identity we value most highly. This third option, reflecting the philosopher's bias for conscious choice, is similar to the religious concept of being
"born again." A choice is made, in an enlightening moment or a gradual
sustained effort in self-definition, that provides new life for the individual.
The chosen identity is not the passive acceptance of the strongest influences
on his or her development. The choice may be either an affirmation of the
identity provided from birth or a very different one.

The Choosing Process

No one would suggest seriously that the choice of an identity, whether an
affirmation of one provided from birth or an alternative, is a simple matter
of making up one's mind. It is our contention that identity is learned
consciously or subconsciously with the nurturing support of at least one
other person. Usually more than one supportive individual is involved;
often an entire supportive group is involved such as family, religious
community, friends, and so on. The complete choosing process does not
ordinarily involve reading a book, hearing a lecture, or making up one's
mind in isolation.

Significant choices and their subsequent supports are most effective
when two or more caring persons are involved in the process. Both mind
and heart—intellect and feelings—are components of such decisions; it is
not a solo act. One reason for the organized aspect of religious and political
movements is that organization provides the emotional/intellectual setting
in which individuals can make important decisions and be nurtured in
their choices. (How well the movements implement this context is another
matter!) Required attendance at meetings of business clubs, fraternities and
sororities, some religious communities, and political clubs reflects a recognition of the fundamental human need for ongoing involvement of the
whole person if the individual is to be nurtured in an organization's tenets.
Our understanding of this aspect of human nature may assist the reader:
we feel that *any significant decision you would make about your identity as a
result of reading these pages would be incomplete; for any view to take hold, it must
be shared with another in a vital, ongoing way.*

MASKS

The Wearing of Masks

It is perfectly acceptable for children to wear masks on Halloween and for adults to do the same at some parties. Hiding their identities and becoming the masks they wear is also suitable for performers on stage. The children and partygoers wear masks of cloth or plastic; the performer wears the mask of a role being played.

The identities of many persons are like masks. In some cases the masks are put on so the person becomes something other than what he or she has been in full or in part. In other instances the person takes on the identity of the mask from birth, a mask provided by family and society.

Some individuals wear masks all the time. No one really knows the real human being behind the mask. "I thought I knew Pat, but I guess I really didn't," is a friend's reaction to some unexpected decision or action from Pat. Perhaps Pat, the real person, was not fully disclosed to the friend; or perhaps only a part of the real person had been shown to the friend. Perhaps Pat, the real Pat, was masked fully or in part even from Pat!

The Mask of Negativity

Have you ever heard anyone say "That's human nature" when something good has been done? Probably not. An official is caught embezzling and people say, "What else can you expect! That's human nature!" We have learned to invest human nature with inborn evil inclinations. Some theologians teach their communities just that. One pastor was overheard saying of his crying infant, "Listen to that crying, a sure sign of selfishness and inborn sinfulness."

This negative attitude toward humanity includes our bodies. Study the advertisements in the newspapers, magazines, and on television. Most carry an underlying denigrating message about your body: "You are defective! We offer a remedy!" We are told that we smell, have offensive breath, need shaping, require supports, have a poor shade of hair that's too flat, are showing wrinkles and lines, possess boring eyes/eyelashes/eyebrows/eyelids or skin and lips that are colorless, have dark teeth, too much hair there and too little here, plain fingers and toe nails! We believe this negative message and spend billions annually on so-called remedies.

Consider another negative attitude toward our bodies. Think for a moment of four of the most vulgar words used as expletives. There is a good chance that all four, or at least three, will have to do with the human body: a place or a function of our physical nature. The "worst" expression is a less than elegant synonym for sexual intercourse! When some people are really angry at someone, they shout two words at the offender that are expressive of human reproduction. (If we valued our bodies positively, the same two words could conceivably be an uninhibited compliment!) We construct our vulgarities largely on our negative attitudes toward the human body.

Many would argue that this negativity is not a mask, that the physical nature as well as the spiritual essence of humanity is essentially depraved or inclined toward wrongfulness. Such religious positions generally provide a rite of cleansing, but the believers are still affected by the negativity the overall culture takes for granted; the negative mask remains in spite of spiritual cleansing.

THE MASCULINE MASK

Most individuals have no difficulty in discovering their sex. Few persons experience any delay in checking the "male" or "female" option on an application or information form. Masculinity and feminity are less clear. A male or female may be labeled masculine or feminine in terms of appearance, attitudes, mannerisms, and roles. This is a different matter from one's sex.

The masculinity of males in the United States has been for some time a concern of the highest priority. In an intentionally humorous poke at this near obsession, one writer has made some suggestions to parents.

1. If you catch your son playing with his sister's dolls, clip out a centerfold and hang it in the dollhouse "den." Hopefully he'll get the message.

2. And since he likes to play with dolls, go buy him one. A Barbie-type is best, with sexy hair, shapely buttocks, and perky little breasts.

3. Too much reading is a surefire danger sign. If Junior wears a pair of reading glasses, smudge them up a bit. And slip a couple of Sgt. Rock and Tarzan comic books into his copy of *Jane Eyre.*

4. Take him bowling. Let him use the little balls, but make him swear every time he misses.

5. No matter what he wants for Christmas, buy him power tools. Great big noisy dangerous power tools.

6. Teach him how to smoke cigars. If he won't smoke cigars, then give him cigarettes, but no low tars and *no* menthol 100's.

7. Take him hunting. Make him kill an animal he's seen in cartoons or in children's books. If he starts crying, cook it up and let him watch you eat it.

8. Get him drunk. This one's easy with a kid of five or six. A couple of sips should more than do the trick.

9. Now take him to a porno movie. If he gets scared and starts to bawl for Mommy, ...

10. Beat him up. You're not trying to hurt him, just to help straighten him out. Once he learns what being unmanly is going to

mean in terms of constant pain and suffering, he'll shape up fast . . . the little fruit. [2]

Although the list is humorous in intent, it does not seem so farfetched when compared to the characteristics of masculinity we have come to recognize and accept.

Appearance. The biological "given" of a male, "masculine," is defined by an angular, tall, muscular, and hard appearance. The roundness of fat is acceptable under a hard-hat or some other uniform that masculinizes the curves.

Attitudes. Shaped by culture, traditional masculine attitudes encompass being competitive, aggressive, distant, detached, unemotional, outgoing, independent, self-confident, and adventurous. *Real* men don't cry, show dependence, hesitation, or vulnerability.

Mannerisms. Approved by culture, traditional masculine mannerisms, a man's "body language," include any posture that does not suggest either ballet or graceful gesturing. A sharp, salute-like wave is all right; the twiddling of fingers is not. Crossed legs with an ankle resting just above the knee is fine; knee planted above knee with pointed foot in motion is forbidden. Swishing like an excited woodfairy is censurable; the swish-swagger of a cowboy movie star in dirty jeans is laudable. Slugging a male on the arm while yelling "Ahr right!," a firm handshake in a business meeting, even a pat on the buttocks while in an athlete's uniform are all appropriate signs of approval; a hug or a pat on the buttocks out of uniform is a scandal (unless one's immediate ancestry can excuse the expressive behavior).

Roles. Set by recent culture, traditional masculine roles, things real men do, are characteristically rough, active, controlling, spatial (engineering, building), protective, supervisory, judgmental, success oriented, and colored blue. Contact-sports athlete, ingenious criminal, hard-nosed businessman, "boss," knowing auto mechanic, provider, and decision maker are examples of successful masculine roles.

Masculinity and Morality

Many of our standards of personal and social morality for males are linked profoundly with how we believe "real men" ought to behave. We assume that if I am male, I ought to exhibit masculine appearances, attitudes,

---

[2]From "Calling All Parents . . . ," *Stag Party* (June/July 1979). This article was given to one of this book's authors by a student, as an example of a prevalent narrow view of masculinity.

mannerisms, and roles; if not, there is something abnormal and *wrong* with me. For example, men readily approve of males who are aggressive—regardless of the goal of the aggressive behavior. Hidden admiration for Hitler, rapists, uncaught criminals, ruthless businessmen, and public admiration of any record setter (no matter how worthless the task) is woven into the fabric of praiseworthy masculine behavior. How many men in the United States would dare question publicly the value of professional sports as this industry has been shaped in recent years? How can one question openly any aspect of activities that so reinforce and symbolize American masculinity?

The High Price of Masculinity

In recent years the traditional understanding of masculinity has been undergoing study. The results are not good for men who embrace the usual masculine forms. Though one's appearance is a matter of the biologically given, the many learned aspects (attitudes, mannerisms, and roles) have males in trouble. Some of the conclusions attributed to masculinized behavior are:

1. Males are dying long before females.
2. Males are more susceptible to death-dealing diseases and suicide.
3. Men are emotionally more devastated by divorce than women.
4. Friendships between men are often shallow and unrewarding with a constant undertone of competition and toughness.
5. Significant, wholesome emotion is often lacking in sexual expression.
6. Sports for men have become compulsive rather than pleasurable.
7. Men are constantly striving to measure up to masculine ideals—whatever the price—and are rarely satisfied with their lives or fulfilled in their relationships.[3]

If these observations are correct, it is fair to ask, "Is it wise or moral to be traditionally masculine? Is there an alternative?"

Masculinity and Identity

It is our conviction that answering the "Who am I" question with "I am a man" (meaning, "I am a male who behaves in a traditionally masculine

[3]See Sidney Jourard's "Some Lethal Aspects of the Male Role" in *The Transparent Self* (New York: Van Nostrand, 1972); Peter Fuller, *The Champions: Psychoanalysis of the Top Athletes* (New York: Urizen, 1977); Leonard Kriegel, *On Men and Manhood* (New York: Hawthorn, 1979); Marc Fasteau, *The Male Machine* (New York: McGraw-Hill, 1974); Herb Goldberg, *The New*

way") is a mask; it is, for the most part, a covering image. Valuing this identity results in a particular quality of relationships, praising moral standards that produce a psychologically and physiologically damaging identity, and moral endorsements that call for more of the same. It is, nevertheless, an option for those who accept "masculinity" as an identity.

THE FEMININE MASK

"Sugar and spice and everything nice, that's what little girls are made of." So goes one picture of traditional femininity. Being "nice" or "ladylike" continues as a norm for female behavior and appearance in many circles today. It is, however, far less obsessive than is masculinity for males; tomboys are tolerated with surprising latitude whatever their ages. Outweighing this toleration, nevertheless, is a history of general negativity toward women and their roles. Consider the following quotations intended by their compiler to demonstrate how many secular and religious sources have viewed women:[4]

> The female requires the male not only for procreation, as in other animals, but also for governance, for the male excels both in intelligence and in strength. (St. Thomas Aquinas)
> Women are created with large hips in order that they should stay home and sit on them. (Martin Luther)
> As long as woman is for birth and children, she is as different from man as body is from soul. (St. Jerome, who had a low regard for the body)
> Women are designed in their deeper instincts to get more pleasure out of life when they are not aggressive. (Dr. Spock)
> Even school children know that the male is by far the more important sex. (John Calvin)
> What a mad idea to demand equality for women! Women are nothing but machines for producing children. (Napoleon)
> Woman is wholly subject to nature, and hence only aesthetically free . . . she becomes free only by her relation to man. (Kierkegaard)
> Woman is a weakling before a show of strength, and a tyrant if she has her will. (St. Ignatius Loyola)
> When a woman thinks at all, she thinks evil. (Seneca)
> Woman's greatest chance for making marriage a success depends upon her willingness to lose her life in that of her husband. (Peter Marshall)

Male: From Self-Destruction to Self-Care (New York: Morrow, 1979); Joe L. Dubbert, *A Man's Place: Masculinity In Transition* (Englewood Cliffs, N.J.: Prentice-Hall, 1979); Fred Hapgood, *Why Males Exist: An Inquiry Into the Evolution of Sex* (New York: Morrow, 1979).
[4]Rebecca Wenger, "Quotations from Chairman Male," in Harry B. Adams, ed., *Reflection* 69, no. 4 (May 1972), p. 16.

From the beginning, nothing has been more alien, hostile, and repugnant to woman than truth—her great art is the lie, her highest concern is mere appearance and beauty. (Nietzsche)

Order includes the primacy of the husband, the ready subjection of the wife, and her willing obedience. (Pope Pius XI)

The fact that women must be regarded as having little sense of justice is no doubt related to the predominance of envy in their mental life. (Freud)

It is shameful for a woman to even think of what nature she has, let alone glory in it. (St. Clement of Alexandria)

Most women have no characters at all! (Alexander Pope)

Sugar and spice, yes; but traditional femininity obviously has its darker side, too. Subordination and acceptance of an inferior status combined with honored niceness is material of the traditional feminine mask. Some of the characteristics of femininity we have come to recognize and accept are as stifling and damaging as are those of masculinity.

Appearance. The biological "given" of a female, "traditional femininity," is defined by roundness, modest height, smoothness, and a generally soft appearance. However, even very angular and otherwise "masculine" women are not disqualified from their femininity as readily as "feminine" appearing males. For some strange reason vulgarities such as "Queer" and "Dyke" are not hurled as readily at a rugged woman—a degree of toleration not enjoyed by her male counterpart.

Attitudes. Shaped by culture, traditional feminine attitudes encompass being passive and accepting, close, romantic, personal, warm, tender, emotional, reserved, dependent, hesitant, and preferring safety. A woman may cry, show dependence, uncertainty, and vulnerability.

Mannerisms. Approved by culture, traditional feminine mannerisms, a woman's "body-language," include any posture that does not suggest either a boxer or severe gesturing; women have more latitude in mannerisms than do men. Crossed legs with an ankle resting just above the knee is not ladylike; knee planted above knee with pointed foot in motion is fine. Swishing like an excited woodfairy is laudable; the swish-swagger of a uniformed male cowboy star is at least questionable. Slugging someone on the arm while yelling "Ahr right!" is inappropriate; in a business meeting a *gentle* handshake is all right. A pat on the buttocks (anyone's buttocks) by a woman, while not causing a scandal would certainly be considered odd; a hug anywhere, anytime is almost always considered nice. Within the boundaries of niceness, expressive behavior is an ingredient of traditional American femininity.

Roles. Set by culture, traditional feminine roles, things *real* ladies do, are characteristically gentle, passive, caring, submissive, verbal (poetry, music, reading), receiving, obedient, neutral, home oriented, and colored pink. Noncontact recreation, knowing how to cook and sew, nursing, accepting whatever financial support a husband is willing to share, and subservience are examples of successful feminine roles and traits.

Femininity and Morality

As with masculinity, many of our standards of personal and social morality are linked closely with how we believe "real ladies" ought to behave. We assume that if I am a female, I ought to exhibit feminine appearances, attitudes, mannerisms, and roles; if not, there is something abnormal and *wrong* with me. We are apt to approve of females who, for example, are home oriented regardless of the quality of the homemaking. A general acceptance of tyrannical or negligent mothers, nagging wives, sloppy housekeepers, and lazy female TV addicts is woven into the fabric of moderately praiseworthy feminine behavior (At least she's in the home where she ought to be!). How many of us would dare question publicly the "right" of all women to be mothers? How can an American question "motherhood" at all? How can one question openly any aspect of activities that so reinforce and symbolize American femininity?

The High Price of Femininity

Subtle and obvious penalties have resulted from the traditional understanding of femininity. Words such as "Dame," "Madame," and "Mistress" have negative connotations, while the male equivalents "Lord," "Sir" and "Mister" are free from derogatory meanings. "Womanly" is frequently negative; "manly" is positive. The English language uses words referring to males as the standard, normal, complementary way to praise; words referring to females have a lesser or negative standing.[5]

In a speech in the late seventies, a female judge observed that for most of the young women going before the courts the "offense" is nonconformity to a social model of what is accepted behavior for young girls. This reflects an attitude not significantly different from the nineteenth-century position that caused girls to be institutionalized for such offenses as stubbornness and disobedience. The controllers of these institutions then felt successful if the offender married and bore children after serving time. Rehabilitation was considered a failure if the offender remained unmarried, became an unwed mother, or was separated or divorced. Even today, girls not boys are brought to court for being promiscuous or fornicating; girls not boys are forced to accept the humiliation of an examination of their bodies—all in the name of protecting the helpless female.

[5]See Casey Miller and Kate Swift, *Words and Women* (New York: Doubleday, 1977).

In many homes the woman's place is still the kitchen, sometimes the family room, rarely the garage. In advertisements a woman is inadequate because she fails to remove the "ring around the collar" from her husband's shirt. The female is exploited as a sex symbol and seducer journeying from sexpot to dishpan with little in between.[6] Inequality between men and women in salaries and employment opportunities has not been removed from American society. Though some would say "They've come a long way" (which may be true), for the most part, the norms for traditional femininity are founded on a particular, limiting notion of appropriate feminine appearances, attitudes, mannerisms and roles.[7] Exceptions are tolerated more for legal reasons than from moral conviction. If these observations are correct, it is fair to ask, "Is it wise and moral to be traditionally feminine? Is there an alternative?"

Femininity and Identity

It is our conviction that answering the "Who am I" question with "I am a lady" (meaning, I am a female who must behave in a traditional feminine way) is a mask; it is, for the most part, a covering image. Valuing this identity results in a particular quality of relationships, praising moral standards that produce a psychologically damaging (or at least artificially limiting) identity, and moral endorsements that call for more of the same.

SOME GENDER TERMS

femaleness: Anatomic and physiologic features which relate to the female's procreative and nurturant capacities.

feminine: An adjective to describe a set of sex-specific social role behaviors that are unrelated to procreative and nurturant biologic functions.

gender identity: The inner sense of maleness or femaleness which identifies the person as being male, female, or ambivalent. . . . Group values may cause conflicts about gender identity by labeling certain nonsexual interests and behavior as mas-

---

[6]See the documentary film "Killing Us Softly: Advertising's Image of Women" (Cambridge Documentary Films, Cambridge, Mass.) and Erving Goffman, "Genderisms," *Psychology Today* (August 1977), pp. 60–63.

[7]See U.S. Dept. of Labor, Bureau of Labor Statistics; *Women in The Labor Force: Some New Data Series* (rev. periodically); Milton Cantor and Bruce Laurie, *Class, Sex, and the Woman Worker* (Westport, Conn.: Greenwood, 1977); Viola Klein, *The Feminine Character: History of An Ideology* (Urbana: Univ. of Illinois Press, 1972); Betty Friedan, *The Feminine Mystique,* 2nd ed. (New York: Norton, 1974); Mary Vetterling-Braggin, et al., *Feminism and Philosophy* (Totowa, N.J.: Littlefield, 1977).

culine or feminine. Gender identity is distinguished from sexual identity, which is biologically determined.

gender role: The image the individual person presents to others and to the self that declares him or her to be boy or girl, man or woman. Gender role is the public declaration of gender identity, but the two do not necessarily coincide.

maleness: Anatomic and physiologic features which relate to the male's procreative capacity.

masculine: An adjective to describe a set of sex-specific social role behaviors that are unrelated to procreative biologic function.

From Shervert H. Frazier et al., *A Psychiatric Glossary*, 4th ed. (Washington, D.C.: American Psychiatric Assoc., 1975), pp. 55, 58, 98, 100.

THE MASK OF ETHNIC ORIGIN

An aquarium of tropical fish in a home is a never-ending source of curiosity, beauty, harmony, struggle, and diversity. Each color, each shape, each temperament and the contribution of each fish (whether by presence or function) is significant to the overall quality of the contained community. For any one kind of fish to claim overall superiority to other occupants would be ludicrous to a human onlooker. All the fish are equal in the sense of their common "fishness." All the fish are not equal in a sense of precise sameness.

Admitting to flaws in this analogy, we find some insights. You're white, black, brown, yellow, red, or various shades thereof; your ancestry is European, Middle Eastern, Near Eastern, African, Asian, native American, or whatever. While social scientists fight over inborn capacities versus cultural influences among human beings and behaviors, we are living on the same small planet, journeying within a largely unknown universe. Assuming we have more reasoning powers than do tropical fish in an aquarium, we wonder legitimately why our "aquarium" is filled with unreasonable striving for superiority among people of differing ethnic backgrounds.

In recent years an "ethnic revival," and in some cases a new ethnic separatism, has emerged. It is one thing to search harmlessly for ancestral roots and to preserve the diverse arts of the multitude of human cultures. It is less innocent if such roots and arts are symptoms and further causes of socially explosive reactions to past and present injustices. Ethnic chauvinism as a source of one's fundamental identity has consequences very different from natural curiosity about one's roots or the preservation of enriching ways of human life. In the words of one scholar

> Ethnicity emphasizes the trivialities that distinguish us and obscures the overwhelming reality of our common genetic and human heritages as well as our common needs and hopes. By emphasizing differences, ethnicity lends itself to the conservative belief in the inevitability of inequality.[8]

It is our contention that each person's ethnic background is important as a contribution to the human community. It is understandable that oppressed groups of human beings have taken an interest in their ethnic heritage; the discovery of positive roots can contribute to legitimate ethnic pride. However, "I am a white of European stock" is more adequate as history or biology than as a basis of identity. As a clue to identity, such an ethnic statement is a superficial mask or image; when valued more or less than another ethnic mask, such a statement can lead to needless disharmony and separation.

One such institution that fosters disharmony and separation is the *Social Register*. Referred to as "that archaic anachronism that presumes to extract the socially prestigious from the rest of us,"[9] the *Social Register* functions for some individuals as a high valuing of who they are. Founded in 1887 by "a socially ambitious son of a patent lawyer whose first publishing venture was a gossip sheet,"[10] the *Social Register* has never disclosed its criteria for its listings. No doubt ethnicity has some relationship to the standards. It is our conviction that whatever its criteria and uses, the *Social Register* and other such listings function poorly as a measure of human worth or adequate identity.

THE MASK OF PERFORMANCES

You have just walked into a social gathering made up of people you don't know. Your hostess introduces you by name. Very quickly you are being identified further by your hostess, or being asked by someone, or you are explaining yourself with a direct or subtle reference to what you *do.* Your name is insufficient; information about what you do is required.

If this scene were only an effort to find something to talk about, what you do may be a good beginning. If you say that you are a student, the

---

[8]Orlando Patterson, "Hidden Dangers in the Ethnic Revival," *New York Times* February 20, 1978, p. 17. See also his *Ethnic Chauvinism: The Reactionary Impulse* (New York: Stein and Day, 1977) and Nathan Glazer, *Affirmative Discrimination: Ethnic Inequality and Public Policy* (New York: Basic Books, 1978).

[9]Carey Winfrey, "Society's 'In' Book: Does It Still Matter?" *New York Times*, February 2, 1980, p. 14.

[10]Winfrey, p. 14.

subject of your studies could begin a congenial conversation. As the con-versation proceeds, however, some evaluations begin to take place. If you name philosophy as an interest, or more specifically ethics, your very being and worth may be invested with whatever your conversation partners think of philosophy; as an ethicist you may be invested with superior moral qualities that inhibit any earthy comments at that gathering. On the one hand, if the other guests learn that you are studying ethics at Harvard, not only might you be of moral excellence but your overall value will increase markedly; being a Harvard student might even compensate for studying ethics in the eyes of those who view ethics as another one of the useless humanities. On the other hand, if you are studying ethics at a public community college in South Dakota, you may be identified as a lesser being! Perhaps *you* view yourself as a superior or inferior human being in terms of what you do and the status accorded by society.

You Are What You Do

We learn very early that to a large extent "I *am* what I *do*." Too often we offer praise and show affection to very young children *only* when they do something acceptable. We reinforce the baby whose bowel movement is performed at the right time; we become ecstatic when our child takes its first steps in front of critical Aunt Wretchny and Uncle Tode. Through the use of this system, successes in school, in the playground (especially at Little League), and at home multiply. If our praises and affection are most demonstrative at these moments, we give a clear message to our children: "You are worthwhile when you perform well; you are what you do." We seal and reseal this sense of identity by asking "What are you going to be when you grow up?" We have implied that you are little or nothing of significance now as a child; your worth depends on what you do as an adult. You will be justified by good works.

Advertisements intended to attract young people to the armed forces or to colleges are often phrased: "Be somebody. Join (or attend) _____!" You will be a nobody until you do.

The masks of our performances, roles, or activities have become en-grained in our culture. We perceive ourselves, we are perceived, and we perceive others according to what is performed and the value attached to the particular role or activity. Some common identities and their conse-quences are as follows:

Child. If individuals consciously or subconsciously answer the iden-tity question with "I am my parents' child," certain consequences may follow. Their value of themselves depends on their fulfillment of the "child" role as they understand it; they judge themselves "good" to the extent that they fulfill the role.

Their relationships with others are morally good to the extent they fulfill the role; their primary moral obligation is to their parents—not to a spouse, their children, or friends. They are worthwhile as children, whatever their ages.

But who are they when their parents are dead? Possibly there will be no dilemma; the role may be well engrained, and the deceased parents' photographs remind them who they are and of their primary loyalty. Acting the part of their parents' children is good; to do differently, bad. Otherwise, an identity crisis develops.

Parent. A mother and father who view the parental role as the source of their identity value themselves to the extent that this role, as understood, is fulfilled. Their relationships with others are morally good to the extent that they are parental; their self-worth depends on parenting. Their children's successes and failures reflect directly on the quality of their parenting.

But who are they when the children grow up and leave home? An identity crisis may surface. A way of avoiding the crisis is not to "let go." They seek out continuous parenting moments with their children. In doing so, they may either alienate their children or become legendary "in-laws." In their own eyes the parents are good as long as they perform at parenting; without a parenting role they lose a sense of worth, identity, and goodness.

Spouse. Being a wife or a husband can also be a source of identity, worth, and goodness. For such a person, a divorce or the death of one's partner is more than grief; it is devastation, a loss of being someone. The possible new identity—"divorcee," "widow," or "widower" has few gratifications and a rather narrow range of good behaviors. The "other half" is gone; only half remains.

Athlete. The aging athlete stares mournfully at the trophies; they show who he or she *was!* Now, this person is an ex-athlete. Being an ex-anything is hardly an in-depth source of identity, worth, and moral rightness. And yet we reinforce this identity, especially among males; we forget that few senior citizens will be able to find a satisfactory identity as an athlete.

Some individuals who yearn to be athletes but who have not had the opportunity and/or ability become avid fans: they may live a fantasy life of sports statistics and voyeuristic pleasure. An identity as a fan, though less than the real thing, permits some fans to feel right with the world, though second-best.

Possessor. Cedric feels proud of his achievements, for which he has worked hard. Strolling around his home, he sees the results of his labor:

the cars, the comfortable house and its contents, and the yard. His summer cottage comes to mind, the trips abroad with his family, and so on. In theory, he could be well satisfied. But there is that gnawing sensation within; a larger house with more furniture, perhaps an additional car, a more expensive country club, more extensive trips, and a guest cottage for the cottage—why not add these items to his possessions? He might then be satisfied with who he is, his self-worth, and the good life. Or, Cedric is hit with unexpected medical bills just as his business folds because of a competitor's unsuccessful invention; not worth much now, not living the good life, Cedric no longer knows who he is.

Leisure Activities. In his newsletter *Context*, editor Martin Marty (April 1, 1980) comments on an observation by O. C. Edwards, a fellow scholar. Marty wrote

> He quotes a *New Yorker* cartoon which shows a newcomer at a cocktail party introducing himself; "Bixby of Palisades Park. I'm into wine-making and the martial arts, Gregorian chant and Zen Buddhism . . ." One could almost affirm: "I have hobbies. Therefore, I am."
>
> Once upon a time people derived identity from jobs. That has changed. Today they use their leisure activities to demonstrate who they are. "When consensus breaks down in a society, one can no longer depend on social reinforcement of one's identity. Rather, the sense of who I am has to be sought privately. That sense of identity is necessary for sanity, and so the question must be answered. If the world does not tell me who I am, I have to find out for myself."

An extention or version of possessor, the individual who derives a sense of identity, self-worth, and a good life by means of leisure activities runs similar risks. How many activities are required to be somebody? What if someday the individual can't pursue as many? What if the person becomes ill and is confined to bed? Who then is he or she, and of what value? What is a good life for an individual confined to bed and wheelchair?

The Cult of Activity

"Keeping busy?" asks a friend you've not seen for a while. Most of the time we reply positively, and we are probably telling the truth. We are so busy that we schedule in moments, brief periods, for "relaxing" activities such as jogging, shopping, and gardening. Perish the thought that we should just sit quietly. We must perform at something to be someone of worth; being good is bound up with keeping busy. While sitting quietly, we're nobody, of little worth, and not really good. *Being someone of value means being active at something.*

And yet we read about excessive stress leading to ill health and poor human relationships. In an essay, a suburban New York youth worker wrote

> Last year seven high school students from an exclusive New York suburban community attempted suicide, all within six months. Two succeeded, five failed. . . . Each year an estimated 5,000 young Americans, ages 15 to 24, succeed at suicide. . . . Measuring up in our success-oriented, competitive culture subjects young people to unbearable pressures. From their tenderest years they are prodded to produce, to excel, to be somebody special. Their lives are regimented like a factory assembly line. Be busy, they are told; maximize every moment.[11]

The next time a friend asks, "Keeping busy?" say "Not really; my life is rather quiet right now." But be prepared to be perceived as an individual who is not somebody of worth and high moral character.

THE MASKS AS IDENTITY

One view of the masks of masculine and feminine gender roles, other roles and performances, and ethnicity proposes that the sum total of the masks and any other behaviors is the only real you. You are what you seem to be; anything else is a fantasy. There is no "self" behaving.[12]

This view claims that the word "mask" is inappropriate as we have used it. Nothing is being covered up, at least no private unobservable "you." "What you see is what you get!" A person is whoever he appears to be in any particular situation; a person becomes his gender images, family roles, and other activities and performances.

If this view is correct, I am my image of the moment. My identity, worth, and goodness depend on what we have called masks in this chapter. Identities are discarded as circumstances require; I *am* according to the situation of the moment. Wife today; widow tomorrow. Athlete today; invalid, ex-athlete after the accident. Company manager this week; retired employee next week. I am a combination of inherited appearances, learned attitudes, mannerisms, negative and positive feelings, roles, activities, and performances. These images are linked to the current appraisals of the worth and goodness of each.

An extreme example serves to illustrate our reservations about this view: "I am an uneducated, poor, nonwhite, old, quadraplegic lesbian." If one is in this situation, is the acceptance of this identity, worth, and perception of moral rightness the only option? Or should we seek the combinations of

---

[11]Edward R. Walsh, "Freeing Children From the Cult of Activity," *New York Times*, June 3, 1979, Sec. 23, p. 16.

[12]"Denials of the Existence of a Self" among Buddhists, Hume, and Behaviorists is discussed in *Living Issues in Philosophy*, pp. 54-59.

ingredients judged most worthwhile by society in order to "be some-body?" Should formal education encourage particular appearances, at-titudes, feelings, mannerisms, and performances so that students fit right? At this point it would be better to search for an alternative.

Those of us who differ with the masks-as-identity position will look further. We cannot disprove this "sum total" position. We acknowledge candidly, however, that it is not a persuasive axiom for us; its implications are inadequate for our perceptions of life.

In looking for an alternative, we can rule out the discussed ways of answering "Who am I?" For us, an adequate identity will not rely on images. We must look for an identity that will hold all our changeable appearances, activities, and so on in perspective. We search for an identity that will provide a satisfactory answer both for the extreme situations and the day-to-day changing circumstances of our lives.

BENEATH THE MASKS

Let us now consider some of the characteristics rooted in our very beings and not dependent on the masks we may wear. Following is a list of such basic qualities and capacities we shall call "givens":

1. *Self-consciousness*   Whereas all animals are conscious, we are self-conscious. We are not only conscious, but we are conscious of the fact that it is *we* who are conscious.

2. *Abstract thought or the power of reflective thinking*   We can search for truth, and we have some ability to distinguish between truth and falsity.

3. *Ethical discrimination and some freedom of choice*   We are conscious of a distinction between what is and what ought to be. We can distinguish between right and wrong, according to our norms, and feel responsible for our actions.

4. *Aesthetic appreciation*   We search for aesthetic pleasure and make dis-tinctions between beauty and ugliness.

5. *Discrimination among ultimate meanings of life*   We are able to decide whether there is any meaning to life and which ultimate meaning suits us. As far as we know, dogs, cats, apes, goldfish, and trees cannot.

6. *Creativity*   We can improvise and invent repeatedly, make complex tools, wear ornaments, fly in the air, travel beyond the earth's atmosphere, journey under the sea, and project pictures around the globe. We are creative artists and technicians.

7. *Sociability*   We reach out for companionship, organization, and

cooperation; we communicate in a variety of ways from a simple touch to complicated languages. We are in relation to others; we are not isolated creatures.

8. Embodiment   We are psychosomatic agents who interact with our environments and whose complex biological processes are dynamic, vital, interwoven aspects of our whole beings. We are not minds or souls trapped within an alien, incompatible body. Each of us is a unique, embodied creature.

Potential Abuses and Distortions

Each of these ingredients, characteristics, qualities, and capacities is subject to distortion. Philosophers and theologians disagree among themselves about the extent to which, if at all, any of these givens are naturally distorted in some or all individuals as they emerge from the womb. Clearly some human beings are born with biological handicaps; our evaluations of and responses to our handicaps vary. Whether some or all people are born with a natural tendency toward passivity, a search for ugliness, and (sinful or) antisocial behavior is still debated. That some individuals make choices that twist the givens in abusive, distorted, and alienating ways is a supportable conviction. The givens can be abused and distorted.

A Useful Concept

If the givens rooted in my nature provide an answer to who I am, we might locate a concept that can summarize them. A recitation of these eight, and perhaps more, characteristics would be burdensome and awkward in any identity affirmation.

The ordinary word *person* may be useful. Although it sounds less than exciting to exclaim "I am a person!" the concept can acquire a new meaning; the ordinary, familiar, and dull—even negative—use of "person" can be buried and a new meaning resurrected. Some reflections on "person" follow:

> What does it mean when we say a human being is a person? First of all, it means that each individual human is not just an instance of mankind in the same way a piece of copper is an instance of copper. Each individual is an original center of being and action. His actions are his own. . . .
> With humans . . . there is a distance between what they are and what they do, on account of the fact that they are knowing subjects with a certain degree of freedom.

... being a person is a kind of dynamic process.... *Being* a person means, therefore, the possibility of *becoming* more and more of a person.[13]

Whatever else is true of him, then, a person is a self-conscious knower who can guide himself by norms of consistency and reasoned investigation.... a person experiences himself not only as a self-conscious knower but also as a complex unity of remembering, feeling, desiring, perceiving and we shall argue, of willing and oughting. ... a person [is] a self-identifying active unity continuing in and constituted by basic unlearned psychic and physiological capacities.[14]

PERSONS AND ROLES

Let me distinguish here between role relationships and interpersonal relationships—a distinction often overlooked in the spate of literature that deals with human relations. Roles are inescapable. They must be played or else the social system will not work. A role is a repertoire of behavior patterns which must be rattled off in appropriate contexts, and all behavior irrelevant to the role must be suppressed. But what we often forget is the fact that it is a person who is playing the role. This person has a self, or I should say, *is* a self. All too often the roles that a person plays do not do justice to all of his self. In fact, there may be nowhere that he may just *be* himself. He may be self-alienated. ... It is possible to be involved in a social group such as a family for years and years, playing one's roles nicely with the other members—and never getting to know the *persons* who are playing the other roles.

Sidney M. Jourard, *The Transparent Self* (New York: Van Nostrand, 1971), pp. 30-31.

Sidney Jourard (1926–1974) was professor of psychology at the University of Florida. Also a psychotherapist, Dr. Jourard wrote several books, including Healthy Personality: An Approach From the View-Point of Humanistic Psychology.

---

[13]A. G. M. van Melsen, "Person," *Encyclopedia of Bioethics*, vol. 3, pp. 1207–1208.
[14]Peter A. Bertocci and Richard M. Millard, *Personality and The Good* (New York: McKay, 1963), pp. 172–173.

For the humanist, "person" may well conceptualize who he or she is. Those with a theological perspective may prefer "child of God." A "child of God" is also a person and, in addition, in a caring relationship with the Creator, like a child to parent. This meaning is conveyed well here:

> The person belongs to the realm of quality, not quantity. It is suddenly manifested in a powerful inner movement which partakes of the nature of the Absolute. However many things we accumulated, that would bring us no nearer to it. The person resides in being, not in having. . . .
>
> Thus the infirm, the neurotic, the aged, can experience this flowering of the person, in spite of all that hinders and limits their existence, much more intensely, sometimes, than those who are loaded with the good things of life. . . .
>
> We must resist the temptation to give a doctrinaire answer to the question . . . "Who am I?" We must give up the idea that knowing the person means compiling a precise and exhaustive inventory of it. There is always some mystery remaining, arising from the very fact that the person is alive. We can never know what new upsurge of life may transfigure it tomorrow.
>
> The person is a potential, a current of life which surges up continually, and which manifests itself in a fresh light at every new blossoming forth of life. At the creative moment of dialogue with God or with another person, I in fact experience a double certainty: that of "discovering" myself, and also that of "changing." I find myself to be different from what I thought I was. From that moment I am different from what I was before. And yet at the same time I am certain that I am the same person. . . .
>
> Our life is a score composed by God. The person is the conductor who is assuring its performance by directing the orchestra—our body and mind. But the composer is not absent. He is there during the performance. He leans over to the conductor and encourages him; he whispers in his ear, making clear his intentions and helping him to put them into execution.[15]

Who Am I?

"I am a person" or "I am a child of God." These identities are constant. It is the person/child-of-God who is embodied male or female.[16] The person or

[15]Tournier, *The Meaning of Persons*, pp. 231–233.

[16]Discussions about what is learned and innate to male and female behavior may be found in five essays in the section titled "Genetic Aspects of Human Behavior" in the *Encyclopedia of Bioethics*, vol. 2, pp. 527–548; Robert C. Solomon and Judith Rose Sanders, "Sexual Identity," *ibid.*, vol. 4, pp. 1589–1596; the November 1978 issue of *Psychology Today*; and Robert May, *Sex and Fantasy: Patterns of Male and Female Development* (New York: Norton, 1980); "The Sexes: How They Differ—and Why," the cover story of *Newsweek* (May 18, 1981), pp. 72–83.

child of God is not identified as a performance or as an inherited ethnicity, social status, or physical structure. "You are NOT what you do nor necessarily what you appear to be!" Instead, you are a person or child of God who has many changeable gender images, secondary inheritances, roles, performances, and activities. As these change or are discarded, the person or child of God as the basic identity remains constant. The "I" is the same basic "I" growing in the givens of personhood. A diagram may be helpful here.

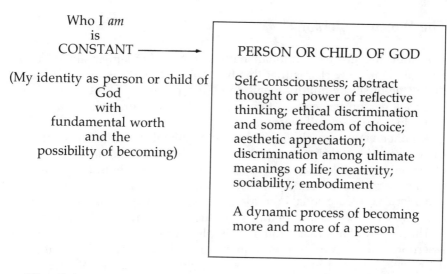

Who I *am*
is
CONSTANT ———————▶

(My identity as person or child of God
with
fundamental worth
and the
possibility of becoming)

PERSON OR CHILD OF GOD

Self-consciousness; abstract thought or power of reflective thinking; ethical discrimination and some freedom of choice; aesthetic appreciation; discrimination among ultimate meanings of life; creativity; sociability; embodiment

A dynamic process of becoming more and more of a person

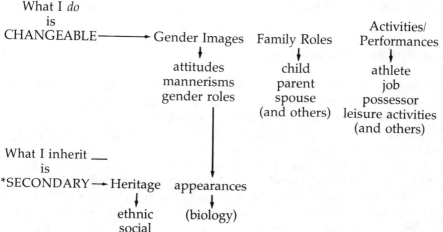

What I *do*
is
CHANGEABLE————————▶ Gender Images   Family Roles   Activities/
                                                      Performances

                         attitudes   child   athlete
                         mannerisms   parent   job
                         gender roles   spouse   possessor
                                          (and others)   leisure activities
                                                          (and others)

What I inherit __
is
*SECONDARY —▶ Heritage   appearances

              ethnic   (biology)
              social

*It is our position that a person cannot do much about his ethnic and social background or his basic physical structure; these factors are not considered as primary in being a person or a child of God.

The changeable aspects of our lives become masks when in combination or singularly they hide the real person from herself or himself and/or others. When the person is mistakenly *identified* as "macho" or "ladylike," as white or nonwhite, wealthy or poor, professor or student, and so on, the real person is obscured. Kept within the perspective of a constant identity as a person or child of God, the changeable "doings" and secondary inheritances can become positive factors in one's life.

The Worth of Persons

If I value the givens of human nature, then I fundamentally value all persons. One view claims that this fundamental worth is inalienable and cannot be offset by anything evil done in a person's life; no matter how terribly a person has chosen to act, his or her fundamental worth determines his or her overall worth.

Another view says although this fundamental worth is inalienable, it can be offset by evil choices and acts. The individual sentenced to die for a capital crime is still fundamentally worthwhile, but hateful decisions and actions override that basic worth. Or, in another example, a great physician and a local crook are equal in fundamental human worth, but their choices and behaviors add to and detract from their respective overall value.

These views have many differing implications. Common to both is the assertion that every person is fundamentally worthwhile just because of their *being,* not their *doing.* A person or child of God does not need to be justified as a human being of fundamental worth by busy good works!

Persons and Morality

By viewing oneself and others as persons and/or children of God, we develop a basic moral sense that includes self-respect and respect for others; I value myself and others and treat myself and others with concern. Never an It–It, I–It, or It–Thou relationship; morally good relations are between and among *persons:* "I–Thou."

Let us conclude this exploration by restating an earlier idea of this chapter: any significant decision you would make about your identity as a result of reading these pages would be incomplete; for any view to take hold, it must be shared with another in a vital ongoing way. The nurturing process of affirming the real you beneath the masks can occur with one or more friends, a religious or humanistic group, a therapist, or other human supports. Books can provide some clarification of alternative views about identity; only live persons interacting deeply can provide the relationships needed for ongoing personal growth.

CHAPTER REVIEW

A. Identity, values, and morality

1. Everyone has a sense of identity, an answer to "Who am I?"—whether thought through or not.
2. A customary philosophical approach to the issue of identity is to raise such questions as "Am I more than my body? Am I my mind?" and so on.
3. This chapter's focus is on the day-to-day issue of identity: the images we have of ourselves as we live out who we are.
4. My own answer to "Who am I" and its value to me determines how highly or poorly I regard myself.
5. Other people's views of my identity determine their values of me.
6. I value other persons according to how I view their identities.
7. An individual's identity as valued by himself and by others *and* the value the individual places on the images he or she perceives of others are crucial to the individual's relations with other human beings; my sense of morality depends to a large extent on my self-regard and on my value of others' identities.

B. Identity is learned

1. We absorb a sense of who we are from our relationships.
2. More than just an intellectual matter, the conscious choice of an identity requires support from others for it to take hold emotionally as well as intellectually.

C. Masks

1. The identities of many persons are like masks; they prevent disclosure of the wearer.
2. The mask of negativity is worn by many persons.

D. The masculine mask

1. The mask of masculinity provides culturally accepted appearances, attitudes, mannerisms, and roles for men; how "real men" ought to behave is linked with such masks.
2. Men pay a high price for wearing the masculine mask.

E. The feminine mask

1. The mask of femininity provides culturally accepted appearances, at-

titudes, mannerisms, and roles for women; how "real ladies" ought to behave is linked with such masks.
2. Women pay a high price for wearing the feminine mask.

F. The mask of ethnic origin

1. In recent years an "ethnic revival" and in some cases an ethnic separatism has emerged.
2. As an identity, ethnic masks can lead to superficiality in relationships, needless disharmony, and separation.

G. The mask of performances

1. We learn, to a large extent, that we *are* what we *do*.
2. Each performance mask has certain potentially negative consequences.
3. "Keeping busy" reflects the valuing of someone active, performing at something.

H. The masks as identity

1. One view holds that all the "masks" combined are the real you.
2. An alternative view proposes a "real you" beneath the masks.

I. Beneath the masks

1. The word "person" can be given new life by valuing the "givens" of personhood positively. "Child of God" is a theological phrasing of "person."
2. "I am a person" or "I am a child of God" can provide a valuable, constant identity.
3. Consequences of this identity include the development of self-respect and respect for others on an I–Thou basis, a fundamental ingredient for one view of morally good relations.

SUGGESTED READINGS

Berenson, Frances M. *Understanding Persons: Personal and Impersonal Relationships.* New York: St. Martin's, 1981.

The conceptual significance of the notion of personal relationships and its relation to a clearer understanding of persons and the self; the author argues that since persons are "entities" who stand in various relationships with one another, an understanding of persons must necessarily involve an understanding both of these relationships and of their diverse emotional components.

Gould, Carol C., and Wartofsky, Marx W., eds. *Women and Philosophy*. New York: Putnam (Capricon), 1976.

A collection of papers about women and philosophy, including insights about the journey of several women as philosophers; many issues of a philosophical nature raised by feminists and women philosophers are joined in a book of papers that concern women in one way or another.

Jourard, Sidney M. *The Transparent Self*. New York: Van Nostrand, 1971.

A classic study by a psychologist of the chosen roads of personal concealment, this plainly written book raises the question "Shall I permit others to know me as I truly am, or shall I seek instead to remain masked and be seen as someone I am not?"

Kriegel, Leonard. *On Men and Manhood*. New York: Hawthorn, 1979.

An examination of masculinity with its shallow bases in athletic and sexual competition rather than humanhood.

Lee, Donald, and Stern, Carl. "Philosophy and Masculinity," *Southwest Philosophical Studies* 3 (1978), pp. 120–125.

A reflection on the possibility that the practice of academic philosophy has been distorted by masculine values; masculine values, their undesirable effects, and suggestions for amelioration are included.

Morrow, Lance. "What Is the Point of Working?" *Time*, May 11, 1981, pp. 93–94.

The centrality of work to the American sense of personal identity and worth is explored briefly.

Richardson, Mary Sue and Alpert, Judith Landon. "Unisex vs. Androgyny," *New York University Education Quarterly* 8, no. 4 (1977), pp. 29–32.

In an essay reviewing three recent gender identity studies, the authors explore androgyny as an alternative to unisex and rigid categories of masculinity and femininity.

Vetterling-Braggin, Mary; Elliston, Frederick A.; and English, Jane. *Feminism and Philosophy*. Totowa, N.J.: Littlefield, 1977.

A collection of contemporary writings by philosophers that ranges over all the feminist issues and is readily intelligible to professionals and nonprofessionals alike.

6

Love and Friendship

In this life we have three lasting qualities—faith, hope and love. But the greatest of them is love.[*]

WHAT THE WORLD NEEDS NOW

Several years ago a popular song echoed a theme present for centuries in literature, music, philosophy, and religion: "What the world needs now is love. . . ." Psychologists and other students of human behavior see the age-old call for love as being central to human relations. Smiling flower children of the sixties bounced their way through that decade with simplistic slogans of love. Greeting cards for all occasions sell well with verses of love and friendship. A television preacher tells his contributing national audience that God loves them and so does he—and a medal so inscribed is available from his corporation without charge. With so many words about love for so many centuries, we might assume that the idea has caught on and all would be well with the world. But it hasn't, and it isn't.

A Gnawing Void

Unhappiness. Surveys by the University of Michigan's Institute for Social Research have since 1957 shown a clear deterioration in Americans' feelings of happiness with life and their sense of well-being.[1] Doubts about education and employment, marriage and family life, friendships, finances, mental health, and global affairs are particularly bothersome to young adults. Unclear goals and a general loss of confidence in life's possibilities contribute to these feelings of depression that affect people of all ages.

[*]First Letter to the Corinthians, I Corinthians 13:13.
[1]Angus Campbell, *Sense of Well-Being in America: Patterns and Trends* (New York: McGraw-Hill, 1980).

108

Asked what they want out of life, many individuals respond, "I want to be happy." Yet the quality of happiness achieved seems mediocre. Given the predominance of "love" among words said and sung, it is interesting that more people do not respond with "I want to love and be loved." Perhaps we have not settled whether love is one ingredient of happiness or whether happiness is an aspect of love. In any case there is a prevailing sense that something is missing.

Loneliness.　Both the Bible and biologists, as well as psychologists, agree that it isn't good for people to be alone. Feeling alone occasionally, though, is very common. Some individuals, however, feel alone chronically.

> Lonely people are dissatisfied with everything about their lives: their living arrangements (whether solo or with others), the number of friends they have, the quality of those friendships, their marriages or love affairs, the number of conversations they have each day, and their sex lives.[2]

Regardless of the circumstances that help create occasional or chronic loneliness, the accompanying feelings of dissatisfaction and insufficient love accentuate any gaps between what *is* and what we believe ought to be. A lonely person senses something is missing.

Common to many forms of chronic unhappiness and loneliness is a gnawing void, a sense of incompleteness. The individual often feels that the quality and the quantity of love in his or her life is insufficient to meet his or her needs.

"Love" as Purpose and Basic Moral Norm

The clue to feelings of happiness, well-being, and belonging is caring, concern, or love. Successful performances and being good at something do not guarantee happiness or satisfying relationships. Achieving is not the answer. We share the assumption that love is essential to human fulfillment.

Who am I? I am a person/child of God. What is the fundamental purpose of my life? It is to love and be loved. Whatever changeable gender images, roles, activities, performances, or secondary inheritances enter my life, my identity can remain constant. Rooted in this identity is a basic calling, a common human vocation of mutual love.[3]

[2]Carin Rubinstein, et al., "Loneliness," *Human Nature* (February 1979), pp. 58–65.

[3]See Willard Gaylin, M.D., *Caring* (New York: Knopf, 1976); *Feelings: Our Vital Signs* (New York: Harper, 1979); Ashley Montagu, *On Being Human* (New York: Hawthorn, 1966); Norman Pittenger, *Loving Says It All* (New York: Pilgrim, 1978); and Joseph Fletcher, *Situation Ethics* (Philadelphia: Westminster, 1966).

We are convinced that implicit in this view of human identity and purpose is the basic moral norm—love. (Whether love is to be applied situationally or legalistically is another matter.) We are among those persons convinced that caring makes the difference in life; love is the fundamental standard by which human moral behavior should be guided and evaluated.

Another song a few years back began "What is this thing called 'love'?" Have all the songwriters, authors, and scholars meant the same thing by "love"? Is there a consensus on what love is? We shall describe some views of love we believe are deficient in various ways and then consider an interpretation of interpersonal love proposed by Ashley Montagu; we are convinced that interpersonal love satisfies human needs most adequately.

RECIPROCAL LOVE: A ROOT NEED

That there is a need for reciprocal love is a widespread assumption within contemporary psychiatry. The evidence seems to indicate a human necessity both to give and receive love.... "Love" is difficult to define precisely, but in this sense we may characterize it as a state of responsiveness with others as its goal. ... there does seem to be some evidence that it is a root need, not only in humans but in other living beings as well.

Paul Kurtz, *Decision and the Condition of Man* (New York: Dell, 1965), p. 152.

Paul W. Kurtz is professor of philosophy at the State University of New York at Buffalo. (He is quoted also in Chapter 2, p. 32).

VARIETIES OF LOVE

Springtime Love

Some individuals thoroughly enjoy the feelings of the chase and the initial phases of a relationship. This "springtime love" may be an early ingredient in a relationship; it is often a feeling of attraction, exhilaration, newness, testing, flirting, hoping, and tentative acceptance. The ego is fed; life is wonderful! The feelings accompanying the courtship and romance are valued perhaps more than the other person. "Falling in love with love is wonderful!"

Such infatuation is common and normal at the outset of a relationship, but some individuals identify these feelings as perfected love. These emotions persevere as long as both partners nurture them. These emotions, however, unfortunately serve as masks covering the actual individuals. In most cases, an ongoing relationship begins to strip away some of the masks, and real persons with strengths and weaknesses are revealed in whole or part. The illusion of absolute perfection with every moment aglow begins to crack. If the initial feelings have been identified as mature love and "right," the lovers are now likely to withdraw from the relationship; "We aren't in love anymore." The relationship is now "wrong." The search for the initial springtime feelings begins again, and again, with person after person—a regrettable cycle continues.

If we have understood the initial feelings not as love but as normal infatuation, we are more willing to let reality replace illusion. The initial "up" feelings can give way to a deeper relationship with another person; being in love with love can be replaced with a different, deeper emotion between persons, that of interpersonal love.

Dependent Love

The feelings of needing someone are familiar to many individuals. The needing, though, can be more acute than the basic desire for companionship. The needing, instead, can be a sense of inability or lacking in oneself. Clinging rather than sharing is a dominant feature of dependent love. "I need particular strengths you have that I lack; I cannot function well without being fed by those strong points."

The strengths may be real in the other person. The love can then flourish as long as the feeding continues. If the needed strengths are not actually present and only imagined, the relationship can suffer with chronic unmet expectations or rupture.

The individuals involved in parasitic, dependent love evaluate their relationship as good as long as the dependency is fed; it is evaluated as bad when lackings in one are not compensated for by the other. Labeling a person "my other half" may be in some cases an indication of some degree of dependent love.

Dependent love is like springtime love in that each is a relationship between images instead of persons. In springtime love, the images are feelings. In dependent love, the images are selected real or imagined features of a partner. Images are masks, however, not whole persons.

Solo Love

Self-infatuation owns the themes "I am the center of the universe" and "The best things in life are *me*." The word "love" means little when directed outwardly to someone else. When used in regard to others it designates a feeling of inner satisfaction: "I love you" means "I feel good inside me about myself because I have been entertained and/or praised." Solo love is evident when "he's all wrapped up in himself." It may also take the form of continuous self-focus; for example, some gurus enable disciple solo lovers to raise their individual consciousnesses and to regard that as the primary emotional goal of life. An exaggerated sense of self-importance, general indifference to others (except as others can be used), exploitation, and ongoing applause-seeking are other signs of solo love.

Curiously, the real person engaged in solo love usually wears two masks: the image of low self-esteem covered with another layer as solo lover.[4]

Debit Love

"I owe you/you owe me" is central to the emotions between persons in debit love. "You do for me and I'll do for you" is a bargaining quality found in such relationships.

A co-worker goes out of the way now and then to be nice to you. Coupled with the niceness is the follow-up: "Will you do such and such for me?" After you complete the task, the co-worker "owes you one" (unless the original niceness was prepayment).

Some relatives who receive emotional satisfaction from frequently giving have, in their minds, purchased a response; they are owed. Particularly obnoxious relatives love with the debit system; one hand offers, but the other hand is held out (or is keeping score).

Debit love can be very controlling and manipulative for the participants, but its rewards can include a sense of well-kept records and productivity. Morally responsible behavior consists of a good inventory and accurate payments; irresponsible behavior is incorrect billing and not paying up.

The emotions of debit love are not essentialy between persons, but rather between the masks of performances, things done. "I have feelings for what you do for me, and for what I do for you." There is little deep involvement in another's life; the relationship is based on bargaining and manipulation.

Aggressive Love

A primary ingredient in feelings of aggressive love is a sense of contest or victory. "Love" on the part of one or more individuals loving in this way is stimulated by challenge, attack, and/or winning. Constant competition dominates most of the togetherness.

---

[4]See Otto Kernberg, M.D., *Borderline Conditions and Pathological Narcissism* (New York: Aronson, 1975).

The person as a human being is not the object of aggressive love; the object of such love is the competitive feeling itself or the images projected by the aggressor on to the victim. Extreme examples include rape and sadism in which the rapist or sadist might interpret his attacks as making love to the conquered. More common is the couple who seem to thrive on psychological warfare and are, in their own view, very much "in love." The feelings of the relationship are in some ways gratifying and are the satisfying focus. Without the contest, the persons in such relationships may have little in common.

Martyr Love

The emotions of misery are idealized by some persons as love. Not to be confused with the self-sacrifices we may be called on to offer, martyr love is the active, subtle, sometimes subconscious collection of injustices. The "poor me" feelings that result can be valued highly.

Some individuals choose to be "losers." Though positive options are in fact open to them, they consistently select alternatives that backfire. Their hobby appears to be collecting injustices.

Jay is bright, from a good home of hard-working parents who are emotionally supportive, willing to contribute significantly to Jay's educational costs, and who continue to provide a place in their home for Jay, even though Jay is an adult. Jay chooses, instead, to live with an unstable drifter, parent a child, wallow in complaints, and attribute the misery to fate. In addition, Jay is miserable to the parents. Jay glows as the misery is nurtured and identifies the glowing feelings as love: "Of course I love my parents, my lover, my child, and myself! Things aren't perfect, but there's plenty of love in my life." In fact, the more miserable things and relationships are, the more Jay glows.

The courting of injustices and other forms of masochism can be understood in terms of various psychological theories, some of which would deny that a choice is involved at all. Disappointment is provoked by the subtle misuse of crucial or routine situations. After achieving the setback, the injustice collector indulges pleasurably in self-pity.

Regardless of psychological explanations for such self-defeating behaviors, we offer this capsule summary: the glow of misery and joyful self-pity are identified as loving emotions by martyrs who nurture such feelings in their own lives.

Possessive Love

"You belong to me" characterizes relationships between or among individuals who enjoy the feeling of power, control, and/or ownership. One type of possessive love involves a dominating person who exerts power and control in a relationship with a submissive counterpart who welcomes being possessed. (Such feelings duplicate dependent love.) Statements such as "my woman" and "he's all mine" may be indications of possessive ingredients in a relationship.

Another type of possessive love is one in which everyone involved possesses everyone else. Two examples follow:

> As the necessary signatures are gathered after a wedding, the guest minister is astonished to hear the new husband firmly warn his wife to be near enough to the telephone to answer within three rings whenever he calls from work. She counters by announcing that his Tuesday nights out with the boys are over. The guest cleric wonders what type of premarital guidance has taken place, if any!
>
> This relationship does not consist of a possessor and dependent, but two possessors. If they remain together, the emotional content of their marriage will be governed by feelings of ownership, with each partner setting aside respective privileges of ownership or domination. In their view, they are very much in love!

> The Weaver family does everything together. Grandmother, mother, father, the married son and his wife and children, and the married daughter and her husband and children are always together—on vacations, weekends, parties, and so on. If one is invited, it is assumed that all are invited; and if they're not, they all come anyway or all stay home! What a loving family! When you see one, you see them all. Individuality is practically nonexistent.

Possessive love can take two primary directions: managerial feelings of the possessor toward the dependent person(s) or feelings of mutual control shared between or among possessive persons. In both cases, genuine freedom is limited and nonconforming initiatives have no place. Individual, authentic personality is discouraged, not by words but by assimilated restrictive patterns. Interpersonal addiction is masked by "togetherness."

Longing Love

In general conversation, erotic love refers to sex acts. A motion picture labeled an "erotic film" is assumed to be sensual and explicit. "In some Greek theories of nature *eros* was the basic creative energy that could 'move worlds.' In the psyches of individual human beings, it has a strength that threatens to overcome reason."[5] Longing love is the main ingredient in this use of eros.

[5]Tom L. Beauchamp et al., *Philosophy and the Human Condition* (Englewood Cliffs, N.J.: Prentice-Hall, 1980), p. 398.

For Plato, longing at its highest level is of a different sort. In an analysis of eros, Nygren has written

> The Platonic eros is desiring love. As such it is marked by two elements: the consequences of a present want and the direction of this want toward the freedom of a higher and more blissful state. . . . Eros is rightly called a "wanting to have." . . . Its desire is, however, not directed toward the nether world of the senses. Eros is love directed toward the higher regions; it is the longing upward toward the world of ideas, and in relation to the present world it assumes the form of fleeing from the world.[6]

Interpretations of eros have ranged from the sexual cravings of one person for another to spiritual longings. In these contexts, "to love" may have different meanings that have in common a "wanting to have," an "urge to merge" with something beyond ourselves: a longing or a craving.

Selfless Love

Some individuals have been taught that true love means the utter abandonment of any self-concern or self-regard. Not necessarily infused with self-contempt or martyr-love components, selfless love means that one's feelings of affection and implied service are directed exclusively to the needs of others. Such an interpretation of love could be considered religious or secular; its proponents usually view selfless love as the heart of their religions.[7] Any love of self in this interpretation is equated with self-centeredness, deification of one's self, pride, and what we have called "solo love." Therefore selflessness is the norm.

True love, wrote Nygren, "is selfless, serving, and helping love."[8] In his classic volume comparing love (*agape*) in the New Testament with eros, Nygren proposed the following understanding of selflessness or opposition to self-love.

> This brings us to one more feature that is specially characteristic of the Pauline idea of Agape: its opposition to all that can be called "self-love." It has often been thought necessary to distinguish between a right and a wrong self-love, and the attempt has been made to give a place to the former as a third kind of love alongside of love to God and neighbourly love. Indeed, it has even been supposed that a commandment of self-love was implicit in the commandment of neighbourly love. But we have already seen the error of any such

---

[6]Anders Nygren, "Eros and Agape," in *A Handbook of Christian Theology* (New York: New American Library, 1958), p. 98.

[7]See John F. Crosby, "On the Origin of the Taboo Against Self-Love," *The Humanist* (November–December 1979), pp. 45–47.

[8]Nygren, p. 98.

attempt to read the idea of self-love into the Gospels, and it is equally wrong to try to find a place for it in Paul's outlook. Self-love is excluded by Paul's fundamental principle. "The love of God which is in Christ Jesus" (Rom. viii. 39) is for him the archetype of all that can rightfully be called Agape, and it is characteristic of this love that it gives itself, sacrifices itself.... [Paul is condemning] all self-love whatsoever, even in its most highly spiritual forms.[9]

Selfless love is by nature not mutual or reciprocal; it is unconditionally given. Some theological contexts for selfless love view human beings as not having the capacity for such love; the true source of selfless love is God; only God's *agape* channeled through persons can be true love.[10]

Selfless love can demand from persons the mask of "giver." Individuals who adopt this understanding of love from religious or secular sources frequently recoil from receiving. They can provide but are difficult to provide for. They are willing to "give you the shirt off their backs" but cannot joyfully accept gifts from others; they are ready to help but cannot easily ask for help. Counselors may hear from an individual in isolated anguish: "People are always coming to me for help, but where are they when I need them?" Chances are the mask of omnipotent giver has been so constantly worn that no one would imagine the giver could ever need help! Parents and people in the helping professions (nurses, clergy, social workers, teachers, doctors, and so on) may view selfless love as the best way of relating to others. The results will frequently be "burn out" or a depletion of "giving energy." The idealization of selfless love in religious literature and among some saints fails to give an accurate picture of the extent of their actual wholesomeness, true state of mental health, and actual interpersonal relationships.

Interpersonal Love

If I embrace my identity as a person or a child of God, I have reached a basic sense of positive self-acceptance; this does not imply that I affirm every aspect of my life as good or perfected. Self-acceptance does not automatically promote springtime love, dependent love, solo love, debit love, aggressive love, possessive love, craving love, or selfless love; it does not mean that everything about me and you is o.k. Self-acceptance means that my identity, who I really am, is fundamentally worthwhile. To feel good about my identity fosters a sense of being "at home" with who I am, of being concerned about *me*, of loving myself, and of becoming more human as my life progresses.

There are theologians who view *agape* not as selfless but as involving "I"

[9]Anders Nygren, *Agape and Eros* (London: SPCK, 1957), pp. 130–131.
[10]See Daniel Day Williams, *The Spirit and the Forms of Love* (New York: Harper, 1968), p. 71 and Chapter X.

as well as "Thou" as both a source and receiver of love. One such theologian has written that

> love includes the following ingredients: commitment or engagement for the good of the other or others, mutuality or openness to others and willingness to give and take, faithfulness to those whom we say we love, hopefulness or expectation that from our relationship better and more enriching life will follow, and an urgent desire for as intimate and complete a communion between persons as is possible for both parties.[11]

More emphatically an evangelical preacher has written

> Love yourself or die—physically and spiritually.... Lack of self-love definitely affects the physical organism. Lose your sense of self-love and you will be depressed, discouraged, and lacking the enthusiasm which is the great energy-producing force of life.
> Love yourself or you will die spiritually. If you do not love yourself, you cannot love your neighbor. If you do not love yourself and do not love others, you are merely a dead man who is walking, sleeping, working, breathing, eating.[12]

The element of mutuality absent from selfless love is integral to interpersonal love. Communion with others instead of merely giving is a goal.

Among some social scientists, interpersonal love, love of self and others, has been valued for many years. One of the most articulate scholars to have written on the nature of humanity and love is the anthropologist Ashley Montagu. In one of his major books he argues well for interpersonal love based on a positive view of human nature. Montagu's view of the qualities and characteristics of love follows:

> *Love implies the possession of a feeling of deep involvement in another,* and to love another means to communicate that feeling of involvement to them. Essentially this means that while love begins as a subjective state, it must be activated and made objective, that is, it must be demonstrative if it is to be fully realized. Love is not passive, it is active, it means involvement.
> *Love is unconditional, it makes no bargains and trades with no one for anything.* It is given freely and without any strings attached. It says, in effect, to the loved one: "I am for you because you are you—and not because you are going to be something I want or expect you to be, but simply because you are you as you now are."
> *Love is supportive.* It conveys to the loved one that he can depend upon those who love him, that they will always be standing by to give him the support he most needs, with no questions asked, neither condemning nor condoning, but endeavoring sympathetically to

---

[11]Pittenger, p. 60.
[12]Robert H. Schuller, *Self-Love: The Dynamic Force of Success* (New York: Hawthorn, 1969), p. 43.

understand, that no trust will be misused, that no faith will be broken; that he will never under any circumstances be failed in his needs.

Love is firm. Love is characterized by a firmness and integrity which not only conveys a feeling of security to the loved one, but serves also as a discipline in that it helps the loved one to respond in kind. But love continues even though we know that the loved one may never respond in kind. The firmness of love conveys to the loved one that both one's "Yea" and one's "Nay" are equally the firm evidence of one's love. The loved one, therefore, comes to incorporate this kind of firmness within himself. . . .

Love is most needed by the human organism from the moment of birth. Our evidence indicates that love is the birthright of every human being, the birthright which is indispensably necessary for the optimum development of the person. It seems to be clear that the best environment, in which love is most efficiently and satisfactorily provided, is within the warm ambience of the bosom of the family. The pattern of love which the child learns within the family, if he learns it well, he will later extend to all human beings.

Love is reciprocal in its effects, and is as beneficial to the giver as it is to the recipient. To love another means to love oneself as well as the other; in this sense, love is the highest form of selfishness as well as the highest form of unselfishness, the best of all forms of conduct for the development of the self, one's own self, and the selves of others.

Love is creative in that it actively participates in the creative development of the loved one as well as contributing toward the further development of the lover.

Love enlarges the capacities of those who are loved and of those who love so that they become increasingly more sensitive in probably all areas of their being.

Love continually elicits, by encouragement, the nascent capacities of the loved one. In the absence of love, those capacities will either fail altogether to be elicited or fail of healthy development. For example, the capacity to feel sensitively, to feel warmly toward others, the capacity to perceive rapidly the changing character of a situation, the capacity to identify with others, the ability to adjust rapidly to rapidly changing conditions, and the like. In all these capacities the person who has been loved is more efficient than the person who has been inadequately loved.

Love is tender, with a tenderness that abjures every form of insensitivity and every form of violence.

Love is joyful, it is pleasure-giving, happiness-producing, it is goodness itself. This does not mean that love is necessarily associated with states of ecstasy or gaiety. Love may produce temporary states of nonpleasure or displeasure, as for example, in children and others who are forbidden some immediate satisfaction for their own "good." Prohibitions stemming from love contribute to the development of the capacity for love and mature character.

Love is fearless. Love has no element of fear in it, and produces no fear in others. Love braves all conditions and situations in a security-producing manner; hence, love tends to reduce fear, allay suspicion, soften all harshness, and produce peacefulness.

Love enables the person to treat life as an art which the person, as artist, is continually seeking to improve and beautify in all its aspects.

Love as an attitude of mind and as a form of behavior is adaptively the best and most efficient of all adjustive processes in enabling the human being to adapt himself to his environment.

For the person and for the species, love is the form of behavior having the highest survival value. [13]

We do not suggest that within this view a person can say "I love you" only if all these qualities and characteristics are fully matured. It is our understanding that interpersonal love is a growing process with the various components reaching varying plateaus at different times for different individuals. To say "I love you" means the relationship is on a progressive journey; integral to the process is the intention to live toward or in conformity with the view of love set forth by Montagu. An ongoing sensitivity to the likely intrusions of incompatible or wounding forms of love is called for; if these intrusions are effectively guarded against, the ingredients of interpersonal love can deepen throughout the relationship.

Supports for Love.   In an interpersonal love relationship, a readiness for patience, for errors confessed and forgiven, and for appropriate self-sacrifice is supportive. Patience is helpful because the rates of progress differ for different persons. For example, two friends may differ in their respective degrees of tenderness, thereby requiring a patient tolerance by one or both of them. Too, mistakes will be made in relationships; debit love or even a serious betrayal might intrude. Wrong decisions, when acknowledged and regretted, can be forgiven and buried. Finally, without adopting martyr love, one person might in a given situation set aside his own needs and desires for the sake of another; patient self-sacrifice in this sense is not the context or goal of the relationship, but a caring act in a particular situation.

In interpersonal love a relationship becomes something different when the qualities and characteristics surveyed in this text are replaced by contradictory ingredients. Though there is no exact science by which we can measure the irretrievable breakdown in interpersonal love, in principle, a relationship is no longer loving in this sense when its quality and characteristics have changed decisively. What may start as interpersonal love can alter; to begin the journey does not guarantee its continuance. An occasional realistic audit can help prevent or accurately declare bankruptcy.

[13]Ashley Montagu, *The Direction of Human Development,* (New York: Hawthorn, 1970), pp. 296–298.

Choice of Loves

It is our conviction that interpersonal love, like the other forms of love, can be established between spouses, between parent and child, among other family members, among friends, and so on. Entire communities can be characterized by one or more types of love. It is not enough to agree simplistically that love is the moral norm for human relations; we must also choose the kind of love from the varieties available.

If the fundamental purpose of each person or child of God is to love, it is crucial that an informed choice be made from among conflicting or contrasting "loves." At stake are the relationships each type of love creates and sustains. If love is selected as the fundamental moral norm as well as life's purpose, we benefit by understanding the basic moral implications of each interpretation. In any case, we are again confronted with a pluralism: love has more than one meaning; longing love, selfless love, and interpersonal love are among the historic interpretations chosen by philosophers and theologians, religious and secular. A choice of "loves" and its consequences for a sense of purpose and morality are open to each of us; a mixture of more than one love in a relationship is common and consequential, too.

Love of One's Neighbor: A Moral Norm

Many religious and humanistic moral norms focus on, or at least include, neighbor love. "Love at work" involves paying attention to those people whom our love must reach or encounter. To round off a discussion of love we need to look at its impact on (and our moral obligations toward) neighbors and friends. In the preceding sections we have seen that "love" can mean different things to different people. So can "neighbor."

The Franciscan Neighbor. For St. Francis of Assisi (1182–1226) there were no limits to "neighbor."

> Franciscan monks observe the divinity in all created beings. They are remarkably Eastern in the extent of their reverence for all of life. Much of Christianity has been human-oriented, viewing the human species as God's noblest creation, alone possessed of soul and reason. Francis, however, taught that God was everywhere and in everything and every creature. The Franciscan way is, therefore, one of total humility, the total rejection of ego and the pride engendered in man by his achievements. There can be no meaningful distinction among people or between people and animals. Hence there can be no meaningful separation between oneself and all that is not oneself.[14]

[14]Richard Paul Janaro, *Philosophy: Something to Believe In* (Beverly Hills: Glencoe, 1975), p. 314.

PARABLE OF THE GOOD SAMARITAN

But the man was anxious to justify himself and said to Jesus, "And who is my neighbor?" Jesus replied, "A man was once on his way down from Jerusalem to Jericho and fell into the hands of brigands; they took all he had, beat him and then made off, leaving him half dead. Now a priest happened to be traveling down the same road, but when he saw the man, he passed by on the other side. In the same way a Levite who came to the place saw him, and passed by on the other side. But a Samaritan traveler who came upon him was moved with compassion when he saw him. He went up and bandaged his wounds, pouring oil and wine on them. He then lifted him on to his own mount, carried him to the inn and looked after him. Next day, he took out two denarii and handed them to the innkeeper. 'Look after him,' he said, 'and on my way back I will make good any extra expense you have.' Which of these three, do you think, proved himself a neighbor to the man who fell into the brigands' hands?" "The one who took pity on him," he replied. Jesus said to him, "Go, and do the same yourself."

Luke 10:25–37 (*The Jerusalem Bible*)

In this view all creation is one's neighbor and should be loved accordingly. The Good Samaritan parable teaches mankind to reach out with love to all. (An ecological implication of this position will be considered in Chapter 16.)

The Universal Neighbor. A second understanding of "neighbor" is based on a prior understanding of something we share in common with all human beings—the gift of creation, the gift of human life. We are automatically neighbors with those with whom we share this common gift, that is, with all other human beings. We are so personally related to the rest of the world that one could argue that the roads down which we walk, directly or indirectly, circle the entire earth. We are living in a time when our responsibility to those who are beaten and lying beside the road must be recognized; we must take into account the fact that we are all part of an international community, we have international institutions that reach to all parts of the globe. The Parable of the Good Samaritan teaches humankind to reach out with love to all fellow human beings. The Danish philosopher

Kierkegaard interpreted the universal neighbor (without reference to international institutions) as follows:

> The category *neighbour* is just like the category human being. Every one of us is a human being and at the same time the heterogeneous individual which he is by particularity; but being a human being is the fundamental qualification. . . . No one should be preoccupied with the differences so that he cowardly or presumptuously forgets that he is a human being; no man is an exception to being a human being by virtue of his particularising differences. He is rather a human being and then a particular human being. [15]

The Individual Neighbor. A third understanding of "neighbor" is based on an interpersonal view of love, that to "love" one's neighbor includes the qualities and characteristics of reciprocity as an actual possibility. This kind of love is very much person-to-person, individually and communally. Neighbor loves neighbor face-to-face in the wider context of the human community.

This interpretation does not exclude persons not identified as neighbors from one's concern, compassion, or outreach. It holds that for love to be truly personal, love for neighbor is different from the broader caring for persons throughout a nation or the entire planet. I *love* my neighbor as myself; I am *concerned about* and *care for* humanity in general. A contemporary theologian has put it this way:

> Love of man is still too general a description. We are speaking certainly of universal humanity, but we must be more precise. In Jesus' way of speaking, there is not even a hint of "embracing millions," of "a kiss for the whole world," as in the poem by Schiller, turned by Beethoven in the Ninth Symphony into a great hymn to joy. A kiss of that kind costs nothing: it is not like kissing this one sick, imprisoned, underprivileged, starving man. . . . love is *not simply love of man but essentially love of neighbor*. It is a love, not of man in general, of someone remote, with whom we are not personally involved, but quite concretely of one's immediate neighbor. . . . But *who is my neighbor?* Jesus does not answer with a definition or a more precise qualification, still less with a law—but—as so often—with a story, an exemplary narrative. According to this, my neighbor is not merely someone who is close to me from the very beginning: a member of my family, my circle of friends, my class, my party, my people. My neighbor can also be a stranger, anyone who turns up at this particular juncture. It is impossible to work out in advance who my neighbor will be. This is the meaning of the story of the man fallen among thieves: my neighbor is *anyone who needs me here and now*. [16]

[15]Søren Kierkegaard, *Works of Love* (New York: Harper, 1962), p. 142.
[16]Hans Kung, *On Being a Christian* (Garden City, N.Y.: Doubleday, 1976), pp. 255-258.

The primary difference between the "universal neighbor" and the "individual neighbor" is a matter of scope, or in other words, the boundaries of the neighborhood. The former excludes no one from love; the latter distinguishes between neighbor love and concern (not "love") for all persons. Love for my universal neighbor calls for my active, personal, moral responsibility and affection for all persons; love for my individual neighbor implies primary personal moral responsibility and affection for anyone who needs me at this particular juncture here and now, wherever we meet face to face. (Whether a legitimate need consists only of a *victimized* person on the road or of anyone with *any* need is an issue for additional consideration and debate.)

Unlike love for a Franciscan or universal neighbor, love for an individual neighbor can accommodate a prioritizing of love and personal moral responsibility. My love can be limited to my "significant other(s),"[17] my family, my friends, and any others (co-workers, residential neighbors, and strangers) I meet on the road.

Others beyond my neighborhood, that is, persons I do not meet face to face on the road, I do care about, seek justice for, support the real needs of as I am able—but with a lesser degree of personal, moral responsibility than for my individual neighbor. In the view of individual neighbor, I *love* my neighbor as myself; I *care* actively for the rest of humankind. (Within the individual neighbor view, it is arguable whether one's moral responsibility and affection are merely different from what one feels for the rest of humankind or simply engender less personal involvement.)

A Choice of Neighbors

"In our law, there's no duty to rescue someone or save someone's life. . . . Our society is based on the right and the sanctity of the individual." . . . As a factual claim about the law in the United States, Judge Flaherty's statement is essentially correct. Furthermore, it is probably true that the law as it is today reflects a conception of the rights and sanctities of the individual that has prevailed throughout much of our legal history. But it is not uncommon for legal theorists and philosophers to bemoan the opinion cited by Judge Flaherty and to argue for the introduction of Bad Samaritan laws. Such laws would place civil or criminal liability on an individual for failing to rescue another, even if the parties are strangers.[18]

"And who is my neighbor?" (Luke 10:29) has been answered pluralistically within secular and religious contexts. Franciscan, universal, and indi-

---

[17]By "significant other(s)" we mean the person(s) with whom a person is most intimate emotionally, the one(s) with whom a person is bonded and self-disclosed. Examples may include one's spouse or lover, celibate men and/or women living in community, and so on.
[18]Eric Mack, "Bad Samaritanism and the Causation of Harm," *Philosophy and Public Affairs* 9, no. 3 (Spring 1980), p. 230.

vidual models of "neighbor" can be found among poets, legal theorists, philosophers, theologians, social scientists and citizens. Those persons committed to a conservative interpretation that "our society is based on the right and the sanctity of the individual" may find these three models of "neighbor"—and perhaps all views—incompatible with their convictions. Not only do we have before us a choice of "loves" but also a choice of "neighbors"—and we have the option of rejecting them all!

We now turn our attention to a particular type of neighbor with whom love is fundamental—those neighbors we call friends.

FRIENDSHIP

Someone Else Should Be Your Friend

Independence when carried too far can lead to isolation. In the extreme, "Do your *own* thing" fails to account for the other things that can be shared by companions. Doing my thing independently can permeate institutions that by their very nature are communal rather than lone ventures. An elderly, self-sufficient New Yorker commented in one brief conversation on both her loneliness and her fondness for the large cathedral in which she worshipped—where she "didn't have to bother with anybody." (No doubt in lonely leisure she enjoyed the book *How To Be Your Own Best Friend*.) She perceived no sense of community at her place of worship; if friendship were there, she probably would have rejected it as an invasion of her privacy and self-sufficiency. It is our belief that friendship is not an optional luxury or nuisance; it is essential to the social or communal nature of human beings. We propose further that friendship is best shared with other human beings, not with oneself, a book, a car, hobbies, or pets. It is pathetic to believe seriously that "a dog is man's best friend."

The topic of friendship has surfaced recently in magazines and books.[19] However, there has been surprisingly little focus on friendship in religious literature.[20] Instead the religious groups that do talk about human relations appear to be preoccupied almost exclusively with the nuclear family. Family relationships, as central to life as they are, do not meet all the relational needs of most people. Many individuals want relationships of significance beyond immediate blood-family bonds. Those persons with few or no family ties may seek fellowship, too. This is not to downgrade nuclear family relationships (which we shall examine in the next chapter); it is to affirm the goodness of other consciously chosen relationships, relationships usually labeled "friendship."

[19]See Charles Fried, "Love, Friendship, and Trust," chapter 5 in *An Anatomy of Values* (Cambridge, Mass.: Harvard Univ. Press, 1970); Christine Leefeldt and Ernest Callenbach, *The Art of Friendship* (New York: Pantheon, 1979); and *Psychology Today* 13, no. 4 (March 1979).
[20]Religious explorations include Andrew M. Greeley, *The Friendship Game* (Garden City, N.Y.: Doubleday, 1970) and Martin E. Marty, *Friendship* (Allen, Texas: Argus, 1980).

The Meaning of "Friend"

At the outset we ought to distinguish between "friendship" and "being friendly." Friendliness is being well-disposed toward people or having a friendly disposition. However, one can be friendly but not have one single friend; friendliness does not imply the actuality of friendship.

The word "friend" originates from an Anglo-Saxon verb meaning "to love." A dictionary meaning is "one attached to another by esteem, respect, and affection; an intimate." Less formally, "a friend is simply someone you spend time with because it's enjoyable to do so and not because it's profitable, useful, or necessary. Friendship is a free and equal nonutilitarian relationship."[21] In a sense, a friend is an intimate neighbor.

The Bonding Principle

A key to understanding human relationships is the "bonding principle." When we walk into a room full of people we don't know, we look for something we have in common with the people we meet. As conversations begin, we listen for something that will bond us with others: a common interest or experience, persons known in common, and so on. Whatever bonds us for the moment or longer can be called the "bonding principle" for a particular relationship.

The bonding principle sets the boundaries and style of a relationship. If we bond as co-workers, we are likely to "talk shop" and relate as colleagues (not necessarily agreeably). If we bond as students, we will probably focus on school experiences. Bonds such as these, while perfectly wholesome, are not friendships. Collegial relationships are not personally close, affectionate or intimate, although they may be very congenial in terms of a particular limited experience. Yet it is not uncommon to be introduced or referred to as so-and-so's *friend*, even though the most you've shared are desks in the same room, income from the same employer, or beds in the same hospital room! (Perhaps a new use of "neighbor" would be better.)

Investments and Expectations

We frequently expect too much from relationships bonded by work and other limited aspects of life. "We've got to get together sometime" is said frequently by co-workers who get along well on the job. If they do visit, they may experience a let-down feeling; everyone is a congenial person, but, at least initially, conversations about the few matters known to be in common may be sparse. If too much is expected from new relationships, if

[21]Leefeldt and Callenbach, p. 6.

people visit initially with a pretense of intimacy, disappointment can result. We often invest more in new relationships than is actually there; our unrealistic expectations for instant companionship cannot deliver the quality of a relationship nurtured by years of love.

Visits with relatives can likewise be a disappointment. We may assume that because we're related biologically, we have a great deal in common and will get along well. With great anticipation we host or vacation with cousins, aunts and uncles, and even brothers and sisters. In fact, some relatives for whom we have a genuine fondness and concern are not friends. We do not spend much time with them, and we are not attached to them by esteem and respect, though elements of affection are genuine. The bonding principle may be a combination of a nostalgic affection and biology rather than an active common history of ongoing love. Consequently, many central holidays spent with some relatives are anticipated with much excitement but cannot provide more than a somewhat hollow, congenial tolerance. In some cases such occasions result in cold or hot wars as individuals compete for status.

Workers who bond with co-workers solely on their common experiences on the job are destined to isolation or reminiscences after retirement. Alumni gatherings every five or ten years can be of the same quality.

We are not proposing that we ought, therefore, to ignore all our relatives, co-workers, fellow alumni, and the like. Instead, such relationships can be seen for what they are; as with any relationship, they have boundaries and styles determined by whatever bonding principle exists in fact, not fantasy. We cannot expect more from any relationship than has been actually invested by the persons involved.

"Friendship," by its root meaning, implies the bonding principle of love, not merely biology, performances, roles, a common ethnic background, gender, or sexual orientation. The very essence of friendship depends on which view of love is linked to the meaning of friendship. Friendship consisting of selfless love as the bonding principle will differ somewhat from longing love or from interpersonal love. Each can give substance to "friendship" as can any combination of "loves." (Leefeldt and Callenbach's informal definition of "friend" seems to imply interpersonal love as ideal.) Friendships sour when the quality and type of love we believe is essential is inactive; sometimes friendships are doomed to failure because each persons brings to the relationship a different view of love. For example, if one person's idea of love is debit love and the other's is possessive love, the relationship in fact has two different bonding principles, each labeled "love."

MORALITY, LOVE, AND FRIENDSHIP

A discussion of love, neighbor, and friendship is integral to the study of morality because we can safely predict that most people will continue to echo the theme "what the world needs now is love. . . ." We can be equally sure that most individuals will seek to bond with others casually or as neighbors and friends, and we will find love proposed as the ideal norm for human relations and morality by the majority of scholars and citizens.

We cannot expect, however, a consensus on the meaning of "love," "neighbor," or "friendship." We shall not be surprised to discover interpretations of love that imply a set of absolute rules as moral maxims; other interpretations will be applied situationally with moral guides.

The inevitability of pluralism on these and other issues does not necessitate moral chaos, but moral differences. Some remaining questions confront us: Which interpretations of love, neighbor, and friendship can coexist in peaceful tolerance? To what extent can we agree to differ? By what method do we rule out particular views? As an individual, what are my criteria for choosing or rejecting a particular interpretation of love, neighbor, and friendship, and a particular method of moral decision making?

CHAPTER REVIEW

A. What the world needs now

1. For centuries "love" has been seen as central to human relations.
2. In recent years a clear deterioration in feelings of happiness and well-being prevails among Americans.
3. A sense of loneliness accompanies much unhappiness; a sense of incompleteness and a feeling that the quality and quantity of love in the individual's life is less than what is needed.
4. Our assumption is that love is essential to human fulfillment; to love and be loved is the fundamental purpose of life and the basic moral norm.
5. "Love" has been interpreted with various meanings.

B. Varieties of love

1. The various meanings of "love" include springtime love, dependent love, solo love, debit love, aggressive love, martyr love, possessive love, longing love, selfless love, and interpersonal love.
2. Each has a different impact on human relations.
3. A choice of "loves" and its consequences for a sense of purpose and morality is open to each of us.
4. Neighbor love can mean the "Franciscan neighbor," the universal neighbor, or the individual neighbor.
5. Respective answers to "Who is my neighbor?" have consequences for the scope of neighbor love.

C. Friendship

1. Friendship is best shared with other human beings, that is, in chosen relationships among men and women not limited to one's biological family.
2. Friendship is a free and equal, nonutilitarian relationship of interpersonal love.
3. The bonding principle, whatever bonds people for a particular relationship of any duration, sets the boundaries and style of a relationship.
4. Unrealistic investments and expectations in a relationship cannot provide a friendship, bonded by interpersonal love nurtured over a period of years.

D. Morality, love, and friendship

1. Love will continue to be proposed as the ideal norm for human relations and morality by the majority of scholars and citizens.
2. The *meanings* of love, neighbor, and friendship will continue to vary, thereby offering options as choices are made.

SUGGESTED READINGS

Blum, Lawrence A. *Friendship, Altruism, and Morality*. Boston: Routledge and Kegan Paul, 1980.

A study of the nature and moral significance of friendship and a defense of sympathy, compassion, and concern for other human beings; also, a critique of moral views that have their roots in Kant's philosophy.

Boas, Charles. "Love," *The Encyclopedia of Philosophy*, V (89–95). New York: Macmillan, Free Press, 1967.

An historical survey of love from classical mythology through Freud; an excellent bibliography of primary and secondary sources concludes the essay.

De Rougemont, Denis. "Love," *Dictionary of the History of Ideas*, III (94–108). New York: Scribners, 1973.

Five basic concepts of love and their manifestations in Western civilization; a useful but limited bibliography.

Leefeldt, Christine and Callenbach, Ernest. *The Art of Friendship*. New York: Pantheon, 1979.

A human relations study that draws on the actual experiences of hundreds of men and women as they provide insights on how friendships are built and preserved.

McGinnis, Alan Loy. *The Friendship Factor*. Minneapolis: Augsburg, 1979.

A pastoral counselor's views with case histories and anecdotes.

Outka, Gene. *Agape: An Ethical Analysis.* New Haven: Yale Univ. Press, 1972.

> The most comprehensive account to date of modern treatments of the love commandment bringing together analytic moral philosophy and theological ethics; liberal footnotes provide valuable bibliographical data.

Yankelovich, Daniel. *New Rules.* New York: Random House, 1981.

> A psychologist's proposal that Americans are moving culturally further and further away from a common, rigid set of personal and social values, toward a widening acceptance of cultural pluralism and at the same time toward an ethic of interpersonal commitment.

7

Marriage
and the Family

The family is the civilian equivalent of Marine boot camp. It is supposed to prepare people for the combats and joys of life. Let us look at it, however, in the light of the fact that one out of every three spouses checks out of his first attempt at marriage. And let us review the family in light of the hypothesis that rigid conformity to the middle-class design for marriage and family life is the prime cause of physical and psychological breakdown in our time. Many families simply are not fit for their members to live in. The hypothesis asserts that conformity to familial roles produces dispiriting, stressing untenable situations which culminate in physical illness for some and neurotic or psychotic breakdown in others. The role definitions and modes of relating designated "normal" serve more to produce a cosmetic image of family life and to maintain the status quo than they do to foster personal growth and full functioning.*

MORAL ISSUES IN FAMILY LIFE

Our customary values are the bases for the high regard most Americans have for marriage and the family. One *ought* to be married to one person of the opposite gender until one of the partners dies; one *should* maintain an unquestioned loyalty to blood relatives; one *ought* to parent children, if medically possible. These and other like-minded moral rules are taken for granted by most senior citizens and many others. These rules provide a basis for the morally good way to live. Members of younger generations and some seniors are questioning our nation's customary values and the morality of the rules governing family life. They are asking such questions as: Should formalized marriage and the certificate be required for a moral relationship? Why should a couple have any children? Isn't divorce often a good solution? Do I have any obligations to relatives I don't know or don't like? Isn't the quality or substance of a relationship far more important than the certified or acceptable form it takes?

In this chapter we shall consider several views on the nature of "family" and "marriage." By doing so, we shall be in a better position to answer for

*Sidney Jourard, "Reinventing Marriage and the Family," in *The Transparent Self* (New York: Van Nostrand, 1972), pp. 103–104.

ourselves these types of moral questions. (Specific matters of sexuality will be discussed in the chapter "Sexual Ethics.")

WHAT IS A FAMILY?

In response to a political statement opposing "more power over families" by the federal government and the Supreme Court's intrusion into the family structure, the leading editorial in *The New York Times* of July 10, 1980, raised the question, "But what family are they talking about?" If we can assume that prominent editorials in nationally circulated newspapers reflect vital issues of the day, the meaning(s) of "family" is not a closed matter.

In ordinary conversation, "family" can refer to the closest biologically related persons or to Cousin Jane twice (or more) removed. We occasionally honor an old friend of our parents with aunthood or unclehood and "like one of the family" modifiers. Family members who cause public embarrassment are called "black sheep of the family" but are still considered family; "ex-family" or some equivalent has not been invoked to designate these individuals, and they are probably invited to weddings, however reluctantly, because "they're family." Such traditional views of family have strong roots in our culture. However, other interpretations have arisen not as an abstract exercise, but because people find themselves in other patterns of human relations for which they claim a legitimate use of "family." Should we reserve "family" for our customary views? Is the traditional family the only normal and moral family? Should individuals and groups forming different patterns find or create their own labels and leave "family" alone? Who are some of these innovators tampering with tradition?

The Couple.   Married in the 1970s, Alice and Ted have no children, and no one else is living with them. They live at a great distance from any relatives, and their only contact with relatives is the exchange of holiday greetings. Without hesitation they speak of themselves as a family unit. If their future includes only the two of them, they will be a family of two as far as they are concerned. However, they are looked on as odd by many others; in fact, without children they are judged to be incomplete as a family. A *real* family, claim their critics, is no less than a traditional nuclear family with father, mother, and children. (One child barely qualifies a couple as a family; two or more suggests normality.)

The Extended Family.   At weddings and funerals we meet the extended family. They are "the relatives" from near and far, the public embarrassments, individuals loved and cherished, persons repulsive or indifferent, all sharing a common biological linking of genealogical significance.

Some members of the extended family remain close emotionally and geographically; they are friends, too. With others there are lesser ties, though warm and congenial. Perhaps among some of them there is an irreparable feud. But social scientists view them all as extended family or tribe.

The Single-Parent Family.   One parent has died, or a divorced parent has custody of the child(ren), or the parent raising the child(ren) has never been married; these are three examples of single-parent families. Although in each case such a group could be, say, a father with his child(ren), the classification "family" is used cautiously. In the first example, a widower and his child(ren), "family" is used readily, though with a sense of incompletion. In the second example, however, a divorced man with his child(ren), the group is more often referred to as a "broken home." The third example (with just a hint of moral judgment), an "unmarried father with his kids," is certainly not a family. ("Bastards" would be in poor taste; "illegitimate" too Victorian!) In these three examples of a father with his child(ren), "family" is reserved for the widower and his child(ren) to express understanding approval of the widower's moral innocence. The familial category is withheld from the other two for moral reasons.

The Blended Family.   Husbands and wives with children from previous marriages appear on the surface to be a nuclear family. Yet, qualifiers such as half-sister, step-brother, step-mother/father, *her* children, *his* children, and so on are more than legal distinctions. They remind us that this family is not quite ideal.

One of the most respectable versions of the blended family is the marriage of a widow and widower and the consequent mingling of their children. Least respected may be the group formed by the marriage of two divorced persons and the gathering of their offspring. Although the group may feel themselves very much a family, persons and groups that do not recognize the validity of a marriage of divorced individuals would hardly call such a group a family.

Same-Sex Couples.   For the majority of citizens, this is going too far! Liberals prefer to call this type of couple "lovers"; conservatives prefer "perverts." In the case of same-sex couples, does anyone seriously use "family?" If not, why?

Living Together.   Some of the world's greatest religious leaders lived with—that is, shared life with—a group of disciples. They "lived together" not as we use the phrase commonly today, but as a community. Convents, monasteries, celibate rectories, some schools, and helping institutions constitute communities bonded by common principles, beliefs, or tasks. Members of these communities, as do some religious congregations, refer to themselves as families. In some cases they view these community families as being more authentic than their nuclear families. Society regards this use of "family" as acceptable poetry if the group is generally approved. When suspect or disapproved, "family" is set aside for "hippie commune," "cult," "bunch of weirdos," and other negative labels.

A man and a woman "living together" is generally tolerated in some geographical areas. "Living in sin," however, is by no means a dead phrase; it is a clear moral judgment. Many so-called liberals betray their traditional images of family and values when they defend such arrangements with comments such as "they are *like* a real family."

THE **Family.**   Some political and religious sources have sounded the alarm in recent years: *the* family is falling apart. They have the traditional, nuclear family in mind. They are convinced the nuclear family is the primary backbone of the nation. Although some couples, some extended families, some single-parent families, some blended families, and some celibate communities are approved, they regard the nuclear family as the foundation of all moral variations. They view as destructive the many deviations and perversions trying to claim family status, thereby undermining the nation's moral fiber. The alleged decline and fall of ancient Rome's family life is called forth as a warning to today's citizens.

Philosophers and many others are less ready to accept the nuclear family as *the* family. Mere biology seems insufficient as the primary ingredient of a family relationship. As we look at the condition of the nuclear family, we may ask: Is it worth preserving? What has happened to family life? Are there coequal moral varieties of family instead of *the* family?

DIAGNOSING THE AMERICAN NUCLEAR FAMILY

In ancient Hebrew civilization a family or household could consist of a husband with more than one wife, concubines, children, blood relatives, slaves, and hired servants. It is curious that in the Gospels, Jesus never condemned polygamy and other family practices of the time, except for the rather harsh form of divorce then in practice.[1]

Prior to the eighteenth century few distinctions were drawn between the goals of the community and the objectives of the American family. Often, families actually consisted of unrelated apprentices and boarders. In the nineteenth century the family became a refuge to protect its members from excesses of capitalism. From that time on the nuclear family gradually gained status as THE family in American life.[2] The nuclear family, though

[1]See C. R. Taber, "Kinship and Family" and "Marriage," *The Interpreter's Dictionary of the Bible—Supplementary Volume* (Nashville: Abingdon, 1976), pp. 519-524 and 573-576.
[2]See Virginia Tufte and Barbara Myerhoff, eds., *Changing Images of the Family* (New Haven: Yale Univ. Press, 1979).

prized highly by many contemporary political and religious spokespersons, is a relatively recent development.

Current departures from the nuclear family model are legion, as implied by these estimates:

1. The divorce rate has doubled in the past ten years, but remarriage has become so frequent that divorce is viewed by some as part of a system of marital transfer. About 20 percent of all married persons have been previously divorced.

2. Single parent families are increasing. Nearly two of five children born at this time will live in such households for at least part of their childhood. Women are heading more households than ever before, about eight million in number.

3. About one and a half million heterosexual couples live together unmarried (2 percent of U.S. households).

4. Only 16 percent of all households with children are ones in which the father is the sole wage earner and the mother is a full-time homemaker; that is, the traditional nuclear family with one worker.

5. Twenty-three percent of all households are single persons living alone—by choice, widowed, or divorced—without children living with them.

Factors Contributing to Changes in the Nuclear Family

Expanding Views of Women.   Women are divided over their identities and purposes. Some believe they were born to be wives and mothers; they are willing to be wage earners only if necessary. Others are convinced that they are primarily persons who may choose various roles; the roles of wife and mother are open to them but are not required. As persons, they share equal rights in all spheres of life with persons who are male. Women who from the outset consciously choose to accept the responsibilities of maintaining a nuclear family with their husbands' understanding and support can shape and share in their families' life without trauma; their identities are not grounded in their familial responsibilities, and they are likely to have interests beyond their homes.

Women who enter nuclear family life with the belief that they were born to be wives and mothers but later reject that view for a liberated or feminist outlook invite understandable difficulties. "She's not the girl I married, and I don't like what's going on" is on the lips of many a husband who has been told to fix dinner for himself and the children on evenings her ethics course meets. Some husbands cannot adjust to their wives as coequal persons; resulting incompatibility that leads to divorce is not uncommon. In extreme cases, also leading to divorce, a newly liberated woman may run away from home; she totally rejects her passively accepted roles as spouse and mother. A real moral dilemma confronts women who change their identities from wives/mothers during the course of their marriages. To what extent, if any, are they obligated to continue functioning in roles they assumed at the time of making the contract called marriage? Are there responsible alternatives to running away from home? When, if ever, does a woman have a moral right to walk out on her husband and children?

Expanding Views of Men. American men have been raised to be "providers." A man's family nurtures his identity and purpose as a provider; he may justify his long hours of striving for success by claiming, "Everything I do is for the good of my wife and kids." Such men cannot function well without a nuclear family; the absence of children or the death of the wife is not only grievable but also shattering to any personal meaning and fulfillment.[3]

Some men, far fewer than women, are seeking choices for themselves. Rather than the fate of provider, they are viewing themselves as persons with options. One alternative is giving work a higher priority than providing. Though they do not exclude marriage and children, such work-oriented men delight in the game of work not necessarily for the money or "for the family."[4] If male workaholics are family men, they will obviously assign their wives and children to a lesser place in their lives. They may choose instead to be single and create a life congenial to their priorities, more easily accomplished with today's greater tolerance of diverse lifestyles.

Men who view themselves as persons with options prior to making personal commitments have, like women, many alternatives. They may enter marriage and parenthood consciously choosing them instead of subconsciously fated to them; their fulfillment may be found within these choices. However, as with many women, a discovery of personhood after assuming family responsibilities and thereafter wanting choices poses moral dilemmas. To what extent, if any, are they obligated to continue functioning in roles assumed at the time of making the contract called marriage? Are there responsible alternatives to running away from home? When, if ever, does a man have a moral right to walk out on his wife and children?

Changing Attitudes Toward Children. The National Alliance for Optional Parenthood based in Washington, D.C., would have been unthinkable a few generations ago. Unless a couple could not have offspring for medical reasons, it was assumed that all marriages ought to result in descendants. "Be fruitful and multiply" (within marriage) was the unques-

---

[3]See George Gilder, *Naked Nomads* (New York: Times Books, 1974).
[4]Male and female workaholics are defended in Marilyn Machlowitz, *Workaholics* (Reading, Mass.: Addison-Wesley, 1980).

tioned moral norm, and it remains so today for many religious communities. Among persons with different values, children are not integral to married life and should be consciously wanted and planned for. Charges of selfishness continue to be hurled at couples who remain childless by choice, but selfishness is an inadequate explanation; it is more in the nature of an *ad hominem* attack.[5]

In July of 1980 the Department of Housing and Urban Development reported that 26 percent of the rental units for housing prohibit families with children; this figure is increasing. This 26 percent does not include condominium or cooperative units; however, many of these have a "no-children" policy. The pitter-patter of little feet (which is sometimes the screaming and crashing of undisciplined children) is not a pleasant reminder of future generations for many adults. Some property owners do not want to rent to nuclear families because landlords have no effective legal recourses for dealing with offensive tenants, and they believe the presence of children increases the probability of trouble for owners. In addition, some tenants want to live free from the noises of normal children. They are not antichild, they are anti-noise and, as do some landlords, they believe the chances for quiet living are greater among adults. Although discriminating against a whole class of persons (i.e., children), these landlords and seekers of quiet know of no other way to own property as safely as possible and live as serenely as possible than to exclude children.

TOO MANY CHILDREN

Children were once the sure symbol of continuity and hope, the one certain value which brought all other values into focus. But today there is a growing ambivalence all around the world, a feeling that there are too many children, too many of the wrong kinds of children—too many affluent children, each of whom is consuming more than his or her share of irreplaceable resources, and too many poor children in poor countries where every gain their countries make is swallowed up by the sheer number of children. So children are becoming a less certain rallying point.

Margaret Mead, *Culture and Commitment*, rev. ed. (Garden City, N.Y.: Doubleday-Anchor, 1978), p. 128.

Margaret Mead (1901–1979) was one of the best known anthropologists of this century. Educated at Barnard College and Columbia University,

[5]See "Childless by Choice," *Newsweek*, Jan. 14, 1980, p. 96; and Nadine Brozan, "New Marriage Roles Make Men Ambivalent About Fatherhood," *New York Times*, May 30, 1980, p. B5.

> *Dr. Mead held, among many others, the positions of curator emeritus of ethnology at the American Museum of Natural History, adjunct professor of anthropology at Columbia, and visiting professor at the University of Cincinnati's Medical College. She authored, coauthored, and edited no fewer than thirty-five books, while also being a parent.*

Even many grandparents more readily admit today that it was great to have the grandchildren visit and leave, all within a reasonable time period. Parents are more outspoken than ever before about their own eagerly awaited graduation day—when the children have all left home. In contrast, there remain those mothers who say, "Who will I play with when the children grow up and leave?" or "What will I do when they're gone?" But more and more mothers disagree that all children are blessings from above.

The Era of Family Violence.   A recent study has shown that the extent of family violence is far greater than the general population may have suspected.[6] Among the findings are these statistics:

Sixteen of every 100 couples have violent confrontations of one sort or another during a 12 month period.

About 4 of every 100 wives are seriously beaten by their husbands.

Three of every 100 children are bitten, kicked, or punched by their parents.

About one-third of all brothers and sisters attack each other severely.

Under stressful conditions, 20 of every 100 wives assault their husbands and 14 of every 100 husbands assault their wives.

Family violence has become a theme of television documentaries and dramas. One such program noted that

In the six years from 1967 to 1973, 39,521 Americans were killed in Vietnam. During those same years, 17,570 Americans died from domestic violence, the result of physical assaults on husbands or wives or children. One aspect of this violence that is increasingly coming to public attention is violence by husbands against their wives: wife beating. There are estimates that one million American women are beaten up by their husbands each year.[7]

Far from "Home Sweet Home," many nuclear families are disaster areas, arenas used for punching, kicking, torture, screaming, and death.

---

[6]See Murray A. Straus and Richard J. Gelles, *Behind Closed Doors: Violence in the American Family* (Garden City, N.Y.: Doubleday, 1980).

[7]"Wifebeating Update," *The MacNeil/Lehrer Report*, December 22, 1978 (Transcript #845-4125 available from WNET/Thirteen, 356 West 58th Street, N.Y., N.Y. 10019).

Teenage suicides are increasing at an alarming rate, students in the junior high age group are very vulnerable. And, juvenile crime is reportedly on the rise. Violence as a tolerated aspect of American life has become an increasing factor contributing to the changes in the nuclear family.

Diagnosis

A glance at the expanding views of women and men, changing attitudes toward children, and family violence does not constitute a thorough analysis of the American nuclear family. We can conclude, however, that components of family life are becoming different, attitudes are changing, and not all is well. We can safely condemn the violence, whatever its causes; however, we are also faced with placing a value on the other changes. Are all the expanding views of women and men desirable? Are changing attitudes toward children for the better?

Options for the Future. One moral choice open to us is to struggle for reestablishment of the nuclear family as idealized by many religious and political spokespersons. Many forces in society are pressing for a revitalization of this form of family life and a devaluation of or legislation against some of the alternatives outlined at the beginning of this chapter.

A second moral choice is the redesigning of the nuclear family. The recognition of each individual in the family unit as a unique person with fundamental equal rights and responsibilities can be accommodated within this plan. A focus on mere form (father + mother + children = family) is set aside for concentration on the quality of relationships among the living family members; form becomes subordinate to real substance. As Jourard wrote,

> The criterion of a successful solution to marital and family relationship problems is not the *appearance* of the relationship, but rather the *experience of freedom, confirmation and growth* on the part of the participants. . . . The criterion of . . . success [is] not "saving the family" in its present form, but rather a richer, fuller experience of growing existence and honest relationship.[8]

Realistic investments and expectations in nuclear family life can replace romanticized visions. Being a spouse and parent cannot deliver utopia to individuals whose identities are as persons not roles. Going through the motions of family life, merely accomplishing a prearranged list of requirements for "success" in family life (e.g., a job with status, a secure income of x dollars, a house in a nice neighborhood, and so on) is only superficially satisfying. As an ever-changeable adventure in interpersonal love among

[8]Jourard, *The Transparent Self*, p. 109.

its members as persons, the nuclear family can be redesigned more realistically. As an adventure, "the family structure . . . cannot be prescribed or
described in advance, only invented. It is for each couple to commence the
project of reinventing their family with imagination and courage."[9]

The third moral choice is to legitimize the previous option as a coequal
with other valuable forms of family life, such as the single-parent family
and the blended family. (We do not intend to exclude additional forms, but
for the moment these two will serve as sufficient examples.)

RELATIVES: THE EXTENDED FAMILY

"Over the river and through the woods to grandmother's house we
go. . . ." On the dining room table there is a perfect turkey and everyone is
smiling. At least the holiday seasons' ads and TV specials would have us
believe that the realistic norm is "one big happy family." No one has died;
grandmother and grandfather are there along with a discreet sprinkling of
the two genders representing all ages. Aunts, uncles, cousins, parents, and
grandparents are alive, well, and cherish each other's company. Walt Dis-
ney and some religious communities seem to acknowledge the existence of
only this ideal quality of family life.

Yet most persons experience a less than ideal family life. The *appearance*
of family may be there at "family occasions," but the bonding principles
may vary from relationship to relationship. More common than we'd like
to admit is the presence of debit love, possessive love, solo love, martyr
love, dependent love, pressures to conform, and clear competition mixed
with enough civility to allow dessert to be finished without a major inci-
dent. The "thank heaven that's over with for another year" is a frequent
indictment of some holiday and family occasions. As mentioned in the
previous chapter, the bonding principle of biology cannot enhance genuine
friendship.

Of rising concern is the place of the elderly in family life. Love and
respect for older people are not universal values in the United States; we
now turn to the issue of abuse of elders.

The Elderly

The deterioration of some nuclear and extended families is shown most
clearly in tragic cases of abuse of the elderly. The chairman of the Select
Committee on Aging of the U.S. House of Representatives summarized
some committee conclusions on elder abuse in these words:

[9]Jourard, p. 109.

As part of the investigation, we sent questionnaires to a random sampling of police chiefs over the country.

The police chiefs, in their replies, made these points:

Elder abuse is not limited by geographical or regional boundaries; it is a major national problem.

Statistics indicate that it is increasing.

Authorities do not know about many cases of elder abuse—they go unreported out of fear of reprisal or embarrassment.

Lack of intervention, due mainly to inadequate machinery and lack of resources, results in repeated abuse of the victim.

The police chiefs gave these examples:

In California, an elderly woman's home was sold and she was divested of her holdings while she was comatose following a stroke.

In Texas, a middle-aged son who lived with his elderly mother sexually abused her on a number of occasions and drained her bank account.

In Tennessee, a nephew killed his 70-year-old uncle and his 65-year-old aunt.

In Georgia, a 27-year-old son repeatedly beat his 60-year-old mother. He was ultimately prosecuted and the mother now lives at an address she is careful to keep secret from him. . . .

There are somewhere between a half million and 2.5 million cases of elderly abuse reported annually in the United States. . . . Some authorities estimate that of elderly people living with family members, 10 percent are abused in one way or another.[10]

Diagnosis and Options for the Future

All is not well with the extended family nor the nuclear family. One moral choice open to us is to value highly those holiday ads and sentimental movies and struggle to make them become real life.

Another moral choice is to rethink the extended family; is it really necessary to let biology dictate familial or pseudofamilial relationships? Perhaps there is no moral obligation to love and visit obnoxious and cruel cousin Susan who will be seen only at an occasional funeral. We might sensitively rethink how holidays could be better spent. As we examine the extended family, ought we consider the quality of life issue for the elderly—their use of leisure, their health needs, their possible places in the extended family

[10]Rep. Claude Pepper, "Abuse of the Elderly," *Fort Lauderdale News/Sun-Sentinel*, July 13, 1980, pp. H1–2.

and other forms of family life (e.g., with single-parent family or younger unmarried relative)? One old model may be appropriate in some situations—elderly parents living with their own children as the welcomed *normal* cycle, not as the last intruding resort before a nursing home or death. The extended family might be reclaimed and broadened with an emphasis on quality rather than structure.

THE SINGLE PERSON AND THE FAMILY

We reported earlier in this chapter that about one of five households in this country is composed of a single person. The designation "household" is useful; it is not a lesser word than "family," only different. We use household here because "family" denotes more than one person. An individual is not a family.

Religious and political groups exploit "family" often insensitively and superficially. In most churches and synagogues, family services and family events have been so normative that the single person has felt out of place with the congregation. Couple's Clubs have had rude and appropriate awakenings when a death occurs in their group; should the survivor be excluded because (s)he is no longer a couple? Now jolted, the group may notice all the other single persons who have been treated as third-class oddities. Inconsistencies in religious groups are glaring: one group demands an unmarried, celibate clergy, other faiths virtually insist on the nuclear family model for their clergy. Neither considers openly and seriously the varied personal needs of individual ordained leaders. Yet even from some religious sources, a greater awareness of the single person is emerging, however slowly.

BEING SINGLE CAN BE GOOD

There is evidence that we have oversold marriage in our society. Since it is a Good Thing, we have acted as though everybody ought to be married. We try to match up our single friends. We treat marriage as a cure for personal shortcomings. We treat single people as though they suffered from some moral defect and we often exclude them from our company.

We live at a time, however, when there is no longer any compelling reason why everyone should be married. We certainly do not need the help of every adult to sustain the population. And when we consider the difficulties inherent in contemporary marriage, we are forced to conclude that many otherwise adequate and attractive adults may simply not be cut out for the married life. Thus we ought to accept and affirm the decision to remain single, just as we affirm the married state.

There are signs that we are beginning to make this shift. Single people are more generally accepted today than they were a generation ago. Still many married people leave their single friends out of their social lives. And churches which emphasize a family orientation often act as though single people did not exist, except perhaps for a special "young adult" group, which often serves as an informal dating bureau.

The Christian community, because it affirms and exalts the married state, has a peculiar obligation to affirm the legitimacy of staying unmarried. Churches need to open themselves to greater participation by single people, in interaction with the married, so as not to treat singleness as a form of social disease.

Earl H. Brill, *The Christian Moral Vision* (New York: Seabury, 1979), p. 112.

Earl H. Brill is an Episcopal priest whose book quoted here is part of the new "Church's Teaching Series" of his faith. A Ph.D. from American University (Washington, D.C.), Fr. Brill has served in parish ministry, college chaplaincy, and as chairman of the American studies department at the American University. He is presently director of studies at the College of Preachers and Canon of the National Cathedral, Washington, D.C.

The attempt to exploit the nostalgic emotions about "family" is not limited to the religious sphere. The 1980 national political conventions entertained themselves and the nation with continuing appeals to "family life," insensitively ignoring the single voter, who, for example, may have just been widowed and very much alone.

Our cultural biases are evident when we examine comments about individuals single by choice (neither widowed nor divorced): "What a waste!" "What a shame!" "I wonder why (s)he's not married!" Further, our inability to pigeonhole the sexual life of all single persons is an unspoken concern of many employers, relatives, friends, and so on; some of their outrageous inquiries and assumptions are crude and repugnant to single people. If single individuals offered similar comments to their married friends and inquired or assumed things about their private sexuality, society would be aghast.

The "single" issue raises new questions about family. Is the real issue the form of family—extended, nuclear, or other forms—or is it a matter of the quality of relationships a person has? Is the rigid conformity to biology (being a relative) as important as the quality of interpersonal love in an individual's life?

We are not suggesting that an isolated, lonely individual state is wholesome or fulfilling. We are wondering whether there is a need to redefine family in terms of the quality of relationships rather than the mere form or structure or, in Jourard's words, the *appearance* versus the actual *relationships*. If we base an understanding of family on the substance of relationships rather than form alone, all of us—including single persons—may create families, perhaps based on interpersonal love instead of only prepackaged forms. Groups such as churches and synagogues might become extended families for single and married persons alike.

MARRIAGE AND COMPANIONSHIP

It is largely because marriage (and monogamy) is so widespread that arriving at a definition of it is so difficult. That is, the practice of marriage transcends our society and its customs, habits, legal systems, social institutions, and ways of life. Any attempt to define marriage would have to define it in terms of social institutions or practices that were necessarily present wherever marriage could occur. . . .[11]

To most Americans, "marriage" means the legal, public contract into which a man and a woman enter voluntarily. A civil, religious, or humanistic ceremony is the setting for validating the contract. Religious traditions consider marriage to be "til death us do part," at least as the initial intention.

In addition to conventional monogamy, other forms of marriage are developing in the United States and elsewhere. Nonexclusive monogamy (which permits sexual expressions outside the marriage relationship), child-free monogamy, contractual monogamy (with a specified agreement on duration and other matters), trial marriage, communal marriage, and polygamy, though not all recognized by law, are viewed as marriages by their participants.[12]

Nonmarital relationships such as "living together" by members of the

---

[11]David Palmer, "The Consolation of the Wedded," in *Philosophy and Sex,* eds. Robert Baker and Frederick Elliston (Buffalo, N.Y.: Prometheus, 1975), p. 179.
[12]See "New Forms of Marriage," the cover theme of *The Humanist* (March/April 1974); "Polyfidelity: The Kerista Village Ideal," *Psychology Today* (May 1980), pp. 42–43; and Charles Westoff, "Marriage and Fertility in the Developed Countries," *Scientific American* 239, no. 6 (December 1978), pp. 51–57.

opposite or same sex, are forming other models of companionship for which the term "marriage" is less frequently used.

The morality of each marital and nonmarital arrangement can be debated without end. In the last analysis any moral approval or disapproval will depend on "what's taken for granted" about the purpose(s) of intimate companionship. For example, it is taken for granted by many persons that the purpose of marriage is for the lifelong union between a man and a woman and for the procreation of children and that such a marriage is the only good form of intimate companionship. Variations in this traditional view include approved modifications such as moral grounds for annulments and divorces, intentionally childless marriages, and so on.

Some traditional-appearing marriages are motivated by money, status, fear of loneliness, sexual security, professional and business benefits, and covers that mask an individual's real needs, desires, or exploits (e.g., the hiding of Don Juan encounters). The substances of some marriages are aggressive love, debit love, dependent love, and other types of love or "loves" in various combinations. For the benefit of those who choose interpersonal love as the norm for intimate companionship, the following questions may be asked prior to making a commitment.[13]

1. *Do we really enjoy each other as companions?* Some persons considering a commitment of marriage or another arrangement have not thought of each other as friends or companions. They may view each other as sexual partners, providers, caregivers, lawgivers, and/or obedient housekeepers. The relationship is more an assignment of duties than an interpersonal adventure. If one partner hopes for interpersonal love as the bonding principle but the other intends a congenial sharing of tasks, a conflict exists from the outset. Or, if their respective feelings of love are incompatible (one feels debit love, the other solo love), conflict is inevitable. Because individuals are often on their "best behavior" prior to making a commitment, these types of incompatibilities might not be evident; in some other instances people see what they want to in their beloved rather than what is really there. This question attempts to "get it all out in the open," so that the individuals themselves may have greater clarity about their hopes and intentions.

2. *Do we intend our commitment to be for a fixed duration or until death separates us?* Either alternative has consequences. The choice of a fixed term

---

[13]Many couples resist a process of premarital or precommitment counseling. They rightly do not want invasions of their personal privacy, an incompetent series of lectures on how they must live in order to be good, or a sense of having to qualify for a counselor's approval. However, an opportunity to communicate with each other on some matters, with the guidance of a prepared counselor, can expose major problems prior to the commitment or develop some awareness of areas needing future consideration.

carries with it not only a sense of open-endedness if the relationship does not work out, but also the possibility of an undercurrent of insecurity and instability, even fear by one partner of the impending termination. A term suggests that emotional investments can be turned off at a certain date. The choice of a lifelong commitment can bring about a trapped feeling and the possibility of a messy divorce if the relationship falters. On the positive side, by commiting themselves to one another in a relationship intended to be permanent—for better or worse—the partners create a climate of security and stability within which they can deal with difficulties inevitable in all human relations; divorce is still an option when irreconcilable differences solidify. The intention of lifelong companionship sets a psychological tone different from one with a fixed term.

3. *What promises or vows do we actually want to make?* It is hypocritical for partners to echo beautiful words that have little or no meaning for themselves. Promises of love, honor, and fidelity for life compromise the integrity of an individual whose heart and mind do not reflect the words.

4. *As individuals and as companions, what do we want out of life?* "When we made the commitment, I didn't realize (s)he'd spend so much time working; I thought our home life would be top priority." Different or conflicting priorities provide contrasting satisfactions. What priority, if any, does a child or children have in the relationship? What about family planning? What methods of family planning can be used in good conscience? Perhaps what we want out of life is compatible, perhaps not.

5. *How open are we to each other as unique persons?* Some partners wear masks; some classify and categorize their companions in certain defined roles, as discussed in the chapter on identity. Is the commitment being made to a whole person or to a mask worn or imposed?

6. *What do we want to do separately?* Few companions are identical in their interests and friendships. Is there room in the relationship for some separateness? If one partner dies, does the whole existence of the survivor(s) crumble, too?

7. *Do we intend to change each other?* The fundamental personality of an adult is quite firm. Though some habits can be changed voluntarily and behaviors modified willingly, the intention to change a companion after making the commitment is misplaced.

8. *What dislikes have we acknowledged, discussed, and accepted in each other?* Some things about each other annoy the most devoted companions. How significant are the dislikes? Would it be a better life without him/her and these irritants? Can annoying moments be transformed into symbols of a partner's preferred presence rather than empty absence?

9. *What, if anything, are we holding back from each other that someday could be hurtful?* We are not suggesting that every negative thought, word, and

deed be confessed; some things are better left unsaid. However, if a potentially damaging event lurks in the background, it may be prudent to deal with it prior to the commitment being made.

10. *How do we resolve our differences?* By silence? (An inflaming punishment). Sulking? Getting even? Being sweet and calm all the time? Talking matters through with real feelings exposed is another alternative.

11. *What will our relationships be with our "in-laws" and our own parents?* To what extent, if at all, is it necessary to defer to the wishes of one's parents or "in-laws"? If there is to be a wedding ceremony, who is doing the major planning, the persons being married or a partner's parent(s)? In the case of illness or death of a partner's parent, what responsibilities, if any, does the son or daughter have? Is it necessary to spend a day every week or particular holidays with parents and/or in-laws? Are they free to "drop in" at your home unannounced?

12. *What are our respective attitudes toward money?* How important is money to us? Who is a spender? Who is a saver? Will there be a major conflict here? What about buying on credit, budgets, separate and/or joint savings and checking accounts?

13. *Are we established in jobs? Whether yes or no, what are the implications for our relationship regarding child care, household chores, schedules for work and leisure, and so on?*

14. *Are we interested in living in the same part of the world?* Does a partner have a hidden intention to live in California while the other yearns for his New England home town?

15. *Are our respective jobs of equal financial reward and potential? If not, how do we feel about the difference?* Can a man (or woman) be comfortable with a woman's (or man's) higher income? Can a man (or woman) accept the role of homemaker while the woman (or man) earns the living, if this arrangement develops? If partners are working and one is to be transferred by the employer, how will this dilemma be resolved?

16. *Are our educational backgrounds similar? If not, how do we feel about the difference?* Does one partner feel stupid because (s)he hasn't the formal schooling of the other? Does a companion with more formal education feel superior?

17. *Are our ages similar? If not, how do we feel about the difference?* Can we accommodate accidental or vicious remarks, such as "This must be your parent!" Or, "Cradle Robber!"

18. *Have we admitted that we will find other persons attractive, both physically and emotionally?* Do we feel something is wrong in our relationship when other persons are appealing?

19. *Is total sexual fidelity to be part of our relationship? If not, what guidelines*

have been established? (The chapter on sexual ethics includes a discussion of various forms of sexual intimacy).

20. *Have we talked, or will we communicate, about our individual sexual preferences and satisfactions?* (See the chapter on sexual ethics.)

21. *If we are considering a religious ceremony, what does this mean to us?* Can we use the prescribed words with integrity? Are we yielding to family pressures that will force public hypocrisy on us? Do we intend any continuity with the religious tradition after the ceremony?

These 21 questions and their subquestions can be adapted for use by any model of intimate companionship. Though participants can offer what they believe to be "correct" or ideal answers, only honest disclosures can accomplish the purpose. Whether the commitment is made by means of matrimony or verbal agreement to live together, the partners' feelings are usually involved deeply. Incompatible or unrealistic expectations and investments on anyone's part can, from the very inception, lead to mere coexistence, ongoing friction, or breach.

DIVORCE

No matter how much effort and counseling goes into an attempt to salvage a relationship, separation is sometimes the most responsible decision. Remaining together in an irreconcilable relationship violates the norm of interpersonal love whether in a humanistic or theological context.

Christian absolutists apply words attributed to Jesus (Mark 10:2–10) such that divorce is never possible, except (in another passage) for adultery (Matthew 19:3–9). Other Christians interpret these passages to mean the type of divorce in Jesus' own time that was especially cruel to women, but not as permanent legislation against all forms of divorce and remarriage.[14]

In the vast majority of cases, separation or divorce is painful and perilous. For some partners, emotional trauma not unlike widowhood can ensue; for others feelings of bitterness, vindication, revenge, anger, desperation, helplessness, numbness, depression, rejection, abandonment, and so forth can combine in any mix. We still believe, however, that the alternative of "staying together for the children" or other such motives may be, in the long run, worse than the feelings and adjustments of separation or divorce. Whether a legal divorce of married companions or the permanent separation of committed partners living together, the emotional content can be the same for adults and children.[15]

[14]See C. R. Taber, "Divorce," *The Interpreter's Dictionary of the Bible. Supplementary volume* pp. 244–245; and Hugh MonteFiore, "Jesus on Divorce and Remarriage," in a Commission Report, *Marriage, Divorce and the Church* (London: SPCK, 1971), pp. 79–95.
[15]See "The Children of Divorce," the cover story of *Newsweek* (February 11, 1980).

MARRIAGE AND THE FAMILY: MORAL OPTIONS

Form and Substance

The debate over the nature of "family" and "marriage" has not arisen among classroom philosophers; it has emerged in society among citizens. The issue has come to the fore because there is a wide gulf between a moral ideal on paper and what is in practice; a growing conviction is evident that a collection of related birth certificates do not alone qualify for the category "family." Likewise, more and more persons are certain that a marriage certificate alone does not guarantee or indicate the reality of a caring relationship. A dissatisfaction with mere conformity to form minus substance in matters of marriage and the family is a sign of integrity in the citizenry.

Moral Options

It is our belief that marriage and the family are not dying out. Instead we are involved in an ethical upheaval over the forms that "family" and "marriage" may take with moral approval. Previously unthinkable questions related to form and substance are being asked such as, "Should people be required to obtain a license to parent children?"[16] These questions and those introduced and posed throughout this chapter are not raised to shock us, but to focus on concerns of *quality in our relationships*. This is the heart of the moral matter.

The authors of an MIT–Harvard report, "The Nation's Families: 1960–1990," warn against a public policy that clings to romantic images of the American family as it was formed during the immediate post-World War II period when individuals married quickly and had large families. Instead, diversity is predicted. In 1977 Vice-President Walter F. Mondale wrote, "This administration understands that we are a diverse and pluralistic nation, that there is no single, ideal model of family, and that government must not try to impose one."[17]

Our toleration as a nation of diverse values and moral norms will set the boundaries on approved forms and substances of marriage and the family. Even the selection of one standard, such as interpersonal love, in theological or secular perspectives, broadens the forms intimate companionships and relationships may assume with moral approval. Marriage and the family may indeed be in a painful condition. But is it the pain of a cruel death due to rigid customary values, a moral decay? Or is it the pangs of a new birth—a wider vision of authentic human relationships?

---

[16]See Hugh Lafollette, "Licensing Parents," *Philosophy and Public Affairs*, 9 no. 2 (Winter 1980), pp. 182–197.

[17]Walter F. Mondale, "The Family in Trouble," *Psychology Today* (May 1977), p. 39.

CHAPTER REVIEW

A. Moral issues in family life

1. Customary values of family life continue to provide norms for the morally good way to live for many persons.
2. Customary values, however, are being questioned by a significant number of citizens.
3. Issues opened for discussion include legalized marriage, parenting, obligations to relatives, form and substance in relationships, and so on.

B. What is a family?

1. The meaning of "family" is not a closed matter.
2. Should "family" be used for the couple, the extended family, the single-parent family, the blended family, same-sex couples, a man and woman living together, as well as the traditional nuclear family?
3. Some sources believe *THE* family is falling apart.

C. Diagnosing the American nuclear family

1. The nuclear family is a relatively recent development.
2. Expanding views of women and men have contributed to dramatic changes in family life.
3. Changing attitudes toward children are also contributing to changes in family life.
4. Family violence is far greater than previously suspected.
5. Options for the future include the reestablishment of the idealized nuclear family, redesign the nuclear family, or expand legitimate understandings of "family."

D. Relatives: The extended family

1. The *appearance* of the ideal extended family may be evident at "family occasions," but the bonding principle may be other than interpersonal love.
2. The elderly are subject to unsuspected abuse in the United States.
3. All is not well with the extended family as well as the nuclear family.
4. Options for the future include efforts to establish the idealized extended family or rethinking the extended family (including the elderly) in terms of quality rather than mere structure.

E. The single person and the family

1. Although a single person is not a family, a need remains to incorporate the single state as a wholesome, legitimate option.

F.   Marriage and companionship

1. The very nature of "marriage" is not a closed matter; varying views of relationships labeled "marriage" exist in fact.
2. The morality of each marital and nonmarital arrangement is an issue, as is the purpose(s) of intimate companionship.
3. Before making a commitment based on interpersonal love, a couple may benefit from exploring certain aspects of their relationship.

G.   Divorce

1. Separation may be the most responsible decision when a relationship cannot be salvaged.
2. Prohibitions on divorce among Christians are rooted in a particular interpretation of the New Testament.

H.   Marriage and the family: Moral options

1. A dissatisfaction with mere conformity to *form* minus *substance* in matters of marriage and the family is a sign of integrity in the citizenry.
2. Marriage and the family are not dying out; we are instead involved in a moral upheaval over the forms families and marriages may take.

SUGGESTED READINGS

Edwards, James C., and MacDonald, Douglas M., eds. *Occasions For Philosophy.* Englewood Cliffs, N.J.: Prentice-Hall, 1979.

> Section four, "Philosophy and Personal Relations," includes three recent essays on monogamy, marriage, and adultery.

Kierkegaard, Søren. "The Aesthetic Validity of Marriage." In *Ethical Choice,* edited by Robert N. Beck and John B. Orr. New York: Free Press, 1970, pp. 105–116.

> A discussion of love and marriage from the ethical viewpoint of the well-known nineteenth century existentialist pastor of Copenhagen, Denmark.

Levitan, Sar A., and Belous, Richard S. *What's Happening to the American Family?* Baltimore: Johns Hopkins Univ. Press, 1981.

> A social science study of the diverse types of households in the United States from The George Washington University's Center for Social Policy Studies.

Norman, Michael. "The New Extended Family," *New York Times Magazine,* Nov. 23, 1980, pp. 26–29, 44, 46, 53, 54, 147, 162, 166, 173.

> The instant expansion of families caused by remarriage after divorce has altered the meaning of "family."

O'Neill, Onora, and Ruddick, William, eds. *Having Children: Philosophical and Legal Reflections on Parenthood*. New York: Oxford Univ. Press, 1979.

> Considerations of public policy issues such as population control, abortion, adoption, and genetic counseling as linked to bearing and rearing children.

Russell, Bertrand, *Marriage and Morals*. New York: Liveright, 1929.

> Written by the twentieth-century British philosopher over fifty years ago, this well known book anticipated many current philosophical concerns.

PART 3
HEALTH AND SEXUALITY

8

Mental
and
Physical
Health

Health ... is an almost universally valuable state. Yet many are imprudent in the extreme in regard to their own health. It would be hard to argue convincingly that one literally owes it to oneself to be healthy, no matter how desirable health is acknowledged to be. But most owe it to others, for a variety of reasons, to seek to maintain good health. Those who lack any such obligation are free to abandon their health, their bodily integrity, and even their lives without fear of thereby violating a moral obligation. But that freedom exists only in consequence of the chilling impoverishment of their lives.

HEALTH AS A MORAL OBLIGATION

The people of our nation are more health conscious today than ever before. They are more aware than their ancestors of nutritional needs, physical fitness, mental health issues, and medical developments and care. We suspect, however, that the public views "a sound mind in a sound body" as a morally neutral option; the thought of mental and physical health as a moral obligation will strike many persons as odd, perhaps an exaggeration of "health fanatics." One might ask, "Isn't my body my own to do with as I please?" "Isn't my state of mind my private domain?"

This chapter's exploration of mental and physical health proposes that one's health is to a large extent a matter of choice not fate and that health of mind and body is a matter of moral obligation not individualistic license or neutrality. We shall support this assumption by arguing for the importance of one's mental and physical health to both the individual *and* the community, thereby broadening health from a private to a community issue. We shall also propose some philosophical principles of mental health and some issues of physical health. The *principles* can serve as practical guides toward greater mental health; the *issues* will bring to your attention several areas requiring additional study. We believe that an individual's moral obligation

*Samuel Gorovitz, "Health As An Obligation," *Encyclopedia of Bioethics*, 2, p. 609.

155

to himself or herself and the community can be met to a great extent by choosing these philosophical principles and by applying a further knowledge of the medical issues. The same components constitute the bases of the community's moral obligation to the individual.

We recognize fully, however, that our proposals will have little or no significance or moral weight to those persons who make contrary assumptions such as "My body is my own to do with as I please" and "My state of mind is my own private domain." Furthermore, ascetic philosophic positions that view this world as *apparently* real rather than *really* real and/or the mortal body as an unworthy concern do not value health as a high priority. The hermit living in an isolated cave and seeking only spiritual salvation or a whole society idealizing other-worldly attitudes have very different priorities from Americans eager for various degrees of material comforts, including reasonable health. (It is almost paradoxical that so many Americans appear to be concerned with health but do not think of physical and mental health as a moral issue.)

Before proceeding further, we can benefit from asking a basic question, what is "health?"

PREAMBLE TO THE CONSTITUTION OF THE WORLD HEALTH ORGANIZATION

The States Parties to this Constitution† declare, in conformity with the Charter of the United Nations, that the following principles are basic to the happiness, harmonious relations and security of all peoples:

Health is a state of complete physical, mental and social well-being and not merely the absence of disease or infirmity.

The enjoyment of the highest attainable standard of health is one of the fundamental rights of every human being without distinction of race, religion, political belief, economic or social condition.

The health of all peoples is fundamental to the attainment of peace and security and is dependent upon the fullest cooperation of individuals and States.

† *The Constitution was adopted by the International Health Conference held in New York from 19 June to 22 July 1946, and signed on 22 July 1946 by the representatives of 61 States (Off. Rec. Wld Hlth Org. 2, 100). Amendments adopted by the Twentieth World Health Assembly (resolution WHA20.36) came into force on 21 May 1975 and are incorporated in the present text.*

The achievement of any State in the promotion and protection of health is of value to all.

Unequal development in different countries in the promotion of health and control of disease, especially communicable disease, is a common danger.

Healthy development of the child is of basic importance; the ability to live harmoniously in a changing total environment is essential to such development.

The extension to all peoples of the benefits of medical, psychological and related knowledge is essential to the fullest attainment of health.

Informed opinion and active cooperation on the part of the public are of the utmost importance in the improvement of the health of the people.

Governments have a responsibility for the health of their peoples which can be fulfilled only by the provision of adequate health and social measures.

Reprinted from World Health Organization: Basic Documents, *26th ed. (Geneva: World Health Organization, 1976), p. 1.*

What Is Health?

One view of health limits all considerations to an individual's biological condition. Another view includes the biological and the mental aspects; a third extends issues of health to include the quality of a person's social interactions. We shall discuss health in its physical and mental dimensions, and interpret social interactions within the mental dimension.

Good Health: Being "Healthy." Is an individual healthy only when no disabilities, discomforts, or ailments are present? If you answer "yes," conditions that disqualify a person from a claim of being healthy would include wearing glasses, a headache, sadness, or a chronic allergy. Being "healthy" in this view appears to mean a state of complete well-being—biological and mental.

The word "complete" creates a problem in defining good health or "healthy." It is doubtful that the "Preamble to the Constitution of the World Health Organization" would insist that persons wearing glasses, suffering a headache, experiencing some sadness, or coping with a chronic allergy should be labeled "unhealthy." Yet an extreme position could demand total, unblemished functioning as the criterion for good health. A more reasonable view of good health, in our judgment, values the capacities of a person to make decisions and to love mutually while coping well with some physical and/or mental flaws. The flaws one allows while still labeling a rational, loving person "healthy" becomes a judgment based on one's own values: if perfect eyesight is of high priority, then wearing glasses may constitute an unhealthy condition; if the loss of a limb is relatively inconsequential to an individual's life, the individual may still be regarded as healthy. The point at which a condition is disabling to a person's valued needs and goals gives meaning to the use of "unhealthy;" prior to that subjective disabling point, one may regard oneself in good health—but with one or more flaws.[1]

THE IMPORTANCE OF MENTAL HEALTH

Mental health cannot be separated in any clear-cut way from physical health. We are increasingly aware of the psychosomatic interrelatedness of mind and body. Though some philosophers retain a concept of the unrelatedness of the mental and the physical, the trend today among philosophers and scientists is either to link the two in a dynamic interaction or to deny that there is any such thing as the mind at all![2] Contemporary medicine assumes that a person's mental condition may affect bodily functions for good or for ill. It can weaken resistance to infection and disease, cause changes in vital organs, and upset the normal functions of the body. For example, anger and other emotional disturbances can speed up the action of the heart, increase blood pressure, and affect the flow of hydrochloric acid, which aggravates the stomach. A knowledge of a patient's frustrations, worries, or fears is often as important as a chemical blood analysis in discovering the causes of an illness. Some physicians claim that a knowledge of the mental outlook of a patient is as important as a knowledge of what disease the patient has. Even a patient's desire to get well may be a critical factor in recovery.

An individual's mental health is important not only to the person but also to the community. To be a contributing participant in one's community, even within one's family, a person must be able to relate positively to others. Individuals who are chronically hostile, suspicious, jealous, disruptive, sour, or self-seeking cannot participate well in the life of any segment of a community. In severe cases a person may not be able to contribute economically and may become only a financial receiver, in no way a giver.

[1]See the section "Health and Disease" (including the essays "History of the Concepts" and "Philosophical Perspectives") in the *Encyclopedia of Bioethics,* vol. 2, pp. 579–605.
[2]See "The Mind," chapter 4 in *Living Issues in Philosophy* (New York: Van Nostrand, 1979).

Emotionally and economically, such an individual must rely on the community. If institutionalized, a patient costs the community the economic and human participation that cannot be offered.

Choices, Responsibility, and Accountability

Some mental disorders are caused by brain damage or chemical imbalance. Other illnesses are caused by conscious choices or conditioning, perhaps the unfortunate learning of self-defeating "things taken for granted" (see chapter 2). We cannot hold a person responsible for mental illnesses caused by factors beyond personal control, such as brain damage, chemical imbalance, or conditioning. However, we can hold morally accountable those individuals (e.g., the burned-out drug user) who through conscious bodily abuse create conditions that result in mental illnesses. To the mentally ill person who is innocent of creating the condition, the community gives assistance (and should probably provide even more); from the individual who deliberately charts a course toward mental disaster, the community can rightly insist on moral accountability.

Mental health, therefore, is an important obligation of the individual for personal well-being and for the community's well-being. Choices that cause mental illness deny wholeness to the individual and fullness to the community; for such choices, individuals are morally responsible and accountable.

We must remind ourselves that persons who hold ascetic and highly individualistic attitudes will not find these arguments persuasive. Some ascetics can logically claim that notions of health for themselves and the community are of a spiritual quality, not bodily. Some individualists view their own degrees of well-being as a wholly private matter, accountable to personal, private senses of morality.

SOME PHILOSOPHICAL PRINCIPLES OF MENTAL HEALTH

Mental health is not necessarily achieved by adapting to readily available principles or ideals. An individual may be exposed to conflicting combinations of ideals, such as martyr love and the need for commercial success, that can result in havoc for the individual. In this example, the conflict between the ideal of being a giver who ignores his own needs (the martyr) and the ideal of making a large amount of money prevents a wholesome integration of an individual's mental outlook. We suspect that a person who merely adapts to whatever principles are at hand runs the risk of personal conflict or disintegration. We should like to suggest some principles of mental health.

Principle of Self-Acceptance

"You can be anything you want to be." "You can do anything you really want to do." Many children are raised with a false notion of their unlimited potential. With this ideal taken for granted, they see about them national idols of brilliance, beauty, and achievement. Through advertisements, films, and other media, they learn that a mind of high intelligence, a body of stunning form, and a record of exceptional achievements ought to be among everyone's realistic goals.

The vast majority of men and women are not intellectually gifted, do not have the basic skeletal frame for a "perfect body," and cannot claim distinction in their achievements. For the majority who continue to take these goals for granted, as in fact within their reach if they would only work harder, two alternatives are available.

1. They may give them up as a lost cause, suffer a nagging guilt that they have "accomplished nothing," and live with a certain degree of self-contempt. They certainly do not accept themselves.

2. They may continue to strive desperately for so-called successes in mind, body, and for achievements that are unattainable because of personal limitations and/or circumstances. Such people live with a sense of incompletion or failure; they do not fully accept themselves either.

Attempts to set new records in almost anything are, in many competitors, symptoms of personal dissatisfaction and of the need to be "successful" at something in order to feel good about oneself. Such individuals may live constantly trying to justify their existence and seeking recognition.

One must reject the ideal of unlimited potential in mind, body, and achievement to successfully walk the path to genuine self-acceptance. It is very difficult to set aside this ideal; it has become engrained in our culture. Though you might agree intellectually to reject it, the desire for its fulfillment may have become rooted in your emotions: "I know the ideal is unrealistic, but how I wish I could be that smart, look that good, and accomplish that much!" The transformation of these feelings requires ongoing support from like-minded family or friends or from a therapist; it is unlikely that such culturally conditioned images can be purged by one's own efforts.

Genuine self-acceptance means accepting our handicaps or limitations as well as our abilities and talents. To accept oneself and the conditions of one's existence does not mean resignation or passive submission to all present conditions. This principle means *the intellectual and emotional affirmations of one's identity as a person or child of God, of one's purpose in life as interpersonal love, and of one's natural abilities and physique.*

The development or growth of an individual's natural abilities and physique is best begun on the foundation of self-acceptance. Dreams of accomplishment can be designed and realized when they are grounded in realistic self-inventory and acceptance, not in the unlikely or impossible dreams of culturally conditioned fantasies.

As a result of genuine self-acceptance, individuals are free to be themselves; each can develop mind and body, and each can accomplish selected realistic goals. However, all growth and achievement is accomplished in the spirit of stretching one's accepted self, not in the context of desperate climbing and reaching toward an imaginary state of perfection that supposedly will "someday" provide satisfaction. Today more than ever counselors are working with men and women who are returning to or entering college for the first time. These people are in their late twenties through retirement years. A common anxiety expressed by many of them is the conviction that they have "wasted" so many years. Their sense of self-acceptance has been diminished by their failure to assess the many positive events in their lives to that point and, above all, by their failure to perceive their whole notion of self-acceptance as linked to unrealistic, utopian goals. On the other hand, those adults continuing their education within the context of genuine self-acceptance can view their present learning as a new adventure, a new chapter in their process of steady growth. Their goals can be set according to established identities, an overall life purpose, and actual capabilities.

Principle of Adjustment

It is unlikely that a particular individual's vision of what the world should be like is precisely the way the world is. In fact, a person's view of what *ought* to be may be in sharp contrast to what *is*. One might become cynical, sour, passive, reclusive, or anxious, or a crusading, scolding, and ever-present spokesperson. Any of these alternatives will eventually earn the individual a loss of credibility in the community as well as personal martyrdom. The transformation of a community to a higher plain or civilization requires a slow, steady witness and effort, not necessarily withdrawal, aggression, or total selflessness.

An adjustment to present conditions does not mean an endorsement of the status quo. The principle of adjustment means *the ongoing process of relating to oneself and to others such that an individual's identity and purpose remain intact while he or she interacts with a pluralistic environment.* Far from a passive conformity to the multi-faced world as it is, adjustment in our interpretation denotes continuous, creative tension between who I am, my purpose, my abilities and achievements, *and* the status quo, including varied expectations of me by others. While not endorsing reality as it *is* in human relations, adjusted persons can, under most circumstances, carve out oases of sustaining harmony and empowering spirit for themselves and a few others. At the same time, they, knowing they are not almighty, can design, where possible, some lasting changes for the better. Such an adjustment includes the toleration of the slow pace with which groups change in both heart and mind and a knowledge that quick revolutions dealing with externals alone may change forms but not substance. We would not, however, preclude violence from all aspects of adjustment; as a final or only just alternative, an adjusted person might be called upon to use force, lethal or otherwise. Amidst all encounters and confrontations, in all conditions in which one finds oneself, the adjusted person knows who and why he or she is.

Some men and women go from spouse to spouse, job to job, location to location, and friend to friend in search of the ideal spouse, job, location, and/or friend. Unable to adjust to less than their image of the ideal, a never ending search occupies their lives. It has probably never occured to them that the ideal *real* person, job, or location has flaws (except for God, heaven, and whatever jobs are available there!). Growth and improvements can occur in people, in jobs, and in locations, but none will probably be found perfected. Demanding such perfection, "idealistic" individuals will be discontented no matter where they are or whom they are with. An adjusted man or woman is not only self-accepting, but also able to interact well with others and various settings.

Principle of Creativity

"Let's see what happens." "What will be will be." "Have a nice day!" Slogans such as these, when they are axioms of a person's philosophy, result in passivity that in turn molds an individual as a victim. Life is received by or happens to such people. They wait for something to happen; they accept "what's in the cards;" they merely *have* days. Nothing is more foreign to them than initiating events or relationships, reasonably planning what will be, and creating a nice day. They appear to accept for themselves some form of fate.[3] Regardless of the origins of their outlook (psychological or otherwise), they are like imprisoned robots waiting for the next programmer to direct them. From our viewpoint, this is unhealthy.

The principle of creativity means *individuals possess innately, within their moral limitations and with the encouragement of others, the capacity to shape their days and years.* Despite limitations shared by all humans—restrictions imposed by one's economic and societal conditions and the confines of one's specific mental and physical endowments—men and women are inherently creative architects who can freely build their own

---

[3]See our discussion of freedom in chapter 2.

lives. Many restrictions that crush creativity are actually self-imposed; when individuals say "I cannot," they may in fact be saying "I'm afraid to" or "I have made prior decisions that preclude this new choice." In reality, they can often (in the sense that they have the actual ability), perhaps with assistance, do such and such.

We are not proposing that in the name of creativity a person should act out every desire and wish. However, knowing and feeling that one could create Plan "A" and choose whether or not to implement Plan "A" is a sign of a person's mental health. The capacity to create and do loving or hateful things is a marvelous facet of human nature. (In any situation, however, whether to love or to hate is a separate, moral matter.) The principle of creativity asserts that with the support of others we are capable of designing, choosing priorities, and planning and that it is a component of good mental health to do so!

Principle of Community

It is possible to think of man as distinguished from plants and animals by the fact that human life—in a very real and not only a purely literary or imaginary sense—requires interchange with an environment which includes culture. When I say that man is distinguished very conspicuously from other members of the biological universe by requiring interchange with a universe of culture, this means, in actual fact, since culture is an abstraction pertaining to people, that man requires interpersonal relationships or interchange with others. While there are apparent exceptions . . . it is a rare person who can cut himself off from mediate and immediate relations with others for long spaces of time without undergoing a deterioration in personality.[4]

No serious student of human nature advocates prolonged individual isolation. Men and women who are isolated from other human beings by choice or circumstances do deteriorate mentally. Watching television, reading, enjoying pets, traveling alone may fill one's hours, but the principle of community means (consistent with Chapters 5 and 6) *that individuals must be involved in a caring, unmasked, trusting relationship with not less than one other person for good mental health.* As Jourard observed,

Self-disclosure is a symptom of personality health and a means of ultimately achieving healthy personality. When I say that self-disclosure is a symptom of personality health, I mean a person who displays many of the other characteristics that betoken healthy personality *will also display the ability to make himself fully known to at least one other significant human being.*[5]

[4]Harry Stack Sullivan, *The Interpersonal Theory of Psychiatry* (New York: Norton, 1953), p. 32.
[5]Sidney Jourard, *The Transparent Self* (New York: Van Nostrand, 1972), p. 32.

The failure to be in an interpersonal relationship with someone produces illnesses of varying kinds and degrees. A community of (an)other person(s), which may include one's real family (not necessarily relatives) and true friends, is the natural context for self-acceptance and creativity; self-acceptance and creativity require for their maximum realization at least one another, whether therapist or comrade.

One distressed individual who thought that prayer alone would overcome loneliness said it well: "God is not enough." Far from heresy, this exclamation is consistent with the Judaeo-Christian wisdom that love of God, neighbor and self—all three—is at the heart of a full life.

The need for some form of community for good mental health is particularly evident in times of joy and sorrow. It is difficult to laugh alone; a humorous film watched by oneself is stressful in that laughter is not meant to be a private pursuit. Another example of the human need for others is an occasion to celebrate; genuine community is the setting to celebrate an achievement, an anniversary, or the like. Individuals in superficial or personally competing groups find it difficult if not impossible to celebrate enthusiastically another's significant moments. In some groups such moments become pitiful occasions of envy and jealousy.

At tragic times and at the death of a loved person, community is beneficial to the troubled and mourning. The very presence or written thoughts of others are extremely supportive for persons suffering calamity or loss. However, individuals who limit their community to a spouse or their nuclear family unduly limit their human resources for much needed emotional support; a spouse may die, and the children will eventually leave home. Without sufficient sharing of sorrows and joys, one's mental health is less than it could be. Unresolved grief and hurt can gnaw away at the mind and heart of an individual, thereby contributing to a stagnant or deteriorating mental state.

The principle of community, in contrast to a residual rugged frontier individualism, remains vital. Secular associations, churches, synagogues, families and friendships whose norm is interpersonal love are potentially excellent communal resources for good mental health.

Principle of Balance

For those persons who choose interpersonal love as their life's vocation and the basic moral norm, the principle of balance is significant. The principle of balance means *the art of maintaining a balanced, flexible, comprehensive vision of and involvement in human relations and events.*

An Art. The course of human life is not, in our understanding, a predetermined sequence of events. With room for chance, novelty, and creativity, one's life can be shaped by a balancing of circumstances beyond one's control with realistic possibilities for the future. Like an artist with particular paints and a limited canvas, the human being as artist can paint whatever picture suits him or her.

Flexibility.   Individuals who insist on pursuing a narrow path with unquestioned obedience to all imposed rules and expectations surrender the possibility of responding to new circumstances. Conformity to someone else's artistry produces robots, not free persons. Flexibility provides a balance between useful boundaries and the surprises that call for new frontiers.

Comprehensive Vision.   Knowing alternative viewpoints about human relations and events is neither a danger to or prevention of an individual's own firm convictions. New knowledge may broaden one's beliefs, give firmer support to present understandings, or possibly suggest major revisions. However, some political and religious groups offer only their own vision of human relations and events, so that fated interpretations prevail. We are convinced that the broad view within which choices can be made is a good balance between narrowness and chaos.

Involvement.   In recent years "Get involved" has been a slogan intended to jolt bystanders into the flow of human relations and events. We now know of two extremes: the passive bystander and the "Samaritan burnout." The latter suffers from "neighbor overload," an unbalanced caregiving to "neighbors" that depletes one's giving energies. Many political activists, social workers, teachers, physicians, nurses, counselors, clergy, and others in the so-called helping occupations have not learned to say "no" as well as "yes." Some individuals have not accepted their human limitations, have not learned to distinguish between their own problems that they themselves must solve and others' problems that others must solve. Sometimes "care-giver" becomes the core of a person's identity (see chapter 5); unfortunately, well-intended messianic outreach to almost everyone and anyone normally results in the burning out of a bright light. Humanitarians and theologically rooted people might recall precedents for balance between rest and care-giving: "And on the seventh day God finished his work which he had done, and he rested. . . ." (Genesis 2:2) "The apostles returned to Jesus, and told him all that they had done and taught. And he said to them, 'Come away by yourselves to a lonely place, and rest a while.'" (Mark 6:30–31). Jesus himself took time off in the wilderness for reflection. It is peculiar that so many care-givers, religious and not, fail to accomodate within their lives a comparable balanced involvement in human relations and events.[6]

[6]Jourard, pp. 64–72.

Principle of Wisdom

The principle of wisdom means *a set of consistent ideals or a philosophy of life that is basically life-affirming and capable of accommodating sorrow.* "As a man thinketh in his heart, so is he" (Proverbs 23:7). "There is a deep tendency in human nature to *become like* that which we imagine ourselves to be."[7] If you believe you are a victim of circumstances, you may become just that and suffer mentally. If you beleive life and the world can progress, although you may not achieve all your goals, you are likely to grow toward them and achieve many of them, a contribution to good mental health.

The life of a person who is mentally healthy is integrated around a philosophy of life. From our viewpoint, a chosen philosophy examined from among alternatives provides wisdom; a fated, imposed set of beliefs is not wisdom, but a program. Wisdom acknowledges its own axioms, implications, and rightful place among global philosophies; a program knows nothing but itself as the one obviously "true" set of alleged facts. Wisdom encourages examined and informed belief; a program accepts without question what's taken for granted. Wisdom fosters enthusiastic sharing of convictions; a program demands unquestioning assent. Wisdom enables a willingness to differ; a program is intolerant of dissent. Wisdom includes a spirit of humility with regard to human limitations to know for sure; a program maintains a spirit of tyranny with regard to knowing with absolute godlike certainty. Wisdom embraces the heart and the mind with appropriate joys and sorrows; a program controls the heart and mind permitting only assent *or* hellfire and brimstone. Wisdom contributes to mental health; programs limit or weaken one's mental condition.

Reasonable consistency in one's wisdom or philosophy is not only an intellectual asset but also provides stability to daily life. Contradictory beliefs accompany fragmented and conflicting behavior, another aspect of poor mental health.

If the principle of wisdom is valid, one wonders why philosophy, the "love of wisdom," is not taught explicitly throughout a person's school years. Far from an abstract, academic nicety, the study of philosophical issues can assist individuals with "getting their ideas together," thereby promoting wisdom and perhaps contributing as well to self-acceptance, adjustment, and creativity.

SICKNESS AS PROTEST

The suggested principles of mental health do not guarantee well-being if followed. We cannot overlook the fact that many forms of mental illness or

---

[7]Marie Beynon Ray, *How Never To Be Tired*, rev. ed. (Indianapolis: Bobbs-Merrill, 1944).

less than optimum mental health are caused by chemical, electrical, and other bodily malfunctions, disease, and handicaps. More than one mentally ill patient has been found to have a physiological basis to the illness after years of ineffective psychotherapy!

In many cases, however, the problem or sickness is the direct result of the violation of one of the principles outlined in this chapter. The sickness is a "protest against a way of life that will not support wellness."[8] Diminished mental health occurs with sufficient violation of these principles. In turn, the body may manifest the troubled state of mind (as some ulcers result from too much stress), or the body may be weakened because of stress such that invading germs find a receptive host. The violations may be conscious (as when a person knowingly accepts too many responsibilities) or subconscious (as when an individual's community consists of only one other mortal person). In either approach, less than optimum mental health is achieved. Severe violations result in mental illness, not just a less than optimum condition.[9]

Many well-written popularized articles by fine scholars on mental health issues of great public interest and concern are appearing in various books and periodicals. We suspect that most of these areas can be traced to a violation of one or more of the principles we have proposed.[10] Additional problems, such as unrealistic guilt, poor psychological preparation for retirement, ongoing procrastination, excessive television watching, persistent lying, insistence on a cynical or sour interpretation of virtually everything and everyone, chronic helplessness and indecisiveness, subconscious creation of situations that result in needless stress and hurt for oneself and others, and feeling "pulled apart at the seams" are directly related to the violation of one or more of these principles.

A Moral Issue

Because choice is the basis of either progress toward optimum mental health or continuing mental deterioration, the quality of an individual's condition is a moral matter. Choices that lead to positive results are morally good, and decisions that contribute to negative consequences are morally

[8]Jourard, pp. 76–77.
[9]See the section "Mental Illness" (including the articles "Conceptions of Mental Illness," "Diagnosis of Mental Illness," and "Labeling in Mental Illness") in the *Encyclopedia of Bioethics*, vol. 3, pp. 1089–1108.
[10]Gordon Clanton and Lynn G. Smith, "The Self-Inflicted Pain of Jealousy," *Psychology Today* (March 1977); see the articles on "Depression," a cover topic of *Psychology Today* (April 1975); Sam Keen, "Chasing the Blahs Away: Boredom," *Psychology Today* (May 1977); Alfie Kohn, "Why Competition," *The Humanist* (January/February, 1980); Williard Gaylin, *Caring* (New York: Knopf, 1976); Daniel J. Levinson, *The Seasons of a Man's Life* (New York: Ballantine, 1978); Nancy Mayer, *The Male Mid-Life Crisis* (Garden City, N.Y.: Doubleday, 1978).

wrong. We repeat, however, that mental illnesses caused by factors beyond a person's control or by ignorance exempt afflicted individuals from moral judgments.

In that no human being is "an island unto himself," a person's state of mind affects not only that individual's existence, but also others with whom he or she relates. Consequently, the moral sphere extends beyond any one man or woman. A diminished sense of self-acceptance, mediocre adjustment, lack of initiative, isolated individualism, imbalance, and ignorance shackle the quality of human relations.

Let us not ignore the choices made by the community that weaken the mental health of individuals! A consensus that upholds unhealthy principles is just as wrong as an individual's unwise decisions. The cultural reinforcements of shallow identities, self-defeating meanings of life, and superficial values subject people within the community to mental pollution.

We hold that good mental health, when medically possible, is a moral obligation of the individual and the community. With the currently available insights about human behavior, the individual and the community are morally obligated to cultivate optimum mental health by means of informed and responsible personal choices and consensus, public education, and supportive agencies.

PHYSICAL HEALTH

The Importance and Morality of Physical Health

We need not create a new case for the importance and morality of physical health. The reasons suggested for the importance of mental health support physical well-being as well. The interaction of mind and body is such that the mind affects the body, and the body affects the mind. Malnutrition, over-exertion, chronic pain, and brain damage are among physical causes of mental distress.

The substitution of "physical" for "mental" in a paragraph on page 159 sums up well the issue: *Physical* health, therefore, is an important obligation of the individual for his own well-being and for the community's well-being. Choices that cause *physical* illness deny the individual his wholeness and the community its fullness; for such choices individuals are responsible and accountable. We hold that good physical health, when medically possible, is a moral obligation of the individual and the community. With the available scientific information about hygiene, the individual and the community are morally obligated to cultivate optimum physical health by means of informed and responsible personal choices and consensus, public education, and supportive agencies.

Much Sickness and Pain Are Unnecessary

A shift in health care is taking place. People are expected to assume basic responsibility for their own health rather than be led by the hand by a physician. Periodic check-ups are recommended as complementary to individual self-care. One publication designed to provide accurate and timely health information for a general readership noted:

> The decade of the 70s produced ... a new emphasis on personal responsibility for keeping healthy, rather than fatalistically waiting for illness to strike without notice.... most thoughtful physicians willing to ignore their own income considerations and the expectations of many patients would agree that much of the "comprehensive" annual health examination makes little sense.... increasingly, both medical evidence and financial considerations are pointing in the direction of emphasizing health education, life-style changes, and selective (versus routine testing—rather than ritualistic, nondirected annual check-ups for healthy persons.
>
> In short, visiting one's physician periodically, perhaps every two or three years in adult life, remains reasonable; at the very least the visit sustains a useful doctor-patient relationship. A review of personal habits and health practices should occur, and selected portions of a physical exam can be performed (as well as taught) to encourage frequent self-examination.[11]

The guidance readily available from public health agencies, television documentaries, health periodicals and books, newspaper columns, courses in schools, and so on can assist people with the development of appropriate hygiene. Those who have been exposed to such information can then choose whether to develop and maintain good health practices. Many others are unaware of public health agencies, avoid documentaries, and neither read nor study. Although people cannot be forced to learn, we propose that the community has a moral obligation to offer the information via methods and media from which all people are able to learn. Much sickness and pain are unnecessary; however, it exists because some men and women choose to ignore what they've been taught and because some have never been taught good health practices. The former can blame themselves for some of their poor health; the community can be held responsible for not informing the latter.

Personal Health Issues. Among the topics with which men and women ought to be familiarized in order to assume major responsibility for their personal health care are the following: nutrition and weight control,

[11]G. Timothy Johnson, ed., "Periodic Health Exams in Perspective," *The Harvard Medical School Health Letter* V, 9 (July 1980), pp. 1–2.

physical fitness, causes of disease, prevention and treatment of major diseases, health and the environment, the aging process, health care delivery, and death and dying. Because these are clearly medical matters rather than philosophical principles, we shall leave the responsibility with the reader to consult books on health for needed information.[12]

The Use and Abuse of Chemicals

Bridging the categories of nutrition, fitness, causes of diseases, and prevention and treatment is the issue of the use and abuse of chemicals. In this area, high emotion and propaganda have confused the nation. When the question is asked, "Does the use of certain substances affect life beneficially or adversely?" scientific evidence is needed to answer the question adequately. If the use of a particular chemical results, in the long run, in a negative impact on the mental and/or physical health of an individual or of most human beings, lack of restrictions on its use is wrong. The issue is really a medical one: Does the use of chemical "A" offer greater benefit or a greater degree of harm? A related matter is: Who is to judge the benefit (value) or harm—the "average citizen" or the scientists equipped to provide the results of research?

THE MORALITY OF "POT"

After exaggerated assertions have been discounted, the serious business of responsible evaluation remains. What are we to say of the experience of smoking marijuana? After a little practice, most people find this experience very pleasant. The Le Dain Commission concluded that a major factor in the contemporary marijuana explosion in the adult population as well as among young people is the simple pleasure of the experience. For example, a teacher and mother of four testified, "When I smoke grass, I do it in the same social way that I take a glass of wine at dinner or have a drink at a party. I do not feel that it is one of the great and beautiful experiences of my life; I simply feel that it is pleasant."

Marijuana typically produces an experience free from anxiety, unusual in interesting ways, including intense sensations and emotions, and stimulating to the imagination. For these reasons it is no exaggeration to say that the experience is *very* pleasant. Since I believe that pleasure is intrinsically good, I conclude that

---

[12]An excellent, introductory book covering these and other health areas is Samuel H. Bartley et al., *Essentials of Life and Health,* 2nd ed. (New York: Random House, 1977).

the experience is good for its own sake. I do not conclude, however, that it is *very* good for its own sake. Why not? It seems to me that traditional hedonism has misinterpreted the nature of value experience because it has emphasized the role of feeling and ignored the element of significance in such experiences. If an experience feels good it is good (judged in itself and apart from its consequences), but the intensity of the feeling is no reliable measure of the degree of value. Most of the value or disvalue of our experiences comes from their significance or meaning. The experience of receiving an A on an exam feels good, but most of its value comes from the awareness that this grade is the product of past effort and one step toward passing the course, earning a degree, and pursuing a vocation. Only as one is aware of the place an experience has in the larger context of one's own life and the lives of others does the experience have any great value or disvalue. Because the experiences of smoking marijuana tend to be isolated from the mainstream of the user's life and to contribute very little to achieving personal goals or to advancing the welfare of others, these experiences, although very pleasant, are relatively meaningless. In my judgment, the experience of using marijuana usually has a genuine but very limited value.

From Carl Wellman, *Morals and Ethics* (Glenview, Ill.: Scott, Foresman, 1975), p. 73.

Carl P. Wellman (b. 1926) is professor of philosophy at Washington University (Missouri) where he has taught since 1968. Having received a Ph.D. degree from Harvard in 1954, he is also the author of The Language of Ethics *and* Challenge and Response: Justification in Ethics.

HEALTH, FINANCES, AND MORALITY

"If you've got your health, you've got everything" is an overstatement, but it points to the desire of most people to have a "sound mind in a sound body." Health fanatics appear to believe that devoted hygiene will prevent all diseases, aging, and death. Abusers of chemicals (including alcohol, nicotine, and tranquilizers), avoiders of sound nutrition, and violators of mental health principles appear to believe that their indifferent or casual hygiene will be inconsequential. Most men and women on both sides will lose because of their own choices. And, ascetics may be disinterested.

Help Needed to Change. Individuals with poor health habits, mental or physical, may need professional help to change to better hygiene. It is fairly easy to say "I want to accept myself" or "I want to stop smoking" for the sake of my health. Some people seem to be able to make such changes with comparative ease; for others, perhaps the majority, professional assistance is needed. A known physician, a hospital, a mental health agency are among the resources that can help a man or woman select the appropriate assistance. It is very risky to seek help from just anyone called a therapist, counselor, or consultant; these terms can be used by anyone with or without suitable training. It is also unwise to walk through the doors of just any clinic that promises weight loss or an end to smoking; a fancy building or a large newspaper ad does not guarantee medically sound personnel or safe procedures! Even the use of over-the-counter drugs or do-it-yourself mental health manuals to alter poor health habits are poor substitutes for professional guidance suited to an individual's personality, physical make-up, and lifestyle. To be sure, we often recognize the need for help; too often, though, we settle for inadequate help.

We propose a middle ground of optimum health that considers one's circumstances, and this degree of health can be achieved only by careful, thoughtful choices. Beyond the issues of personal and community responsibility raised in this chapter, the moral issues are many. We close this discussion with a quotation that raises additional, related questions.

> If public funds are used to pay for medical care, should those individuals whose lifestyles are not conducive to good health shoulder a higher share of the tax burden for medical care? It is widely believed today that one of the most important factors in remaining healthy is individual lifestyle. Heavy smoking, for example, is linked with cancer; heavy drinking, with cirrhosis of the liver; obesity and inadequate exercise, with cardiovascular and other diseases. In view of this, should smokers, alcohol consumers, and others indulgent in high risk-running behavior, pay additional taxes on products such as alcohol in order to provide money for additional care? If they were required to do so, then smokers, alcoholics, etc., as groups, and not the general public, would pay the extra burden for that medical care.[13]

A financial consideration of health issues may motivate the public to consider the ethics of mental and physical health, especially the matters of

---

[13]Thomas A. Mappes and Jane S. Zembaty, *Biomedical Ethics* (New York: McGraw-Hill, 1981), p. 520. More will be said about the moral implications of public funding of health care in our chapters on politics and economics.

choices and their consequences, the individual's obligation to the community, and the community's responsibilities to the individual.

CHAPTER REVIEW

A. Health as a moral obligation

1. Mental and physical health as a moral obligation will strike many persons as odd.
2. If an individual's health is "his own private business," health as a moral issue related to the community may sound peculiar and unconvincing.
3. This chapter explores mental and physical health as a matter of choice, not fate, and as a matter of moral obligation, not individualistic license or neutrality; for persons who feel their mental and physical health is a private matter and for ascetics, such an exploration will have little value.
4. Our discussion of "health" includes its physical and mental dimensions; we do not suggest that being "healthy" demands physical and mental perfection.
5. We propose that a healthy person is one who has the capacities to make decisions and to love mutually while coping well with some physical and/or mental flaws.
6. The point at which a condition disqualifies an individual from being regarded as healthy is subjective.

B. The importance of mental health

1. Mental health cannot be totally separated from physical health.
2. An individual's mental health is important both to the person and the community, so that the individual may participate fully with others on a mutual basis.
3. Mental illnesses caused by factors beyond an individual's control exempt the individual from moral responsibility for the condition.
4. Mental illnesses resulting from willful actions of an individual involve moral responsibility and accountability.
5. Mental health is an important obligation of the individual for his own well-being and for the community's well-being.

C. Some philosophical principles of mental health

1. Among the principles by which a person can grow in mental health are self-acceptance, adjustment, creativity, community, balance, and wisdom.

D. Sickness as protest

1. Diminished mental health results with sufficient violations of the suggested principles, except in cases in which illness has a physiological basis.
2. Except for the illnesses caused by factors beyond a person's control, individuals choose progress toward optimum mental health or continuing mental deterioration.
3. Cultural reinforcements of unhealthy principles engrained in society subject people to mental pollution.
4. Good mental health is a moral obligation of the individual and the community; optimum health can be encouraged by means of informed and responsible personal choices and consensus, public education, and supportive agencies.

E. Physical health

1. Physical health, as well as mental health, is an important obligation of the individual for his own well-being and for the community's well-being.
2. Much sickness and pain is unnecessary but exists because some men and women choose to ignore what they've been taught, and some others have never been taught good health practices.
3. Personal health issues include many topics readily discussed in current resources on health.
4. The issue of the use and abuse of chemicals can focus on whether the use of a particular chemical offers greater benefit or a greater degree of harm to a person.

F. Health, finances, and morality

1. We propose that an individual's optimum health depends on one's circumstances and that such optimum health can be achieved only by careful, thoughtful choices.
2. Related moral questions include whether persons whose choices may cause illness ought to assume greater financial burdens for their medical care.

SUGGESTED READINGS

Butler, Robert N., and Lewis, Myrna I. *Aging and Mental Health.* 2nd ed. St. Louis: Mosby, 1977.

> The nature and problems of old age *and* health issues of evaluation, treatment, and prevention are the two major parts of this comprehensive study; a

helpful glossary and directories to helping agencies and associations are included.

Johnson, G. Timothy, ed. *The Harvard Medical School Health Letter* (79 Garden St., Cambridge, Mass. 02138).

A monthly authoritative newsletter offered by subscription contains information for the general reader about human health and disease.

Johnson, G. Timothy, and Goldfinger, Stephen E. *The Harvard Medical School Health Letter Book.* Cambridge, Mass.: Harvard Univ. Press, 1981.

Staying healthy, hazards of living, reproduction and child care, diseases mainly of adulthood, some problems of aging, and you and the doctor are the main parts of this book which, like the *Letter* (see previous entry), contains latest findings of interest to the general public.

Mowrer, O. Hobart, ed. *Morality and Mental Health.* Chicago: Rand McNally, 1967.

A collection of seventy-five articles within six parts: popular appraisals and protests; psychiatry and moral issues; clergymen on 'the cure of souls'; psychology in a new key; social science, law, and philosophy; and, literature, biography, and art.

Reich, Warren T., ed. *Encyclopedia of Bioethics.* New York: Free Press, 1978.

Essays on smoking, alcoholism, drug addiction, mental illness, and Hinduism are among the many explorations of the moral dimensions of various issues and heritages. The epigram introducing this chapter is from a rare philosophic source considering health as a personal moral issue.

9

Medical Ethics

To be blind to moral dimensions of what human beings do to one another is as much of a handicap as to be visually blind or unable to have memories. But [the former] is a more insidious handicap since it is often not recognized as one. Those who are thus deprived stumble through the world of humans unaware that their perception is flawed—and do untold harm to those whose lives they affect. It is in this category that we must place those who insist that there are no ethical considerations in science or in medicine.*

MEDICINE AND HUMAN VALUES

Medical ethics is not new; the practice of medicine in primitive societies required moral judgments grounded in their respective values. The systematic study and teaching of medical ethics is only now emerging as a major interdisciplinary field. In the last half of the 1970s, suitable textbooks in medical ethics became available for classroom use, signaling a new curricular role. Public awareness surged in 1975 with the New Jersey Superior Court's decision concerning the maintenance or withdrawal of life-preserving treatments of a comatose patient, Karen Ann Quinlan. Six years earlier, however, the Institute of Society, Ethics and the Life Sciences (also known as "The Hastings Center") was founded by an interdisciplinary group of physicians, biologists, philosophers, theologians, lawyers, and social scientists. The Institute developed through a shared concern that advances in medicine, biology, and the behavioral sciences were confronting humanity with enormously difficult ethical dilemmas involving significant social, cultural, and legal implications. Organizers of the Institute believe that ethical and value questions are fundamental and are best pursued in an interdisciplinary fashion.

*Sissela Bok, "The Tools of Bioethics," in *Ethics in Medicine: Historical Perspectives and Contemporary Concerns,* eds. Stanley Joel Reiser et al. (Cambridge, Mass.: M.I.T. Press, 1977), p. 138.

A Subject of Irresolution

General principles of personhood and interpersonal love combined with an awareness of moving from fate to choice (see Chapter 1, pp. 6–7) and of concern for substance rather than mere form (see Chapter 7, pp. 147–148) undergird our moral convictions. The presuppositions or axioms expressed in those chapters continue in this chapter on medical ethics. However, additional principles and concepts are needed in medical ethics.

Our purposes in this chapter include: (1) stimulating the readers' moral imagination beyond the convictions taught to them as they were being raised; (2) developing in the reader a greater awareness of the value dimension of medical care; (3) eliciting an appropriate sense of personal responsibility for one's own role in medical decisions; and (4) heightening sensitivity to the inherent ambiguity and pluralism in these matters. We shall not offer neat resolutions or indisputable principles. Instead, we shall explore the irresolutions of some important philosophic concepts and principles in the spirit of "ground work" for further study.

Following the "can do/ought to do" issue that raises the moral aspect, we shall categorize medical ethics as an area within bioethics, note that medical ethics cannot be avoided, and introduce decision making and other issues of communication. The reality of pluralism will again come to the fore as we explore several philosophic issues and some moral dilemmas in medicine.

The "Can Do/Ought to Do" Issue. "Why did you climb that dangerous peak?" asks the curious bystander. "Because it was there!" replies the proud performer. And the public pays homage. One of the fundamental American values now being called into question is the rather strange notion that if something *can* be done it *ought* to be done. The rather silly books listing records of trivial achievements also exemplify this "virtue." The media faithfully covers marathons of any sort—even the riding of a roller coaster a record number of times. "What can be done ought to be done" is thereby further programmed into the population.

Applied to science, this axiom opens the door wide to any procedure, development, invention, or gadget. One consequence of this mentality has been the undisciplined "progress" that has resulted in untold ecological damage. (The ecological issue will be examined in Chapter 16.) Ethically concerned observers of nature, including some philosophers, have become quite vocal in attempts to draw the public's attention to the danger of doing whatever is possible.

Bioethics and Medical Ethics. "Bioethics" is the comprehensive classification of ethical considerations implied by some biological developments such as moral dilemmas about population growth and environmental quality. Medical or biomedical ethics is the area of bioethics that concentrates on moral questions raised in the practice of medicine; for example, a physician *can* sterilize a retarded teenager, but under what circumstances, if any, *ought* the physician do so? The boundaries of bioethics and medical ethics are not set with finality because they overlap, because of ongoing new developments in the various sciences with implications for bioethics, and because of medical advances. Bioethics as a field attempts to respond to whatever value issues or moral questions are created by new knowledge about humanity in relation to nature. Hence, bioethics remains open to results of human ingenuity and the sorting out of "can do/ought to do" problems.

A BIOETHICAL CREED FOR INDIVIDUALS

1. Belief: *I accept the need for prompt remedial action in a world beset with crises.*
   Commitment: I will work with others to improve the formulation of my beliefs, to evolve additional credos, and to unite in a worldwide movement that will make possible the survival and improved development of the human species in harmony with the natural environment.
2. Belief: *I accept the fact that the future survival and development of mankind, both culturally and biologically, is strongly conditioned by man's present activities and plans.*
   Commitment: I will try to live my own life and to influence the lives of others so as to promote the evolution of a better world for future generations of mankind, and I will try to avoid actions that would jeopardize their future.
3. Belief: *I accept the uniqueness of each individual and his instinctive need to contribute to the betterment of some larger unit of society in a way that is compatible with the long-range needs of society.*
   Commitment: I will try to listen to the reasoned viewpoint of others whether from a minority or a majority, and I will recognize the role of emotional commitment in producing effective action.
4. Belief: *I accept the inevitability of some human suffering that must result from the natural disorder in biological creatures and in the physical world, but I do not passively accept the suffering that results from man's inhumanity to man.*
   Commitment: I will try to face my own problems with dignity and courage, I will try to assist my fellow men when they are

afflicted, and I will work toward the goal of eliminating needless suffering among mankind as a whole.
5. Belief: *I accept the finality of death as a necessary part of life. I
affirm my veneration for life, my belief in the brotherhood of man,
and my belief that I have an obligation to future generations of man.*
Commitment: I will try to live in a way that will benefit the
lives of my fellow men now and in time to come and be
remembered favorably by those who survive me.

From Van Rensselaer Potter, *Bioethics: Bridge to the Future* (Englewood
Cliffs, N.J.: Prentice-Hall, 1971), p. 196.

---

*Van Rensselaer Potter (b. 1911) is professor of oncology and assistant
director of the McArdle Laboratory for Cancer Research in the Medical
School of the University of Wisconsin. Honored several times for his
research in cancer, he is also the author of* Nucleic Acid Outlines,
vol. 1, and editor of Methods in Medical Research, *vol. 1.*

Medical Ethics Cannot Be Avoided

It is probable that everyone reading this book has consulted a physician.
Many employers and schools require a minimal check-up at some time. You
may have had surgery, been treated for a "bug," delivered a baby, been
tested for glasses by an ophthalmologist, and so on. Occasional involvement with professional medical care has become commonplace in the
United States, except for the uninformed or reluctant poor.

Whether or not a person consults a physician reflects the person's values. Whether a check-up is required by an employer, school, or other
source; whether a person gets a check-up simply to be in good standing
with whoever requires the consultation; whether the person gets a complete examination because of an actual concern for the status of his or her
health—the reason doesn't matter. The choice to go to the doctor stems
from the individual's values and judgment: "I *ought* to go." Motivations
vary, but actually "to go" is a moral choice, an implementation of one's
values.

Decision Making.   Once a conference with a health care deliverer
(physician, nurse, physician's assistant, etc.) is in process, the ethical issues sharpen. The professional can diagnose, recommend, urge, prescribe,

describe alternatives, and offer forecasts, but unless patient incompetence is evident, the decision to take any particular action rests with the patient. The decision-making responsibility is well outlined here:

1. The primary decision-making responsibility rests with the patient, so long as he is competent.

2. When the patient is incompetent, the socially designated next of kin and other close relatives should be allowed to speak for the patient.

3. If the physician has reason to doubt whether the above individuals are representing the patient's best interests, he may choose other individuals to involve in the decision process, or, as a last resort, may make the decision himself; however he assumes the responsibility for demonstrating that his doubts were based on reasonable evidence.

4. Any of the above individuals, except the doctor, may opt out of the decision process by being unable to decide or by refusing to take responsibility. In such a case the doctor must seek the opinion of an alternative patient representative (such as a court order or a more distant relative) if there is time, or make the decision himself if there is not. The doctor cannot opt out of the process.

5. As a general rule, all the above individuals must act within the usual constraints imposed by society. Where these constraints have become so rigid as to constitute a conflict between society's best interests and the patient's best interests, the case must be decided individually by careful consideration of the consequences.[1]

The patient's decision is based on many values, whether formally considered or not. The physician's recommendations are also interwoven with the physician's own value system, articulated or not. In recommending or choosing a course of action based on medical evidence, physician and patient evaluate such matters as: (1) is living with chronic pain *preferable* to risky surgery? (2) is prolonged suffering *better than* death? (3) is it more *desirable* to relieve present suffering with addictive drugs or to endure pain to prevent the possibility of long-term addiction? (4) *should* valium or a mental health counselor be the treatment?

CHOICES ARE BASED ON VALUES

[E]very medical decision has a value component. The first skill needed by one who takes medical and biological ethics seriously is that of recognizing the evaluative dimensions of cases which otherwise appear to be mundane and value-free. In some medical decisions, to be sure, the value choices may seem utterly trivial. One must have a blood transfusion *if* he *wants* to live—

---

[1]Howard Brody, *Ethical Decisions in Medicine* 2nd ed. (Boston: Little, Brown, 1981), p. 111.

but the fact that some people, such as Jehovah's Witnesses, value other things more than continuing life in this world reveals that even when the values are so readily assumed, evaluations are still present. Many moral disputes in fact arise because the value alternatives are not recognized and spelled out. . . .

In virtually every medical situation, more than one plausible alternative exists: experimental surgery or standard treatment, salt-free diet or diuretic, psychopharmacological agent or psychotherapy, scientifically trained physician or folk healer. . . . If it is true that more than one plausible alternative exists at some point in the treatment of virtually every patient, then choices must be made based on some system of values.

From Robert M. Veatch, *Case Studies in Medical Ethics* (Cambridge, Mass.: Harvard Univ. Press, 1977), pp. 17, 19.

Robert M. Veatch (b. 1939) earned a Ph.D. degree in ethics at Harvard. Formerly senior associate at The Hastings Center, he is professor of medical ethics at the Kennedy Institute of Ethics, Georgetown University. His writings include Death, Dying, and the Biological Revolution *and several journal and encyclopedia articles.*

The practice of medicine cannot escape value issues. Health care deliverers and patients have moved from fate to choice among options and therefore are participants together in applied medical ethics. A sensitivity to some primary moral problems in medicine enables professionals and patients to make informed decisions. The days of "Do what you think is right, Doctor" are coming to an end as responsibilities for health care are shared significantly with the patient.

Related Issues of Communication. A patient's decision, reflecting values, is linked to the related issues of informed consent and truth-telling. If the patient is to make a sound decision, truth must be communicated effectively; then informed consent can be given by the patient as decisions are made. On further examination, many questions can be raised such as: When is consent informed consent; that is, how much information must be given to a patient before consent is fully informed? Which patients are competent to give consent? When is consent fully voluntary and not strongly influenced by overwhelming fear? Are doctors ever morally justified in lying to patients? The patient-physician relationship depends significantly on the various answers to these questions.

PHILOSOPHIC ISSUES

As we consider several basic philosophic issues related to medical ethics and then some moral dilemmas in medicine, we shall raise many pertinent questions. We shall offer no neat resolutions, because to do so would misrepresent the medical ethics field. You and your physician, and others involved in your health care, will have to reach your own thoughtful conclusions.

As one may expect, many vexing questions face medical ethicists. Although patients and professionals may avoid formal consideration of some of the questions, their assumed answers permeate their chosen moral directions. Let us give attention now to some of the philosophic questions that are linked to moral considerations in medicine.

What Is "Life"?   "It's great to be alive!" Perhaps so, but what is it that makes a person alive or "with life"? One answer claims that life exists when a "vital force" is present that distinguishes the entity from inorganic nature. The exact nature of this vital force, however, is elusive; no one seems to know the exact conditions for or ingredients of life throughout nature. Is the vital force different among human beings, parakeets, flowers, and bacteria? Is the vital force a biological essence, a spiritual quality, or a combination of both?

In what sense is it true to say that life is present in a "dead" tree? Is cellular activity in the "dead" tree such that the tree has life in some sense? If there are varying degrees of life present in several trees, what qualifies one tree as "alive" and another "dead"?

What is *human* "life"? Do we look for a biological, spiritual, or mental definition or a combination of the three? What are the implications for "life" if one believes in life after death?

When Does One Become a "Person"?   There is no consensus on the nature of "person;" discussions of this issue continue.[2] Yet this is a pivotal matter in decisions related to abortion, care of the profoundly retarded, the senile, and so on. One view is that an individual is a person from the moment of conception until death; the killing of an innocent person at any time between conception and death is murder.

Another view (the "developmental view") makes a distinction between

---

[2] See "The Concept of a Person in Ethical Theory," *The Monist* 62, no. 3 (July 1979) and Michael B. Green and Daniel Wikler, "Brain Death and Personal Identity," *Philosophy and Public Affairs*, vol. 9, no. 2 (Winter 1980).

human life and a *person*. Human life exists from the moment of conception, but a *zygote* (the fertilized entity not yet implanted at the uterine wall) is not a person. From about two weeks after fertilization until about the end of the eighth week (when brain waves can be detected), the entity is an *embryo,* not a complete person. The *fetal* stage lasts for about the final seven months. Developmentalists disagree as to when the fetus can be regarded as a person: At four months from fertilization when it noticeably moves? At seven months when it may survive on its own outside the mother's womb? At birth? The key to defining "person" among developmentalists is the developmental stage selected for personhood; this is a philosophic judgment.

Other views further qualify "person" among born individuals; not all born human individuals are persons. Proponents of these views have developed several criteria for personhood, such as:

the ability to reason

minimal intelligence

self-awareness (versus mere consciousness)

being an autonomous and free origin of activity (versus a robot-like automaton)

the presence of a soul

a capacity to communicate by any means

the capacity to make basic moral judgments

a sense of the passage of time and of the future

a capability of relating to others

Scholars differ as to which of these characteristics are essential to personhood and the precise meaning of each.

What Is the Value of Life?　Many viewpoints take it for granted that life has an intrinsic value. Theologically stated, "life is sacred"; life derives its value from the Creator. On further thought, the question becomes complex. Whether interpreted theologically or humanistically, are we to assume that *all* life is of equal value? Members of the Jain religion are vegetarians, strain their beverages, and sweep their paths as they walk, in order to protect bugs. Having ruled out the sacredness of vegetable life, they value more highly other living creatures. "Life is sacred" means something different to them than to humanists and religious communities that value *human* life most highly.

In the United States we don't eat dogs and cats; in India cows are not food. We eat turkeys and chickens, but not robins and canaries. Swordfish will be on a menu, but not goldfish or guppies. Ancient Romans regarded roses as a delicacy; we use them as ornaments. The President of the United States would receive excellent medical care in a hospital emergency room; would an unshaven recluse be valued such that he would receive the same quality care in the same emergency room? When it comes to the value of life, we discriminate; we choose the kinds of life that we believe have greatest value. We make these choices among species and within species. With what justification do we assign such contrasting values to the lives of different creatures?

What Is Meant by "The Right to Life"? The belief that life from conception has an intrinsic value or is sacred often exists in conjunction with a "right-to-life" position. In an attempt to get beyond a poster slogan, we can raise the following issues for clarification.

Who or what has a right to life? The bugs protected by the Jains? Cows, dogs and cats, turkeys and chickens, robins and canaries, swordfish, goldfish and guppies, roses, the President and/or the unshaven recluse? Is the right to life an inalienable right? If absolutely so, no exceptions can be made; every living creature must die naturally, without interventions that hasten death. As a result, we would have no meat, fish, poultry as food, or ornamental flowers. If the inalienable right is linked only to persons, we could not kill in self-defense, and the issue of capital punishment would be resolved.

Strictly speaking, few men and women support an absolutist right-to-life position for all human beings. Exceptions are made especially in some occasions of self-defense. However, once an exception is made, the absolute quality is lost. The question is transformed to "under what conditions does a person lose his right to life?" In other words, under what circumstances can one's right to life be waived?

Advocates of lethal self-defense believe that some unjust aggressors have waived their right to life; they may be killed by their victims as a last resort. Proponents of capital punishment believe that with the commission of certain crimes, an individual waives his right to life and may be put to death. Supporters of suicide hold that an individual may waive his own right to life in particular circumstances (e.g., deliberate martyrdom or unbearable terminal illness). By what criteria can the discrimination among creatures or among only human beings be justified with regard to the right to life?

What Is an Acceptable Quality of Life? "Goodbye To Our Good Life?" is the featured cover story of an issue of *U.S. News and World Report* (August 4, 1980, p. 45). The article reports "The great bulk of this country's people have managed to retain the trappings of a high standard of living: A decent home, good food and clothing, quality education and health care, access to jobs and promotions, and leisure opportunities." Are these "trappings" the standard by which one's quality of life is measured?

A few years ago a television documentary included an interview with a woman confined to an "iron lung" for about 20 years. She was happy, content, able to do many things by orally manipulating various controls and, in her view, had an acceptable quality of life.

Is quality of life measured by moral, biological, psychological and/or economic criteria? Are there levels of quality, and who decides?

When Is Death? Is it possible to pronounce a tree or a person dead only when all cellular life has ceased? If so, quite a period of time would have to elapse between usual reckonings of death and cutting down a tree or embalming a person. On the other hand, the removal of a wanted tree where there is hope of revitalization or the premature burial of a human being is undesirable! At which point is it safe to assume that a person is dead: At heart failure? One year in a coma? When there are no signs of brain activity for one hour, twenty-four hours, forty-eight hours, or _____? A combination of these conditions?

To What Extent Does Humanity Share with God and/or Nature the Responsibility to Begin, Shape, and End Lives? If you have taken an aspirin, cut your fingernails, worn glasses, or taken vitamins, you have intervened in nature. You did not leave it to God or nature to cure the headache, manicure your nails, correct your vision, or manage your vitamin intake. One could argue that wearing clothes, except for protection from environmental nuisances or dangers, is unnatural. The vast majority of civilized men and women accept the principle of intervention in nature; the issue is, to what extent? For therapy? For cosmetic reasons? For control of future human characteristics? As we shall learn later in this chapter, this is a crucial philosophic issue in medical ethics.

If a Practice or Procedure has the Possibility of Abuse, Ought It Be Forbidden? "Doing *this* might lead to *that!*" By itself this degree of caution would prevent any and all changes, developments, and progress. Risks are involved in most situations: a new religion in town *might* create aggressive bigots; allowing ice cream to be served publicly *could* be detrimental to the health of lax diabetics; removing tonsils surgically *may* eventually lead to the disintegration of family life because children forced to go to the hospital may resent their parents; studying philosophy involves questioning what has been taken for granted, which in turn *may* lead to conflicting viewpoints and nuclear war!

We are not suggesting that cautious consideration of possibilities be entirely set aside. We propose instead that the realistic beneficial and harmful probabilities of a practice or procedure be studied with care. We reject the notions that in all instances "A" *must* lead to "D" and that all ventures must be wholly risk free. These faulty notions would have precluded the discoveries of the beneficial uses of fire, the wheel, all surgical procedures, and even initiatives in the risky human relationships we value! Likewise, issues of intervention such as selecting the gender of a child, sterilization, cloning, and suicide can be explored thoughtfully.

Improbable fantasies of "one thing leading to another" as well as appeals to noninterference with "God's Will" in nature are neither convincing nor supportive; after all, left to itself, God's natural environment produces Siamese twins and sustains syphilis. Human medical intervention in these and other "natural" occurrences is usually welcome!

Can Distinctions Be Made Between...?

Killing and murder.

"Then David said to the Philistine (Goliath), 'You come to me with a sword and with a spear and with a javelin; but I come to you in the name of the Lord of hosts, the God of the armies of Israel, whom you have defiled. This day the Lord will deliver you into my hand, and I will strike you down, and cut off your head....; for the battle is the Lord's and he will give you into our hand.'" (I Samuel 17:45-47)

Is there a contradiction between the Lord's apparent approval of David killing Goliath and one of the Ten Commandments? The consensus of scholars is that no contradiction exists because the accurate translation of the Commandment is "You shall do no *murder*." In fact, "Biblical law distinguishes the following types of homicide: murder, accidental homicide, the goring ox, and justifiable homicide."[3] The ethical issue becomes: By what criteria can a distinction be made between murder (wrongful killing) and justifiable killing? In considerations of abortion, suicide, and inducing death, this issue is especially significant.

Medical aid and medical interference.   Surely, one may think, an innoculation against polio is medical aid for everyone. Proven routine assistance that helps prevent disease is routine and clearly beneficial. However, if one's religious convictions prohibit injections, an order to be immunized constitutes intolerable medical interference, a violation of personal rights and liberties.

Another more extreme example is the elderly woman who refused to give permission for the amputation of a leg, although without the surgery she would die. A court declared her incompetent (because of her refusal of relatively safe surgery and her willingness to die), and her leg was amputated. Is this medical aid or is it interference? By what standards can aid be distinguished from interference?

Extraordinary and ordinary means.

Ordinary means of preserving life are all medicines, treatments, and operations which offer a reasonable hope of benefit for the patient and which can be obtained and used without excessive expense, pain, or other inconvenience.... In contradistinction to ordinary are *extraordinary* means of preserving life. By this we mean all medicines,

---

[3]J. Greenberg, "Crimes and Punishment," *The Interpreter's Dictionary of the Bible,* vol. A–D, p. 738.

treatments, and operations which cannot be obtained or used without excessive expense, pain, or other inconvenience, or which, if used, would not offer a reasonable hope of benefit.[4]

This attempt by Roman Catholic theologians at clarification of extraordinary and ordinary means makes it clear that *vitalism,* the prolonging of life no matter what, is not a moral principle of the Roman Catholic Church. We are not aware of any religious or humanistic group in which vitalism is an axiom. However, the "Sacred Congregation" admits to the difficulty, which all persons face, in definitively distinguishing between ordinary and extraordinary means.

> In the past, moralists replied that one is never obligated to use "extraordinary" means. This reply, which as a principle still holds good, is perhaps less clear today by reason of the imprecision of the term and rapid progress made in the treatment of sickness.[5]

The 1980 Declaration proceeds to offer guidelines for making the distinctions; but this effort, in our judgment, does not remove the ambiguities and uncertainties.

The subtle difference between medical aid and interference and extraordinary and ordinary means is that the former issue focuses on whether the intervention itself is *personally valued* as helpful, whereas the latter concentrates on the *professional complexity* of the intervention. For example, a blood transfusion will be regarded as *interference* by a Jehovah's witness and as *ordinary means* by a physician. Or, you may regard your request for $1,000,000 experimental surgery and care that may prolong your life for one year as medical *aid*; those receiving your request may view it as *extraordinary*. The subjective nature of these terms are imprecise and debatable.

Philosophic Pluralism. Philosophic pluralism emerges in its most perplexing and critical forms in medical ethics. The issues discussed in Chapter 2 that led us to philosophic pluralism are important and significant; but the ambiguity surrounding moral dilemmas in medicine are *acute.* A hospital emergency room has an urgency about it that a classroom discussion of freewill versus determinism lacks.

Before we venture into some issues of medical practice, we might reflect for a moment on what we are doing. We are not providing obviously true solutions; we have no method by which the Final Truth on these matters can be established. *We can, however, introduce competing insights and hope to learn to tolerate ambiguity even in acute situations.*

Let us consider only a sampling of medical concerns and their respective

---

[4]Gerald Kelly, S.J., *Medico-Moral Problems* (St. Louis: Catholic Hospital Assoc., 1958), p. 129.
[5]"Declaration On Euthanasia" issued by the Vatican's Sacred Congregation for the Doctrine of Faith, May 5, 1980.

moral dilemmas. Within the scope of this chapter we can develop a modest awareness of the complexity of some moral issues of reproduction, living, dying, and death.

SOME MORAL DILEMMAS IN MEDICINE

Family Planning

An unwanted child, for whatever reasons, begins life with a disadvantage. With varying rationales, contemporary philosophers and theologians agree that planning the number and approximate intervals of children is to the advantage of all concerned. Sharp disagreements arise over the methods of family planning.

Contraception.   One view of preventing conception holds that all devices (such as condom or pill) are immoral intrusions into nature, hence "unnatural." Men and women have no right to intervene in the natural process with devices or chemicals. (See Chapter 4 on Thomistic natural law ethics.) Instead, a careful observation of the laws of nature can assist with scheduling intercourse such that conception occurs only as desired; in fertile periods, disciplined abstinence is the natural method of family planning.

A contrasting view values intervention by medically approved devices and chemicals. More accurate, such approaches encourage greater spontaneity between partners and fewer surprise pregnancies. This position views reliable contraceptive devices and chemicals as natural, equating such assistance with the use of eye glasses and aspirin.

Involuntary Sterilization.   It is rare that pleas to clothe and feed the poor are coupled with equally strong petitions for effective family planning among deprived people. Even more rarely will a politician or religious spokesperson hint at required sterilization of individuals or groups whose prolific child-bearing aggravates their chronic poverty. The right to have as many children as one wants is in the public's mind an unchallenged axiom that is contrary to notions of involuntary sterilization. In recent years in the United States, an informal belief has arisen that fewer children in a family benefits the family and society in general. However, the federal income tax structure continues to reward taxpayers who have several dependents with increasing tax deductions; no one has seriously proposed a greater tax on parents producing more than a certain number of offspring. To intervene in someone's life through involuntary sterilization or taxing parents for exceeding a recommended number of children presupposes a moral right for authorities to do so; those opposed to such interventions call instead for the treatment of social conditions through acts of justice, not through acts viewed as being *against* the poor and ignorant. The right to reproduce without restrictions remains supported and intact.

A different view rejects the belief that every man and woman has the inalienable right to reproduce. This view points out that the law already restricts marriage between close relatives or individuals with certain diseases—a nonsurgical form of involuntary sterilization. Because babies are more tolerated now among unmarried persons, such required "involuntary nonsurgical sterilization" could be extended further; subcultures that promote child-bearing for larger welfare checks could be subjected to such sterilization. Forced family planning has come of age for the ignorant, irresponsible, chronically pregnant, retarded, and mentally ill; this view does not question anyone's right to appropriate sexual intimacy, only to unrestricted conception. The alleged right to reproduce without restriction is challenged by this position.

New Methods of Conception. The fertilization of a human egg has, until recent years, been accomplished by means of sexual intercourse. And that's the way it should always be, according to one side of the argument. Humanity has no right to intervene in this natural process of conjugal love; interventions are dehumanizing.

In vitro fertilization. The other side of the debate views human intervention as compassionate assistance to prospective parents who have medical problems preventing conception. On July 25, 1978, Louise Brown was born at Oldham General Hospital in England; her parents had tried for nine years to have a child. British physicians were able to extract an unfertilized egg from her mother's body, place it in a laboratory dish (*in vitro* means "in glass"), fertilize it with her father's sperm, and insert the fertilized egg into her mother's womb for nine month's development.

Objections to the process include not only the charge of a dehumanizing and unnatural intervention, but also murder. In the process, several unsuccessful attempts may result in the discarding of fertilized eggs; if all conceived human life are persons, then it follows that innocent persons have been discarded.

Because *in vitro* fertilization makes possible the current use of donor sperm, donor eggs, substitute females for the period of pregnancy, and perhaps some day a full-term pregnancy in an artificial womb, objections multiply with charges of adultery and disintegration of family life. Frozen sperm, frozen fertilized eggs, and unmarried individuals who want to raise children add further possibilities and occasions of moral resistance.

Artificial insemination. The use of a syringe to deposit semen in the vagina is also supported and objected to along the same lines of argument: those *for* the process see it as medical assistance and one more therapeutic intervention; those against it summon the arguments of unnaturalness and of abuses that defy what God and/or nature intended.

Abortion

Groups favoring abortion do not endorse abortion as just one more method of contraception. Regardless of how early in a pregnancy an abortion takes place, it is medically more risky than the use of contraceptive devices and chemicals. Repeated abortions increase the medical risk to a woman.

Most individuals supporting abortion to some extent or wholeheartedly do not view the human life present during some or all of the nine month's pregnancy as a person. The removal of such human life from a woman's body is similar to the removal of tonsils or the appendix—both also human life but not persons. Supporters have varying views on the stage at which the individual human life becomes an *actual* person. They may agree that each fertilized and unfertilized egg is a *potential* person, but not a complete person with a right to life. They point out that the body itself discards eggs on a regular basis. Unfertilized eggs degenerate, and miscarriages account for abortions of fertilized eggs. As noted in a widely used text:

> Spontaneous abortions, also called miscarriages, occur at a much higher rate than many people realize. It has been estimated that about 33 percent of all fertilized eggs abort before the next menstrual period is overdue. In these cases most women never realize that they are—or were—pregnant. An additional 25 percent of all pregnancies miscarry between the time of fertilization and labor, meaning that almost 60% of all pregnancies end before a viable birth occurs. These abortions and miscarriages occur, of course, without any human intervention.[6]

The body itself aborts human life on a regular basis. According to advocates of abortion, human intervention inducing abortions (like many other medical interventions) supplements what nature is already doing: the discarding of human life, not the murder of persons. Some other defenders of abortion focus on claims of the woman's rights over her own body; the rights of citizens to their individual choices about abortion; the benefits of having wanted, planned-for children; and the value of licensed physicians performing abortions legally and safely. A philosopher has proposed other considerations in the issue of abortion.

> The following factors should then be weighed by the mother before she can be confident that abortion is the right way out of her dilemma, and one she will not come to regret or view with guilt:

> whether or not the pregnancy was voluntarily undertaken.

> the importance and validity of the *reasons* for wanting the abortion.

> the technique to be used in the abortion; the extent to which it can be regarded as "cessation of bodily life support," rather than as outright killing.

[6]James Leslie McCary, *McCary's Human Sexuality*, 3rd ed. (New York: Van Nostrand, 1978), p. 205.

the time of pregnancy.

whether or not the father agrees to the abortion.

whether or not all other alternatives have been considered, such as adoption.

her religious views.

And the father, if he weighs these factors differently, may feel the grief and responsibility differently too and wish to take over the care of the baby after birth.

Abortion is a last resort, and must remain so. It is much more problematic than contraception, yet it is sometimes the only way out of a great dilemma. Neither individual parents nor society should look at abortion as a policy to be encouraged at the expense of contraception, sterilization, and adoption. At the same time, there are a number of circumstances in which it can justifiably be undertaken, for which public and private facilities must be provided in such a way as to make no distinction between rich and poor.[7]

Opponents, who frequently label themselves as "pro-life," view the fertilized egg not only as human life but also as a person or potential person with the right to life from conception to natural death. Abortion by human intervention is unnatural, the killing of the innocent, and therefore murder. They raise a concern for the devaluation of all human life, such that killing elderly people, the mentally ill, and so on could be legally sanctioned along with abortion. Life throughout the continuum from fertilization to death is equally sacred; abortion is immoral.

The choices on abortion before society as seen by one medical ethicist are summed up as follows:

Only if we can decide where we stand on these issues can we decide where we stand on the morality of terminating pregnancies. In practical policy terms, there are four positions to choose among, and our choice will depend on what we decide about the status and quality of the fetus. (1) We can condemn abortion altogether or, at most, justify it to save the pregnant woman's life. (2) We can favor a limited permissiveness to prevent ill health, to prevent defective babies, or to prevent the product of rape or incest. This is a policy of compulsory pregnancy but with escape clauses. (3) We can approve of abortion for any reasons prior to the ability to survive outside the womb—possibly on the grounds of social needs or some question of justice, although these grounds are not so apparent as they were when we lacked enough labor power and needed lots of soldiers. (4) We can oppose any and all forms of compulsory pregnancy, making the ending of pregnancies, like their beginning, a private or personal matter.[8]

[7]Sissela Bok, "Ethical Problems of Abortion," *Hastings Center Studies,* vol. 2, no. 1 (January 1974); available as Reprint #122 of "Readings" from The Hastings Center.
[8]Joseph Fletcher, *Humanhood: Essays in Biomedical Ethics* (Buffalo, N. Y.: Prometheus, 1979), p. 138.

Shaping Persons

A fairly good rate of success has already been achieved at preselecting the sex of a child. Sperm that create males can be separated quite reliably from those that spark female life; the chosen specimen is then artificially inseminated, and nine months later, the patient has a very good chance of giving birth to a baby of the chosen sex. Not only can a married couple utilize this opportunity, but donor sperm could be used in conjunction with sex selection.

In 1980 a "sperm bank" came to public notice. Using sperm from Nobel-prize winning scientists from the "bank," several women of high intelligence reported their resulting pregnancies. Advocates view this intervention in shaping lives as improving the genetic stock of humanity by freezing gifted men's sperm for current and future insemination of bright women. Assuming that "brighter is better," which in turn can lead to social usefulness, sperm bank promotors see their efforts as humanitarian.

The new science of splicing genes, which control the development of individual cells, is another controversial area. The production of insulin, new foods, and possible cancer cures are among the potential benefits to mankind. However, at least in theory, the creation of new forms of persons (e.g., with very short legs for space exploration and habitation) will be possible in the distant future.

Technologies involving the developing zygote may someday include parthenogenesis (development to birth of unfertilized egg) of a person and cloning (development of many persons identical to a parent).

Shaping persons also comes under the general label "genetic engineering." Ethicists differ on the morality of various aspects of shaping persons with regard to the purposes of such efforts, the standards by which "desired characteristics" are measured, the value and quality of life of any resulting defective people, and whether such nontherapeutic interventions are moral at all!

Other Moral/Medical Issues of Living, Dying, and Death

Repeatedly we discover the same or similar essential philosophic questions being raised about the nature of life itself, the meaning of "person," the value of life, the right to life, quality of life, the extent of human intervention, whether *this* will lead to *that,* and the distinctions between killing and murder, aid and interference, and extraordinary and ordinary means. The conditions and morality of various forms of behavior control, confidentiality, truth-telling, organ transplants, and experimentation are additional issues not so much of reproduction but of medical treatment for the living and the dying.

Death itself raises questions of when death occurs and what it is: an annihilation of a person or a birth to a new plane of personal life? The rightfulness or wrongfulness of prolonging life of a dying person, of letting nature take its course with a terminal patient, and of inducing death by one's own hand (suicide) or with another's assistance (voluntarily or involuntarily) are dilemmas in daily newspapers, magazines, and on television documentaries and dramas. (See "When Doctors Play God: The Ethics of Life-and-Death Decisions," *Newsweek* cover story, August 31, 1981.)

BENEFITS OF MEDICAL ETHICS STUDY

"I have hated you since you introduced me to issues of medical ethics," was an overstatement by a nurse-colleague to a friend-philosopher. Preferring as little ambiguity as possible and trained for exactness, the world of health care deliverers welcomes the pluralistic insights of medical ethics with mixed emotions. The public at large may react in similar fashion.

But what are we to do? As professionals and layfolk we can stumble through our lives blind to the options, or we can become familiarized with the moral dimensions and major ethical positions of medical care in which we and those we love are or shall be involved. The benefits of understanding the inevitable pluralism include development of our own informed choices as well as respect for the thoughtful, informed choices of those with whom we differ. The framing of laws consistent with the Constitution on these matters will be a persistent challenge for decades to come. It is hoped that our lawmakers, courts, health care deliverers, patients, and moral spokespersons will come to a greater awareness of alternative views so that humanity can move from shallow slogans and responses to informed consciences and choices. We hope this glance at medical ethics will stimulate your interest in further study of these life issues so that you may develop principles and concepts for your use.

A TASK FOR PHILOSOPHERS: CLARITY ABOUT IMPORTANT QUESTIONS

I should like to say at once that if the moral philosopher *cannot* help with the problems of medical ethics, he ought to shut up shop. The problems of medical ethics are so typical of the moral problems that moral philosophy is supposed to be able to help with, that a failure here really would be a sign either of the uselessness of the discipline or of the incompetence of the particular practitioner. I do not want to overstate this point, however. It could be the case that, so far as practical help goes, philosophy is at the stage now at which, not so long ago, medicine was. It has been said that until fairly recently one was more likely to survive one's illnesses if one kept out of the hands

of the doctor than if one allowed oneself to be treated—and this
was at any rate true of the wounded on battlefields, because the
surgeons' instruments were not sterilized. Yet all the same
medicine *has* now progressed to a stage at which it saves lives.
The change came when certain *methods* got accepted: I mean, not
merely such things as aseptic surgery, but also the application to
medicine of the scientific method in general, which meant that
firm and reliable procedures were adopted for determining
whether a certain treatment worked or not; and also the relation
of medicine to fundamental knowledge about physiology and
biochemistry, which made possible the invention of new treatments to be tested in this way.

The same could be true of philosophy. There have been great
philosophers in the past, just as there were great doctors before
the advent of modern medicine; but it is only very recently in the
history of philosophy that general standards of rigour in argument have improved to such an extent that there is some hope of
our establishing our discipline on a firm basis. By "standards of
rigour," I mean such things as the insistence on knowing, and
being able to explain, exactly what you mean when you say
something, which involves being able to say what follows logically from it and what does not, what it is logically consistent
with, and so on. If this is not insisted on, arguments will get lost
in the sands. Even now it is insisted on only in certain parts of
the philosophical world; you are very likely to meet philosophers who do not accept this requirement of rigour, and
my advice to you is that you should regard them in the same
light as you would regard a medical man, whether or not he had
the right letters after his name, who claimed to have a wonder
drug which would cure the common cold, but was not ready to
submit it to controlled tests. It is undoubtedly true that many
patients will feel much better when they have taken his drug;
but since we simply do not know whether it is the drug that has
made them feel better, or his personal charisma, or natural
causes, he has not contributed to the advance of medicine.

I do not want to give the impression that nobody insisted on
rigour in argument until recently; indeed, it was the insistence
on knowing what you meant that really got philosophy started.
Socrates, Plato, and Aristotle, as well, probably, as some other
great men of their time whose works have not come down to us,
knew how philosophy ought to be done and made great pro-

gress in it; and there have been other periods in which philosophy in this rigorous sense has flourished; but they have always been succeeded by periods of decline in which a kind of superficial excitement was prized above rigour in argument, and so philosophy got lost. It is very important not to let this happen again. For the true philosopher the most exciting thing in the world—perhaps the only exciting thing—is to become really clear about some important question.

R. M. Hare, "Medical Ethics: Can the Moral Philosopher Help?" in Stuart F. Spicker and H. Tristram Engelhardt, Jr., eds., *Philosophical Medical Ethics: Its Nature and Significance* (Holland, D. Reidel, 1977), pp. 49-50.

R. M. Hare (b. 1919) is White's Professor of Moral Philosophy, Corpus Christi College, Oxford University (England). His many writings include The Language of Morals, Freedom and Reason, *and* Applications of Moral Philosophy.

CHAPTER REVIEW

A. Medicine and human values

1. The practice of medicine throughout history has required moral judgments grounded in values; within the past decade, medical ethics has been emerging as a major interdisciplinary field, as evidenced by increasing numbers of textbooks available for classroom use.
2. This chapter explores the irresolutions of some important philosophic concepts and principles in the spirit of "ground work" for further study.
3. A major issue raising the moral dimension of medical care is the "can do/ought to do" issue.
4. Bioethics is the comprehensive classification of ethical considerations implied by some biological developments; medical or biomedical ethics is an area of bioethics that concentrates on moral questions raised in the practice of medicine.
5. The implementation of one's values in judgments and decisions constitutes a moral choice; medical ethics in this sense cannot be avoided by readers of this book, in that each has or will choose to consult a physician at some time or other.

6. Decision making and related issues of communication have value components and are therefore additional issues.

B. Philosophic issues

1. As we consider several basic philosophic issues related to medical ethics, we shall offer no neat resolutions; readers will have to reach their own thoughtful conclusions.
2. The issues include: What is "life"? When does one become a "person"? What is the value of life? What is meant by "the right to life"? What is an acceptable quality of life? When is death? To what extent does humanity share with God and/or nature the responsibility to begin, shape, and end lives? If a practice or procedure has the possibility of abuse, ought it be forbidden? And, can distinctions be made between killing and murder and extraordinary and ordinary means?
3. Philosophic pluralism emerges in its most perplexing and critical forms in medical ethics; although we cannot offer final truths on these matters, we can be introduced to competing insights and, we hope, learn to tolerate ambiguity even in acute situations.

C. Some moral dilemmas in medicine

1. Family planning involves such moral issues as contraception, involuntary sterilization, and new methods of conception.
2. Abortion, shaping persons, and moral/medical issues of living, dying, and death are also vital matters.

D. Benefits of medical ethics study

1. As professionals and layfolk we can stumble through our lives blind to the options we have, or we can become familiarized with the moral dimensions and major ethical positions of medical care in which we and those we love are or shall be involved. We can choose for ourselves, and we may learn to agree to differ with others personally and legally.

SUGGESTED READINGS

Abrams, Natalie, ed. "Newsletter on Philosophy and Medicine."

A publication of the American Philosophical Association (University of Delaware, Newark, Delaware 1971); the eight-page newsletter, published several times a year, includes committee reports, essays, bibliographical information, and announcements of conferences and programs.

Duncan, A. S. et al., eds. *Dictionary of Medical Ethics*, New Revised Edition. New York: Crossroad, 1981.

> The second edition of a 459-page dictionary in which more than 70 percent of the contributors are physicians; British experience permeates the brief entries.

Durbin, Paul T., ed. *A Guide to The Culture of Science, Technology, and Medicine.* New York: Free Press, 1980.

> An in-depth survey of the literature of the history, philosophy, and sociology of science, technology, medicine, and the expanding field of bioethics. Section III "Bioethics" in Chapter 6 "Philosophy of Medicine" includes a bibliographic introduction to basic sources, reference sources, and journals and series; *a very important bibliographic source.* (The *Hastings Center Report* is one of the important periodicals listed.)

Fletcher, Joseph. *Humanhood: Essay in Biomedical Ethics.* Buffalo, N.Y.: Prometheus, 1979.

> The humanistic ethicist who pioneered the field with his *Morals and Medicine* and explored approaches to ethics in his often misunderstood *Situation Ethics* has gathered essays on a wide range of bioethical topics in a most readable manner.

Mappes, Thomas A., and Zembaty, Jane S., eds. *Biomedical Ethics.* New York: McGraw-Hill, 1981.

> One of the best of the many current college-level textbooks in the field; clear introductions to each topic, representative views by contemporary scholars (with an introductory synopsis of each selection), and excellent annotated bibliographies concluding each chapter provide the able student with a fine survey.

Reich, Warren T., ed. *Encyclopedia of Bioethics.* New York: Free Press, 1978.

> *THE* reference work in the field!

Ruddick, William, ed. *Philosophers In Medical Centers.* New York: Society for Philosophy and Public Affairs, 1980.

> The editor has assembled for the Bioethics Committee of The Society for Philosophy and Public Affairs (New York Chapter) an 82 page booklet of essays by philosophers working in and around two New York medical centers. (Copies are available at a nominal cost from the editor at The Department of Philosophy, New York University, N.Y., N.Y. 10012.)

Shannon, Thomas A., and DiGiacomo, James J. *An Introduction to Bioethics.* New York: Paulist, 1979.

> An excellent introduction to selected issues in the area of bioethics along with an overview of the basic medical and ethical dilemmas that have arisen in the field; useful to the citizen for private reading and in basic courses.

10

Sexual Ethics

In an attempt to build up a new sexual morality, the first question we have to ask ourselves is not, How should the relations between the sexes be regulated? but, Is it good that men, women and children should be kept in artificial ignorance of facts relating to sexual affairs? . . . Sexual morality, I should say, must be such as to commend itself to well-informed persons and not to depend upon ignorance for its appeal.*

THE "PROBLEM" OF SEX

It is curious that many, if not most, moral matters are referred to as issues, concerns, or questions; only the most troublesome are labeled "problems." In the minds of generations of people, sexual matters frequently fall within the "problem" category. Until recent years, informed conversations and questions about human sexuality have been hushed at best, and no doubt a large portion of the citizenry wishes that the near silence still prevailed! Even newspapers reported modestly that so-and-so was arrested on a "morals charge." The public knew what *that* meant; no bank robbery here! Some public media remain modest in this regard.

The uneasiness about sexual issues stems in part from a sense of privacy which holds that some concerns about life are not for public airing or display. A sense of shame has also accompanied much reflection on sex; as an illustration, read an influential 5th century theologian's words.

Of the shame which attends all sexual intercourse, Lust requires for its consummation darkness and secrecy; and this not only when unlawful intercourse is desired, but even such fornication as the earthly city has legalized. . . . What! does not even conjugal intercourse, sanctioned as it is by law for the propagation of children, legitimate

---

*Bertrand Russell, *Marriage and Morals* (1929; rpt. New York: Liveright, 1970), p. 93.

and honourable though it be, does it not seek retirement from every eye?... This right action seeks the light, in so far as it seeks to be known, but yet dreads being seen. And why so, if not because that which is by nature fitting and decent is so done as to be accompanied with a shame-begetting penalty of sin?[1]

Augustine was convinced that marital procreation was moral, but the accompanying lust or desires that activate the sexual organs is part of humanity's sinful nature. Successors to Augustine's thought and the various philosophies that shaped his thinking are legion in Western civilization; their legacy has promoted a sense of shame surrounding human sexuality.

CELEBRATING SEXUALITY

THE BRIDE
My Beloved is fresh and ruddy,
to be known among ten thousand.
His head is golden, purest gold,
his locks are palm fronds
and black as the raven.
His eyes are doves
at a pool of water,
bathed in milk,
at rest on a pool.
His cheeks are beds of spices,
banks sweetly scented.
His lips are lilies,
distilling pure myrrh.
His hands are golden, rounded,
set with jewels of Tarshish.
His belly a block of ivory
covered with sapphires.
His legs are alabaster columns
set in sockets of pure gold.
His appearance is that of Lebanon,
unrivaled as the cedars.
His conversation is sweetness itself,
he is altogether lovable.

[1]St. Augustine, *City of God,* trans. Marcus Dods (New York: Modern Library, 1950), book XIV, sec. 18, pp. 466–467.

> Such is my Beloved, such is my friend,
> O daughters of Jerusalem.
>
> From the Fourth Poem in The Song of Songs 5:10–16, The Old Testament.
> The bride's poem is appropriately sensuous, uncharacteristic of later
> Victorian ladies!

Add the individual's need for being considered "normal" to possible senses of privacy and shame and sex becomes anything but a dispassionate subject. One viewpoint combining all three feelings (privacy, shame, and insistent normality) is exemplified by Archie Bunker's sexual sophistication: in his view, sex is not to be discussed, sheepish modesty accompanies intimacies, and nobody is more normal than he! For persons unaffected by extremes of privacy and shame associated with sex, normality is a sufficient concern preventing a neutral reflection on sexuality. An insistence on viewing one's own sexuality as the standard for all humanity may invoke all the obstacles to clear thinking: tradition, common sense, propaganda, authoritarianism, generalization, universalization, *ad hominem* arguments, prejudice, and impatience. (See Chapter 2 and consider how these obstacles cloud much thinking about sexual issues.) Another reason sex is a "problem" is the conviction of many persons that sexual morality has become too permissive; the "problem" is reflected in moral chaos.

THE FUNDAMENTAL QUESTION IN SEXUAL ETHICS

Your answer to "What is the primary purpose of human sexuality?" determines to a large extent your conclusions about sexual normality, naturalness, and morality. Whatever is consistent with your understanding of sexuality's basic purpose will be judged normal, natural, and moral; whatever is inconsistent will be interpreted as abnormal, unnatural and immoral. Four primary purposes represent the contrasting views.

Four Representative Views

Procreation.   The position that having babies is the primary purpose of sexual relations is harmonious with Augustine and other medieval scholars' attitudes toward sex. According to this singular objective, only those acts leading to possible conception are normal, natural, and good. Stimulating events leading to a culmination in sexual intercourse may be justified; however, sperm deposited anywhere but vaginally is abnormal, unnatural, and immoral. The typical expression of the procreative view in Western civilization includes these eight assumptions:

(1) seminal discharge defines the essence of sexual intercourse; (2) the only moral function of sexual intercourse is procreation (hence, the emission of semen in any way that in itself prevents procreation is unnatural and immoral); (3) procreation naturally completes itself in the generation of an adult; (4) those who engage in sexual intercourse should provide whatever is necessary to rear any creature they procreate; (5) an unadulterous monogamous marriage is the vest environment for rearing offspring to become adults; (6) females are inferior to males; (7) the male acts as the female's governor in marriage; (8) divorce is improper. . . .[2]

Variations within the procreative view are possible. The removal of assumptions five through eight would allow for an unmarried couple living together to direct their intimacies only to procreation. As doubtful as this may seem in actual practice, it is a theoretical possibility as a variation on the procreative view more customarily limited to marriage.

Procreation and Unitive Affection.   A different view combines procreation with "making love" as the primary purpose of human sexuality. Love that unites the man and woman in mutual self-giving is added to procreation to form the integral purpose of sexual acts. Those acts that are not within the context of both unitive affection *and* procreative possibilities are abnormal, unnatural, and immoral.

Western religious views normally require that expressions of love and procreative intent be within a monogamous marriage. However, other interpretations of this norm could justify polygamous and nonmarital contexts. As long as conception and unitive affection constitute the inseparable components of the purpose of sex, various forms of marital and nonmarital applications of the norm are logically conceivable. For example, a commune of unmarried, sexually expressive men and women could utilize this norm as could the more traditional Jewish and Christian communities requiring monogamous marriage.

SEX FOR PROCREATION AND UNITIVE AFFECTION

Now in fact the Church throughout her history has always considered a certain number of precepts of the natural law as having an absolute and immutable value, and in their transgression she has seen a contradiction of the teaching and spirit of the Gospel.

Since sexual ethics concern certain fundamental values of human and Christian life, this general teaching equally applies

---

[2]Robert Baker and Frederick Elliston, *Philosophy and Sex* (Buffalo, N.Y.: Prometheus, 1975), p. 3.

to sexual ethics. In this domain there exist principles and norms which the Church has always transmitted as part of her teaching, however much the opinions and morals of the world may have been opposed to them. These principles and norms in no way owe their origin to a certain type of culture, but rather to knowledge of the divine law and of human nature. They therefore cannot be considered as having become out of date or doubtful under the pretext that a new cultural situation has arisen. . . . the use of the sexual function has its true meaning and moral rectitude only in true marriage. . . . according to the objective moral order, homosexual relations are acts which lack an essential and indispensable finality. . . . homosexual acts are intrinsically disordered and can in no case be approved. . . . masturbation is an intrinsically and seriously disordered act. The main reason is that, whatever the motive for acting in this way, the deliberate use of the sexual faculty outside of normal conjugal relations essentially contradicts the finality of the faculty. For it lacks the sexual relationship called for by the moral order, namely the relationship which realizes the full sense of mutual self-giving and human procreation in the context of true love.

Sacred Congregation for the Doctrine of the Faith, *Declaration on Certain Questions Concerning Sexual Ethics* (Washington, D.C.: U.S. Catholic Conference Publications Office, issued Dec. 29, 1975); pp. 5–10.

Unitive Affection.   Mutual self-giving in interpersonal love is a third primary purpose of human sexuality. "Making love" is the purpose; "having babies" (planned or at random) can occur between men and women but is not integral to the interpersonal union.

This purpose also has contrasting interpretations. One view would limit sexually expressed unitive affection to husband and wife. Other views may accommodate one or more of the following sexual alliances: an unmarried man and an unmarried woman, persons of the opposite sex living communally, persons of the opposite and/or same sex living communally, two individuals of the same sex, husband and wives in a polygamous marriage, and so on. As long as ingredients of interpersonal love are intended and basically present in the relationship, sexual expression is normal, natural, and moral.

Pleasure.   A fourth representative primary purpose of human sexuality is pleasure. Neither reproduction nor interpersonal love is the basic goal;

an individual's own concept of pleasure, physical and/or emotional, is sought.

As with the other three primary purposes already represented, variations on this theme are possible, also. An individual may seek pleasure with a total disregard for the "object" or "objects" with whom the sexual encounter is taking place. Or the encounter may include mutual pleasure whereby both or all participants are clearly personal "subjects," not mere objects; but any sense of intentional or actual interpersonal love is not an integral consideration. However one is "turned on," pleasure is normal, natural, and good.

Variations

The four representative primary purposes surveyed do not exhaust the human imagination. They illustrate four familiar basic purposes and their implications for judgments of sexual normality, naturalness, and goodness. Variations on these four might conceivably include integrated, subordinate purposes in many combinations. For example, the purpose of pleasure may or may not include personal mutuality as a secondary feature, as was mentioned in the previous paragraph. Or any of the four representative purposes may or may not include the strengthening of the marital bond as a secondary purpose. It is no wonder that the lay public as well as scholars cannot reach a clear consensus on what is normal, natural, and moral in human sexuality; several philosophies of human sexuality compete with evangelical fervor for our loyalties.

SEX RESEARCH: A HELP TO ETHICS?

The current biological and psychological research into human sexuality is impressive.[3] From a purely descriptive point of view, information about human sexuality is enlightening. For example, it has been found that brains may differ in women and men; the extent to which any differences affect behavior is uncertain. Chemical differences have been found when some heterosexual persons are compared with some homosexual men and

---

[3]See the articles under the general theme "Sex Research: Where Are We Now?" in *The Humanist* (March/April 1978) and those in the category "Sex Therapy and Sex Research" in the *Encyclopedia of Bioethics*. Also useful are the following books: Eleanor Emmons Maccoby and Carol Nagy Jacklin, *The Psychology of Sex Differences* (Stanford, Calif.: Stanford Univ. Press, 1975); Robert May, *Sex and Fantasy: Patterns of Male and Female Development* (New York: Norton, 1980); John Money and Anke A. Ehrhardt, *Man and Woman/Boy and Girl* (Baltimore: Johns Hopkins, 1972); Martin S. Weinberg, ed., *Sex Research: Studies from the Kinsey Institute* (New York: Oxford Univ. Press, 1976).

women and also with transsexuals; whether the differences cause or accompany the particular sexual orientation or condition is unknown.

The sexual preference or orientation spectrum ranges from persons exclusively heterosexual to men and women exclusively homosexual; the large category of "bisexual" or "ambisexual" falls between the extremes. Persons are categorized on the spectrum whether or not they have actually had genital relations with anyone; the inclination classifies a person (e.g., as heterosexual) whether or not the individual has had physical contact.

Reports claiming to be descriptive about sexual conditions and practices (ranging from incest to necrophilia, child molestation to adult rape, sadomasochism to celibacy, anal intercourse to cuddling, prostitution to fidelity, virginity to transsexualism, transvestism to nudity, and other topics) add to the data bank of existing varieties in human sexuality. However, normative ethics does not simply affirm the status quo. Instead, moral judgments are made on the basis of what *ought to be.* A claim that "I was born that way" or "I've been conditioned to behave in such-and-such a way" as justification for a particular sexual expression does not satisfy the ethicist. Perhaps you *are* that way, for whatever reasons, but perhaps you *ought* to change! Siamese twins are born requiring surgery; some babies need transfusions at birth; and abnormal and unnatural sexual conditions and behaviors ought, whenever possible, to be corrected.

The dilemma presents a dilemma in itself, valuing some behaviors as normal/natural/good and others as abnormal/unnatural/bad. No one seriously claims that the majority of anything is always automatically normal, natural, and good; a worldwide consensus on any issue simply describes what *is* among beliefs and practices, not necessarily what is good. And so we return to philosophy *not* for the undoubtable Answer, but for the wisdom to understand that any approval or sanctioning of a sexual condition or practice depends heavily on one's answer to "What is the primary purpose of human sexuality?" Disapprovals (including labeling a condition or practice as abnormal/unnatural/bad) and taboos occur when someone or something is inconsistent with a particular answer about sexuality's purpose.

Sex research supplies many data, interpreted in various ways, about the diversity of sexual expression among human beings. Because of their empirical methods, however, descriptive sciences cannot tell us how human sexuality *ought* to be expressed.

HOLY WRITINGS: A HELP TO ETHICS?

"The Bible says..." is sometimes intended to settle once and for all whatever issue is addressed. The same intention may be in the speaker's mind who says "The Holy Koran says..." or "The Holy Scriptures of Hinduism/Buddhism/Confucianism/ and so on tell us..." To each community of faith, its own writings are inspired, revealed, and/or enlightened. The ethicist is confronted with many claims of "moral truth" by the various world religions (as well as by secular philosophies); most of the faithful appeal to their own holy writings as a major source of objective moral standards. A comparison among them results in contrasting emphases and incompatible conflicts as to the primary purpose of human sexuality.[4]

Within a particular religion there may be significant variations on several important matters: What do the scriptural words mean as intended by the author? Was the author writing for a specific event or historical period, or was he communicating a message literally applicable to all people forever? Are the words in the quotation below binding today on those persons who regard them as scriptural? What did the author intend by this passage?

> If a man has a stubborn and rebellious son who will not listen to the voice of his father or the voice of his mother, and even when they punish him still will not pay attention to them, his father and mother shall take hold of him and bring him out to the elders of the town at the gate of that place. And they shall say to the elders of his town, "This son of ours is stubborn and rebellious and will not listen to us; he is a wastrel and a drunkard." Then all his fellow citizens shall stone him to death. You must banish this evil from your midst." (Deuteronomy 21:18–21)

Or this passage:

> Slaves, be obedient to the men who are called your masters in this world, with deep respect and sincere loyalty, as you are obedient to Christ . . . (Ephesians 6:5)

Or this:

> Similarly, I direct that women are to wear suitable clothes and to be dressed quietly and modestly, without braided hair or gold and jewelry or expensive clothes; their adornment is to do the sort of good works that are proper for women who profess to be religious. During instruction, a woman should be quiet and respectful. I am not giving permission for a woman to teach or to tell a man what to do. A woman ought not to speak, because Adam was formed first and Eve afterward, and it was not Adam who was led astray but the woman who was led astray and fell into sin. Nevertheless, she will be saved by childbearing, provided she lives a modest life and is constant in faith and love and holiness. (I Timothy 2:9–15)

It is possible to interpret these writings literally as binding on all persons living at the time they were written and for the indefinite future. It is also

[4]See Geoffrey Parrinder, *Sex in the World's Religions* (New York: Oxford Univ. Press, 1980); Cherry Lindholm and Charles Lindholm, "Life Behind the Veil: Sexual Codes in the Moslem World," *Science Digest* (Special ed., Summer 1980), pp. 42–47, 106–107.

possible to discover contrasting views on many matters, including human sexuality, in the Bible. In these instances, which passage prevails? A controversial study by a Roman Catholic theological commission includes the following summary of its chapter on "The Bible and Human Sexuality":

> The foregoing survey, schematic as it is, demonstrates clearly that the Bible does not provide us with a simple yes or no code of sexual ethics. No single text or collection of texts constitutes anything like a coherent biblical theology of human sexuality. Scripture is not even concerned with sexuality as such, regarding it instead as one aspect of life, properly viewed only within the context of the whole person and the whole of human life with all its relationships and responsibilities.
>
> The Old Testament contains such a plurality of customs, laws, and insights related to sexuality, that no single voice can be said to prevail. Throughout the Old Testament, however, one can clearly perceive the influence of taboos regarding cultic purity and of the patriarchal form of marriage and society. While monogamy seemed to be held up as an ideal state (Gen 2:24), polygamy and, for the male, even concubinage were tolerated. Only adultery with the wife or betrothed of a fellow Israelite was consistently condemned, and this in such a way as to make clear that the reason for the condemnation is to be found not in the nature of human sexuality but in the familial and societal responsibilities owed to members of the same community. The Old Testament view of women ranged from regarding them as chattel (Exodus) or objects of disdain (Sirach) to the affirmation of their personhood (Deuteronomy). Women function in the biblical narratives in a variety of ways from leaders, prophets, and judges to mere sex objects. Recognized as good in itself, sexual activity was condemned when even remotely associated with the fertility rituals of Israel's heathen neighbors. Yet marriage and erotic imagery were often used (Hosea, Canticle of Canticles) to describe the sacred covenantal union between God and Israel.
>
> As in the Old Testament, every statement in the New Testament regarding human sexuality is historically occasioned and conditioned. Jesus did not proclaim any new sexual ethic as such. Of indirect but profound significance for any Christian ethics of sexuality, however, are Jesus' teaching on the essential equality of men and women, his prohibition of divorce affirming fidelity within marriage for both sexes, and the primacy he gave to the law of love; in short, his personalism. Jesus' affirmation of human dignity led him to resist legalistic casuistry and to insist on the "weightier matters" of the Law, namely, its spirit and intent. Jesus humanized the Law in the sense that, for him, it was precisely our joy, our holiness as wholeness, human welfare and well-being, that constituted the will of God.
>
> Jesus' affirmation of human dignity and his attitude toward law resounded in St. Paul, particularly in his championing of Christian equality (Gal 3) and freedom (Gal 4). In opposition to exaggerated asceticism, St. Paul affirmed the goodness and lawfulness of sex (1 Cor 7) but unhesitatingly expressed his personal preference for celi-

bacy in light of the return of Christ in glory, which Paul regarded as imminent. St. Paul's eschatology, the depraved moral climate of his day, and the influence of Stoic philosophy on his thought must all be kept in mind for the correct interpretation of his references to marriage and sex related matters.

Employing the historical critical method of interpretation, contemporary biblical scholarship makes it clear that we cannot validly abstract statements regarding sexuality out of their biblical context and use them as proof texts to validate any twentieth-century theology of human sexuality. It is not that Scripture has failed to answer current problems and questions regarding premarital sexual intercourse, masturbation, birth control, and the like. Our questions simply were not asked by the biblical authors; hence, answers to these questions should not be expected from them.

Looking at the plurality of the statements and attitudes on human sexuality in the Bible, the inconsistencies among them, and the historical circumstances that gave rise to them, critical biblical scholarship finds it impossible on the basis of the empirical data to approve or reject categorically any particular sexual act outside of its contextual circumstances and intention. In view of the weight of contrary historical evidence, anyone who maintains that the Bible absolutely forbids certain forms of sexual behavior, regardless of circumstances, must likewise bear the burden of proof.

This is not to say, however, that the Bible leaves us without ideals or any guidance whatever. Scripture provides us with certain fundamental themes as a basis on which to construct a modern theology of human sexuality. Despite changing historical circumstances and perspectives, the biblical authors consistently give common witness to the nature of God as gracious and loving, and to the ideal of fidelity as a foremost expression of our loving response. While the Bible does not provide absolute dictates about specific sexual practices, it declares that sexual intercourse is good, always to be seen, however, within the larger context of personhood and community.[5]

Because this contemporary study as a whole offers conclusions supporting a "unitive affection" purpose of human sexuality, it represents a shift from the modern Roman Catholic "procreation and unitive affection" stance. "Official" theology has not shifted and has disavowed the Commission's findings. This example of one religious community's diverse philosophy of human sexuality serves to illustrate well the scholarly pluralism within one conservative religious tradition; the Bible itself has not settled once and for all the issues of human sexuality, even for all Roman Catholics. On a global basis we can discover other communities of faith using their holy writings with similar divergencies. The ethicist will discover applications and var-

---

[5]Anthony Kosnik, et al., *Human Sexuality: New Directions in American Catholic Thought*. A Study Commissioned by The Catholic Theological Society of America. (New York: Paulist, 1977), pp. 29-32.

iations of the four primary purposes of sex among holy writings but neither unanimity nor an obviously superior presentation of one particular viewpoint.

PLURALISM AGAIN[6]

"Between consenting adults" and "do no harm" are minimal moral standards undergirding most legal and ethical systems. Because four primary purposes of human sexuality (and their variations) are plausible among reasonable people, American social law today is reluctant to enforce one of them as the norm for all citizens. To promote a particular view as the only outlook is to support one faith or philosophy among others, thereby denying a latitude of informed belief intended by American law. Not all local communities are convinced of the legitimacy of such pluralism and its implications, nor have all states and the Congress enacted laws that embody the pluralism we have suggested. If pluralistic sexual philosophies are ever recognized by law, they will no doubt incorporate such moral norms as "between consenting adults" and "do no harm." Pluralism does not foster chaotic license wherein one citizen may impose on another; consent and a freedom from harm are essential for civilized expressions of diverse sexual philosophies.

"Abnormal," "unnatural," and "immoral" as value judgments will acquire meanings according to the particular view of the primary (and secondary) purpose(s) of human sexuality. A particular behavior or act forced on another person or a medically harmful act will be likewise labeled. Such value judgments find justification within the frame of reference of a particular philosophy of human sexuality.

HOMOSEXUALITY: A PERVERSION?

It is not clear whether homosexuality is a perversion, but it seems unlikely. For such a classification would have to depend on the possibility of extracting from the system a distinction between male and female sexuality; and much that has been said so far applies equally to men and women. Moreover, it would have to be maintained that there was a natural tie between the type of sexuality and the sex of the body and that two sexualities of the same type could not interact properly.

Certainly there is much support for an aggressive-passive distinction between male and female sexuality. In our culture

---

[6]See the discussion of philosophic pluralism in Chapter 2.

the male's arousal tends to initiate the perceptual exchange; he usually makes the sexual approach, largely controls the course of the act, and of course penetrates whereas the woman receives. When two men or two women engage in intercourse they cannot both adhere to these sexual roles. The question is how essential the roles are to an adequate sexual relation. One relevant observation is that a good deal of deviation from these roles occurs in heterosexual intercourse. Women can be sexually aggressive and men passive, and temporary reversals of role are not uncommon in heterosexual exchanges of reasonable length. If such conditions are set aside, it may be urged that there is something irreducibly perverted in attraction to a body anatomically like one's own. But alarming as some people in our culture may find such attraction, it remains psychologically unilluminating to class it as perverted. Certainly if homosexuality is a perversion, it is so in a very different sense from that in which shoe fetishism is a perversion, for some version of the full range of interpersonal perceptions seems perfectly possible between two persons of the same sex.

From Thomas G. Nagel, "Sexual Perversion," *Journal of Philosophy* 66, no. 1 (Jan. 16, 1969).

Educated at Cornell, Oxford (England), and Harvard, Dr. Nagel is professor of philosophy at Princeton University. He is the author of The Possibility of Altruism *and associate editor of* The Journal of Philosophy and Public Affairs.

SAME-SEX ORIENTATIONS: VARIATION OR PERVERSION?

Popular and scholarly articles and books on human sexuality are available in a new explosion of interest and research. Never before has so much information been gathered and published, and the traditional "marriage and the family" is no longer the only suitable subject for discussion. In 1975 (Sept. 8) the cover of *Time* magazine jolted some sensibilities with its picture of a uniformed member of the armed services captioned "I Am A Homosexual." In March of the same year a psychologist had boldly proposed "Homosexuals May Be Healthier Than Straights" as his essay's title in *Psychology Today*. To conclude the year, the Episcopal Bishop of New York ordained a professed homosexual woman as a deacon (and early in 1977 as a priest)! The topic, which had been among the most hushed yet joked about aspects of life, became a living ethical issue among the military, psychologists, clergy, and the public at large.

Although it is among the most controversial "problems" in sexual ethics, we have chosen same-sex orientations as a "case study" for several reasons: (1) it is a living ethical issue; (2) much new information is available about homosexualities; and (3) it can serve well as an example of an ethical examination of an emotionally explosive sexual issue.

We shall proceed by reflecting on some obstacles to clear thinking about same-sex orientations, by reporting some information about this human experience, and by reflecting on some ethical implications.

Obstacles to Clear Thinking

Masculinity–Femininity. In Chapter 5 we discussed the masculine and feminine masks that many men and women wear as components of their identities. We should not underestimate the importance of "masculine" appearances and behaviors, as culturally defined, to the American male, who defines his maleness by his "manliness."

The public has confused masculinity/femininity, manliness/femaleness with being male or female. Actually, one's genitals have little to do with a man or woman's masculinity or femininity! According to cultural traditions, certain attributes labeled "masculine" are linked with males and others labeled "feminine" are linked with females. We reinforce our sense of maleness with masculine characteristics and our sense of femaleness with feminine characteristics. These traditional assignments are so precious to us that we often become outraged at males who appear at all "feminine" and, at best, unamused at females who appear too "masculine." On reflection, we may realize that our hostilities are aimed at any apparent role reversals, such as an expressive male gracefully dancing the ballet or a hard-faced female lifting weights.

Homosexual men range from very "masculine" to "feminine" *as do heterosexual men*; homosexual and heterosexual women range from very "feminine" to "masculine." We are as likely to be annoyed at an effeminate heterosexual male as an effeminate homosexual male; we are as likely to be perturbed by a butch heterosexual female as a butch homosexual female. Our animosity exists regardless of who we think their sexual partners may be! "Fag" is shouted at a male's feminine behavior and appearance even if the name-caller knows the male is sexually active with women. The mistaken association of an individual's sex or sexual orientation with a person's degree of masculinity or femininity is an obstacle to clear thinking; if we can admit to our impatience or anger about alleged "misplaced" masculinity or femininity, we can consider more clearly *the separate issue of sexual orientation*.

Aesthetics.   A husband and wife may enjoy many sexual acts, yet one or both of them may find certain other physical expressions disgusting. One's aesthetic response to sexual expressions is highly individualistic and personal, a matter of taste for the most part. Nibbling gently on an ear may be highly erotic to you, yet revolting to someone else. Yet you would resent it if someone labeled you "sick" because you were stimulated by such contact. We propose that an individual's condemnation of any act solely on the grounds that it is personally repugnant is an obstacle to clear thinking; one's own aesthetic response is not the norm for humanity. Sexual expressions between persons of the same sex may be aesthetically pleasing to one individual and revolting to another; therefore, neither person can morally condemn the acts by other than his own response.

Intimacy.   Some individuals fear that emotional and sensual intimacy and genital sex are synonymous; they need not be. It is very possible for an adult to deeply love another adult or a younger person of the opposite or same sex without that love being expressed genitally. Buddying, hugging, walking arm-in-arm, even (literally) sleeping together can be beautiful expressions of such intimate mutual affection. If one does not understand that such same-sex intimacies as well as opposite-sex intimacies are healthy, one could panic at one's own inner emotions or another's displayed feelings of love; to assume that all persons of the same sex showing emotional and/or sensual *intimacy* are leading one inevitably to genital relations is utterly foolish. The fear that genital contact is the goal of all same-sex affections can prevent some deep relationships of love; such fears can result in a blanket condemnation of in-depth same-sex friendships and a misplaced disapproval of homosexual men and women. In other words, mistaking healthy feelings of love toward friends of the same sex for fears of genital eroticism can evoke confusions; homosexual men and women can become scapegoats for those who are unable to distinguish between intimacy and genital sexuality. Clear thinking is prevented if one fails to make such a distinction.

Other Obstacles.   In addition to masculinity/femininity traditions and personal aesthetics clouding a fair consideration of same-sex intimacy, other obstacles are employed by self-appointed moral guardians. One 1977 crusader against homosexuality effectively combined several obstacles and myths to convince much of the public of homosexuality's alleged menace to the country. This particular moral guardian, totally sincere and committed, proclaimed that innocent children needed protection from recruiting homosexual predators; holy writings were quoted, *ad hominem* attacks were utilized, and so-called 'traditional American religious and family values' were invoked. Sincerity, an alarming need to protect the innocent, quoted Scripture, character assassination, and appeals to nation, family, and religion are (especially in combination) powerful obstacles to clear thinking; a man or woman who has a public forum can produce mindless responses when these techniques are employed and misinformation is aired.

Building on good intentions, fears, ignorance, traditions, and falsehoods, anyone as wise as a serpent can victimize a large portion of humanity for virtually any cause. When the object of the crusade is homosexuality, such idols of the mind persuade a public ready to vent its rage on an "enemy," real or imagined. We may read newspaper accounts such as "Hunting Gays in Central Park," (in New York City's *The Village Voice*, July 24, 1978), in which these shocking words report:

> A gay man claimed he saw the gang clubbing away at another man and shouted, "Why are you beating him?" "Because he's a fag," was the answer. "Just like you." The inquirer didn't linger for a further response. Dialogue was sparse throughout the rampage. Each attack was guerilla-like—swift and without warning. Quick clubbings, then onward to the next target.

One can only speculate about the personal phobic insecurities of individuals who hunt and club unarmed human beings admittedly different in some respects from themselves. Why such hate? Whatever the reasons, homosexual persons have not only been hunted in New York's Central Park but also by Hitler as objects of extermination along with Jews, anti-Nazi intellectuals, Poles, Russians, and Gypsies. The Holocaust, known primarily for its brutal destruction of several million innocent Jews, was also responsible for the annihilation of hundreds of thousands of innocent homosexual individuals.[7]

Information About Same-Sex Orientations

Definition Problems. If someone were to proclaim "I am heterosexual," we would know little about the individual. We may wonder (1) what that label means to the person, (2) whether (s)he is well-adjusted psychologically, (3) if (s)he is celibate or sexually active, (4) whether (s)he has one or more partners inside and/or outside of marriage, (5) what the individual's philosophy of sex is, and so on. We may suspect that at the very least the person is trying to communicate that (s)he is attracted eroti-

[7]See Edward McNall Burns et al., *Western Civilizations*, 9th ed. (New York: Norton, 1980), pp. 862 and 890; Ira Glasser, "The Yellow Star and the Pink Triangle," *New York Times*, Sept. 10, 1975, p. 45; John J. McNeill, S.J., "Homosexuality and Violence," in *The Church and the Homosexual* (Kansas City: Sneed Andrews and McMeel, 1976), pp. 138–141; Heinz Heger, *The Men with Pink Triangle* (Boston: Alyson, 1980).

cally to some members of the opposite sex. We assume that this individual is capable of various important levels of relationships with members of the same sex but that other significant emotional and genital expressions are oriented toward the opposite sex.

If someone were to proclaim "I am homosexual," we would know as little about the individual. The meaning of the label, the individual's psychological adjustment, possible celibacy or activity, partner(s), commitments, philosophy of sex, and so on are unknown on the basis of so little information. We may suspect that at the very least (s)he is trying to communicate that (s)he is attracted erotically to some members of the same sex. We assume that this individual is capable of various important levels of relationships with members of the opposite sex but that other significant emotional and genital expressions are oriented toward the same sex. The recent study *Homosexualities: A Study of Diversity Among Men and Women* suggests that just as differences exist among heterosexual people, one cannot accurately stereotype homosexual men and women.[8]

Bisexuality. We might become very uncomfortable if someone were to disclose "I am bisexual." Men and women who feel oriented toward both sexes defy the neat classifications "heterosexual" and "homosexual." Stereotyping is less possible among these people, and a bisexual (or "ambisexual") revelation may confuse us all the more!

One set of professional definitions may be helpful:

bisexuality: originally a concept of Freud's indicating the belief that components of both sexes could be found in each individual. Today the term is often used to refer to persons who are capable of achieving orgasm with a partner of either sex.

homosexuality: sexual orientation toward persons of the same sex. Not a psychiatric disorder as such.

sexual orientation disturbance: an official diagnostic category for individuals whose sexual interests are directed primarily toward persons of the same sex and who are either disturbed by, in conflict with, or wish to change their sexual orientation. To be distinguished from homosexuality and lesbianism.

lesbian: homosexual woman.

lesbianism: homosexual activity between women.[9]

WHAT ONE HOMOSEXUAL WOMAN WANTS

The only difficulty in being lesbian is the fact of falling perhaps
for a woman and not knowing whether she is also gay. This can

---

[8]See Alan P. Bell and Martin S. Weinberg, *Homosexualities: A Study of Diversity Among Men and Women* (New York: Simon and Schuster, 1978).

[9]Shervert H. Frazier et al., *A Psychiatric Glossary*, 4th ed. (Washington, D.C.: American Psychiatric Assoc., 1975), pp. 27, 62, 140, 96, and 97.

be tricky and not always turn out satisfactorily. Heterosexuals do not have this trouble. Man meets woman and vice versa, and there is nothing to bar their way if they wish to have an affair. However, when woman meets woman there is an interim period of uncertainty, unless of course one meets with an [homosexual] organisation like Kenric.

I would like to settle down with a woman eventually, someone about the same age as myself with whom I am able to share my life and its interests, becoming part of and sharing hers. . . . I don't like one-night stands—they can be cheap and often one can be hurt. Relationships in the homosexual world should have a time for courting as heterosexuals do. Maybe I am old-fashioned in having this view, but it's the way I see things.

From an anonymous interview in Charlotte Wolff, M.D., *Love Between Women* (New York: Harper, 1971), pp. 264–265.

With these minimal definitions we can communicate in only the most general terms; little is known about men and women to whom these categories apply unless they are individually self-disclosing or are observed at close hand.

Incidence.   Among lower animals (such as some birds, apes, and porpoises) homosexual behavior has been observed. In many civilizations past and present and among all classes of society, homosexual behavior has been recorded. The exact number of homosexual or bisexual men and women at any given historical moment is subject to enormous debate and can obscure the ethicist's task. As we have suggested before, what *is* (whether abundantly or scarcely) does not tell us what ought to be.

Causes.   Several theories as to the causes of sexual orientations have been advanced: heredity theories propose that sexual orientation is inborn; environmental theories assert sexual orientations are conditioned; and hormonal theories suggest that one's hormone balance fixes a person's sexual orientation. No contemporary researcher suggests that an individual simply chooses at random a location on the heterosexual-bisexual-homosexual continuum. Researchers in the field of human sexuality clearly do not know for sure which cause(s) bring about any man's or woman's sexual orientation, including any one of the same-sex orientations. (The plural is used here because different degrees of same-sex orientations appear to exist among homosexual and bisexual men and women).

Genital Activities. The aesthetic range of physical pleasures is as wide and varied among homosexual persons as among heterosexual people. An act is heterosexual when performed between individuals of the opposite sex and homosexual when performed between individuals of the same sex. There is no such thing as a "homosexual act," only human acts classified according to the participants' sexes. The only impossible act for same-sex participants is vaginal intercourse possibly leading to procreation, which requires male and female partners.

Life Styles. Homosexual men and women are in all walks of life, as are bisexual and heterosexual persons. The bisexual or homosexual ten-year veteran running back (for the San Francisco Forty-Niners, the Detroit Lions, the Washington Redskins, the New Orleans Saints, and the Green Bay Packers) David Kopay wrote:

> People are always asking me now about the "three quarterbacks" in professional football who are supposed to be homosexual. First of all, I would never have limited the number to just three. The *Washington Star* said that, not I. I don't know if there are three or thirty. Stiles once told me about making it with several other players, and more than one has come up to me recently and confided, "I'm just a big closet case myself—but right now I can't deal with it."[10]

Same-sex inclinations, whether bisexual or homosexual, can be found among athletes (which confounds men dependent on "masculinity" for a sense of manliness), housewives, physicians, soldiers, and so on. No life style is exempt; the diversity is enormous.

One life style, that of unpublicized same-sex couples, experiences some unique restrictions not affecting opposite-sex couples. Two male or two female "lovers" ("lovers" in this context implies a commitment paralleling a marital bond) cannot readily attend family gatherings as an accepted covenanted couple, be invited as a family to weddings or other social events, be observed too often together at the movies or a concert, worship together on a regular basis, refer to themselves as a "couple" or as "we," show strong emotional support in public in times of crisis (family deaths, hospitalization of one partner, and so on), claim legal rights to the partner's estate, visit or make an emergency decision as "next of kin," travel on a family plan, insure a second automobile on a single policy, frequently use each other's cars publicly, publicly share significant birthdays or anniversaries, often go shopping together, obtain a home mortgage together from many banks, greet each other or say goodbye near a visible door or window, receive emotional support from the community when a partner is ill or dies, invite many others (such as co-workers) to a shared home, live

[10]David Kopay and Perry Deane Young, *The David Kopay Story* (New York: Arbor, 1977), p. 148.

together visibly in one apartment or house, or readily find a good counselor in the "Yellow Pages" if their relationship needs some support or sorting out. To imagine the social prohibitions on a same-sex couple, heterosexual couples might try to live publicly as a "proper" brother and sister or as a celibate priest in the company of a celibate nun!

A CHRISTIAN BISHOP'S THOUGHTS ON SEX

I believe sexuality to be a mysterious gift by which we are led to love one another. It also is a gift by which men and women are made different and through the exercise of which new persons are brought into the world. Sexuality, the psychologists teach us, invades all our affective lives, all our desires and emotions of love. Its power, some believe, is the same power from which our longings for God Himself come forth. Tradition uses the love song of the Song of Solomon as a paradigm for Christ's love for the Church.

I personally feel that the day may come soon when a responsible homosexual relationship will be seen as not contrary to God's will. However, at this point in time, an official statement or action to that effect would be premature and inappropriate.

Since all of us are still far from understanding the mysteries of personality and theology, it is most important that every part of the Church continue to study, to talk and to pray that we find God's will.

Paul Moore, Jr., *Take A Bishop Like Me* (New York: Harper, 1979), p. 184.

The Right Reverend Paul Moore, Jr. (b. 1919) has been Bishop of the Episcopal Diocese of New York since 1972. Educated at Yale and the General Theological Seminary in New York, Bishop Moore is a trustee of Yale and also author of The Church Reclaims the City.

Cures. If one's philosophy of human sexuality includes procreation integral to the primary purpose of sex, it follows that nonprocreative sexual expressions are abnormal, unnatural, and immoral; within this perspective, same-sex genital expressions are in themselves symptoms of a deviant, immature, or sick personality. Celibacy or a cure of the perversion would therefore be appropriate. However, changes in actual orientation lack clear documentation. Persons diagnosed as having a sexual orientation disturbance might achieve apparent success in establishing significant heterosexual relationships. This route offers hope to men and women who have been emotionally hurt by unrewarding same-sex relationships, who cannot tolerate society's attitudes toward their orientation, who are plagued with self-contempt rooted in their own incompatible philosophies of human sexuality, and/or who have been psychologically damaged by some pressures associated with their sexual orientation. Successful heterosexual adjustments are most likely to occur among men and women who are to some degree bisexual; their orientation is not necessarily changed, but their same-sex inclinations can be sublimated.

The "unitive affection" or "pleasure" philosophies of human sexuality can accommodate homosexuality as a normal, natural, and moral variation within the spectrum of human sexual behavior. Interpersonal love is the standard for the unitive affection position; pleasure itself for the pleasure philosophy. If as secondary purposes to either philosophy heterosexuality is injected as a "taken for granted" view, homosexuality would not be a variation, but a perversion.

We must recognize, however, that those *philosophies that embrace homosexuality as a variation do not thereby sanction all expressions of same-sex relations.* Likewise, those philosophies that propose only heterosexuality as normal do not sanction every conceivable expression of opposite-sex relations. Heterosexual or homosexual incest, sadomasochism, promiscuity, rape, and so on are not given a Goodhousekeeping Seal of Approval just because the basic orientation is acceptable! What one does with one's heterosexual or homosexual inclinations is a moral matter, and pathologies can be found in either. Within philosophies accepting of same-sex relationships, cures can be sought for those expressions (e.g., injurious sadism) diagnosed as "sick."

Proclaiming One's Same-Sex Orientation

From our study of identity (Chapter 5) we learned that people tend to view themselves and others according to something they do, some label which announces that they do certain things. Some labels seem to imprison individuals in their own eyes and/or in the view of others. Accepting one's identity as a homosexual is as shallow as accepting one's identity as a heterosexual; neither has much depth. Both can accentuate one's sexuality as a preoccupying focus engulfing whatever persons and places reinforce that identity. Accepting one's identity as a unique person or a unique child of God, whose sexual orientation is such-and-such, is another matter; in this view one's genital urges do not determine exclusively one's relationships and life events. Accepting one's sexual orientation, unless it conflicts with one's philosophy, is one thing; elevating it as one's ultimate concern is quite another! To inflict on family, friends, and the public a misunderstood and perhaps repelling same-sex orientation may in most cases include the consequences of being identified from that time on not as a unique person or child of God, but as a homosexual (the most positive label) or as a fag, dyke, queer, and/or pervert. As one sociologist noted:

> To "come out" and accept any identity is not freedom but a renunciation of freedom. The ultimate freedom of a human being is to become what he chooses and wishes to become, restrained only by forces that are genuinely beyond his control. There is no alcoholic, heterosexual, or homosexual identity. There are only people who behave in a given manner, at various times of their lives, in some cases over an entire lifetime. The behavior is real, but the identity is an invention. It is an invention believed in so thoroughly by some people that they have become what they were improperly tagged as being.[11]

To come out of the closet and publicly accept a deviant label is self-limiting, not freedom-giving, in the long run. Regretfully, in our culture we are what we "do," what stands out about us most in the public (or our own) mind. Honesty with one's self and selected others is different from proclaiming insensitively and indiscriminately a self-defeating, superficial label. Some men and women believe that for their own mental health and integrity, they must provide such information; all the consequences of such disclosures cannot be expected to be positive and fulfilling to anyone at this time in history.

Ethics and the Homosexual Person

Those philosophies that take for granted procreation or only heterosexuality as integral to any acceptable purpose of human sexuality would exclude same-sex expressions. Homosexuality does not logically fit within such purposes and therefore would be judged immoral or at best "sick." However, within those philosophies not insisting on procreation or heterosexuality, same-sex relations may be approved by a variety of logically compatible moral standards such as interpersonal love or pleasure among "objects."

---

[11]Edward Sagarin, "The High Personal Cost of Wearing A Label," *Psychology Today*, 9 (March 1976), pp. 25–27. See also Lorenzo Middleton and Anne C. Roark, "Campus Homosexuals: Out of the Closet but Not Out of Trouble," *The Chronicle of Higher Education* XXII, 21 (July 13, 1981), pp. 3–4; "How The Military Hunts For Homosexuals" in *Civil Liberties*, no. 338 (June 1981), p. 6.

A SECULAR HUMANISTIC MORAL PRINCIPLE

Sexual morality should come from a sense of caring and respect for others; it cannot be legislated. Laws can and do protect the young from exploitation and people of any age from abuse. Beyond that, forms of sexual expression should not be a matter of legal regulation. Mature individuals should be able to choose their partners and the kinds of sexual expression suited to them. Certain forms of sexual expression are limiting and confining, for example, prostitution, sado-masochism, or fetishism. However, any changes in such patterns, if they are made, should come through education and counseling, not by legal prohibition. Our overriding objective should be to help individuals live balanced and self-actualized lives. The punishing and ostracizing of those who voluntarily engage in socially disapproved forms of sexual conduct only exacerbate the problem. Sexual morality should be viewed as an inseparable part of general morality, not as a special set of rules. Sexual values and sex acts, like other human values and acts, should be evaluated by whether they frustrate or enhance human fulfillment.

From "A New Bill of Sexual Rights and Responsibilities," *The Humanist* 36, no. 1 (January/February 1976, p. 5).

This bill of sexual rights was signed by several humanists as listed with the entire document in The Humanist.

GUIDES TO MORAL SEXUAL CONDUCT

Theologian W. Norman Pittenger has provided a summary of ethical standards for heterosexual and homosexual men and women. From a Christian theological view affirming the basic goodness of sex, he offers food for thought within the "unitive affection" philosophy of human sexuality; those who view the unitive affection philosophy other than in a theological context may discover a usefulness for Pittenger's reflections (just delete the theology!).

1. Whatever one does, in terms of sexual manifestation, is to be an expression of love, rather than an effort to satisfy the merely animal

lusts. Yet we must not forget that those "animal" desires are part of the total human structure, in themselves good, but needing right control lest they get "out of hand."

2. In all sexual activity, coercion and pressure can have no place, for they are a denial of love. This rules out seduction of the unwilling and any form of "rape."

3. Cruelty, whether subtle or vicious, is the denial of love and cannot be permitted. Sadism and masochism are the extreme cases of such cruelty, inflicted either upon others or inflicted (or desired) on oneself: in whatever form these show themselves, they are inhuman.

4. Nobody should be urged into kinds of sexual activity that are offensive to him or seem wrong in his own eyes. Whatever sexual practices are adopted, they must be pleasing to both parties involved.

5. In any and every sexual activity, those who engage in it must accept the responsibility for whatever it entails, whether this is the emotional state of the other person, a child who may result from that contact, or anything else. We cannot contract out of this responsibility without showing ourselves callous, indifferent, hence inhuman and unloving. To attempt to contract out is to deny our responsible manhood and to cut off the possibility of growth.

6. For most people, most of the time, in most places, the usual way of finding sexual satisfaction will be through a commitment in married life. That commitment will arise from love one for the other; the sexual activity, in the physical sense, will then be an expression and a strengthening of the love they share. There will be some (in actual figures, a considerable number) whose only way of sexual expression is homosexual, with another person of their own sex. In their case, the aim should be at establishing a relationship with another that will be as permanent as possible, marked by the same qualities of commitment, mutuality, giving-and-receiving, union, and tenderness, as will be found in the heterosexual relationship.

7. When a man or a woman "sins," sexually speaking, by actions which deny his faithfulness, mutuality, commitment, tenderness, etc., he may be restored to the path of proper and healthy growth. Ultimately, this forgiveness is from the divine Lover whom we call God; that Lover accepts the "sinner" in the confident hope that through the influence of divine grace (i.e., the empowering possible to those who open themselves to, and ask for, continuing love) something good may be won, in spite of what has been wrong in the past. Proximately, forgiveness is through acceptance in love by other human beings, who surround the "sinner" with their concern and provide opportunities for him to make a fresh start.

8. In sexual life, as everywhere else in man's existence, he is part of society. Hence any decisions he makes, any good that he achieves, any failures that he makes too, affect others and seriously influence the social life. Thus one must ever be mindful of the wide-range consequences of actions for which one decides.

9. In any and every yearning really to love, really to be open to another's love, God is present and God is at work. This tells us that

no human being should be *afraid* to love or *fearful* of accepting love. At the same time, since God as Love seeks always the right growth of his human children, their proper movement toward fulfillment, their genuine "making" of personality in social intercourse, this also tells us that we need to be alert to his "guiding." The "guidance" of God is not dictation nor verbal direction; it is found when a man keeps his eyes open, uses his head, and thus sees opportunities for good opening before him. One of those opportunities is given when he meets another with whom he can share life. Yet the sharing of life itself demands that one shall be loyal, controlled, ready to sacrifice for the other—even to sacrifice what may appear attractive possibilities of sexual contact with a third person. And it is right there that love demands more even than control: it demands difficult decisions of a negative sort, precisely in order that the earlier positive decision for the loved one may be maintained.[12]

Each philosophy has its own spokespersons and moral rules or guides. Pittenger is but one example of one particular philosophy. A challenge for decades to come will be the clarification of our capacity to accommodate reasonable philosophic pluralism in our laws so that justice[13] is accorded to men and women whose informed faiths differ about sex; perhaps someday, sex will be less of a "problem" and more of an issue about which we can agree to differ.

INTEGRATING SEX AND LIFE

The basic problem of sex today is what it always has been—to integrate it properly into the whole of life. We have erred in the past by imposing undue restrictions. Since we found it hard to accept sex as a real and proper part of life, we made it a kind of disreputable relative who had to be acknowledged, but was admitted through the back door and had to live in the cellar. No wonder that we have had not only revolt, but a constant emphasis, by well-intentioned but mistaken people, that sex is necessarily wholesome and good.

Today, the problems of sex arise mainly not out of undue restrictions, but from the assumption that sex can run "hog-wild" without being significantly related to the rest of our lives. Sex is hereby dissociated from its relationships to, and its effects upon, the values and goals of our society. We fail to understand that sex is part of the total personality structure....

The task of the educator and the religious leader is not to beat

---

[12]W. Norman Pittenger, *Making Sexuality Human* (New York: Pilgrim, 1970), pp. 87–89.
[13]See chapter 15 in this book, pp. 317–338.

the drums on behalf of a misguided liberalism, or to seek a resurrection of the past taboos. It is, instead, to help people, young and old, to fit their sex interests and behavior into a total and constructive concept of self and life, and to develop the moral standards that are required by valid personal, social, and lasting goals. We rightly begin by discarding the fictions that still delude us; but before us lies the far greater task of developing those deeper insights that will enable us to make sex a happy and meaningful part of our lives.

From Sylvanus M. Duvall, "Sex Fictions and Facts: A Social Scientist Destroys Some Myths," *Look Magazine,* 24 (April 12, 1960), pp. 47–48, 52.

Sylvanus M. Duvall (b. 1900) has taught in the fields of the social sciences and religion at George Williams College since 1933. His specialty is in family and marriage relations, and his writings include Before You Marry; Men, Women, and Morals; *and* The Art and Skill of Getting Along With People.

CHAPTER REVIEW

A. The "problem" of sex

1. For generations, sexual matters have been viewed within the "problem" category of life.
2. Privacy, shame, and individual senses of normality combined with obstacles to clear thinking and fears of permissiveness contribute to the view of sex as a problem.

B. The fundamental question in sexual ethics

1. "What is the primary purpose of human sexuality?" is the fundamental question in sexual ethics.
2. A particular answer to this question implies a standard for normality, naturalness, and morality.
3. Four representative views are procreation, procreation and unitive affection, unitive affection, and pleasure.

4. Variations on the four representative views are possible in several combinations.
5. Several possible philosophies of human sexuality prevent a clear consensus on what is normal, natural, and moral.

C. Sex research: A help to ethics?

1. Sex research supplies many data, interpreted in various ways, about the diversity of sexual expressions among human beings.
2. Because of their empirical methods, descriptive sciences cannot tell us how human sexuality *ought* to be expressed.

D. Holy writings: A help to ethics?

1. The ethicist is confronted with many claims of "moral truth" by the various world religions as well as by secular philosophies.
2. Most of the faithful appeal to their own holy writings as a major source of objective moral standards.
3. On a global basis, we can discover the various communities of faith using their respective holy writings with much diversity; unanimity within a religion or among religions cannot be expected.

E. Pluralism again

1. Because four primary purposes of human sexuality (and their variations) are plausible among reasonable people, we are faced again with pluralism.
2. Pluralism does not foster moral chaos, but rather broad legal boundaries among civilized people.

F. Same-sex orientations: Variation or perversion?

1. We have chosen same-sex orientations as a "case study" because it is a living ethical issue, much new information is available about homosexualities, and it can serve well as an example of an ethical examination of an emotionally explosive sexual issue.
2. Obstacles to clear thinking include confusions about masculinity and femininity, aesthetics, intimacy, and other obstacles.
3. Hatred of homosexual human beings has led to many murders of homosexuals by gangs and by Hitler.
4. Labels such as "heterosexual" or "homosexual" reveal little about a person; just as differences exist among heterosexual people, one cannot accurately stereotype homosexual men and women.

5. "Bisexual," denoting men and women who feel oriented toward both sexes, can also be a confusing label.
6. Researchers do not know for sure which cause(s) bring about any man's or woman's sexual orientation.
7. Sexual acts are classified according to the participants' genders; there is no such thing as a "homosexual act."
8. Homosexual men and women are in all walks of life, as are bisexual and heterosexual persons.
9. Same-sex couples experience many unique restrictions not affecting opposite-sex couples.
10. The degree of normality, naturalness, and morality of homosexual orientations and expressions depends on one's answer to the fundamental question in sexual ethics.
11. Philosophies that affirm homosexuality as a variation of human sexuality do not necessarily approve all expressions of same-sex relations.
12. A general announcement of one's homosexual orientation will probably, at this time in history, result in one's being perceived primarily as "gay" instead of as a person; however, for their own mental health, some homosexual men and women choose to "come out" publicly.

G. Guides to moral sexual conduct

1. Theologian Norman Pittenger has suggested a summary of ethical standards; his view is within a "unitive affection" philosophy and may be useful, minus his theological convictions, to humanists, as well as to those of a Judeo-Christian faith.
2. Perhaps someday, sex will be less of a "problem" and more of an issue about which we can agree to differ.

SUGGESTED READINGS

Baker, Robert, and Elliston, Frederick. *Philosophy and Sex.* Buffalo, N.Y.: Prometheus, 1975.

> The essays in this book cover such topics as an analysis of our vocabulary about sex; the pros and cons of promiscuity, monogamy, and birth control; the meaning of perversion; adultery; feminism; and abortion.

Boswell, John. *Christianity, Social Tolerance, and Homosexuality.* Chicago: Univ. of Chicago Press, 1980.

> Yale historian Boswell shows that Roman Catholic Europe of the Middle Ages was not hostile to homosexuality and that there were centuries when the church accepted and even canonized homosexual persons; the origins of opposition are also explored.

Hunter, J. F. M. *Thinking About Sex and Love.* New York: St. Martin's, 1980.

> The author addresses the moral considerations attached to sexual behavior in contemporary society; a philosophical inquiry into the theory and practice of personal sexual morality.

Jones, Clinton R. *Understanding Gay Relatives and Friends.* New York: Seabury, 1978.

> The senior canon of Christ Church Cathedral, Hartford, has drawn on his secular training as a marriage, family, and sex therapist to provide eleven readable case studies, including a homosexual son, daughter, brother, sister, husband, wife, father, teacher, and clergyman, as well as a transvestite husband and a transsexual son.

Kelly, Gary F. *Sexuality: The Human Perspective.* Woodbury, N.Y.: Barron's, 1980.

> An excellent college or young adult text, useful as a reference in a home library. Thirteen chapters are organized around four parts (Male/Female, Women/Men; Human Sexual Behavior; Dealing with Sexual Problems; Sex and Contemporary Society) and an appendix, "Resources in Human Sexuality."

McCary, James Leslie. *McCary's Human Sexuality.* 3rd ed. New York: Van Nostrand, 1978.

> Since its first edition in 1967, this college textbook has become a standard source of sex education; twenty-one chapters are organized around six parts: introduction, the human sexual system, the sexual act, present-day sexual attitudes and behavior, sexual complications, and sex and society.

Reich, Warren T., ed. *Encyclopedia of Bioethics.* New York: Free Press, 1978.

> Excellent articles with bibliographies include "Homosexuality," "Sex Therapy and Sex Research," "Sexual Behavior," "Sexual Development," "Sexual Ethics," and "Sexual Identity."

Verene, D. P., ed. *Sexual Love and Western Morality.* New York: Harper, 1972.

> A philosophical anthology of major thinkers, from ancient to contemporary periods, on the nature of sex, the sexes, and sexual love.

Vannoy, Russell. *Sex Without Love: A Philosophical Exploration.* Buffalo, N.Y.: Prometheus, 1980.

> An analysis of the major issues of both sex and love; the book's thesis is that a sexual relationship between individuals who are not in love can be meaningful and fulfilling.

PART 4
SOCIAL ETHICS

11

The Political Order

If Liberty and Equality, as is thought by some, are chiefly to be found in democracy, they will be best attained when all persons alike share in the government to the utmost.*

THE MORAL CONTEXT

The words "government, politics, and economics" are often regarded as foreign to or at least at the very edge of the study of morality. For many people these three things seem abstract, impersonal, and "out there," removed from the kinds of moral decisions we normally associate with ethics. All three seem so large and so immune to change by individual moral decisions that we take them for granted, part of the "givens" with which we work when we do ethics.

In the next two chapters we will see that despite their tendency to overwhelm us with their enormity and complexity, all three aspects of living together have a moral foundation and must be evaluated by moral norms. Essentially, government (or the state), politics, and economics have to do with the relations of persons living together in some kind of social order. Government ensures the order of the relationship and carries out the decisions of the community regarding its welfare, defense, and the adjustment of the interests of the various subgroups within it. Politics is the process by which these decisions are reached and implemented. Economics is the process by which the community produces and distributes the material goods necessary for its welfare.

Because there are many different ways to create and maintain social order, to come to and implement social decisions, and to produce and distribute material goods, there are moral choices that any society has to make about each of these areas of human action. Many of our everyday moral choices are made within the context of given political, governmental,

*Aristotle, Politics, Book IV, The Pocket Aristotle, trans. W. D. Ross. (New York: Pocket Books, 1958), pp. 32–321.

and economic structures and presuppose their implicit values. However, on occasion, people are faced with moral choices relating directly to the very foundations of governmental or economic systems. Most of us, for instance, simply assume the rightness of democracy as the governmental system within which to act. Some people, however, choose alternative forms of government such as socialism or libertarianism. Therefore, it is important for any student of morality to know and to reaffirm if necessary why he or she accepts a particular form of government or a particular economic arrangement.

Moral choices relating to political decisions are based on the principle that a political order, as an arrangement of persons and resources, must reflect some understanding of justice.

In considering a political order we are focusing primarily upon the social arrangements (laws and institutions) by which a community governs itself. Justice is the moral concern for how these arrangements balance the right of the individual to make choices for him/herself against the need for the society to place limits on individual liberty in order to ensure that peace, order, and social responsibilities are maintained and met. The weight given to social constraint as opposed to individual freedom will differ according to different social philosophies. But in a representative democracy, which will be our primary object of attention in this chapter, justice means that a moral evaluation of political decisions must take into account not only their effect upon the individual but also their effect upon the laws and institutions designed to restrain individual behavior (e.g., judicial or penal) or to meet social obligations which individuals alone cannot meet (e.g., welfare or defense).

In order to implement a concern for justice, it is necessary to know how the political system within which one must act works in practice. In this chapter an overview of areas of concern primarily within representative democracy will be given. Specific issues, such as racial justice, resort to war, dissent, freedom of expression, and ecological responsibility, will be discussed in separate chapters. This chapter will focus upon the social and political context within which these particular issues occur.

We will begin by setting forth some political philosophies regarding the function and limits of the state. We will then examine the generally agreed on obligations of any government, the legal process by which those obligations are carried out, the way a social order gets the money it needs to meet its obligations, and, finally, the way it elects persons who will determine its policies and the means to implement them.

The Functions of Government

The functions of government are many. Whether human beings are inherently fulfilled by living in community with each other (as we have maintained) or simply have to adopt social behavior because they are forced to live together by circumstances, persons do inevitably come together into groups. Some groups represent the narrow interests of their members: other groups represent broader, more diverse interests. Ultimately, the interests of individuals and the various groups to which they belong must be harmonized so that the peaceful pursuit of all interests is made as effective as possible. Providing the order and peace that makes the harmony of interests possible is one of the most important roles for the state. This means that it must be recognized by all members of the community as the overriding authority that determines what is legally acceptable behavior on the part of member groups and individuals. The exercise of power to compel or restrain behavior is one of the most important functions of any government.

In modern society, the instrument through which the government exercises its power is the law. Laws require us to do some things (like pay our taxes) and prohibit us from doing other things (like stealing). The power of the law is the power of compulsion, and the state has the effective means (and must be recognized as such) of enforcing the power of the law. The state, through the law, *coerces* behavior by threatening consequences for a violation of the law that offset the rewards anticipated through breaking the law. If the threat does not keep me from breaking the law, the state will punish me such that it is to my advantage not to break laws.

Groups within society will, of course, have their own internal rules and laws. However, for the state to work, the laws of any group must receive ultimate sanction from the state, and the state must be acknowledged to have the power to overrule or annul any secondary law. The function of government as the coercer of action and the sanctioner of law presupposes that persons will not always act for the benefit of others. As persons act out of self-interest, some regulating device, with power to enforce its decisions, is necessary to adjust and harmonize the various self-interests. This device is the state.

The Limits of Governmental Power

Most theories of government would accept the principles just outlined. However, significant disagreement occurs over how far or to what extent the power of law, coercion, and regulation should go. Some have argued that the role of the state is essentially repressive. The state should be limited to those acts of prohibition that keep people from interfering in the pursuits of others. We have seen such a theory in the moral philosophy of Thomas Hobbes. The state is a necessary evil that exists because of the conflict between competing self-interests. Its role is to keep the damage from such conflict to a minimum and to forbid individuals and groups from violating the rights of others. One assumption on which this position rests is that if individuals are free to pursue their own self-interests, they are more likely to know what is in their best interest than is a sovereign body ruling over them. Some have even argued that the power of the state should be limited to prohibiting fraud or deceit and punishing the violation of contracts. All other decisions and acts should be left to free individuals and the groups that represent their particular interests. Generally, the position just outlined is known as the *laissez-faire* (to allow to do) doctrine, and it has been the foundation of much of the rhetorical support (if not the substance) of government in this country.

In practice, laissez-faire has received substantial modification primarily because of the influence of an alternative view of the function of government. This view holds that in addition to sanctioning legal obligations, the state has the responsibility for ensuring the welfare of its members, particularly those who are unable to provide for their own. This position, sometimes known as the theory of the welfare state, maintains that the power of the state must be used to promote the welfare of the community as a whole and to protect those members of it too powerless to protect themselves. The state, it is argued, must (for example) provide for the medical needs of those who cannot save enough money to pay for medical care themselves. The provision of a common education to all citizens must be the responsibility of the state, to use another example, because private agencies cannot be counted on to make the same education available to everyone at a price they can afford.

At this level of disagreement, it may be hard to see the practical implications of adopting one or the other of the alternative understandings of the state. In order to see those implications, we need to raise some more basic questions. What is the view of human relationship assumed by each one? How does each position handle the issue of justice? These are the essential questions for moral evaluation.

Fellowship or Individualism?

Those who argue for a minimal interference by the state in the affairs of the individuals and groups that comprise the society generally assume that the relationship between persons is incidental to their primary goal, which is the pursuit of self-interest. Friendship and group solidarity may be important but primarily as ways of enhancing the interests of the individual or of the group itself. Justice, therefore, is the adoption of principles that will protect persons in their drive toward the fulfillment of their desires. A key assumption here is that as some are successful in pursuing their interests, others will fail. Those who achieve success do so primarily because of their greater skill, intelligence, and ambition. Those who fail do so because of their lack of ambition, skill, and intelligence. It thus is to the benefit of the group and the community as a whole for the weaklings to fall by the wayside, thereby making it impossible for them to weaken the social organism by their presence.

Employing the analogy of the organic body, this notion of the state sees the health of the society as deriving primarily from permitting the strong elements of the system to thrive while eliminating the weaker elements so as to avoid infection and debilitation. It is also assumed that as each part of the organism strives for its own interests, the harmony of the system will emerge. We will see the full explication of this in our analysis of the economic dimension of the community. It should be clear that this position has some affinity to the positions sketched earlier under the rubric of Darwinism, evolutionism, and Nietzsche's will to power.

The position of the welfare state, expressed in an extreme form in various socialistic systems, assumes that the relationship between persons is essential to their well-being and fulfillment. Friendship and group solidarity may have the incidental effect of enhancing individual self-interest, but they are primarily enjoyed for their own sake. Persons are happier on the whole when they live in bonds of affection with and compassion for all others. From this assumption flows the understanding of justice as the expression by the community, through its institutions and laws, of concern for the welfare of the community as a whole and in particular of those members who have been disadvantaged by a lack of power, education, skill, or resources.

Assuming that a community is more fulfilled when all its members are treated as equally important contributors to communal enterprises, this view of the state requires that it actively involve itself in equalizing opportunities for all to contribute and in negating the effects of those groups whose activities create inequities and disadvantages for some at the expense of others. Although those holding this view of the state are not as likely to adopt the analogy of the healthy organism, it could be utilized to suggest that the vision of the community implied by the welfare society is one in which the whole body is not healthy unless the weaker elements are made stronger by the compassion and action of the already strong.

In our chapter on social justice (Chapter 15), we will examine in more detail some of the concrete effects of this alternative view of the state. What is important at this point is to see that there are two different views of the role of the state, that each has a particular notion of human relationship at its base, and each has a consequent view of what justice means and what the obligation of the state is to implement it.

Who Shall Rule?

Once it has been determined what the general purpose of the government is, it is necessary to determine who shall carry it out. This is the question of who shall rule, or more specifically, who shall be in positions of power to determine what the laws governing all shall be. Who is the government?

Historically, all sorts of alternatives have been tried and advocated. Some argue that incorporating all ultimate decision making and power in a single individual or elite works best for efficient, orderly, and wise governance. The more power is dispersed among many people, the more chaotic and uncertain become the rules by which order and justice are preserved. Those who should rule are those who have demonstrated their fitness to do so by their wisdom, by their previous contribution to the welfare of the society, or by hereditary right.

At the opposite end of the spectrum is the view, associated with socialism or communism, that only the people as a whole have a right to rule. This argument is based on the assumption that the purpose of the state is the welfare of all. Since all are to benefit from the actions of the state, all should participate in determining those actions. Any theory that denies the right of the people to govern themselves winds up justifying the arrogation of power by small groups that will pursue their own self-interest at the expense of others.

The difficulty with this view, of course, is that it is notoriously hard to see how all the people can carry out the responsibilities of decision making effectively. Thus, a middle position (known as representative government) has generally been adopted by most western societies. With a wide variety of forms, this position maintains that the will of the people can be the determiner of law and government but only through representation of the society at large by a much smaller group of individuals. *Politics* is the process by which these representatives are brought to power and by which they carry into effect what they perceive to be the will of those whom they represent.

THE DILEMMA OF THE DEMOCRATIC IDEAL

From the ethical point of view . . . it is not too much to say that the democratic ideal poses, rather than solves, the great problem: How to harmonize the development of each individual with the maintenance of a social state in which the activities of one will contribute to the good of all the others. It expresses a postulate in the sense of a demand to be realized: That each individual shall have the opportunity for release, expression, fulfillment, of his distinctive capacities, and that the outcome shall further the establishment of a fund of shared values. Like every true ideal, it signifies something to be done rather than something already given, something ready-made. Because it is something to be accomplished by human planning and arrange-

> ment, it involves constant meeting and solving of problems.
> ... There is no short-cut to it, no single predestined road
> which can be found once for all and which, if human beings
> continue to walk in it without deviation, will surely conduct
> them to the goal.
>
> John Dewey and James H. Tufts, *Ethics,* chapter 17 in John Somerville
> and Ronald E. Santoni, *Social and Political Philosophy: Readings From Plato
> to Gandhi* (Garden City, N.Y.: Doubleday), pp. 498–499.

---

*John Dewey (1859–1952) was one of America's foremost philosophers,
known primarily for his work in education and for his development of
pragmatism. He was also a prominent social critic.*

It could be said that politics only really exists in a representative system since it is the art of the possible. That is, it is the complicated way by which the society determines how to adjust the interests of the largest number of constituencies to each other and to the society as a whole. This means that politics is also the science of compromise because no single interest can be fully dominant if other interests are also to be represented effectively. Some of the most interesting of all moral problems in the area of government occur in and through moral issues that emerge as governments carry out their functions.

OBLIGATIONS OF THE POLITICAL ORDER

National Defense

A universally agreed to obligation of any government is to protect its citizens from attack by other countries. It must provide for a national defense. It is not, of course, inconceivable that a community should be so dedicated to the principles of nonviolence and pacifism that it would, as a body, prefer to be overrun or destroyed rather than resort to violent defense of its territory. (Such a case occurred when the Quakers who controlled the government of Pennsylvania voluntarily abdicated power rather than provide arms for the defense of the frontier against hostile Indians).

Nevertheless, pacifism for an entire society is extraordinarily rare. The consensus in most democratic societies is for protection and, therefore, for an effective military defense. Moral questions begin to develop when the society has to determine the size of its defense capabilities: Should it seek merely to achieve parity or equality with the defense of those nations most likely to attack it, or should it strive for clear superiority? The question becomes particularly important when an "arms race" develops between two or more countries, each spending more and more to stay ahead of the others. With a limited budget, more money for defense necessarily means less money for other concerns, especially domestic needs.

A second issue has to do with how broadly national defense is interpreted. It could mean simply defending one's boundaries if they are physically crossed by an enemy. Or it could mean defending what the nation perceives to be its self-interest in parts of the world not under its flag. In recent years, we have seen nations' defense budgets escalate dramatically to provide support for other nations whose defense is considered vital to national self-interest. Critics have argued that in an economically and politically interrelated world, it is so difficult to separate national self-interest from the affairs of other people that to identify national defense with a broad conception of national self-interest makes it impossible to control the allocation of funds to a military budget.

Militarism Is Itself a Danger.   Because appeals to self-defense and the pride of a nation are so easily converted into an uncritical support of military spending, a nation can avoid raising serious moral questions about the values that are threatened by slashing monies for social welfare while building a military posture. If a nation's self-image becomes identified with the size of its military weaponry or armies, its understanding of itself as a community dedicated to the social values of domestic justice and compassion may be seriously damaged.

Another factor that must be considered is the complexity of military spending. Because armaments and military technology are so highly complicated and beyond most citizens' understanding, it becomes easy to defend any military budget request simply on the authorization of those agencies with a self-interest in perpetuating military spending. President Eisenhower warned the United States as he left the presidency to beware of the military-industrial complex. He pointed out that large segments of the economic community were dependent on military spending. Allied with those who were part of the enormous military establishment, they could create a climate of pressure for uncritical support for ever-increasing military budgets that could not be scrutinized intelligently by the average citizen.

Finally, the danger of militarism can be seen in its creation of an attitude that might lead to the actual use of military force simply because so much of it has been developed and because the nation's image has been tied to it. If a nation brandishes its military might too often, as its claim to be taken seriously by the rest of the world, it might push itself by the logic of its own claims into using its force and thus initiating military conflict.

The International Community

Beyond the arena of military defense, any society must consider its other obligations to the international community of nations. This may involve negotiation over mutual reduction of military armaments (see Chapter 17), it may involve trade agreements, economic assistance, and cooperation in dealing with problems of hunger, education, health, and political refugees. It may also involve a commitment to working through international organizations like the United Nations or the International Monetary Fund to secure these ends. No nation, in today's increasingly interdependent world, can afford to stand aloof from the agencies that try to make relations between countries more harmonious and equitable.

Domestic Obligations

Turning from international obligations to the domestic scene, all political systems are required to provide certain basic services to their citizens. Bodies or agencies are organized to implement the provision of these services. Among these are a body for making laws, a judicial system, agencies for providing protection against crime, punishment for convicted criminals, some public schooling, access to medical care, relief from the ravages of natural disasters, aid in cases of extreme poverty or disablement, preservation of natural resources, and raising the revenues to carry out these tasks. In addition, some political philosophies maintain that government must provide for the regulation of industries whose activities and products affect the public good, such as airlines, drug manufacturers, food preparers, etc. There is a great deal of disagreement, as we indicated earlier, over the legitimacy of any intervention by a federal government into the activities of private enterprise. Even when some consent is reached as to the right of government to so intervene, wide disagreement still exists as to the degree of intervention considered appropriate.

Legislation and Legislators

The creation of laws to prohibit certain acts and require others is necessary for order in any society. Each person and group within a social system must be able to know what the limits on its freedom to act are and what the consequences of violating those limits will be. One of the most important political tasks, therefore, is the election of persons to those bodies whose primary task it is to write the laws of the society. In this country, the Congress (consisting of a House of Representatives, elected every two years and comprising representation based on population, and a Senate, elected in staggered terms for six years and based on the principle of two senators for each state) is the legislative body.

One of the basic issues faced by every national legislator is how far to extend the domain of national laws and how much latitude to give to each state to determine its own laws. The genius as well as the frustration of the United States Constitution is that it divides the legislative powers between federal and state governments. The question of "states' rights" has remained alive for many years as a result. It was experienced most dramatically over the issue of slavery: Was it within the purview of each state to determine the legality of slavery or was slavery to be the subject ultimately of federal law binding on and superior to state law? The same question now troubles many people with respect to the rights of women to equal treatment under the law. Some argue for a constitutional amendment guaranteeing that equality for women under federal law supercedes any other policies or laws written by states. Others argue that each state should handle the question of womens' rights individually.

Another issue faced by legislative bodies is the degree of protection for minority groups regardless of the desires of the majority of the electorate. Are there certain rights (to be enshrined into law) possessed by all persons that cannot be legislated away even if that should be the expressed desire of a majority of the country? Traditionally, legislation has protected some such rights, such as the right to assemble, to speak peacefully on controversial matters, or to propogate unpopular views.

Regulation

Legislators must also address the question of how far laws should go in protecting people from possible dangers. The issue of regulation of business practices enters at this point. Is it the obligation of government to pass laws protecting the minds of children from exposure to advertising designed to get them to eat cereals that contain large amounts of sugar, known to be detrimental to their health? Should the government limit by law the amount of violence shown on television to persons likely to be unduly influenced by it? Should the federal government require drug manufacturers to submit their drugs to federal testing procedures prior to putting them up for sale to the public? Should the federal government hold commercial enterprises accountable for accurate and nonmisleading advertising? Should the government, in the name of the public good, require car manufacturers to produce by a given date automobiles that meet a certain gas mileage ratio? Should the federal law provide regulations regarding air safety standards? The list of concerns is almost endless but must be faced in a practical way by those we elect to legislative office. (Since so much of what determines the appropriate scope of legislation is based on a more fundamental ideology of economic justice and freedom, we will examine some of the issues in legislation affecting the distribution of and access to economic resources in Chapter 12.)

The Enforcement of Law

Once laws are passed within a political order, they must be enforced. Generally, citizens experience the enforcement of the laws by those agencies whose job it is to protect against crime and to seek out those who have committed crime. The primary agency is, of course, the police. Society normally entrusts them alone, at the domestic level, with the power of violence against those who have lawlessly used violence in the carrying out of a crime. In recent years, as people have become aware of the degree to which police are not immune from the biases and foibles of the community from which they are recruited, concerns have been voiced about the need for review of and limits on police activity by citizens' groups. These concerns are particularly acute in communities that have a large minority population and a police force drawn primarily from the majority population. The result has often been charges of police harassment and brutality, and less serious, insensitivity to the needs of the minority community.

More traditional problems faced by all groups, including enforcement agencies from the police to the FBI, are graft, corruption, and bribery. Excessive use of force has also been added recently to the list of citizen concerns. Much of the debate centers around the question of who should review police action: professional police panels or citizens' review boards.

Under the rubric of protection, the political order must also deal with the degree of freedom it wants to permit its citizens in buying and possessing dangerous weapons. The issue is one of public safety in conflict with individual freedom. Opponents of control, through registration and limited sale, of guns argue that such restrictions would infringe the liberty of private citizens to "bear arms" and would constitute an unwarranted intrusion of governmental regulation into the domain of personal choice. Proponents of gun control point out that the consequences of rejecting it are the easy availability of guns even to persons with criminal records and the subsequent temptation to employ a lethal weapon in the commission of a crime (not to mention the increased likelihood of accidental death or injury from an inexperienced person playing with the accessible weapon). Through the political order, it must be decided whether the actual danger to the public safety from having no control over the purchase of guns warrants the restriction on the freedom of choice such control would entail.

The Judicial Arena

More serious questions arise as we look from the enforcement of law to its interpretation and the determination of punishment for those accused of breaking it. The third branch of government, alongside the legislative and executive, is the judicial. The courts have the job of interpreting the law, making sure it is in conformity with the Constitution. They also have the

job, through the complicated processes involving judges, juries, prose-
cutors, defense attorneys, trials, hearings, etc., of determining the guilt or
innocence of persons accused of breaking the law and of determining the
appropriate punishment. There has been much controversy in recent years
over the role of the courts in placing limits on material that can be introduced into a trial. For example, courts have ruled that evidence obtained
without a search warrant or confessions extracted without prior counsel are
inadmissible. This has meant, in some cases, that persons "known" to be
guilty have been released due to erroneous police procedures.

A serious moral dilemma is thereby revealed: Can the safeguards provided by correct legal procedure to protect the innocent be modified or
lifted in cases in which there is general consent that the accused is really
guilty? To release someone whose conviction was overturned on a legal
"technicality" seems, to some, a mockery of the spirit of justice. To others,
it is the price a society must pay if it wishes to protect all the rights of the
accused. As one advocate of strict protection put it:

> [I]n totalitarian countries, five people were executed in order to en-
> sure that the one guilty person was punished; in a democracy, five
> people were let go in order to ensure that the four innocent persons
> were not unjustly punished.

Another festering moral issue facing the judicial system has to do with
the scope of the courts' interpretive activity. In some decisions, the courts
have required action of federal, state, and municipal agencies to remedy
what (in the courts' mind) are social ills or injustices. They have required
schools to desegregate, reviewed desegration plans, and insisted that
companies engage in "affirmative action" hiring to rectify past discriminatory hiring practices. Critics of the courts argue that they are engaged in
"social engineering," performing work properly left to the legislative
branch of government. Defenders of the courts point out that unless the
courts interpret the laws in an activist way, the laws will remain a dead
letter, ineffective in carrying out the purposes for which they were enacted.
The basic question has become: What role should the judicial system play
in implementing a society's vision of social justice?

Punishment and Prisons

One aspect of this question has to do with the nature and reform of the
country's penal institutions. The courts normally determine the kind of
punishment or incarceration appropriate for a convicted criminal. However, they sometimes take into account the condition and effect on the
criminal of the penal institution to which he is being sent. One of the basic
questions courts face in this regard is whether imprisonment is essentially
retributive or punitive, i.e., a punishment for crime, or rehabilitative, i.e.,

designed to help and educate the criminal to return to a socially useful life when released. It is a shocking fact that many convicted criminals are recidivists—they return to jail after release for having committed further crimes. Recent atrocities at major penal institutions, such as Attica in up-state New York and a penitentiary in New Mexico have dramatized the horrors of life behind bars.

Brutality, corruption, and forced homosexuality are only some of the conditions faced by prisoners in many American jails today. First offenders often are bred into a further life of crime while behind bars. The social cost of returning likely recidivists back onto the street is thus quite high. Critics point out, however, that the social cost of making prisons truly rehabilita-tive would be enormous as well as demoralizing to the society since it would appear to give the criminal special attention and training not avail-able to those who have not committed a crime. At issue is the fundamental question of whether the society wishes to pay primarily for the satisfaction of knowing that criminals are being punished, often brutally and with little chance of becoming socially responsible on release, or to pay primarily for the rehabilitation and long-term welfare of those who have broken soci-ety's laws. Either way, the cost is enormous but the moral alternatives must be faced directly and with full knowledge of what actually happens as a result of each choice.

Budgets and Taxes

No matter how long the list of responsibilities laid on the government, it is necessary to pay for each one. This involves the raising of revenues from the citizenry. In our federal system, taxes are laid on persons and corpora-tions in order to meet a federal budget (not to mention state and municipal budgets). The setting of the budget is an exercise in moral choice because revenues allocated to different areas of governmental obligation reflect the degree of moral commitment the society has made to those areas. A budget that allocates more money to national defense than to the eradication of poverty within has clearly made a moral decision that the latter is less morally urgent than the former. A decision to grant more funds for public highways than to public transportation reveals the moral priority of con-tinuing to reaffirm the interests of the automobile makers and the freedom of those with money to use however much gasoline they can afford. One can trace the moral choices of a society right down through the entire budget, whether it be federal, state, or local.

Once the budget is determined it is necessary to raise the money to carry it out. We will discuss some of the underlying moral problems such an economic decision entails in the next chapter. In the present context, it should be remarked simply that no government can implement the will of the people it represents unless the people provide it with the necessary money. One often hears complaints about the agency, the Internal Revenue Service, authorized to collect taxes. But there should be no fundamental moral question about its right to do so and the corresponding obligation of the citizenry to pay the taxes levied.

The more complicated moral issues have to do with the way in which the taxes are levied, on whom, and by what standards of equity. For example, some argue that an income tax that is progressive (i.e., taxes larger incomes at a higher rate) is equitable since it is based on the ability to pay. Others argue that it is inequitable since it discourages those very people whose higher incomes reflect their greater productivity and ambition—the very people, it is argued, upon whom the productive capacity of the nation's economy depends. As we have already seen, and will see in economic terms later, this argument reflects the fundamental dispute between those favoring a limited government and those advocating some form of a welfare state. And that argument, in turn, depends on basic assumptions about the nature of human beings and their relationships with each other in community.

THE POLITICAL PROCESS

Representation

Because most people experience the workings of government or participate in it most directly in the election of legislative representatives, we need to outline some of the more pressing moral issues that occur in this area commonly known as politics. The words "politics" and "politician" have in recent years come to be associated with what is less than honorable, slightly corrupt, and influenced by the basest motives. If these impressions are correct, it is not because of the nature of politics but because of a lack of informed participation by citizens in the political process.

LIMITS ON CONSENT TO POLITICAL AUTHORITY

Consent theory does not insist . . . that a man must stand on his own judgment in everything. That would be an anarchistic denial of all authority and of all political obligation. But it maintains that there must be good reasons for handing over to someone else one's right to decide. . . . Fundamentally, then, the theory of consent "moralizes" political authority and obligation. When Locke said that men were free by nature, he surely meant, at the very least, that no one can deprive another of the right to form his own judgments. . . . In that capacity, no man can put his conscience in the permanent keeping of any authority, whether party leader, lawyer, or priest. Every man, therefore, must decide for himself whether he has a duty to accept a given authority; for no one else can decide that for him. Similarly, he can accept authority only with reservations. For he yields his freedom to act on his own moral estimate of situations, or as Locke put, to do "whatsoever he thought fit for the preservation of himself and the rest of mankind," only "so far forth as the preservation of himself and that society shall require."

S. I. Benn, and R. S. Peters, *Principles of Political Thought* (New York: Collier-Macmillan, 1964), pp. 388, 386.

S. I. Benn (b. 1920) is Senior Fellow, Department of Philosophy, Institute of Advanced Studies, Australian National University. R. S. Peters (b. 1919) is reader in philosophy and psychology at Birkbeck College, University of London. He is author of The Concept of Motivation *and* The Concept of Character.

Politics is the process by which conflicting interests are reconciled so as to best represent the will of the various constituencies that comprise the public. Politics is, necessarily, the art of the possible: the art of compromise between positions. Most bodies to which people are elected deal with a wider range of issues than simply those concerning the single area or majority of the constituency from which a person has been elected. Therefore, it is impossible for politicians to represent without modification the will of each group within his or her electoral area. One rarely expects an elected official to be a computer, tallying up in machine fashion the wishes of a majority of the constituency and voting without deliberation for whatever wish emerges on top.

Single Issue Politics

Recently in American politics, "single-issue" electing has become popular. Proponents of a single issue, such as those in opposition to school busing or the pro and con forces on abortion or those advocating a repeal of taxes, have announced that they will either vote for or against a candidate solely on the basis of that candidate's position on their particular issue. While this tactic focuses attention on the candidate's views on that issue, it often obscures and frustrates the political process because it excludes from consideration other issues that will necessarily have to be considered by the candidate once in office. It may also defeat persons whose over-all views are more in line with the general interests of the constituents but with whose specific view on the one issue are at odds with theirs. In a generally conservative district, for example, a proven conservative politician whose long-run voting record represents the constituency well, may go down to defeat to a liberal simply because the latter is closer to the "required" position on the single issue in question. An informed electorate must weigh both long-term as well as short-term consequences of voting exclusively on "single issues."

Conflict of Interest

Regardless of how broad a view a political candidate has on the many issues in question, it is true that some groups and some ideas will be more influential than others. An informed electorate owes it to itself to become as familiar as possible with the interest groups to which a candidate is indebted or with which the candidate has special ties. The most troublesome problem in this area is that of conflict of interest. If banking practices have become a matter of concern, electing a banker (whose livelihood depends on the maintenance of present banking practice) to deal with that issue may very well put that banker/candidate in a position of conflict of interest. As a human being, he or she cannot help but allow decisions to be influenced by his or her dependence on the banking profession and may not, therefore, be able to take a strictly objective or broad view of the problems within that profession. Electing lawyers to bodies that have the responsibility of creating laws may involve some conflict of interest simply because each new law created produces more work for the legal profession.

It would be foolish to suggest that people can be found who have no interests they might come in conflict with at some time in such a position. But it is not foolish to insist that those conflicts be made public so that the electorate knows what they are and can judge the degree of conflict involved.

It used to be that the groups to which politicians were most heavily indebted were those that made the greatest contributions to their campaigns. A large contributing group, like the National Rifle Association, would provide such generous campaign support that the elected candidate then felt obligated to vote in whatever way best represented the wishes of that group. The obvious corruption to which such practices led has been modified somewhat in recent years due to campaign disclosure laws and requirements that place limits on the amount any single group or person can donate to a campaign.

Lobbies

One of the most effective ways to reach an elected official to convince him or her of your group's position is through the process known as "lobbying." A lobby is an official representative (or group of representatives) for a special interest (e.g., the automakers, the tomato-growers, the NAACP, etc.). These people visit elected officials in order to inform them of their group's positions. Apart from the occasional petty bribery (giving expensive, unrecorded gifts to the elected official), there is the larger question of whether lobbies create undue pressure on elected representatives. It is clear that only those interest groups large enough and wealthy enough to afford them can effectively utilize lobbies. This gives them disproportionate influence on the legislative process. In the past, lobbyists often went about their work unregistered and unidentified to the general public. Once again, public disclosure of who they are is one step toward providing the public with the kind of information it needs to make intelligent judgments about the wisdom and positions of its elected agents.

THE ELECTIVE PROCESS

The fact that most legislators are elected brings its own moral problems. Although election permits the people to have their views represented more precisely than does appointments to office, the election process is so complicated that it is difficult to ensure that the best candidates are the ones who survive its many stages. Office-seekers normally run as the candidates of one of two major "parties," Democratic and Republican. This makes it difficult for "third party" candidates, who are dissatisfied with the positions taken by the two established parties, to secure the necessary financial and campaign support. Historically, third parties have not been successful in electing their candidates to office, though they have drawn votes away from the established party candidates. They have, on occasion, focused attention on an issue that, over time, has forced the main-line parties to accommodate the third party position. But those who consider a third party approach must recognize that while this might permit them to vote on a more precisely defined principle (the larger parties necessarily having to make their principles somewhat more vague in order to appeal to larger, more diverse groups), it may also permit the election of the poorer of the two candidates running within the established parties.

Limits of Party Politics

Being registered in either the Democratic or Republican party is a particular advantage at the outset of an electoral campaign since it permits one to vote for those people who will later run as candidates of that party. In the selection process, known as primaries, many candidates within a party compete to be the nominees of that party. Unless one is registered as a member of that party, it is impossible to have a say in which persons emerge as nominees. Some have argued that this gives an unfair advantage to political parties and to their registered members—others argue that without this weeding out process, the final election would be chaotic and unmanageable. But it does pose an interesting moral dilemma: it forces a person to join a single party that may on occasion adopt positions the joiner does not agree with.

An independent, who might desire to steer clear of the petty details and party loyalty demanded of members of particular parties, achieves political "purity" at the price of political impotence at the primary level. The independent, of course, can point to another price he or she is glad not to have to pay: that of having to support an entire "team" of nominees. A party might endorse a "slate" of candidates and members of the party are expected to vote for the entire slate. It is argued that unless the team is elected, nothing effective can be done in the legislative assemblies since the votes of most of the party are normally necessary to pass laws. This creates a problem for those who wish to support the team but feel strongly opposed to one or more of its members. Do they risk losing the advantages of team votes in the assembly in order to vote against a member of their team and for a member of the opposition, who as an individual, they find more attractive?

Financial Obligations

Once nominated, a candidate must find financial support for his or her campaign. In order to compensate for the obvious advantages of incumbency and wealth, campaign laws have been passed to limit spending and to provide some support for those not presently in office. But enormous sums of money are necessary for a campaign, and the increasing length of campaigns drains financial resources that some argue might be better spent elsewhere. The time and money necessary for campaigning for an office make a successful run almost prohibitive for those with no personal wealth and those who cannot afford to give up full-time jobs for the duration of a campaign. This has meant, in practice, that more and more politicians are drawn from the ranks of the well-to-do or from professions that permit lengthy absences. Thus, factory workers and others who are paid by the hour are effectively barred from running for office.

Campaigning

Perhaps the most disturbing part of any political process is the way in which campaigns are carried out. It would be nice to think that candidates spend most of their time debating the issues of the day and setting forth their political philosophies. But election depends primarily on the image of the candidate the public has when it goes to the voting booth. In a society that projects images primarily through the media and through advertising, much of political campaigning is the packaging and distribution of the image the candidates want to present. The shallowness and superficiality of such an approach are obvious. Yet, it is replied, most people do not want to take the time to read lengthy position papers or to struggle with the intricacies of complicated issues. It is also pointed out that since many of the issues an official must face have not even arisen at the time of election, it is more important to vote for the character of the candidate than for his or her stand on this or that specific issue.

The problem with concentrating on the personal integrity or virtue of the candidate is that it so easily degenerates into a popularity contest revolving around "personality." Effectiveness as a legislator, as someone who can carry into effect the programs he or she represents, is often forgotten. It is possible to favor someone with whose principles you agree but who is notoriously ineffective in implementing them through the legislative process. It is also possible to favor someone with whom you are not always in agreement but who has the proven capacity to utilize the legislative machinery successfully. Or one could support a candidate whose views are not always one's own but who has shown courage and trustworthiness in the political arena and reject a candidate who represents one's views more consistently but who is personally untrustworthy or weak. Few candidates possess all the best qualities at once. The voter, therefore, must sort out the moral options and make the best, but necessarily qualified, choice possible.

Should the Uninformed Vote?

It has long been a truism in American politics that one should vote in elections, from local to national. Americans exercise their right to vote in far fewer numbers, relative to those who are eligible to vote, than most democracies in the world today. However, an argument has recently been heard urging people to stay away from the polls if they are not informed about the candidates and issues to be voted on. An uninformed electorate is more dangerous than an informed but smaller electorate. People who vote without knowledge are more easily swayed by extraneous factors, e.g., the splashiness of the candidates' ads, word of mouth from neighbors, long-time party loyalty, and so on. Encouraging an uninformed electorate may be to the advantage of some candidates with a high degree of superficial appeal and a low degree of political wisdom, but it works against the long-run interests of the country. Whether this argument is ultimately persuasive (its opponents point out that the habit of voting is in itself important; that the less the ordinary citizen votes, the more special interest groups will dominate political decisions, etc.), it is true that moral integrity requires the analysis and evaluation of a whole range of issues, some of which have been outlined here. In the world of politics, it is impossible to ignore the effects of its decisions on the lives of people. Therefore, it is imperative that morally sensitive persons inform themselves about how those decisions are reached and how their own participation in the electoral process affects the decision making that goes on.

In this chapter we have given an overview of the political order within which moral agents act. The broad scope of political responsibilities has been canvassed in order to convey a sense of the interrelationship of moral issues for persons living together in a community. The principle of justice as a balance between individual liberty and the obligations of government to meet social needs underlies and informs the moral dimensions of political choice. In later chapters we will take up some specific issues in greater detail.

CHAPTER REVIEW

A. The moral context

1. Government and politics are arenas of moral action because they are constituted by choices based on values.
2. A government seeks to provide peace and order for its citizens. One way it does so is through legal sanctions.
3. There is much disagreement about the extent to which law should govern individual and group behavior.
4. The disagreement reveals differing views of human relationships. Some believe that social relations serve the primary end of individual interest. Others believe that social relations are the primary end of relationship and that the individual is fulfilled through his or her contributions to the community.
5. Every political order must decide who is to rule: one person, a few, or all. If the latter, then how are the opinions of all effectively carried into practice? Representative government has been chosen by most western societies.

B. Obligations of the political order

1. National defense must be provided by a government. How broadly this is understood will affect the degree of militarism and military spending within a political order.
2. Each society must determine its obligations within the community of nations.

3. Domestically, a representative government carries out its obligations through the legislative process. One issue in this area is how to allocate responsibilities between the federal and state governments.
4. Regulation of individual and business activity must be addressed by the political order. How far such regulation should extend is a major issue in today's society.
5. The enforcement of law brings with it many problems regarding excessive use of force, the availability of weapons to the public, and the safeguarding of individual rights in police investigations.
6. The political order must also deal with the issues surrounding the punishment of those found guilty of breaking its laws.
7. The creation of a federal, state, or municipal budget is an exercise in moral decision making.

C.   The political process

1. Politics is the process by which conflicting interests are reconciled so as to best represent the will of the various constituencies that comprise the public.
2. In recent years, single issue politics has become a feature of the political order. It raises the moral issue of long-term versus short-term consequences of political choice.
3. Legislators with conflicts of interest raise the moral question of how to represent equitably the views of all their constituents.
4. Lobbies bring particular concerns to the attention of legislators but raise the question of whether they unduly influence them.

D.   The elective process

1. Electing representatives involves the use of political parties, which may limit one's freedom to choose the best person.
2. Elections require enormous expenditures of money, also creating limits on who may run for office.
3. Campaigning for political office sometimes appeals to the baser instincts of the electorate.
4. A final issue in the election process is whether uninformed people should vote, especially if their vote is not swayed by knowledge but by superficial factors.

SUGGESTED READINGS

Benn, S. I., and Peters, R. S. *The Principles of Political Thought, Social Foundations of the Democratic State.* New York: Collier-Macmillan, 1964.

An analytical study from the point of view of "cautious Utilitarianism" of social principles, covering such topics as property, punishment, rights, obligations, and political authority.

Brogan, D. W. *Politics in America.* Garden City, N.Y.: Doubleday, 1954.

An instructive study of the facets of politics, including a chapter on "Politics and Morals."

Girvetz, Harry K., ed. *Contemporary Moral Issues.* Belmont, Calif.: Wadsworth, 1963.

A collection of essays on a number of political issues, including some on the dilemmas of punishment.

Niebuhr, Reinhold. *Moral Man and Immoral Society.* New York: Scribners, 1932.

A classic statement by one of America's major theologians on the moral dilemmas of political decision making.

Rousse, Thomas A., ed. *Political Ethics and the Voter.* New York: Wilson, 1952.

A set of essays covering such topics as lobbies, pressure groups, tax scandals, and moral issues facing legislators and voters.

Sabine, G. H. *History of Political Theory.* Rev. ed. New York: Holt, 1955.

A massive and comprehensive history of the different political theories that make up Western civilization.

12

The Economic Order

We have always known that heedless self-interest was bad morals; we know now that it is bad economics.*

Like a hypochondriac who is so absorbed in the processes of his own digestion that he goes to the grave before he has begun to live, industrialized communities neglect the very objects for which it is worthwhile to acquire riches in their feverish preoccupation with the means by which riches can be acquired.†

THE MORAL CONTEXT

Economic Activity Is Moral Activity

It is sometimes assumed that the economic enterprises of a society run by their own inherent laws not subject to human interference. A view has developed in many circles that the laws of supply and demand, of incentive and production, of allocation and resources, are almost scientific in their rigor and unalterability. From this it has been concluded that political and moral decisions should not affect the running of the economic machine.

Although it may be true that the choices people make about what to buy and what to produce can be reasonably predicted, at least in a general way, it is false to conclude that the way in which a society produces goods, makes them available, and provides the resources for consuming them is value free. Economic systems are value laden and carry within them a whole set of values about the nature of persons and their relationship with each other. It is also true that political decisions necessarily have an effect on the functioning of the economy (a political decision to tax the purchase

---

*Franklin Delano Roosevelt in his Second Inaugural Address, January 20, 1937.
†H. H. Tawney, *The Acquisitive Society* (London: Bell, 1926), p. 241.

of gasoline will affect, to some degree, the amount of gasoline people will voluntarily buy). Therefore, value judgments are always being made implicitly about economic realities. The moral task is to make those judgments explicitly. The key to making them intelligently will depend on how we evaluate the effects of economic practices on issues of justice, equity, and the welfare of persons within the society.

The word "goods," used to refer to what is produced and what is consumed, ironically indicates the moral dimension of economics. For goods are what are good for people: they directly affect the well-being of persons. The moral problems that emerge as we try to sort out the justification for economic systems in terms of their effect on the well-being of people are clearly related to the goals of government and to the political decisions that help achieve those goals. Government, politics, and economics make up an integrated whole with respect to the general social order within which we live and, therefore, raise similar moral problems for us.

Who Controls the Productive Process?

In a system of production, distribution, and consumption, it is inevitable that decisions must be made about who will produce, what will be produced, to whom and by what means it will be distributed, and who will consume it. These decisions necessarily involve moral choice.

At a basic level, economic decisions affect the well-being and welfare of everyone in the social order. The fundamental moral questions, therefore, revolve around an analysis and evaluation of these decisions. Some economic systems will stress the importance of individual free choice in the production and consumption of goods, accepting as a "necessary evil" the inequities of enterprise, ingenuity, and consequent wealth. Other economic systems will stress the importance of equality for all in terms of access to basic goods, accepting as a "necessary evil" the curtailment of individual freedom of choice. The fact that every economic system must make some tradeoffs in the balance of values reveals that no system can ever fully embody all the values it claims to strive for. There are many things that the "best laid plans" cannot anticipate or control. In the following we will deal primarily with the *ideals* espoused by architects of alternative economic orders. It is important to remember that in practice these ideals will always be less than perfectly realized. Moral choice, therefore, will be made not solely in the light of a vision of values in the abstract, but also in the shadow of the actual world, always less than perfect, in which those values are practiced with a greater or lesser degree of faithfulness.

Each economic system has its own moral foundation or, at least, moral implications. Benjamin Ward tried to show that economics is thoroughly permeated by ideology in its structure, in the ways it asks questions and answers them, and in the ways policy implications are drawn from it.[1]

It will be helpful, therefore, to examine in outline the main elements of the major economic philosophies in the world today to uncover their moral foundations and implications. Common areas of concern will be: the understanding of property and the ownership of resources and production; the rights and nature of labor; the determination of what to do with profit; the freedom of individuals to produce and consume what they choose; the understanding of competition and incentive; the nature of obligations to those who are poor and/or economically unproductive; the exercise of power in the political arena based on economic power; the distribution of economic wealth as based on need or on economic contribution; the understanding of the fulfilled life in relation to economic production and consumption.

ECONOMIC PHILOSOPHIES—I

Laissez-Faire or Free Market Economics

At one extreme in the spectrum of economic philosophies is a position that intersects at many points with the political philosophy known as laissez-faire. The economic side of this philosophy stresses the importance of individual initiative and enterprise in producing whatever goods seem desirable to the producer and offering them on the free market for whatever price they will command. This means granting as much freedom as possible to the individual to determine his or her own interests, either in buying or selling. Buttressed by the famous "invisible hand" first propounded by the moralist-economist Adam Smith, this position claims that as individuals pursue their own self-interests, the good of the whole will be enhanced.

> Every individual intends only his own gain, and he is in this, as in so many other cases, led by an invisible hand to promote an end which was no part of his intention.[2]

A basic assumption of the laissez-faire or capitalist doctrine is that human beings are essentially motivated by self-interest. Any attempt to

---

[1]Benjamin Ward, *The Ideal Worlds of Economics: Liberal, Radical and Conservative Economic World Views* (New York: Basic Books, 1979), p. viii.
[2]Adam Smith, *An Inquiry Into the Nature and Causes of the Wealth of Nations*, ed. Edwin Cannan (New York: Modern Library, 1937), p. 423.

regulate that self-interest from the outside (by governmental interference) will result in the curtailment of the initiative and ambition that produces the best efforts from all the members of the social order. In America this ideology has been called the American Way of Life or the private enterprise system and has been identified with what is great and virtuous about the way Americans do business. As the National Association of Manufacturers booklet *The American Individual Enterprise System* put it in 1946:

> We became a nation of free men ... free to pursue our happiness without interference from the state, with the greatest liberty of individual action ever known to man. Individuals, conscious of unbounded opportunity, inflamed by the love of achievement, inspired by the hope of profit, ambitious of the comfort, power and influence that wealth brings, turned with ... vigor to producing and offering goods and services in freely competitive markets. The individual wanted little from the government beyond police protection while he confidently worked out his own destiny.... Our "private enterprise system" and our American form of government are inseparable and there can be no compromise between a free economy and a governmentally dictated economy without endangering our political as well as our economic freedom.[3]

Without a governmentally dictated economy it might be supposed that economic decisions and their effects would be chaotic. Supporters of laissez-faire capitalism claim, however, that the market regulates itself in and through the free decisions of individual producers and consumers. If people are free to offer their products at whatever price they choose, then it obviously is in their best interest to charge a lower price than others who are offering the same thing. It also serves their interests to offer only what others are interested in buying. Thus, nothing will be produced that is not desired, and what is produced will be required, by the influence of the consumer, to be of good quality and low price. If an item is poorly made and overpriced, consumers will seek alternatives to it. This will encourage some producers to bring onto the market a better made, less expensive substitute. Thus both producer and consumer come out ahead and the market is seen to discipline or regulate itself. As Irving Kristol has said, "mere commercial activity—what Robert Nozick so nicely calls commercial transactions between consenting adults—... should be the dynamic force which defines and shapes the civilization."[4]

---

[3]The Economic Principles Commission of the National Association of Manufacturers, *The American Individual Enterprise System.* vol. II (New York, McGraw-Hill Co., Inc., 1946), pp. 1018–1021.
[4]Irving Kristol, "The Disaffection From Capitalism," in *Capitalism and Socialism: A Theological Inquiry,* ed. Michael Novak (Washington, D.C.: American Enterprise Institute for Public Policy Research, 1979,) p. 16.

Incentive Rewarded

In a capitalist scheme, it is argued, there is every incentive for initiative and ambition since, "inflamed by the love of achievement," enterprising entrepeneurs will be creative in coming up with new ways of offering new things to meet new and particular demands by free consumers. The end result, as has been put by Ludwig von Mises, is that

> free enterprise has radically changed the fate of man. . . . It has, in an unprecedented way, raised the standard of living of the average man in those nations that did not too severely impede the acquisitive spirit of enterprising individuals.[5]

The Profit Motive

At the heart of this capitalist view of human beings is the conviction that they are driven by individual self-interest. As long as room is provided for ambition and incentive, competing self-interests will produce the best for all. The economic implication of this view is the notion of the profit motive. People will always seek to make a profit from whatever deals or enterprises they engage in. A profit is simply what is left over after all the expenses of producing and marketing the object to be sold have been met. The capitalist position assumes that everyone wants to make a profit, although it admits that not everyone will want to use the profit made in the same way. Lest this be seen as making a virtue out of selfishness, it is immediately pointed out by defenders of capitalism that the search for profit will induce the producer to serve the needs of those to whom he wishes to sell his product. Thus, self-interest is seen to work for the benefit of all. As von Mises puts it:

> [B]y the instrumentality of the profit-and-loss system, the most eminent members of society are prompted to serve to the best of their abilities the well-being of the masses of less gifted people. What pays under capitalism is satisfying the common man, the customer. The more people you satisfy, the better for you.[6]

Competition

Closely tied to the profit motive is the principle of competition. To achieve more profit, producers must compete with their rivals in the race to offer cheaper, more attractive goods. Without the constant threat of competi-

---

[5]Ludwig von Mises, *The Ultimate Foundation of Economic Science: An Essay on Method* (Princeton: Van Nostrand, 1962), p. 122.
[6]von Mises, p. 128.

tion, producers will become complacent, their goods will become shoddy, and there will be no incentive to keep prices low. Success in the marketplace may not, in and of itself, be the goal of the entrepeneur, but merely the means to the real end: status in the community or power to carry out social goals or to be of service to the larger society. In addition, competition is a stimulus to moral sensitivity. Edward Norman claims that

> the competitive deployment of personal resources and talents is a tremendous stimulus to moral self-consciousness; it encourages, rather than discourages, the individual in the cultivation of a practical scheme of responsibility for his actions, and imposes, as a condition of maintaining living standards, a sense of moral duty.[7]

Private Property

In addition to ambition, profit, and competition, capitalism is linked to the defense of private property. To own personally what one has been able to purchase with the money earned by one's own efforts is a basic right within this system. Any threat aimed at confiscating or limiting the right to private property is regarded as a threat to the rewards that make the system operative. In addition, without the use of private property the entrepeneur is not free to use profits in whatever way he or she deems best. To make the system work, the entrepreneur must have the freedom to use his or her property (whether in the form of money or tangible goods such as land) in whatever way will contribute to his or her own enhancement. This might mean reinvesting the money in upgrading the business, opening a new business, buying out rivals, or in pursuit of luxury items for oneself. Unless entrepreneurs know that their property is their own to do with as they want, their ambition and incentive will be thwarted and the system will start to unravel.

It is often pointed out in defense of capitalism that persons who use their money or property to make more profit are only being rewarded for being willing to risk their money. The system works in large part because capitalists are willing to risk their "capital" in new ventures whose success is not guaranteed at the outset since all success in the market depends on the uncoerced choices of the consumer. Thus, an automobile manufacturer who risks capital in the production of a new kind of car should be rewarded for that risk, should the venture prove successful, by the profits the investment produces. It is always possible, in this arrangement, to lose what is risked in investment. Thus, knowledge, creativity, and skill are encouraged.

[7]Edward R. Norman, "Denigration of Capitalism: Current Education and the Moral Subversion of Capitalist Society," in *The Denigration of Capitalism: Six Points of View*, ed. Michael Novak (Washington, D.C.: American Enterprise Institute for Public Policy Research, 1979), p. 9.

Social Obligations

But what, it might be asked, does this system do for those who are unable to offer anything on the market and therefore are not able to receive its rewards? First, it has been argued, capitalism on the whole creates wealthier countries than do alternative economic systems. Thus, while there may be relative poverty in a capitalist country—between those aged, infirm, and incompetent, on the one hand, and the successful, rich, and enterprising, on the other—there is greater wealth for this country's "poor" relative to the extreme poverty in other countries. In addition, capitalism generally works best when it is producing for mass consumption. As Joseph Schumpeter has pointed out, the rich have always been able to afford whatever they wanted: it is the poor who are best served by the production of cheap goods, mass produced.

> Electric lighting is not a great boon to anyone who has money enough to buy a sufficient number of candles. . . . It is the cheap cloth, the cheap cotton and rayon fabric, boots, motorcars, and so on that are the typical achievements of capitalist production, and not as a rule improvements that would mean much to the rich man. . . . The capitalist achievement does not typically consist in providing more silk stockings for queens but in bringing them within the reach of factory girls in return for steadily decreasing amounts of effort . . . the capitalist process . . . progressively raises the standard of life of the masses.[8]

It is also claimed by the capitalists that it is they who provide the employment that gives the great bulk of workers the money needed to purchase the goods they desire. If the capitalists were unwilling to risk capital in investment in industry or production, there would be no jobs. Therefore, the more the capitalists are encouraged to pursue profit, the more the workers benefit since capitalists depend on the workers' labor to maximize their own income. Workers expend their "capital"—their labor—and are rewarded for this investment with profit—wages. Since the workers have every right to choose for whom they will work, their fundamental freedom and rights are also protected under capitalism.

Finally, it is argued, the obligation to meet the needs of those unable to contribute to the productive process is one that rests on the moral conscience of individuals. As Milton Friedman puts it:

> The capitalist system must leave the ethical problem for the individual to wrestle with. The "really" important ethical problems are those that face an individual in a free society—what he should do with his freedom.[9]

---

[8]J. A. Schumpeter, *Capitalism, Socialism and Democracy*, 3rd ed. (New York: Harper, 1950, 1962), p. 64.

[9]Milton Friedman, *Capitalism and Freedom* (Chicago: Univ. of Chicago Press, 1962), p. 12.

For the state to take from the rich to meet the needs of the poor is to condone stealing since it is unfair to take people's property without their consent. People should pay for the services they demand. Unless the demands of justice are met voluntarily by the conscientious decisions of those able to meet them, morality is not served. In extreme cases, such as those in which persons are victims of circumstances that render them unable to compete in the marketplace, it might be necessary to give them enough money to reenter it. This basic minimum income, achieved through a negative income tax, would replace all forms of social welfare because it would bring everyone back into the free-for-all of the market and would put moral responsibility for their own welfare back where it belongs—on their own initiative and power of choice.

Versions of Capitalism

There are versions of laissez-faire capitalism that accept many of its basic moral assumptions but seek to modify them so as to ameliorate more directly the condition of the poor and disadvantaged. A basic version of the model accepts the premise that capitalism is very useful as a means of production. However, it wishes to supply ends to the economic system from outside itself. Sometimes known as social market capitalism or welfare capitalism, this model wishes the workers, the wage earners, to share more directly and equitably in the achievements of the system. This "mixed economy" is one in which the state controls and plans, in various ways, the activities of the private business sector. The state may also become the owner and producer of some industries while permitting private business people to play a role in the management of other industries.

The state should set the rules within which the capitalist works and should take the primary responsibility for meeting public needs: education, police protection, medical care, social security, and standards for safe products. In other words, the state should be prepared to interfere with the workings of the market to ensure a greater degree of security for that part of the society unable to fend successfully for itself in the marketplace and to provide services required by all persons equally, regardless of their ability to pay for it in full out of their earnings. A political decision might be made, for example to limit the monopoly of one company over all the oil to be developed in a country. Such a decision would be made on behalf of the public to ensure that oil is available at low enough prices so that no one is forced to go without. Or a government might choose to nationalize an industry to control, on behalf of the whole society, both the amount of goods produced by that industry and their price.

Thus, social market capitalism accepts the workings of the capitalist system but modifies their effects on those members of the society who would be seriously disadvantaged or impoverished if they had to rely entirely on their own ability to compete without aid in the marketplace. Much of the moral debate over economic issues in this country revolves around the virtues of social market capitalism as a modifier of strict laissez-faire capitalism. The issue, essentially, is the degree to which governmental interference with the market is warranted in particular cases.

ECONOMIC PHILOSOPHIES—II

A Socialist Critique of Capitalism

In the economic spectrum at the end opposite capitalism are the various forms of socialism. Just as they propose a radically different understanding of economic arrangements, so they build on a very different understanding of human nature and its fulfillment. Although socialist economics has not had much appeal in the United States it is a moral alternative that requires serious attention by Americans because of its attractiveness to large numbers of people around the world.

Historically, the theory of socialism emerged as a reaction to what some regarded as the moral failure of capitalism. Socialism therefore depends on capitalism in a way that capitalism does not depend on socialism. Socialism began as a criticism of capitalism. It cannot be understood except through its criticism. We must examine that criticism, therefore, before looking at the alternative socialism proposes to capitalism.

REFLECTIONS ON FREEDOM IN A MARKET ECONOMY

The passing of market-economy can become the beginning of an era of unprecedented freedom. . . . Yet we find the path blocked by a moral obstacle. Planning and control are being attacked as a denial of freedom. Free enterprise and private ownership are declared to be essentials of freedom. . . . The freedom that regulation creates is denounced as unfreedom; the justice, liberty and welfare it offers are decried as a camouflage of slavery. . . . With the liberal the idea of freedom thus degenerates into a mere advocacy of free enterprise—which is today reduced to a fiction by the hard reality of giant trusts and princely monopolies. . . . This leaves no alternative but either to remain faithful to an illusionary idea of freedom and deny the reality of society, or to accept that reality and reject the idea of freedom. . . . The discarding of the market utopia brings us face to face with the reality of society. It is the dividing line between liberalism on the one hand, fascism and socialism on the other. The difference between these two is not primarily economic. It is moral and religious. Even where they profess identical economics, they are not only different but are, indeed, embodiments of opposite principles. And the ultimate on which they separate is again freedom . . . is freedom an empty word, a temptation, designed to ruin man and his works, or can man reassert his freedom in the face of that knowledge and strive for its fulfillment in society without lapsing into moral illusionism?

Karl Polanyi, *The Great Transformation* (Boston: Beacon, 1957), pp. 258–259.

Karl Polanyi (1886–1964) taught in the fields of politics and economics. He was particularly interested in the social implications of economic theory and practice. He taught at Oxford, the University of London, and Bennington College. He is the author of The Essence of Fascism.

This indictment normally has two dimensions: one lists the undesirable consequences of living under capitalism and the other criticizes the view of human nature capitalism endorses and encourages.

At the heart of the practical rejection of capitalism is the claim that it is unjust in its distribution of the goods of a social order. Critics point out that the laissez-faire model assumes that every member of the market economy has something to sell that is as potentially valuable as whatever can be sold or marketed by every other member. If all enter the market with the same chips or bargaining power, then equity might be served. But in fact we know that not everyone does enter at the same level. If capital (property, money, etc.) is necessary to move forward, then obviously those with inherited wealth start far ahead of those born into poverty, malnutrition, and ignorance. There is no mechanism intrinsic to capitalist values, as such, to remedy the inequities of the starting line.

Distribution of Wealth

The effect of these inequities is dramatically revealed in the picture of wealth distribution in the United States today. Our distribution is roughly the same as India's.[10] Two-thirds of all manufacturing assets are controlled by 200 giant corporations. In other words, the control of the capitalist system is concentrated in the hands of very few persons and corporations. Less than 2 percent of the population owns 80 percent of all corporate stock. Only 74,000 persons own at least 40 percent of all the corporate stock in the country. To put it in terms of income, 20 percent of American families receives nearly 46 percent of America's income, while the 20 percent at the other end of the spectrum receives 14 times less or a little over 3 percent. One percent of American families receives more than twice the income of the 20 percent of families who occupy the bottom rung of the income ladder.

Concentration of Power

This concentration of economic power in the hands of few people obviously makes them able to exert extraordinary and disproportionate influence on the institutions of government that determine policy for the country as a whole. In the 90th Congress, for example, there were ninety-seven bankers, twelve of whom sat on the House Banking Commission, which sets rules for the banking industry. It would be hard to imagine a clearer case of potential conflict of interest. Access to political power by those who profit most from capitalism results in an array of laws permitting what are commonly known as tax loopholes for the wealthy. In 1967 twenty-one millionaires paid no federal taxes at all. In 1966 $250 million was paid in farm subsidies to well-off farmers comprising less than .02 percent of the population in Texas while 28 percent of the people living in that state below the official poverty line received only $7 million in all forms of food assistance.

Most Americans, in other words, are not capitalists: most do not own stocks, most do not invest in their own business. Thus, relatively few persons control the capitalist economic system, while the majority of persons depend on the capitalists' decisions for employment, housing, availability of goods, and revenues to pay for education, medical care, etc.

---

[10]These and other claims about capitalism are taken from Eugene Toland, Thomas Fenton, and Lawrence McCulloch, "Project for Justice and Peace" in *Struggling with the System*, ed. Robert L. DeWitt (Ambler, Pa.: Witness Magazine, 1976).

This means that real power and the enactment of values comes from within

> tiny self-perpetuating oligarichies. These in turn are drawn from and judged by the group opinion of a small fragment of America—its business and financial community. . . . Thus the only real control which guides or limits their economic and social action is the real, though undefined and tacit, philosophy of the men who compose them.[11]

Limits on Freedom

The majority of people in a capitalist system find themselves bound by the restrictions of what is supposed to be a system that rewards freedom. For example, intelligent use of freedom presupposes a thorough knowledge of what one wants to purchase, including its alternatives. It also presupposes that one genuinely has the freedom not to buy what is offered on the market (thus forcing down the price). And it presupposes genuine competition among producers of the same item. None of these presuppositions is fully operative for most consumers today. Most people are not free to choose a house or an apartment to live in; most are not free to choose to seek medical care—neither need can be satisfied without having to purchase, out of whatever resources one can secure, these items from sellers who offer them at whatever price the market will bear. Thus, many people are shut out of owning a home or renting a decent apartment because they don't have the bargaining chips to secure them.

In other service areas, there is little or no competition among providers. A buyer has little choice about who will provide energy in the home or telephone service or transportation. Even in industries in which there are different companies offering a similar product (such as the automobile industry), it is difficult to find genuine competition due to corporate decisions not to seriously undercut corporate rivals.

In addition, most consumers simply do not have the thorough knowledge necessary to distinguish between the services of one company and another. This is particularly true in the field of medicine in which the patient is not expected to pass judgment on the doctor's advice but is expected to pay for it on the market model of consumption.

Labor as a Commodity

Beyond the question of the degree of power the consumer has to exercise assumed freedom in the marketplace, critics point to the problem of the

[11]Adolf A. Berle, *The 20th Century Capitalist Revolution* (New York: Harcourt, 1954), p. 180.

employee, the worker in the capitalist system. For most people, the only bargaining chip is the labor they can provide. Thus, they must offer to the employer their personal capital: their ability to work. Their labor becomes a commodity to be sold on the open market. This puts the laborer in a unique position. The capitalist can risk his monetary capital without endangering his person: the laborer has only his person to risk and thus is bought or invested in as an object.

The Marxist critique of capitalism is particularly sensitive to this issue. It argues that the worker *becomes* an object in capitalism because himself is all he has to offer. Thus, he becomes alienated, that is, separated in a profound way from himself (he comes to see himself only as an object to be used in the productive process), from other persons (they become his rivals since they are competing with him to be bought for labor), and from what he does with his labor (he comes to see his labor not as a creative act arising out of his freedom but as drudgery, as meaningless repetition of meaningless work). At the same time, the worker cannot opt out of this cycle of alienation because if he does not allow himself to be bought, he will find himself unemployed. And in capitalism, without employment there is no income and without income there are no bargaining chips at all. In a system that makes virtually all important services and commodities (including those having to do with medical care, housing, clothing, transportation, and even some forms of education) dependent on the purchasing power of the consumer, the threat of unemployment is the threat of being cut off from any decent standard of living.

COMMUNITY AND CONSUMPTION IN CONFLICT

Poverty is a social and political status involving vulnerability to political and even police intervention in one's life and the lack of any effective power to assert one's wishes and needs. Poverty is bad mainly because it is a condition of powerlessness, not because, in America at least, it involves stark material want. When poverty is chosen, when it is a voluntary status, undertaken for some moral or religious end, it is often a state of joy rather than of suffering, as in the case of Thoreau at Walden, the Peace Corps worker, or the inhabitant of a rural commune. . . . There is every reason to believe that a life of material austerity, of pride and pleasure in the quality of workmanship rather than in the amount consumed, a life lived in a warm and supportive community, would be far healthier for our society, ecologically and sociologically, than our present dominant pattern of ever-accelerating consumption. But our economy could not survive a mass turn to voluntary poverty . . . and our economy exerts all of its enormous power to prevent such a turn. I submit that of the several critical features of our present social situation that leads me to call it America's third time of trial this is the most decisive.

Robert Bellah, *The Broken Covenant* (New York: Seabury, 1975), p. 135–136.

Robert Bellah (b. 1927) is Ford Professor of Sociology and Comparative Studies at the University of California, Berkeley. He has explored the relation between religion and society in a number of books, including Beyond Belief *and* Religion and Progress in Modern Asia. *He is also the author of "Civil Religion in America."*

Racism and Sexism

Because of the need for human labor, capitalism encourages what some have called a "reserve army of unemployed" from whose ranks capitalists can always threaten to draw low paid workers if present workers do not contain their demands for higher pay or better working conditions. There is no incentive for the employer to pay workers more than necessary to get them to accept work. This has led some companies to locate in poorer countries where wages are lower. For the same reason, it is to the employer's advantage to exploit racial and gender differences. As women are forced to return to the marketplace to help supplement their husbands' income, they are forced into accepting lower paying jobs to have jobs at all. The same is true for minority groups who are normally hit hardest by any cutback in employment, thus suffering time and again the "last hired, first fired" syndrome. This puts black people in a peculiarly vulnerable position within capitalism. They

> pay higher rents for inferior housing, higher prices in ghetto stores, higher insurance premiums, higher interest rates in banks and lending companies, travel longer distances at greater expense to their jobs, suffer from inferior garbage collection and less access to public recreational facilities, and are assessed at higher property tax rates when they own housing. Employers, by not discouraging white male resentment of blacks and women entering the labor force, enjoy the benefits of not having this force organized and united in their bargaining position.[12]

[12]From Michael Reich, "The Economics of Racism," in DeWitt, p. 90.

Stimulation Through Advertising

Excessive criticisms of capitalism point to its use of massive advertising to lure consumers into buying items the social or personal value of which is never questioned by the system. Thousands of items are sold every year simply because a producer has found a way, through clever advertising, to stimulate interest in them. Do people really *need* enormous gas guzzling cars, homes with more rooms than can be lived in, home video cassettes, elaborate cemeteries for dogs, and so on? It has been claimed that Americans spend more money every year on liquor and tobacco than on education. Capitalism has no incentive to sell only those things that are socially useful since its basic incentive is to sell what *can* be sold at profit. Thus, capitalism employs thousands of people and agencies simply to stimulate interest in nonessential items. The charge leveled at capitalism in this regard is that it is inherently wasteful and inefficient. It does not provide work for everyone who wants to work,

> much of its men and materials is devoted to the production of the most extravagant luxuries at the same time that enough of the necessities of life for all is not produced . . . in its concern for increased price and profitability instead of for human needs, it sanctions the deliberate destruction of crops and goods.[13]

Capitalism is also wasteful in that there is no incentive to preserve dwindling natural resources. The capitalist system depends on the assumption that there is an infinite supply of the resources from which it makes its products. Even when it becomes clear that some of these resources are soon going to be used up, like oil, capitalism as it now stands has no incentive to cut back on its use since the system is driven by the search for profits. In fact, the more scarce and close to depletion a resource is, the more profit can be made from selling it since people are going to be willing to pay dearly for it. Thus the system, according to its socialist critics, is irrational as well as wasteful. By forbidding any over-all planning of the economy, capitalism necessarily must go through periodic breakdown and crisis: recession, depression, and the resulting unemployment.

Socialist Criticism of Capitalism's View of People

The preceding are some of the alleged factual consequences of capitalism according to its critics; the other dimension of their criticism centers on the view of human nature in the system. Fundamentally, critics point to capitalism's view of people as essentially selfish, driven by the desire to be

---

[13]Leo Huberman, ''The ABC of Socialism'' in DeWitt, p. 110.

superior to others in wealth, status, or power. The profit motive, while it may have produced some creative inventions in the past, has a tendency to exalt the worst aspects of human beings. As John Bennett puts it:

> The profit motive... is morally objectionable. It tends to corrupt the individual and it becomes the source of temptation, even in far-reaching decisions, to put a very limited interest before the common good.[14]

The profit motive is linked, of course, with competition and individualism. In the capitalist system, priority is given to individual interests with the result that other persons are seen primarily as competitors, as things to work against or get the better of so that one may rise above them in status, wealth, or power. Thus, capitalism is essentially destructive of the social, communal impulse in persons. It provides no real incentive to work cooperatively (except to make a better profit at the expense of some other group), and no incentive to work *for* the needs of others or for those aspects of human life that celebrate and enhance the joy of sharing with and acting justly toward others.

The ultimate indictment, for some, of the capitalist system is that it has no way of providing systematically and intentionally for *social* needs. J. Philip Wogaman captures the issue in an imaginary debate between a capitalist and a Marxist critic:

> *Capitalist:* The capitalist... responds to market demand.... He is the servant of the consumer.
> *Marxist:* This may be *somewhat* true—if we could ignore monopoly price-fixing, manipulation by advertising, planned obsolescence, collusion among manufacturers to limit production, and other devices of consumer manipulation. But even if it were entirely true that the capitalist is the "servant" of the consumer, this only begs the question of power. For consumer power only represents a partial interest of society, not the whole interest. The whole interest includes what can be called public goods. Private capital, under pure capitalism, retains the right to determine *that* as well. The market is not a very good mechanism for determining social consumption because it is private and *individualistic....* The individualism of the market... is appropriate to private consumption—not to public expenditures for needed public goods and services.[15]

The moral issue raised by capitalism's critics is the ability of this economic system to serve the needs of the social order rather than the needs of

[14]John C. Bennett, "Capitalism, Ethics, and Morality," in National Industrial Conference Board, *The Future of Capitalism* (New York: Macmillan, 1967), p. 162.
[15]J. Philip Wogaman, *The Great Economic Debate: An Ethical Analysis* (Philadelphia: Westminster, 1977), pp. 94–96.

some at the expense of others. The alternative to the criticism historically has been some real or theoretical version of socialism, with the emphasis clearly on the social dimensions of living together in equity and justice.

THE SOCIALIST ALTERNATIVE

Drawing on Marx's view (see Chapter 4 for a discussion of the foundation of Marxist ethics) that under capitalism the worker is alienated from himself, from other persons, and from the results of his labor, socialist philosophers have insisted that under socialism persons will be able to fulfill their social or communal nature. In communism there will be "the complete return of man to himself as a social (i.e., human) being."[16] Socialists generally admit, however, that it will require a revolution in human consciousness and in economic and social arrangements to bring out the communal impulse so long buried under capitalism.

Under socialism, the first practical goal will be to transfer production from private to social control. There must be public ownership of the means of production if the people are to determine effectively what should be produced for their needs.

Cloth will be made, not to make money, but to provide people with clothes—and so will all other goods.[17]

In place of the competitive free-for-all of the marketplace, socialism would substitute some form of central planning. This would avoid, socialists claim, the wasteful, overlapping efforts of capitalist production, including the enormous waste and debilitating effects of money and energy spent on advertising that appeals to the baser instincts of human beings.

In such a socialist system the worker will no longer be exploited by someone else: he will feel engaged in the productive process because he is working for a community in which he has an important stake and a deciding voice. Critics of socialism point out that this vision is simply naive or utopian. Peter Berger claims that "the fundamental contradiction of socialism . . . is that every empirical attempt to realize its vision of solidarity has resulted in alienations far worse than it protested against in the first place."[18] Or, as Michael Novak puts it, "we live in a world, after all, which has been and is harsh to human beings . . . there is a not-niceness in nature" which the socialist blindly covers over in his unrealistic assumptions about human motivation.[19]

[16]Karl Marx, *Economic and Philosophic Manuscripts of 1844,* trans. Martin Milligan, ed. Dirk Struik (New York: International, 1964), p. 135.

[17]Huberman, p. 127.

[18]Peter Berger, "Capitalism and Socialism: Ethical Assessment," in *Capitalism and Socialism,* p. 98.

[19]Michael Novak, "Seven Theological Facets," in *Capitalism and Socialism,* p. 118–119.

Freedom Within Socialism

One of the most serious problems socialists have to face as they look toward implementing their vision is how much freedom to permit the people as a whole in making the basic decisions that affect their lives. This is the problem of democratic versus autocratic socialism. If it claims that the people are the real determiners of their lives (and thus of the economy and politics that serve them), how can socialism avoid the people democratically making decisions that are hedonistic, selfish, or just plain stupid? Can socialism, in a political democracy, avoid the emergence of self-interest seeking to consolidate power under the rhetoric of "communal interest"? The experience of the Soviet Union is not reassuring on this score. It has been tempting for some forms of socialism to insist on control from the top in the name of the people on the bottom. The result has been the creation of a totalitarian regime in which personal freedom has been reduced or even eliminated. The fundamental human desire for such freedom is witnessed to by the increasing attempts of many within socialist countries to escape them. The presence of the same impulses intrinsic to capitalism (initiative, desire for power, competition) thus becomes as much a problem for autocratic socialism as it does for its hated alternative.

Efficiency

There is also the problem of efficiency. While it might sound nice to talk about the people making decisions, how is this to be effected in a practical way? Wouldn't layer upon layer of a bureaucracy have to be developed? Wouldn't every idea have to pass up and down thousands of channels, be checked out in a multitude of ways by millions of people before it could be enacted? The problems are difficult. Capitalists point to the unenthusiastic mood among workers in socialist countries. Some socialist systems, like Yugoslavia, *are* experimenting with variations in the socialist model to overcome this problem. By decentralizing some decisions and by allowing a limited form of competition among some worker-owned industries, the Yugoslavs are trying to balance the need for overall social planning with the need for greater efficiency and a closer relation between groups of people and their decisions. The capitalist objection to socialist economic *practice* has been to argue that it cannot do what it promises. "It offers redistribution *and* abundance—and on this promise it simply cannot deliver."[20]

[20]Irving Kristol, "The Spiritual Roots of Capitalism and Socialism," in *Capitalism and Socialism*, p. 9.

Capitalism, on the other hand, offers the possibility of continual economic growth—"and delivers."[21] The failure of socialist systems to satisfy
the economic needs of their people is indicated by reports of workers'
dissatisfaction with goods and services from within some socialist countries. The lack of statistical information (which would justify a point-by-
point comparison of such information between this country and many
socialist countries) also indicates the relative lack of openness found in
nondemocratic, noncapitalist societies.

Perhaps the most important issue in this regard in any socialist scheme
is the rights of those members who dissent from the will of the majority.
How will those rights be protected? What role will there be for a critical and
vocal minority viewpoint? A democratic socialism would have less trouble
with this question than an autocratic one, but so far, no completely persuasive models have been realized in practice.

A Comparative Issue: Medical Care

A brief examination of a concrete issue common to both socialism and
capitalism will help, in summary, to illuminate the differences between
these two models of human life. No subject in recent years has stirred up
so much debate (in this country) as the question of whether we should
have a national health insurance scheme. Opponents say that such a plan
smacks of socialism and would undercut the free enterprise system that
has made American medicine the envy of the world.

The issue is essentially one of the right of persons to have medical care
provided without regard to their ability to pay what the market demands
versus the right of the medical profession to sell its services on the free
market according to the rules of free enterprise. The proposal for national
health insurance (in its various forms) rests on the claim that medical care is
a *right* of every person, as basic a right as education or the vote. As a right,
it cannot be made available on the basis of ability to pay. Socialists would
argue that the only way to resolve the problem of providing medical care to
those who cannot afford it is through some control of the medical care
system by society as a whole. Someone will eventually have to pay for the
care provided, but if it is controlled and planned centrally (allowing for
some freedom of choice in areas not affecting ability to pay), people will not
be afraid to seek medical help out of fear that they cannot pay for it.

Socialists also point out that in capitalism consumers (the patients) have
little or no control over what they pay for: they must pay the doctor's fee

---

[21]Kristol, p. 27.

(or the insurance premium) but beyond that are at the mercy of the doctor's decisions about how much more care (and thus how much more money) is needed. The fee-for-service model, basic to capitalism, has a built-in conflict of interest for doctors since it is they who determine how much more service the patient needs and it is they who benefit from that determination. Capitalists reply by pointing out that doctors will not be inclined to do their best work or put in long hours and creative effort if the impersonal, bureaucratic hand of the state controls their activity. They argue that many doctors in socialized medical schemes, such as Great Britain's, are trying to leave and move to countries where no such controls exist. The socialist, in response to this argument, asks whether ministering to the medical needs of other human beings should ever be based on the desire for profit or monetary advantage. Thus, at the very heart of the debate over national health insurance we find revealed, perhaps more clearly than anywhere else, the fundamental differences between those who assume something like the socialist mode of human interaction and those who assume the capitalist values.

A Conservationist Caution

Historically, the debate between capitalism and socialism has occupied most of the space allotted to discussion of economic models and their ethical implications. Recently, however, a third economic model has entered the discussion. It sharply questions some assumptions common to both capitalism and socialism. Known as conservationism, or simply as "the small is beautiful" concept (after its primary spokesman, E. F. Schumacher), this model rejects what it calls the idols of productivity and consumption (no matter who determines them) and replaces them with a vision of life lived simply and in harmony with the environment. (See Chapter 16 for a fuller discussion of the ecological issues underlying this economic model.) We live in a time of rapidly depleting, nonrenewable natural resources like oil and gas. We have been driven in the past by the notion that our standard of living must continually rise and that economic growth is necessary to that end. This has meant greater and greater (material) consumption. Schumacher and others wish to call a halt to this notion of human fulfillment.

It is not the quantity of things consumed, they argue, but the quality of consumption that makes life meaningful. This might mean a return to a form of production that is much more limited in scope and involves the worker much more directly. Production and technology need to be scaled down, not built up, to serve the specific needs of those who will use them. The economic machine must not be out of balance with the sustainable resources of the earth. Reducing levels of consumption need not mean a return to a lower standard of living, but a different standard, one in which work and leisure are more harmoniously integrated and thus more fulfilling.

It might be argued that this model of scaled-down economics is more in line with socialism than capitalism but its advocates point out that many socialist economies have the same uncontrolled urge to increase production as capitalism does despite the different way in which it is determined and its fruits distributed.

Nevertheless, the model of human life suggested by the small is beautiful conservationist idea does, like socialism, point away from the individualism and hedonism implicit in capitalism and toward an understanding of human nature more directly based on the joys of human fellowship and creative activity.

ECONOMIC IDEALS AND ECONOMIC REALITY

It should be clear that in our analysis of alternative economic systems, we have been treating both as *ideals:* We have stressed the values each claims to strive for. But in practice ideals are always less than fully realized. The free market system is not entirely free nor is it wholly a market. Similarly, socialist values have never been fully embodied in any economic or social system. The critic of socialism uses the fact that no ideals are ever actualized in their purity to insist that socialism is naive and that capitalism is realistic about its understanding of human nature. The critic of capitalism uses the fact that ideals are not now being realized as a sign that capitalism prevents these values from being considered seriously and the socialist's values have not yet had a chance to be practiced without the shadow of capitalist hegemony hanging over them.

What this means is that in the real world, moral choices are made within systems that are less than pure. There are many factors beyond our control which impinge upon and impede the successful realization of moral values. It is important, therefore, to know which values can be put into practice with the least amount of distortion. It is also important to know which proclaimed ideals can be exploited most easily in order to justify self-serving or unjust behavior.

Moral reflection upon the values essential to different ways of organizing economic relationships is not complete until one has considered the complete picture of how these values come into play in the course of actual social and economic practice. Nevertheless, such practice should not become the object of attention so exclusively that it obscures the very real, though sometimes hard to reach, foundation of values on which all human institutions are ultimately built.

CHAPTER REVIEW

A. The moral context

1. Economic activity is moral activity because value judgments are always being made about what to produce and what to consume.
2. Each economic system has its own moral foundation.

B. Economic philosophies

1. Laissez-faire or free market economics stipulates that if each individual is free to pursue his or her own self-interest, a social order will emerge in which the good of the whole will be enhanced.
2. In such a scheme, incentive and the love of achievement will be rewarded.
3. The profit motive is the catalyst that drives the economic system and rewards incentive. Closely tied to it are the principles of competition and the defense of the right to private property.
4. Capitalism meets its social obligations by rewarding the production of goods for mass consumption and by providing employment.
5. There are versions of capitalism in which the state plays a more active role in meeting basic public needs such as education, police protection, and protection against deception.

C. A socialist critique of capitalism

1. The socialist criticism of the free market system, echoed by many people around the globe, focuses on what it regards as the failure of capitalism to achieve economic justice.
2. The inequities of capitalism are alleged to be unequal distribution of wealth, the concentration of power in relatively few hands, the limits of freedom for those with little to offer on the market, the treatment of labor as a commodity, and the exploitation of racism and sexism.
3. Capitalism as such has no incentive to sell goods that are essential for human welfare or to refrain from stimulating, through advertising, a desire for goods that are nonessential.
4. A crucial objection to capitalism by its socialist critics is that its view of human nature is demeaning. Capitalism regards human beings as self-centered individuals who are not interested in working communally for the common good.

D. The socialist alternative

1. Drawing on the work of Karl Marx, the socialist alternative looks toward an economic system in which the human being's social nature

will be fulfilled. In such a system production will be under social control and will be centrally planned.

2. The socialist alternative must face the question of whether it permits sufficient individual freedoms and is efficient in providing what it promises.

3. The provision of medical care under capitalism and socialism reveals the fundamental differences between the two systems.

4. A warning to both capitalism and socialism is issued by conservationists who argue that any responsible economic system must learn to conserve its resources.

5. Economic ideals are never realized perfectly. Moral choice will depend in part on which economic values can be realized in practice with the least amount of distortion and which are less easily subverted by self-serving rationalization.

SUGGESTED READINGS

Friedman, Milton. *Capitalism and Freedom.* Chicago: Univ. of Chicago Press, 1962.

A strong defense of capitalism by one of its most famous economic spokesmen.

Kristol, Irving. *Two Cheers for Capitalism.* New York: Basic Books, 1978.

Another strong defense of capitalism by someone who was once attracted to its alternative.

Marx, Karl. *The Economic and Philosophical Manuscripts of 1844.* Edited with an introduction by Drik J. Struik. Trans. Martin Milligan. New York: International, 1964.

The major work by Marx in which he presents his moral objections to capitalism.

McGovern, Arthur F. *Marxism: An American Christian Perspective.* Maryknoll, N.Y.: Orbis, 1980.

A comprehensive analysis of the development of Marxism and a fair comparison of its principles in relation to the principles of capitalism. Also deals with the religious objections to socialism.

Novak, Michael ed. *Capitalism and Socialism: A Theological Inquiry.* Washington D.C.: American Enterprise Institute for Public Policy Research, 1979.

A spirited collection of essays in support of the virtues of capitalism by some of its leading defenders, including Irving Kristol, S. M. Lipset, and Peter Berger.

Wogaman, J. Philip. *The Great Economic Debate: An Ethical Analysis.* Philadelphia: Westminster, 1977.

A masterful explication of the moral values implicit in different economic systems.

13

Freedom
of Thought
and Expression

All reforms owe their origin to the initiation of minorities in opposition to majorities. *

Thomas Jefferson once said in defense of freedom of thought and expression that "it does me no injury for my neighbor to say there are twenty gods, or no God. It neither picks my pocket nor breaks my leg."[1] What a man thinks and says, according to Jefferson, should not be the legitimate concern of government since its powers "extend to such acts only as are injurious to others."[2] In his argument are contained the seeds of all the dilemmas that surround the moral issue of freedom of thought and expression.

An Enlightenment thinker and rationalist, Jefferson was a firm believer in the power of free, critical minds to search out and destroy any errors that infect the body politic. In this belief Jefferson brought fresh support to an ancient assumption: that truth can be reached not by the coercive powers of imposed authority, but by the free exercise of a self-determining rational mind.

DILEMMAS OF FREEDOM OF EXPRESSION

In a perfect world Jefferson's assumption would be unchallenged. But in a morally ambiguous world, is it always true that the free expression of ideas leads necessarily to the truth? Although it may be true on most occasions, it is not hard for us to think of cases in which the opposite result occurs. If

---

*Mohandas K. Gandhi, *Non-Violent Resistance* (New York: Schocken Books, 1961. Copyright Navajivan Trust, Ahmedabad, 1951), p. 18.
[1]Thomas Jefferson, from *Notes on Virginia*, quoted in *Dissent*. Prepared by The Institute for Contemporary Curriculum Development (New York: Cambridge, 1972), p. 18.
[2]*Notes on Virginia.*

274

among three persons, one knows the correct path out of a deep forest and the other two do not, even though all three make the same claim to truth and have apparently equally persuasive reasons for doing so, there is a greater chance of remaining lost if the weight of the two false claims is believed to be greater than the weight of the one true claim. In other words, ignorance is not necessarily overcome by the free exchange of equally ignorant opinions.

There are other, more serious examples of situations in which complete freedom of expression would be problematic. The standard case is that of the freedom to stand up in a crowded theater and yell "Fire" without just cause. We know that some people will react to the announcement in panic, and in their rush for the exit many people will be hurt. Although Jefferson might believe that it will not break his leg for his neighbor to say there are twenty gods, it might very well break his leg if that same neighbor were to yell "Fire" in a theater in which Jefferson was sitting. Jefferson's defense of freedom of thought and expression is disingenuous because it seems to imply that speaking one's mind has no consequences for others. But this implication is clearly false as the examples just cited reveal.

Before pursuing the kinds of qualifications the right to free expression requires, it is necessary briefly to distinguish between two things so far considered together: freedom of thought and freedom of expression. Although morality is concerned with the nature of one's thoughts (e.g., one should not have lustful thoughts about another), the effectiveness of moral legislation is limited to those actions that are publicly *expressed*. This is not to say that the mind is beyond the influence of public action, but it is clearly the case that, even though some societies may have tried to proscribe certain types of thinking, beliefs and opinions cannot realistically be the object of moral legislation. Only the public articulation of them can be effectively coerced or forbidden.

Relative Freedoms

Because expression of thought will necessarily have consequences for others, the real question in deciding the proper place to give to freedom of expression is what weight do we want to give to other freedoms? It has been argued recently by some developing countries that freedom from hunger and chaos, and freedom for the development of basic economic conditions are more important than complete freedom of political expression or freedom of the press. They argue that the latter freedoms depend on and presuppose an already achieved economic freedom from scarcity and dependence on other countries. They also point out that freedom of political expression presupposes a stable enough political process to permit different opinions to be heard without threatening the political order as such. In a social setting rife with dissension and anarchy they argue, it is necessary to impose order and to clamp down, provisionally, on freedom of political expression.

Many people will not accept this argument in favor of curtailing freedom of expression under the conditions listed above. They will point out that anyone who forbids freedom of expression in the name of more basic freedoms, especially in the political realm, is claiming to be in possession not only of truth but also of the right to impose that truth on others. History is filled with examples of self-proclaimed messiahs who impose their visions of right on unwilling subjects.

There is no easy passage between the Syclla of complete freedom of expression and the Charibidis of imposing restraint on the expression of dangerous falsehood. Some degree of responsibility for the consequences of my expression is inherent in my freedom. If I know that I am slandering you when I allege certain things about you, I must be made responsible if that slander causes you harm. If a society permits a corporation to claim certain things about its product that are untrue as well as produce products that are harmful to those who buy them, then that society is being irresponsible to its citizens.

If I as an individual see you about to distribute as a beverage a liquid that I know is poisonous and you proclaim is safe, then I am irresponsible to you and to those whom you have convinced to drink the liquid if I do not snatch it away and forbid you to speak about it any longer.

The problem, of course, is that if we could all agree on the truth, the banning of falsehood would not be problematic. But we don't all agree on what is true. In fact, we don't all agree even on how the truth is to be discovered (some believe that only what science tells them is true, others look to divine revelations, others to intuition, others to what the majority thinks, etc.). Although this fact can be distressing, it is also our clue to the basis of the right to freedom of expression because it reveals one of the most important distinguishing traits of the human person: the capacity for self-determination.

TRUTH'S ADVANTAGE OVER ERROR

But, indeed, the dictum that truth always triumphs over persecution, is one of those pleasant falsehoods which men repeat after one another till they pass into commonplace but which all experience refutes. History teems with instances of truth put down by persecution. If not suppressed forever, it may be thrown back for centuries. . . . It is a piece of idle sentimentality that truth, merely as truth, has any inherent power denied to error, of prevailing against the dungeon and the stake. Men are not more zealous for truth then they often are for error, and a

> sufficient application of legal or even of social penalties will generally succeed in stopping the propagation of either. The real advantage which truth has consists in this, that when an opinion is true, it may be extinguished once, twice, or many times, but in the course of ages there will generally be found persons to rediscover it, until some one of its reappearances falls on a time when from favorable circumstances it escapes persecution until it has made such head as to withstand all subsequent attempts to suppress it. . . .
>
> J. S. Mill, "On Liberty," in *Utilitarianism, Liberty, And Representative Government* (New York: Dutton, 1951), pp. 118–119.

Determining the Truth for Oneself

Part of what it means to be fully human is to be able to determine freely what course our life shall take: to be able to make the basic decisions about the enactment of our intentions without coercion, to be able to enter into loving relations with others of our own volition. If the highest form of human relationship is one of love, then it is clear that we must have the freedom to create it since love can never be imposed or compelled. At the very foundation of our freedom to choose is our freedom to make those choices with the widest range of options possible and on the basis of the most accurate knowledge. Intelligence is a prerequisite for true freedom of action. Although all people are free to vote for whomever they wish, ignorance of candidates' views makes the decision for whom to vote virtually a random one. Freedom is not the same as randomness: it entails, in part, freedom from factors that influence one's choices unconsciously. To be really free to make choices, people need to know their options, what the likely consequences of their choices will be, and they must choose without being influenced by forces of which they are unaware.

Freedom of expression should be defended, therefore, essentially because it is a prerequisite for making self-determined choices with the greatest degree of critical intelligence. Reason and critical thinking may not always lead to the truth. And the right of free expression does not depend on an assertion being true. But apart from critical thinking, there is no way for a person to make intelligent, self-determined decisions. Any restriction on freedom of expression must make its case on the grounds that the consequences of erroneous choice are so obvious and clearly undesirable as to outweigh the negative consequences of limiting expression.

OBSTACLES TO FREEDOM OF EXPRESSION

As we now examine specific cases in which freedom of expression is an issue, we will see the basic conflict between the need of a society to prevent certain undesirable consequences and its need to provide some way in which error and self-interest can be challenged by those whose contrary beliefs are not presently in the ascendency.

We should first turn to those factors in society that, while not deliberately seeking to stifle freedom of expression, nevertheless work against it in subtle ways. One such factor would be habit or the inertia of accepting whatever happens to be the prevailing opinion at any time. Most of us find it easier not to be constantly examining and rejustifying beliefs and opinions. It is far more convenient to accept the general view of those around us on issues not of immediate concern. But while habitual ways of thinking have the virtue of freeing our minds for other matters, they have the vice of closing us off from new and potentially more truthful points of view.

Another aspect of unexamined thinking is prejudice or bias. To be biased per se is not necessarily bad (it means bending toward something) provided it is based on justifiable reasons. But prejudice and unevaluated bias lean us toward views that are more the product of emotional self-interest than disinterested investigation. Not only does prejudice lead to damaging consequences for others who are the target of our views but it also closes us off to insights and truths that, if adopted, could free us for new and exciting encounters with others.

We should also mention the fact of propaganda or self-interested advertising as an obstacle to critical thinking and freedom of expression. While presentation of information about a governmental policy or about a product for sale by a private company is a necessary part of the process of making an intelligent decision (and is itself a form of freedom of expression), propaganda is the presentation of false, misleading, or emotionally manipulative material. By working on parts of our decision-making faculties other than pure reason, propaganda inclines us toward choices over which we have relatively less control than those we make after careful deliberation and weighing of the evidence. When a piece of propaganda subtly questions a man's masculinity if he fails to choose a particular brand of cigarette, his choice is affected by emotional factors that are very powerful but not easily controlled by rational thought.

Another factor working against self-critical thought is the pressure of public opinion. All persons are members of various groups or publics. It is necessary to the success of such groups (from churches to cattle owners' associations) that the members express a high degree of unanimity on issues central to the groups' purposes. In such a context it is difficult for the individual member to express freely and in detail any qualifications or reservations she might want to make about the group's position. Because the group's position must satisfy a wide variety of individual concerns, it must be simply stated and usually winds up being an oversimplification of a complex problem, something that could be put into a slogan such as "No Nukes." While the result may prove quite politically effective, it operates as an obstacle to critical thinking and freedom of expression because it leaves little room for individual dissent or modification. Since the individual does agree with the basic stand taken by the group, she is encouraged (both by her own self-interest and by the group as a whole) not to express her hesitation or engage in what might seem like nit-picking or trivial argumentation. But the end result is a diminution in critical evaluation and an increase in submission to the views of others.

The Opinion Poll

One particularly pernicious aspect of the pressure of public opinion is the emergence in recent years of the public opinion poll. For many people who have succumbed to the obstacles of habit, prejudice, propaganda, and laziness of thought, the public opinion poll becomes a convenient way of deciding what to think. Most of us don't normally like to hold a minority viewpoint. Therefore, we find our thinking aided immeasureably by discovering what the majority of our fellow citizens think. Although this information might be enlightening, it can also be a convenient excuse for having our thinking done for us by other people. It has even been alleged that when the election results from one part of the country are flashed to other parts in which the polls are still open, many people decide to vote for whomever is leading, simply to be on the side of majority opinion.

Ignorance About the Bill of Rights

It is this kind of mindless thinking that has led most of the famous voices of the past to write their defenses of freedom of expression. We have already examined the essence of Thomas Jefferson's position (with its attendant problems). His stand on freedom of thought and expression is, of course, particular pertinent to us since much of it was incorporated into the famous Bill of Rights, the first ten amendments to the Constitution of the United States. The First Amendment is the clearest and most forceful: "Congress shall make no law respecting an establishment of religion, or prohibiting the free exercise thereof; or abridging the freedom of speech, or of the press; or the right of the people peaceably to assemble, and to petition the government for a redress of grievances." As we shall see shortly, there is much debate on exactly how parts of this Amendment are to be interpreted: but its general thrust is clear. What is alarming to many defenders of freedom of expression is the degree to which large numbers of Americans remain ignorant of this vital part of our constitutional legacy. It has now become an almost annual exercise for a researcher to present to citizens a copy of the Bill of Rights without identifying it as such and to ask them whether it is acceptable. A large percentage of persons reject it as being too "communistic" or "un-American." It would be ironic and tragic if this hard-won freedom were to be lost in part because people simply did not know of its origin or place in their own national history.

Jefferson was not, of course, original in his defense of freedom of expression. The English traditions, to take but a slightly earlier example, have long had forceful speakers on the issue. John Milton, one of the most important of English poets, wrote in his "Areopagitica," in opposition to a Parliamentary bill of 1643 that would have made all publications subject to prior approval of Parliament, "Who kills a man, kills a reasonable creature, God's image; but he who destroys a good book, kills reason itself."[3]

Another historic defense of freedom of expression was made by John Stuart Mill (1806–1873) in his essay "On Liberty." There, Mill said "If all mankind minus one were of one opinion, and only one person were of the contrary opinion, mankind would be no more justified in silencing that one person, than he, if he had the power, would be justified in silencing mankind." Even if the one opinion is clearly wrong, society gains by "the clearer perception and livelier impression of truth produced by its collision with error."[4]

We can be proud that our nation has built on and incorporated the ideas of such forceful defenders of a precious liberty. But no freedom is without its complications as it is lived out in the detail of everyday, social life, nor is it without its attackers and detractors. We now must turn to some of the more important specific issues facing us today with respect to freedom of expression.

CONTEMPORARY ISSUES

National Security

It is clear that groups of all kinds have a vested interest in retaining the loyalty of their members. A group shot through with conflicting opinions is rarely able to achieve its purposes. This is especially true of nations: a basic freedom each one desires is from the threat of destruction by external enemies. To secure this freedom, nations develop a security system that includes both military defense and defense against domestic betrayal. Few would challenge the right and need for a country to have a national security system; in fact, many of the most troubling incidents involving free-

---

[3]John Milton, "Areopagitica," *Major British Writers I* (New York: Harcourt, 1954), p. 430.
[4]John Stuart Mill, *Utilitarianism, Liberty, and Representative Government* (New York: Dutton, 1910), p. 79.

dom of expression in recent years have come in areas relating to national security. A recent president of the United States has even been alleged to have broken the law in order to suppress citizen's attempts to publish material critical of this country's handling of the Vietnam War—and the chief executive's action was justified on the grounds of national security. The question raised by this event is whether there are any limits to the use of national security against the right of free expression by those who disagree with a nation's policies. Clearly, handing over to an enemy agent information that could lead to the weakening of a country's defenses in time of war is a treasonous act. But on what grounds should a nation's laws be imposed on someone merely *suspected* of committing such an act? Surely, the legal protection would extend to this person just as it would to a suspected murderer, even though in the eyes of some the former crime is far more heinous than the latter.

The whole purpose of law is to keep individuals (no matter how exalted) from exploiting their power to enforce laws without due process when the accusation is based on mere suspicions or beliefs. In many cases, attempts to block the publication of dissenting views are motivated by a fear that what will be revealed will be damaging, not to the nation, but to a particular party, or person, or set of policies and judgments (the latter should not be identified with the security of the nation at large). Self-interest makes it hard for us to remember that although we might think a particular administration's policies are right, they are rarely, if ever, the only viable and loyal policies conceivable. The individual who sought to publish material damaging to a particular administration's conduct of the war claimed to be loyal to his country's best interests and opposed only to the way in which those interests had been, in his opinion, subverted by the administration in question. In fact the publication of the Pentagon Papers was eventually upheld by the Supreme Court on the grounds that the material contained in them was not detrimental to present security efforts even though it was damaging to the reputation of earlier policies and programs. In striking down attempts to quash the Papers, the Court in effect reminded the country, and especially those in particularly powerful positions, that the power to exercise restraint against free expression in the name of national security is so fraught with potential abuse that it must be employed with extreme caution and with heightened sensitivity to the right of minority viewpoints on national policy.

The Loyalty Oath

A crucial part of the debate over the use of national security to curtail expression is the status of the loyalty oath. Although not as legally well entrenched as national security, the loyalty requirement has been used by many associations to ensure that their members are above suspicion in fidelity to the groups' aims and policies. There are various consequences for failing to take such an oath, for example, the infamous "blacklist" used by many organizations to keep "suspect" people from employment. It is not hard to imagine the chilling effect a loyalty oath can have. Ironically, of course, those who are truly disloyal and are seeking to corrupt a group from within will be the first to sign such an oath since presumably they are not bound by the same scruples as those who are offended by the presumption of someone else questioning their loyalty. It is plain that the effect of the oath and its implied consequences is the stifling of free speech. Many can still remember the midfifties when the McCarthy scene frightened many Americans into silence and fearful conformity to the views of a few self-selected patriots. Hundreds of able writers, actors, teachers, and public servants were blacklisted and lost their jobs simply because they refused to sign a loyalty oath at their place of business. They based their refusal on the proper claim that they had done nothing to have their loyalty questioned in the first place and that the greatest personal safeguard of the American legal system is the presumption of "innocent until proven guilty" in the proper judicial arena.

Even more insidious was the stifling of free expression by self-proclaimed patriots. It became the norm to blacklist someone who refused to answer leading and intimidating questions (despite the fact that silence is no sign of guilt), or who had associations with people who had been blacklisted or suspected of some nefarious deed, or who belonged to an organization that one of the witch-hunters "thought" was in some way suspicious. This country has never passed through a period in which freedom of expression was so greatly in jeopardy as it was in those days.

We must not think that the kind of scare tactics that then threatened freedom of speech are a thing of the past. In less widespread but still chilling ways it is with us today. An actress who had espoused unpopular political views was recently attacked for taking a part in a movie sympathetic to the attacker's position: a singer loses bookings because her open espousal of certain sexual views is offensive to others. It is clearly the prerogative of all citizens to refuse to hear someone with whose views they disagree; however, it is not right to refuse that person employment if the views in question are unrelated to the kind of work or skills involved.

Obnoxious Views

Needless to say there are some very difficult cases in which it is hard to feel strongly about these principles because the views expressed are so obnoxious as to be revolting. But it is precisely in the hard cases that we need to keep the principles visible. It is easy to do right when the situation is uncomplicated: it is hard but necessary to do right when the situation is demanding. If our morality depends on the ease with which it can be implemented but falls apart under pressure, it is hardly a morality that can be counted on to safeguard basic liberties. The real test of freedom of expression comes when we must grant it to those who will use it to express views thoroughly repugnant to us. But unless we are willing to stick to the principle in this kind of hard situation, we may well find that our own views are someday suppressed because another group of people in a position of power find *them* repugnant and dangerous.

Perhaps one of the hardest of recent cases to test the principle of freedom of expression came in the town of Skokie, Illinois in 1978. Skokie is a town where a large number of survivors of the Nazi concentration camps live. Their memories of that holocaust are still vivid and painful. In the name of free speech, The Nazi Party of America asked for the right to demonstrate on the main streets of Skokie, carrying their banners and reading their speeches of vilification against the Jews and praising the work of Hitler in his attempt to exterminate the Jewish people. It is hard to imagine a more morally odious group than the Nazis or a more victimized, traumatized group than the Jewish survivors of the Holocaust. Because of the likelihood of the march stirring up old, painful memories and further traumatizing already damaged people, many persons otherwise sympathetic to freedom of speech sought to have the march prohibited. This was a true test case for freedom of expression. It made the application of the principle of that freedom difficult but admirable in the opinion of many because it had stood up under conditions and opposition with which even the defenders of freedom of speech could sympathize. Many people, in fact, remained genuinely torn in their opinions. One point around which much of the discussion turned was the applicability of the "fighting words" doctrine, which says that if a speaker knows ahead of time that his words will likely cause a riot or lead to damage, he can be held liable for what he says and his actions may be prohibited. Although it was clear that the speech of the Nazis would be troubling to those who heard it and although many of them would be particularly sensitive, given their past experience, to what would be said, it was argued from the other side that if undue consideration was given to how people *might* react or the degree to which they *might* be offended, then free speech was in danger in more than just this situation. Should black civil rights groups, on the same line of reasoning, have been forbidden from marching through racist, segregated neighborhoods simply because racists would be offended, perhaps even traumatized somewhat, by being confronted with the demands of civil rights?

It has been held by courts that if genuine riot or physical violence can reasonably be shown to be probable in the event of a demonstration, it can be stopped. But short of that eventuality, the courts generally have permitted free speech, no matter how morally repulsive its content is to the sentiments of the general population. They have done so in many cases because they believe the right of free expression is so precious that it should be defended especially in the case of minority opinions because it is there that it takes on meaning and its full power and value can be seen. As one Jewish defender of the Nazi's right to speak said, "If we take away this loathsome group's right to express its views, who is to say when we (the Jews) will once again become a loathsome group in the eyes of some other protectors' of the public sensibility?" If the decision as to what views are acceptable and what are to be suppressed depends on popular sentiment, then the rights of minority groups must always remain precarious. The surest way of protecting one's own right to express opinions is to protect the right of those groups most opposed to one's own views.

Scientific "Claims"

Another objection to free speech is that if ideas have consequences, some ideas, expressed often enough and with enough apparent credibility, could lead eventually to actions that would not have been contemplated had the listeners not been exposed to those ideas. A very controversial recent case has involved the expression of views by a prominent scientist (his prominence, incidentally, is not in the field about which he is speaking). Claiming the support of scientific evidence, this speaker asserts the inferiority of black people in the area of intelligence. On many campuses, he has been actively opposed and on some his appearance has been banned. Once again, the issue of freedom of expression is challenged by a hard case. The main argument of those seeking to ban his speaking is that in this particular case, his views could lend spurious, scientific credibility to racism that in turn could be used as justification by those who wish to legislate various forms of racial discrimination. For example, if his views are taken seriously, those who wish to limit funding for predominantly black schools would feel themselves justified in doing so on the ground that it makes no sense to spend money on those who cannot learn as well as their white counterparts. The proponents of limiting this scientist's freedom of speech remind people that if someone like Hitler were permitted complete freedom to express his anti-Semitic views in the guise of scientifically verified principles, he would convince many people who believe anything with scientific backing to support anti-Semitic legislation. They point out that public speaking does not have sufficient safeguards against misleading, distorting, and emotionally charged propaganda presented under the guise of scientific "truth."

Roughly the same kind of argument has been advanced against large corporations engaging in advertising aimed at selling children cereals and other items about which they are in no position to make a reasonable judgment. The advertisers, of course, claim that any attempt to limit the kind of advertising they do is a curtailment of their right of free speech. Their opponents point out that freedom of speech does not entail the right to use persuasive techniques on defenseless people who are unable to sort out truth from fantasy, especially when the fantasy, if acted on, would lead to harm.

It should, of course, be noted that one important difference between the two cases is that in the former, a single individual is involved, and in the latter, the power of a giant corporation. Many would argue that corporations do not have the same kind of rights as individuals. Because their power is so much greater, corporations have a correspondingly greater responsibility to exercise due care in the expression of their ideas. The advertising power of a major cereal manufacturer exercised on Saturday morning television has a much more pervasive effect on the minds of children than does the power of a single speaker addressing an audience of adults.

Nevertheless, the issue of freedom of expression is roughly the same in both cases. To what extent should a society seek to protect people it believes are unable to sort out fact from fiction from the presentation of ideas that are admittedly important enough to cause major changes in the society, if acted on? It should be remembered that the defense of the right of free speech does not derive from the assumption that what is said is true. It is, in fact, the belief that truth can only *emerge* from the confrontation of alternative views that underlies one need for freedom of expression. The real issue, in our opinion, is not whether individuals or groups are free to express their ideas but whether they have a responsibility to avoid distortion and to respond to alternative views.

Responsibility for Nondeception

It is a point of law that a company that deliberately deceives a consumer about the product he has purchased can be held liable for that deception. The right of free speech does not include immunity from damages done when people act on false information contained in the speech. Obviously when the consequences of acting on misleading information are far in the future and mixed with numerous other factors, it is impossible to isolate particular pieces of information as the direct causes of damaging acts. Nevertheless, many feel that speeches directly or indirectly abetting racism have the long-range effect of making racism respectable and thus leading to racist acts. How is it possible, therefore, for a society to ensure that racist speeches are responsibility made? Those who would seek to have free speech with no risk involved want the principle without the price. But the price of free speech is that many ideas will be expressed that are not only untrue but also contributory to harmful acts in the long run. This, we believe, is an expensive price, but the price of not paying it is to sanction the right of a society or powerful groups within the society to censor what at any given time they regard as unacceptable views. The potential abuse to which such a right can be put is far greater than the abuse to which the right of free speech can lead. No right is risk-free.

In a free society, one way of minimizing the risk without eliminating it would be to require speakers to listen to alternative positions (even if they should not be forced to answer questions). The laws against deception would provide an additional boundary beyond which the speaker's claims could not go without some recourse by his opponents. In the case of corporate advertising, the basic principle that could be utilized in opposition to their propaganda aimed at children would be that freedom of expression assumes the encounter of reasonable people with differing ideas. If children have not yet reached the age of reason and yet are being treated as having the capacity to act, to their detriment, on emotions stirred by powerful propaganda, then it would not be unreasonable or an infringement of freedom of speech to restrict the kind of access corporate advertising has to them.

PORNOGRAPHY

Another very volatile area in which freedom of expression is at stake is the question of whether pornography should be permitted to be sold openly to all adults who wish to purchase it. Freedom of expression is involved in the sale of pornography because many people believe that pornography is genuinely harmful to some people. There is much disagreement, even among the advocates of limiting the sale or display of pornography, over what kind of harm is caused and to whom. There are some who downplay the alleged harmful effects of pornography and instead base their desire to ban it on the principle that it is morally offensive to the larger community.

One of the underlying complicating factors in any discussion of pornography and free speech is the difficulty in reaching a single, agreed-to definition of what obscenity or pornography *is*. The root meanings of these two words are clearly related to that which sexually stimulates and that which is morally impure. There are some writers who have argued that to restrict obscenity to sexual areas is to miss the filth and moral impurity of such things as racism, war, and the prostitution of values in the name of money or success. Nevertheless, the difficulty in reaching a decision about the meaning of pornography means that at a fundamental level, the opponents in this debate simply do not agree that what is under consideration is truly, morally impure. The case for censorship holds that exposure of adults (let alone minors) to sexually stimulating material leads directly to various criminal acts. They point out that people who read or watch pornographic material are often involved in sex-related crimes. What is not clearly demonstrated (and, some would argue, has been refuted by counter demonstrations in Denmark where sex crimes went down when the sale of pornographic material became legalized) is that exposure to pornography is a *cause* of sex crimes. It is one thing to argue that the two go together, but the evidence could be interpreted to mean that people who commit sex crimes would do so whether or not they had access to pornography—that their interest in the latter is a consequence of the same factors that lead them into sex crimes in the first place. Despite the conflicting evidence, however, if it could be shown beyond a reasonable doubt that reading pornographic material did have a strong causal effect on sex crime, the case for limiting exposure of pornographic material would be immeasurably enhanced. The point at issue, it should be remembered, is a factual one in this case.

Pornography as Dehumanizing

Also somewhat dependent on factual evidence is the case against pornography based on the belief that a society exposed to it over a period of time will become dehumanized and loveless. It is argued that pornography displays people in mere carnal encounters that inevitably are less than personal, in which there is no room for love, tenderness, and the whole gamut of human feelings that go far beyond the sexual to make up a full personal relationship. A person exposed to enough of this kind of purely sexual emphasis will eventually come to think that sex alone is what makes a person "authentic." Therefore, in the name of a loving society, there is solid ground for limiting or even banning the display of pornographic material.

This position is still dependent on some factual findings: if it could be shown that exposure to pornography does not, in fact, lead to a dehumanizing of personal relations, then the position would be correspondingly weaker. There are even some authorities who have argued that in many cases, exposure to pornography has helped love relationships. They point out that many couples have trouble expressing the sexual side of their relationship because of inhibitions and fear, the result of which is a less than wholesome relationship. By viewing allegedly pornographic material, they have been freed from their barriers to full expression and have gone on to develop full personal relations with others in which sex is an important part but by no means the central or dominating attraction. Those who argue this way claim that a desire to avoid (and have others avoid) sexual material is based on a fear of sex and is therefore ultimately debilitating. A free, open encounter with sex is the only way, paradoxically, that sex can be dethroned from its place in the pantheon of obsessions and reduced to what it should be in a healthy relationship: a necessary but not sufficient aspect.

Community Standards

Finally, and least dependent on factual support, is the claim that pornography is offensive to the moral standards of the community and that the majority has a right to keep out of its sight what it finds offensive. Just as a community, through zoning laws and other legal devices, can prohibit a junk yard from being built on a quiet, residential street, so it can prohibit establishments from dispensing what in its view is moral junk. Many of those advancing this position do not wish to prohibit the sale of pornographic material per se but merely to restrict the location in which it is sold so that nonconsenting adults need not have their moral sensibilities offended. Some cities, for example, have used this argument to "cordon" off a section of town beyond which no pornography can be displayed but within which it can be. All citizens are informed of its location and those who consent to buy pornography are free to do so and those who do not wish to be offended are forewarned to stay away.

Even this expedient, of limiting the location of pornographic supply shops and movies, is not sufficient to meet the demands of some who would argue that unless the exposure to pornography has been demonstrated beyond a reasonable shadow of a doubt to constitute a clear and present danger to the safety or well-being of the community, it should be permitted complete freedom of display. They would argue that it has not, in fact, been shown to lead directly to harmful effects, either for the person who is exposed to it or for others within the community. They reject the argument that pornography leads to a depersonalization of love and they are especially fearful of the argument that a community's moral sensibilities should determine the freedom of expression of members within it. The core of their argument is that as long as the acts of consenting adults do not harm others, it is no business of the society to dictate what they can and cannot do.

AVOIDING THE OFFENSIVENESS OF PORNOGRAPHY

When printed words hide decorously behind covers of books sitting passively on the shelves of a bookstore, their offensiveness is easily avoided.

There is nothing like the evil smell of rancid garbage oozing right out through the covers of a book whether one looks at it or not. When an "obscene" book sits on a shelf, who is there to be offended? Those who want to read it for the sake of erotic stimulation presumably will not be offended (else they wouldn't read it), and those who choose not to read it will have no experience of it to be offended by.

Moreover, no one forces a customer to browse randomly, and if he is informed in advance of the risk of risqué passages, he should be prepared to shoulder that risk himself without complaint. I conclude that there are no sufficient grounds derived either from the harm or offense principles for suppressing obscene literature, unless that ground be the protection of children; but I see no reason why selective prohibitions for children could not work as well in the case of books as in the cases of cigarettes and whiskey. . . .

Joel Feinberg, "Harmless Immoralities and Offensive Nuisances," from *Issues in Law and Morality*, ed. N. Care and T. Trelogan, (Pittsburgh: Case Western Reserve Univ. Press, 1973), as found in Thomas A. Mappes and Jane S. Zembaty, eds., *Social Ethics: Morality and Social Policy* (New York: McGraw-Hill, c. 1977), p. 256.

Joel Feinberg (b. 1926) is professor of philosophy at the University of Arizona, Tucson. He is the author of Doing and Deserving *and* Social Philosophy *as well as many articles in the field of social and legal philosophy.*

In our opinion, there is a clear risk to the full enjoyment of freedom of expression, but once again, we feel it is better to take this risk than risk the dangers of the suppression of free speech. Assuming that it has not been demonstrated that exposure to pornography is a direct causal factor in harmful acts to others, and assuming that even if such exposure could conceivably constitute some kind of harm to the consenting adult, that harm is so hard to measure and would be so loaded with nonfactual interpretations that it is better to permit adults to make their own choices in this area. I may regard Mr. Jones going to see a pornographic movie as a waste of time, as indicative of some values on his part that I do not share, even as a sign that Mr. Jones does not have the capacity for a full personal relationship, but I also respect Mr. Jones' right to make a mistake and to choose to live a life that I find less than satisfying. That is the price of permitting each of us the freedom to determine our own lives. I can insist that Mr. Jones not leave pornographic materials in my mailbox or display them on a street down which I and my children must necessarily pass, and I can keep my mind open for evidence that would demonstrate that Mr. Jones' exposure to pornography is causing him to become a sex criminal, but I would be infringing without sufficient justification on the precious freedom of expression if I prohibited Mr. Jones from using his freedom to see and read what he wants.

It might very well be true that the moral values I feel are important to my community are degraded by an increasing preoccupation with pornography on the part of Mr. Jones and those like him. But, even apart from the fact that clamping down on something is a sure way to excite interest in it, I would have to balance the moral tone pornography represents against the moral tone displayed by a community decision to prohibit freedom of expression. It will not do just to say that a community's moral tone is sufficient to prohibit certain offensive materials. The act of prohibition is itself, necessarily, a moral act and sets a moral tone: it is not a morally neutral event. Prohibition or curtailment of expression, while obviously necessary in certain instances, as we have already seen, can cast a chill over a community that may be, for many, too high a price to pay for staking out a moral claim against offensive literature. A price will be paid in either case: in our opinion the choice for freedom of expression in this instance sets the better moral tone.

Academic Freedom and the Censorship of Textbooks

In a slightly less sensational way than in the case of pornography, many communities experience the dilemmas of freedom of expression in dealing with educational materials in their school systems. In recent years, there has been a wave of concern sweeping many school districts about the kind of "radical" or "subversive" material used in the classroom. On the basis of the principles that the community has a right to determine by what values its children shall be educated and that materials harmful to persons can legitimately be suppressed, many people have tried to remove from school libraries and curricula books that, in their opinion, are damaging because they represent values not held by the community as a whole. Although this issue has sometimes affected institutions of higher learning (and has led to the implementation of such safeguards as tenure and the protections of the right of free speech and research), its greatest effect is felt in those educational systems directly under public control. Although some of the protesters against allegedly controversial material are simply misinformed (many objections are raised against books that are American classics, like "The Scarlet Letter," and are often unread by the objectors), there is clearly an issue involved if a school is requiring its children to read books that advocate values the community finds offensive. Although it is better to err on the side of freedom of expression, the issue is complicated by the fact that, according to the objectors, those who are doing the reading are not yet old enough to form mature, intelligent judgments about what they read and that those requiring the reading are not critical or intelligent enough to put the material into a fair and comprehensive framework.

Although it is clear that some materials do present points of view that many of us would find morally repugnant, it is equally clear that the attempt to suppress the material is morally repugnant. There is a clash of values in this situation. In our opinion, the resolution of the conflict can be approached by a judicious balancing of the need for students to be exposed to ideas that challenge their own and the need to experience that challenge with the tools of criticism, intelligence, and knowledge. Ideas, no matter how disturbing, do not go away simply because the materials in which they are contained are prohibited. The best way to deal with ideas is to confront them: examine their assumptions, their evidence, their consequences. If this kind of critical confrontation of ideas with ideas, values with values, is not done in the supportive context of an educational system, it is unlikely to be done elsewhere as well or as sympathetically.

THE DEMAND FOR EXPRESSION VERSUS THE RIGHT TO PRIVACY

So far our discussion has involved only those cases in which people have sought to express their ideas and found some obstacles to that desire. However, there are cases falling under the general rubric of freedom of expression that involve the need of a society to gather information that individuals may not wish to supply. In these cases, expression of beliefs and knowledge would be withheld in the name of freedom and compelled in the name of overriding social needs.

For example, information about a person's financial dealings or health may need to be divulged if a credit card or an insurance policy is to be issued. A newspaper reporter may have some information relevant to the disposition of a court case that she is not willing to reveal because to do so would jeopardize confidential relations with an important news source. A person called before an investigative body may not wish to reveal information he alone knows about the life of someone else under suspicion of disloyalty.

Does a society have the right to coerce the expression of knowledge and opinion? Are there some things individuals have a right to keep private even though to do so would complicate the work of various social agencies? Some would argue that in a free enterprise system, it is necessary to give up some information about myself (such as my medical history) in order to get health insurance coverage since I am not guaranteed that coverage by the government. In other words, to get something you must give something. Although agreeing in principle, others argue that once that information gets stored in information banks, it can be pried loose by other agencies to whom I have not given my consent. In an age fascinated with the setting of records and the compiling of statistics, it is not too surprising that we are moving, as one critic put it, toward a Dossier Society. The federal government is reported to hold almost four billion (4,000,000,000) records on individuals. In addition, records are kept by banks, credit bureaus, insurance firms, utilities, medical facilities, subscription list distributors, investigating agencies, and even portions of the media.

The horror stories connected with the abuse and misuse of these records are legion. One man was declared dead by the Social Security computer in 1978 and is now spending month after month waiting to be resurrected. (Meanwhile, his checks and other vital services have been curtailed since, with foresight, the government does not expend its energies on dead people). It has been determined that the only way to bring him back to "life" is to "lie" to the computer, defraud it, in order to get it to alter its information. Thousands of people have been denied insurance because neighbors or associates have lied about the person's health or life style, and the lies have been duly recorded as fact without cross-checking and without being made available to the client for refutation.

Despite the injustices to which this kind of activity can lead, there are strong voices that say the risk is worth it. Since much of the illegal operation of business racketeering and white collar crime reveals evidence of itself only through bank records or phone calls, some law enforcement officials argue that unless they have access to such records, they cannot compile a sufficient case against the criminals. Many of the complicated crimes have been solved by knowing who talked to whom when, who made deposits in which bank, and so on. As criminals themselves employ data banks and create computer frauds, it is only fair, many claim, that legal agencies have the same power. (Unfortunately, in one case, the use of data records by the police enabled a convicted criminal to secure from those records the name of the person who informed on him and with that information ordered the murder of the informer.)

The Argument for Complete Privacy

At the opposite end of the spectrum are those who argue for complete privacy: no information to be revealed except at the clients' bidding. Although this position clearly would protect against fraud and the misuses of information, it would effectively eliminate private insurance and credit extension since these agencies could not stay in business if they had to depend only on the information the client was willing to provide them. It would also be extremely difficult for the federal government to develop fair and just policies affecting the distribution of services to people if it had no accurate knowledge of their needs and abilities. Some have argued recently that it will become increasingly difficult to take an accurate census of the United States (required every ten years and used as a basis for all sorts of social planning) since so many people are afraid of what will be done with the information they reveal about themselves to the government.

There is a third set of voices being heard on this issue: those that wish to see complete open disclosure of all information, not just to private and federal agencies, but to the public at large. On the principle that secret information will be used fraudulently, they argue that an honest society needs to be an informed society: that the voters and the general public can make better, wiser choices if all the information is available to them. Unfortunately, this would mean that personal matters, or matters regarding my choice of political groups or reading material or private entertainment could be made public. Whether the benefit to society at large would be worth that kind of public revelation is extremely difficult to determine.

Rights in Conflict

Clearly in this area there are rights in conflict: the right of the society to defend itself against crime that seeks to hide behind the barrier of privacy and the right of individuals to protect their lives from intrusion that has no socially redeeming purpose. One way society can approach a responsible position on the issue might be for it to decide what *kinds* of information it wishes agencies to have. To make that decision wisely it should be presented with clear arguments setting forth the reasons why some information is relevant to policies with which the society agrees, for example, general income range to determine the kind of income supplementation necessary in certain deprived areas or the kind of taxes to levy. Other kinds of information, such as political affiliation, reading material, life style, and the like, would be irrelevant to most agencies' work. If a case could be made that such information *is* essential, then individuals could have a choice as to whether they wish to receive the services of that agency in return for giving up that kind of information. The problem with much information-gathering today is that the person about whom the record is compiled has no way of knowing what is in the file, no way of correcting what is erroneous, and no way of controlling to which agencies, other than the one agreed to, the material will be provided. In the end, society must seek to balance individual privacy against the social need for information.

Informing on Others

Related to the issue of invasion of privacy, but somewhat less threatening to the personal life of the individual from whom information is sought, is the issue of whether people should be compelled to reveal information in court cases or investigative hearings. During the McCarthy scare, many individuals were called before congressional committees and asked to testify against friends and acquaintances. Quite apart from the legality and power of such committees, the question arose as to whether an individual had the right to protect a friend by silence even if he knew the friend to be guilty or suspect with regard to some crime. There is a strong version of private morality which holds that people should not inform on their friends: to do so would betray a basic lack of loyalty and confidence. Let the investigating agency discover in other ways whether there is evidence of guilt or not: morally, I should not be put in the position of being my brother's accuser. As John Steinbeck put it: "To force personal immorality on a man, to wound his private virtue, undermines his public virtue."[5]

On the other hand, critics ask what happens if the situation is not that of a McCarthy-like witch-hunt for suspected traitors, but is rather one in which the investigation is looking for persons suspected of defrauding the poor of millions of dollars? Do I have a right, in the name of private virtue and a sense of personal loyalty, to shield a friend I believe may be involved in such a crime? How is that private virtue weighed against the need of my society to seek out those who would betray its basic principles of justice? To what extent must I as an individual contribute to its task? If I refuse my contribution, how can I expect others to make theirs? Once again, the dilemmas arise because of the need to balance individual liberty against social need. Unless we wish to assert that the individual can live without society, it is inevitable that at some point the needs of the one will have to be modified to meet the needs of the other.

Obligations of the Press

Some have argued that while individuals, per se, do not have the right to arbitrarily choose to withhold information vital to the prosecution of a criminal case, certain classes of individuals do. Reporters, whose job it is to provide the public with the kind of information necessary to enable them to be informed citizens, are singled out as making up such a class. If there is to be a free flow of news, especially from and about places of decision making and power, it is crucial that some individuals provide information to the press that would not normally be forthcoming. These people can confidentially reveal to a reporter what they know to be going on, but the reporter cannot disclose the informer's identity to the public. To do so would automatically make it impossible for the reporter to be entrusted with the kind of information informers feed to the press. Some reporters have argued that even in criminal cases in which they have been asked to testify, the right of confidentiality of sources is so important that it should not be violated even if the information sought would be vital to the outcome of the case. They point out that if the government has the power to compel such information, the result would be a drying up of sources of information about all sorts of important institutions and policies. A government bent on protecting its own mistakes and fraudulent dealings could use such power to prevent damaging information about its illegal doings

[5]John Steinbeck, "The Trial of Arthur Miller," in *Contemporary Moral Issues*, ed. Harry K. Girvetz (Belmont, Calif.: Wadsworth, 1964), p. 73.

from being made public. Only if informants have the assurance that their identity remains inviolate will they provide the kind of assistance a free press depends on.

Opponents of this position argue that it is not fair to single out certain classes, especially the press, for immunity from releasing vital information. They would agree that other classes, such as the clergy, have a special kind of immunity, but that the media is such a diffuse, uncertified, nonaccountable body of persons that it is dangerous to grant it a power not granted to others. Just as withholding information by a government can be an abusive act covering up self-serving interest, so withholding information by a news person can be an excuse for suppression of facts harmful to the self-interests of the news agency. There is no monopoly on employing deceit or using cover-ups to hide self-interest and illegal activities by any one class of people. The press is no more altruistic, despite the vital service it performs, than any other class.

PUBLIC DECISIONS

The ideal way to bring the right of freedom of expression into harmony with the need to restrict that right under certain circumstances would be to have a society decide, through open and critical discussion, those areas of its common life in which it wants some curtailment of freedom of expression. The real dangers of freedom of expression do not lie in those restrictions that have been agreed to by public discussion and selection: they lie in those restrictions imposed subtly, unconsciously, or in the name of arbitrary values by wielders of political power.

Most of the historical objections to curtailment of the freedom of expression have assumed often implicitly, that the real enemy is a coercive majority capable of imposing its view on a relatively powerless minority. Because society is created in part out of a mutual distrust of the self-interest of other people, especially as it congregates in associations that can exercise more power than individuals, freedom of expression is important in keeping the self-interest of one group from interfering with the self-interest of another group.

Truth is enhanced when it is able to be seen as such, which happens only when it can be challenged openly by counter views. If I wish to have you accept, for your own well thought out reasons, my claim that what you are about to drink is hydrochloric acid, I would rather have you challenge me to prove by public test that the liquid is acid rather than simply take my word for it. I know that only in this way will you be thoroughly convinced. As long as people feel that they are being forced to act for reasons they cannot accept, their obedience will be provisional and unstable since their action is compelled from without. If you wish to secure others' assent to your belief, you must provide grounds for the belief that can pass the test of critical evaluation. The only mechanism for providing those grounds is an arena in which competing claims can be put forward for examination and appraisal. The mortar for building the arena is freedom of expression.

Group Self-Interest

We should not be naïve and expect that pure rational discussion will quickly, if ever, lead to the disappearance of error. Self-interest will always incline reason to serve its ends to some degree. But the manipulation of reason and critical thinking can be restrained if everyone has equal access to the arena of rational challenge and debate. Because manipulation becomes increasingly dangerous the more it is under the control of increasingly powerful groups, the more scope should be given to the individual to express his or her views against those of the established authorities. Established, governing groups are particularly susceptible to their own self-interest since they can be more easily lulled into the belief that what they are commanding is for the good of all. They must be especially sensitive, therefore, to those ways in which they retard the free expression of thought on the part of less-established minority groups and individuals. Although there are situations in which restraint on freedom of expression would be appropriate, those who would be the first to urge such restraint should be also the first to explore, with intense self-criticism, what vested interests they have in forbidding alternative views. The most dangerous members of any society are those people who not only claim to know the truth but also claim that their position is unconnected with an advantage to themselves and is only for the good of others. Their claims more often than not are based on a fear of permitting others to reach the same truth (if it be so) on their own, for reasons they can rationally accept. That fear is always a sign that some kind of self-interest is involved and is therefore suspect as a legitimate basis for restraining freedom of expression.

Ultimately there is no pure safeguard against the risks of free speech. The best a society can do is to help its citizens develop the critical weapons of intelligence and wise judgment. The danger of ideas comes when people are fooled into accepting them without sufficient warrant or justification. As long as a society remains ignorant of what a sound argument involves, of what is good as opposed to spurious or irrelevant evidence, of how to anticipate the long-range consequences of following a particular option, of how to sort out self-serving arguments from well-grounded claims, there will be no sure defense against being misled by harmful ideas freely expressed. A well-informed, critically sensitive society is its own best defense against the risks of free speech, and it is the only kind of society in which the excitement and creativity of the free expression of ideas can flourish.

CHAPTER REVIEW

A. Dilemmas of freedom of expression

1. Does the free expression of ideas necessarily lead to truth?
2. There are occasions when expressing an opinion can lead to harm for others.
3. Are there conditions in which freedom of thought is relatively less important than some other freedom, e.g., freedom from political instability?
4. Freedom of expression is a prerequisite for making self-determined choices with the greatest degree of critical intelligence.

B. Obstacles to freedom of expression

1. Some things work indirectly to stifle freedom of expression: ease of conforming to public opinion, emotional self-interest, propaganda.
2. In recent years the use of the opinion poll has led some people to allow others to do their thinking for them.
3. Ignorance about the Bill of Rights creates a climate in which defense of freedom of expression seems unimportant.

C. Contemporary issues

1. The need for national security can lead to restrictions on freedom of expression.
2. The loyalty oath creates conflict in many who want to be loyal to their country's needs without informing on those persons not legally indictable for crimes against the state.
3. The expression of views regarded by nearly all members of the society as morally obnoxious (e.g., anti-Semitism or racism) presents a difficult challenge to the application of the principle of freedom of expression.
4. Equally troubling to many is the right of speakers with scientific credentials to present views that demean ethnic and racial groups.
5. Requiring all expressions of opinion to be nondeceptive can eliminate some of the risks of free speech.

D. Pornography

1. The sale and availability of pornography is one of the most volatile issues falling under freedom of expression.
2. Much of the debate centers around the factual consequences of being exposed to pornographic material.
3. Some argue that pornography is dehumanizing; others argue that it can liberate people from sexual repression.

4. The standards and sensibilities of local communities are often considered in determining the right of pornographic distribution.
5. The censorship or oversight of classroom material by community spokespersons reveals some of the same dilemmas encountered in the question of pornography.

E. The demand for expression versus the right to privacy

1. Are there situations in which we should be compelled to reveal information about ourselves to others, for example, our medical history to an insurance company?
2. Are there dangers in compiling data banks on many aspects of our private lives? If criminals can hide behind the shield of privacy, does their right to privacy outweigh the government's obligation to catch wrongdoers?
3. In this area, clearly, rights are in conflict and a balance must be sought between complete privacy and the divulgence of all aspects of our personal lives to private or public agencies.
4. The conflict is particularly acute for those persons who are privy to information that could prove decisive in a court of law. Do I have a right to withhold knowledge of a crime that a friend committed?
5. Members of the press have faced this conflict recently when, compelled by courts to divulge their sources in legal proceedings, they have refused and have subsequently been jailed for doing so.

F. Public decisions

1. The society should decide publicly what areas of its common life need some restrictions on freedom of expression.
2. Recognizing the reality of group self-interest will help us to guard against uncritically accepting a group's claims to truth.
3. A well-informed, critically sensitive society is its own best defense against the risks of free speech.

SUGGESTED READINGS

Feinberg, Joel. *Social Philosophy*. Englewood Cliffs, N.J.: Prentice-Hall, 1973.

An analysis of issues in social relations including a study of liberty and its limitations.

Hofstadter, Richard. *Anti-Intellectualism in American Life*. New York: Knopf, 1963.

A well-known study by a noted historian on some of the dangers in American life to freedom of thought and expression.

Knight, Harold V. *With Liberty and Justice For All: The Meaning of the Bill of Rights Today.* Rev. ed. with introduction by Roger Baldwin. Dobbs Ferry, N.Y.: Oceana, 1968.

An examination of the relevance of the Bill of Rights for contemporary issues of freedom of thought and expression.

Leiser, Burton M. *Liberty, Justice and Morals.* New York: Macmillan, 1973.

An analysis of how morals are enforced, with particular attention to the issues of pornography and obscenity.

Mill, John Stuart. "On Liberty," in *Utilitarianism, Liberty, and Representative Government.* New York: Dutton, 1951.

The classic and often-quoted defense of liberty by the nineteenth century English philosopher.

Murphy, Paul. *The Meaning of Freedom of Speech.* Westport, Conn.: Greenwood, 1972.

An historical treatment of first amendment freedoms in the period from Woodrow Wilson to Franklin Roosevelt.

14

Dissent

Disobedience can never be anything but a concrete decision in a single particular case. . . . The refusal of obedience in the case of a particular historical and political decision of government must therefore, like this decision itself, be a venture undertaken on one's own responsibility. A historical decision cannot be entirely resolved into ethical terms; there remains a residuum, the venture of action.*

THE FOUNDATIONS OF DISSENT

Dissent's American Heritage

We began our discussion of freedom of thought and expression by quoting from Thomas Jefferson. It would, therefore, be appropriate to begin our discussion of the extreme form of that freedom, dissent, with another set of very famous words from the pen of the philosopher from Virginia. He wrote that all human beings have basic rights, among them,

> Life, Liberty and the pursuit of Happiness—that to secure these rights, governments are instituted among men, deriving their just powers from the consent of the governed—.

He is here expressing the basic justification for any government and its corresponding set of laws. But inasmuch as he was writing to defend a decision to dissent from a particular government, he had to go on to provide a justification for what would become a violent revolution.

> That whenever any form of government becomes destructive of these ends, it is the *right* of the people to *alter* or *abolish* it, and to institute new Government, laying its foundation on such principles and organizing its powers in such form as to them shall seem most likely to effect their safety and happiness. . . . [W]hen a long train of abuses and usurpations . . . evinces a design to reduce them [the people] under absolute despotism, it is their right, it is their *duty*, to

*Dietrich Bonhoeffer, *Ethics*, ed. Eberhard Bethge (New York: Macmillan, 1955), p. 343–344.

throw off such government, and to provide new Guards for their future security.

These are powerful words, enshrined in our Declaration of Independence, and they lay out a rationale not just for free speech and expression but for a morally binding *duty* to so dissent from a particular form of government as to abolish it and throw it off. Unfortunately for those who would stifle dissent or who feel it has no place in modern society, the rationale set forth by Jefferson not only justifies political and military revolution, it also was the basis for the revolution that brought this country into being.

Dissent has a long history in our country. It has included peaceful and violent acts of disobedience against particular laws and in some cases against the dissenters, and it has led to new social legislation aimed at redressing injustices not given sufficient attention until dissent occurred. But dissent is clearly a major step beyond freedom of expression. Although speech is an act, and ideas have consequences, there is an obvious escalation from pronouncing dissatisfaction with the fairness of a law to refusing to obey it. Dissent is opposition to laws and policies that often takes on the form of disobedience. The ultimate form of dissent is rebellion or revolution: the abolition of one form of law and its replacement by another. This usually, but not inevitably, involves the removal of personnel and the profound restructuring of political institutions and legal machinery. Power (political, economic, and social) passes from one set of persons to another and new laws are created to better provide the security Jefferson talks about.

The Justification of Dissent

Dissent of this kind is clearly far more dangerous to the stability, peace, and order of a society than is freedom of expression as discussed in the previous chapter. Consequently, dissent requires a more thoroughgoing, more elaborate justification than do acts that simply put into effect the right of free speech. In some cases dissent involves the repudiation, through political action, of the very laws that provide for the protection of freedom of expression. Because dissent sometimes challenges the justification of the basis of law itself in a given society, it cannot appeal, in those cases, to the society's laws for *its* justification. In some sense, all acts of revolution can be morally justified only by an appeal to some law or principle that transcends the society being overturned.

But revolutions are the final form of dissent. Its preliminary form usually is an act of disobeying a particular law or set of laws regarded as unjust. The charge of injustice is normally based on a claim that the general principles of the society cannot sanction such a law, despite its having been legislated. The most obvious example would be the laws protecting slavery in the years before the Civil War. Although clearly having the force of law, slavery came to be regarded by many as unjust, as not in keeping with the basic principles enunciated in the documents pertaining to the founding of the country. Those who sought to overturn slavery did not repudiate the society as such; they saw slavery as inconsistent with their vision of the highest ideals of the society. As long as slavery enjoyed the protection of the law, however, it could not be removed without violating the laws supporting it.

To get a better sense of what the decision to engage in dissent involves and how dissent can move through various stages, even to the contemplation of revolution, it might be helpful to imaginatively recreate the situation of a young woman in 1850 trying to think through her response to the issue of slavery and justice.

A Sense of Discrepancy

Dissent begins when an individual senses a discrepancy between a set of ideals and current practice. The ideals must not yet have been incorporated into specific laws. If they have, opposition to the practice is simply opposition to what is already illegal, not opposition to a fundamental defect in the law. Dissent can begin only when the law permits something regarded as evil or prohibits something regarded as right. The aim of dissent is to eliminate the discrepancy between law and practice either by altering the law to permit what is right or to pass a law to prohibit what is wrong. Opposition to slavery might begin, then, with a sense that slavery, while legally permitted in 1850, is wrong on the basis of ideals or values not yet given legal enactment. The form of dissent, at the outset, might be appeal to those agencies responsible for changing laws in the constitutional manner, in this case, the Congress. In fact, many individuals did petition Congress to take up the matter of slavery. Today such petitioning might take the form of writing to one's congressional representatives or organizing political rallies to show support for legislative change.

Conflict of Loyalties

At this point, one important question any dissenter must consider is: By what standard, or on what basis have I determined that I can be both loyal to my country and in opposition to one of its duly enacted legal statutes? In the case of slavery it was possible for many people to reconcile the original intentions of the founding fathers with slavery (since slavery was not explicitly forbidden in the Constitution, since slaves were recognized as being equal to only a portion of a free white person, etc.). Others argued that despite these anomalies, the fundamental beliefs enshrined in the Declaration of Independence and in the Constitution regarding the equality of all persons were incompatible with the existence of slavery. With these beliefs as their base, they went on to argue that opposition to slavery was consistent with loyalty to the highest values of the country as set forth in its own fundamental charter.

Had that not been the case, the opponent of slavery would have had to face a more difficult decision: if her country's foundation explicitly approved of slavery and its existence reflected a fundamental ideal in the minds of those responsible for the Constitution, she would have to choose between slavery and infidelity to some of her country's stated values. At this point, she would have to fall back on a set of values that in her opinion are higher than those of her own country. These values might be based on any of the traditional moral positions considered earlier: an intuitive sense of what is just for all human beings, a response to the will of God, a belief about what is ultimately beneficial to the greatest number of people of which her countrymen are only a part, a Kantian sense of a categorical imperative demanding the universalization of justice, and so on.

But she must be clear that if her opposition to slavery is to escalate into full-fledged dissent, it must be based on a moral position transcending at least part of the legally enacted value system of her own country. She would have to accept the dissenter's working premise: Laws, while sometimes expressing morality, are not the definition or source of morality. Laws can be vehicles of justice, but justice sometimes reaches beyond particular laws. As Thoreau once said:

> Law never made men a whit more just; and, by means of their respect for it, even the well-disposed are daily made the agents of injustice.[1]

In other words, obeying some laws that are in conflict with justice can actually perpetuate injustice.

Having made her decision whether the law in question is or is not in keeping with the basic values of her country, she must then decide what action to take. Her petitioning and other appeals to the bodies that have the power to change the laws have gone unheeded. She can choose to resort to other legal maneuvers such as electing to office candidates who promise to take up the issue of legal change, or she can choose to have the laws permitting slavery challenged in court to test their constitutionality. This latter method is often the most frequently employed just prior to nonlegal forms of dissent. It is always possible that a court, empowered to interpret law as being in conformity or nonconformity with the Constitution, could strike down the law in question. She must reckon with the possibility that

---

[1]Henry David Thoreau, *Essay on Civil Disobedience,* quoted in *Dissent:* The Institute for Contemporary Curriculum Development (New York: Cambridge, 1972), p. 19.

her legal appeal will be lengthy (meanwhile the injustice of slavery continues to oppress and degrade thousands of slaves), that it might not even be given legal standing, and ultimately that it might be unsuccessful, i.e., the law permitting slavery might be declared perfectly constitutional.

Passive Disobedience

In the latter case, more forceful forms of dissent become viable options. In this country, one of the most time-honored and respected of these more direct forms of dissent is the tactic of passive disobedience, passively disobeying the law believed to be unjust. At this point the dissenter decides to disobey one or more laws pertaining to slavery, not by violent intervention against it but by refusing to obey it. For example, there was a law requiring that all fugitive slaves be returned to their masters. Many opponents of slavery chose to harbor runaway slaves, thereby directly disobeying the law. Their disobedience did not require them to take up arms against the duly constituted authorities and in that sense was a passive dissent. Much of the agitation against discriminatory, segregationist law in the southern states during the 1950s and 1960s was in the form of passive disobedience. If the law forbade black persons and white persons from eating together at a lunch counter, the dissenters—black and white together—disobeyed the law simply by sitting down as a block and waiting to be served.

If enough people passively disobey a law it will eventually come to be recognized by the official bodies of state that the law simply does not have the kind of social support necessary to make its enforcement possible. The law on prohibition is a case in point. It eventually was repealed because the large majority of Americans said by their disobedience of that law that it did not have enough social sanction to be a law representing the will of the people. Passive disobedience may also lead to a court challenge of the constitutionality of the law: the dissenters, given their day in court, can ask that the law, with whose violation they are being charged, be interpreted by a higher court as constitutional or unconstitutional.

At the very least, passive disobedience normally brings the issue to public attention. It is the hope of most dissenters that the public will eventually come to see the injustice of the law in question and that dissent will then spread widely enough that no further dissent will be necessary inasmuch as public opinion will force a legislative change.

The Acceptance or Rejection of Punishment

It should be recognized by our young dissenter, however, that whether or not public sentiment is aroused in favor of her cause, she may, as the price of her dissent, have to be willing to pay the full consequences of her disobedience. The force of the law requires that its violation be punished in some manner. Normally, this would mean that as long as the law is in effect, and assuming our dissenter has been rightfully convicted of disobeying it, she will have to pay a fine or spend time in jail.

THE DILEMMAS OF DISSENT

It is at this point that a major transition can occur in the form of dissent considered appropriate. Those dissenters who feel that the general premise of law and the legal structure of their country as such are valid will normally accept punishment for violation of a specific law. To fail to do so calls into question the basis of law per se. To refuse to accept the legal consequences of disobedience suggests that the individual's own moral position is not only higher than the particular offensive law in question, but is higher than law in general.

The force of law depends on a willingness of people in a social order to accept the sanctions imposed when law is broken. This acceptance, which might include imprisonment, does not undermine the challenge mounted against the law—it may, in fact, highlight it by evoking in the public a sympathy for the person "unjustly" suffering punishment. That kind of sympathy may be just what is needed to have the law legally overturned. It calls forth a moral response from the onlookers regarding the injustice of the specific law, but it does not call into question the validity of law as such. It undergirds the legal system precisely because it accepts its general premise, that law is respected because it imposes punishment when it is violated.

But some dissenters are led to the position that not only is one law unjust but that the entire corpus of law in a particular society is unjust: that the injustices being perpetrated are so vast and so intertwined in the entire legal system that passive disobedience and a willingness to be punished for violation of one or more laws will either be futile or an excuse for the authorities to act even more repressively. A citizen in Nazi Germany, for example, might understandably have reached the conclusion that the whole array of anti-Semitic, racist legislation was so overwhelming and so much a reflection of the power structure's system of values, that isolated passive protest against a few laws would have been irrelevant and ineffective. At this point, many dissenters make the transition to active disobedience.

Here, many who break the law will not be willing to accept legal punishment. To do so, they argue, tacitly acknowledges the rightfulness of the legal order of that society. Therefore, their dissent must be seen as repudiating that order in its entirety since the individual laws are merely reflections of the fundamental injustice that the legal order represents. To make such dissent requires a profound moral choice. It entails a decision on the part of the dissenter to reject the recourse of legal appeal and to take the law into her own hands. Such a step needs a strong and clearly thought out moral foundation, a foundation so deep as to stand in judgment not just on a single law but on a whole legal system. This kind of radical action is not lightly taken because it makes its appeal beyond the society and that society's principles and values. Certainly no persons whose moral values have been given to them solely by their society could make such a move.

Threat to Order and Law

Even those who feel there is a "transcendent" justification for rejecting the rule of law in a given society must weigh carefully the consequences of their action. Readiness to repudiate a whole legal system may lead to an undermining of social confidence in *any* legal system, which would clearly be disastrous for the kind of just society the dissenter is working toward. Many theologians have argued that our proneness to set up our own sinful desires in place of the needs of others is so strong that *any* rule of law is better than none at all. Law and order at least have the virtue of suppressing chaos or anarchy. If we returned to a state of complete freedom for each individual to do what he or she wanted without restraint, we would be back in a barbarous and destructive situation. Such views lead to the counsel of obedience even to unjust laws (although exceptions are made in religious arguments for those laws that directly contravene a "divine" commandment: no rule of law can be obeyed if it forbids worship of God, for instance). To reject this counsel and to engage in active rejection of a legal order takes the dissenter into the final arena of dissent—rebellion or revolution.

Our dissenter, therefore, faces another choice: She may refuse to accept punishment for her disobedience of the law regarding slavery without intending to call into question the general framework of law in her society. But if that is not her intention, she must show why her decision to refuse punishment does not rely on the principle that the force of law has no validity for anyone who thinks a law is invalid. If that principle is invoked, she has the further responsibility of showing that the order, which is necessary to any society, is not thereby seriously undermined. She would have to show, for instance, what distinguishes her refusal from the refusal of a rapist to accept the legal consequences of his act. She cannot argue that the law she has broken is wrong and the law the rapist has broken is right since, in the eyes of the society and its legal structure, both laws are right. She cannot argue that the purity of her motives, her moral sense of justice, is clearly superior to the lack of morality inherent in an act of rape. That may be true but a society cannot accept as morally binding *any* act an agent declares to be "sincere" or well-intended.

GANDHI ON CIVIL DISOBEDIENCE

The lawbreaker breaks the law surreptitiously and tries to avoid the penalty—not so the civil resister. He ever obeys the laws of the State to which he belongs, not out of fear of the sanctions but because he considers them to be good for the welfare of society. But there come occasions, generally rare, when he considers certain laws to be so unjust as to render obedience to them a dishonour. He then openly and civilly breaks them and quietly suffers the penalty for their breach. And in order to register his protest against the action of the law givers, it is open to him to withdraw his co-operation from the State by disobeying such other laws whose breach does not involve moral turpitude.

Mohandas K. Gandhi, *Non-Violent Resistance* (New York: Schocken Books, 1961. Copyright Navajivan Trust, Ahmedabad, 1951), p. 7.

Mohandas K. Gandhi (1869–1948) was a leader for India's independence from colonial rule and the foremost spokesman for the principle of satyagraha *or nonviolent resistance. He combined political and religious concerns into a life revered by many as saintly.*

Ultimately, our dissenter must argue that social orders and their legal systems are not absolutes: they are relative to the end of justice and/or fellowship. She must be willing to accept the conclusion that, as Jefferson put it in the Declaration of Independence, some abuses of justice are so great that an individual has the moral duty to appeal no longer to the values and laws of a given society for moral justification but must appeal to something universal, transcending that society, such as "the rights of persons in general," or God's will, or a fundamental moral sense not based on social consent.

Active Violation of Other Rights

This kind of appeal was made often in the case of slavery. Its radical injustice united many people not in revolution, but in active, sometimes violent disobedience of the law. This involved in many cases an active violation not only of the rights of other persons but even of their property. Dissenters who do not wish to bring their dissent to the point of revolution must still consider the degree to which they can justify not simply disobedience of law and refusal to accept the legal consequences but also how far they should go in obstructing the rights of others. Recently, a number of incidents have happened in which anti-abortion demonstrators have prohibited persons from seeking abortions even though the latter is presently a right under the law. They have also, in the process, impeded the right of some doctors and nurses from practicing their trade, another right well established in law. In these cases the dissenter must decide on what basis one right can temporarily cancel out another.

In 1850 many people felt that the right of the slave to be free outweighed the right of the slave-owner to own the slave. Clearly both rights could not be exercised at the same time. In many cases of active dissent, the rights being violated are not the direct target of the dissenter (such as the right of access to a public building), but those rights can become the subject in a demonstration designed to call attention to the violation of other rights. Protestors blocked the entrance to public buildings in the late sixties in order to call attention to the injustice of the Vietnam War. In the process they denied some people access to the buildings even though they had no quarrel with that right as such. Part of the dissenters' justification in doing so was their claim that only by inconveniencing previously unconcerned people could they bring the force of their moral position to the attention of those individuals.

There is no way in such situations for each and every right to be harmoniously realized. The dissenter, therefore, takes on a heavy responsibility in deciding for others, in effect, what they will or will not be free to do. There are a number of variations on this problem that the dissenter must consider. Some have argued that destruction of property, while a serious escalation of dissent, is justified if the issue involves the destruction of persons. While seeking to avoid any harm to other individuals, some dissenters have forcefully broken into private homes to free slaves, or have ransacked the offices of people believed to be perpetrating injustice (e.g., the pouring of blood on the draft office files in Catonsville, Maryland, during the Vietnam War protests). Although these acts are not done lightly, it is pointed out by the dissenters that it is better to maim physical objects than to use those objects to aid in the maiming of persons. Also, by destroying objects, they argue, other people can be brought to see the relative values of human well-being versus material well-being. Some dissenters claimed that when a society cared more about the protection of physical objects than about the lives of men being sent off to war, it revealed a priority of values fundamentally at odds with their own. This revelation became, for some, a catalyst into revolutionary action.

Dissent in Democratic Societies

Before moving to a discussion of the moral problems involved in the ultimate form of dissent—revolution—we should note an important distinction often remarked on by opponents of violent dissent. They point out a very important difference between societies with and societies without a democratic process for resolving political conflict. In totalitarian regimes in which the law is determined by the ruler's whim and upheld by military might, dissent, to be realistic, must resort to arms since the force of reason is irrelevant. In democratic societies, on the other hand, the political process "ensures" that if enough people can be brought to see the correctness of a dissenter's position (by free distribution of his ideas, free election of his candidates, etc.), the evil opposed will be eradicated without recourse to violence.

There is great force in this observation. A dissenter who has not tried the legal and peaceful channels available before deciding to engage in violent acts against a social order obviously has little or no place in her scheme of values for law or due process. A person not willing to use the law to remedy a social evil is not normally a person a society should be willing to trust with the defense or enforcement of the law since it is apparent that she regards her claims as superseding any rights the law has on her.

Nevertheless, there are times, in many dissenters' opinion, when the level of bigotry in the populace and the manipulation of the political process by the powers that be are so inimical and so unresponsive to the demands of justice that they are justified in going outside the law to secure their ends. There were those who argued during the slavery debate that given enough time (perhaps another two or three generations), slavery would come to be seen by enough people as either so unprofitable or unjust that it would gradually be made illegal. Their opponents argued that a moral wrong, especially one that involves the degradation and oppression of human beings, cannot wait on the whims and subtleties of a less than perfect political process to bring about its elimination. Some rights, such as the right to be free from bondage to another, should not be held hostage to a process designed to reach a compromise on most issues—for how could there be a compromise on the right of freedom? If a practice is wrong, it should be stopped immediately; and if the legal and political processes are incapable of doing that, they must be transcended by acts of revolution.

REVOLUTION AND VIOLENCE

Revolution implies a complete change either in the persons who control a government or in the distribution of political and economic power. It also requires changes in the legal system greater than the mere abolition of some laws and the addition of others. Revolutions involve a fundamental change of social values for which a change in government and law is a necessary prerequisite.

Revolutions would not be necessary if those who controlled the economic and political power of a society were amenable to change through persuasion or the political process. It is because those in power hold on to it, even through the manipulation and sometimes the subversion of the legal/political process, that active resistance becomes necessary if an alternative set of values is to be enacted.

Violence

Active resistance obviously raises the profound moral problem of violence: To what degree, if at all, is violence justified, against whom, and by what means? The violence done by armies has long been regarded as justified since it is done in the name of the society of which the army is an instrument of policy. The issue is not violence per se but *who* is being violent to whom and by what sanction. If the American revolutionaries had been unsuccessful in the war of independence, they could all have been convicted and punished as illegitimate, violent traitors. Because they won, their violence against the forces of the Crown attains an aura of legitimacy. We should remember that part of what makes violence justifiable is whether those who use it attain their goals.

But for a person struggling to know what is morally correct in this situation, mere success cannot be a sufficient justification for acting violently. Our dissenter must ask herself, Am I morally right in using physical force to restrain a slave owner from mutilating a slave, even though the owner has the legal right to do so under the laws of property and punishment? Her first barrier would be a definitional one. Some people believe that "violence" is only such when it is illegal. A police officer does not do violence when shooting a fleeing bandit but the bandit does violence when shooting the police officer in return. Others would argue that violence is any act that intentionally produces physical harm to another (though some such acts might be legally sanctioned, like those that occur in boxing).

To allow our moral considerations of acts that harm others to be resolved for us by a definition is to short-circuit the moral reasoning involved. Any act of harm to others needs justification: what the morally sensitive individual needs to do is sort out those acts of violence that are justifiable from ones that are not. We are talking here specifically about violent acts in the political sphere.

There are many arguments advanced against recourse to illegal violence. Religiously, many people feel that although they are expected by divine authority to do what they can to help other people, they are forbidden by

God's commands to use violence; if only violence will succeed in righting wrongs, then that "righting" will have to come from God. In the meantime the religious person must be patient if other acts, short of violence, are of no avail. Others have argued that since violence does an injustice to the body and/or mind of another, it cannot be justified since we should always treat others as ends, not as means. To act violently against you, even though you, through your actions are denying justice to others, is to violate your status as a person worthy of dignity and respect. Violence, therefore, directly contradicts in its enactment the very goals for which it is assumed to be the means. Such a contradiction is not morally permissible.

Perhaps the most prevalent argument against violence is one that appeals to its consequences. It is pointed out that when dissenters resort to violence, they normally bring down on their heads massive retaliation and repression. In other words, violence is self-defeating since its use by rebels justifies the established authorities' use of vicious reprisals and police-state tactics. More damaging in the long run is the fact that if a political order comes to power by violence, it creates a precedent for its own overthrow by violence. Violence breeds violence. (This is reflected in the fear of many in our society that too much exposure to the portrayal of violence in harmless settings, like in front of the TV, creates an atmosphere in which violence comes to be an acceptable way of resolving disputes.)

Is violence, then, justified? Those who think it can be point out that violence (harm to others through force) should not be assumed to be absent from even a smooth, well-run society. They argue that violence is done to our minds all the time by the power of false ideas and the propaganda of the power brokers. They also insist that when a regime is corrupt, the police and military forces, in the name of law, do violence to innocent victims continually. When the Nazis exterminated their Jewish victims, in the name of legally enacted statutes, was not violence being done? When slaves were treated as animals was not violence being done? Therefore, the proponents of selective violence conclude that if legality and order are maintained by violence and cloak injustice and brutality, there can be no legitimate objection to using counter-violence to remove the evil.

It should be noted that the end being appealed to here is social: that is, those who would use violence appeal to the need to establish a social order that is more just than the one in power. For those individuals whose highest moral end is not a social order at all but, say, obedience to a religious authority (even at the price of death or isolation), such an end is not ultimately relevant to their decision. If adherence to a moral principle, like "never do harm to another intentionally," is more important than creating a just society, then it would be difficult to find a justification for violence.

For those who hold that the establishment of justice *is* a moral end to be pursued, violence can be justified, according to the proponents, if there is a reasonable chance that its use will succeed in overthrowing the oppressive regime and instituting a just one. The right or end to be achieved must be higher in one's scale of values than the right (e.g., to be spared harm by others) that must be temporarily denied by violence. The amount of violence to be used must be proportionate to the evil being opposed. If destruction of property will succeed in bringing about justice, violence against persons is not justified. If violence against one or a few persons will succeed, it is not justified to kill many.

This line of argument was used by those who collaborated in the attempt to kill Hitler. Although fully aware of the horror of their intended act, they believed that killing one man would have greater effect than a resort to random violence against many. Those against whom the violence is directed must be the most directly responsible for the evil or injustice that the situation permits.

Terrorist tactics are, in this regard, the most difficult of all acts to justify morally, if they can be justified at all, since they are directed against "innocent" people such as children. The justification advanced for terror is that it brings to people's attention the injustice being suffered and forces the perpetrators of injustice to confront the problem. But terror is random: it uses as its means complete disregard for responsibility to others—it is difficult to see how such blindness to the particularities of other persons' lives can ever be a means to a social order in which the lives of others are treated with sensitivity and respect.

AN ARGUMENT AGAINST VIOLENCE

How wonderful it is that freedom's instruments—the rights to speak, to publish, to protest, to assemble peaceably, and to participate in the electoral process—have so demonstrated their power and vitality! These are our alternatives to violence; and so long as they are used forcefully but prudently, we shall continue as a vital, free society. . . .

. . . Violence on the part of a minority is sometimes a means of producing quick recognition of needs. It is not a productive technique for inducing the majority to undertake a job that must be figured in years of time and billions of dollars.

I recognize that there are times and societies in which violence employed to accomplish political ends has been respected. In times long gone by, tyrannicide had its respectable defenders. George Washington and friends were violent revolutionists. It is certainly arguable that slavery was abolished only by force of arms. But these analogies are too facile.

Violence is never defensible—and it has never succeeded in securing massive reform in an open society where there were alternative methods of winning the minds of others to one's cause and securing changes in the government or its policies.

Abe Fortas, *Concerning Dissent and Civil Disobedience* (New York: New American Library, 1968), pp. 39-40.

Abe Fortas (b. 1910) is a former Supreme Court Justice and prominent member of the legal profession.

Violence, then, if it is to be morally right at all, must be selective and guided by full consideration not only of its long-term effects but also of the means used in its implementation. These must be as much under the control of the agents of violence as possible. To rule out violence absolutely would be to sanction it under another name: the state or the established authorities. But when it is resorted to, as Reinhold Niebuhr once said so poignantly

> ... its terror must have the tempo of a surgeon's skill and healing must follow quickly upon its wounds.[2]

THE OPTION OF DISSENT

To return to the dilemma of our young dissenter: She has been struggling to know what to do in the case of slavery. Her dissent has escalated to the point where she has had to consider violence. Historically, of course, that violence eventually came in a legally sanctioned way for her: her government responded to acts associated with slavery by authorizing military conflict. Had the government gone the other way, had it continued to accept slavery as reconciliable with the nation's laws and traditions, she would have found herself much as Jefferson had found himself in 1776—deciding whether a full scale revolution was necessary to abolish this evil once and for all. Had society become "destructive of the . . . life, liberty and pursuit of happiness" of the enslaved black persons? If it had, then Jefferson's words would have special weight:

> [I]t is the right of the people to alter or to abolish it, and to institute new government, laying its foundation on such principles and organizing its powers in such form, as to them shall seem most likely to effect their safety and happiness.

[2]Reinhold Niebuhr, *Moral Man and Immoral Society.* (New York: Scribners, 1932), p. 220.

We can count ourselves fortunate that history did not take this turn, that the government came to see that slavery was not compatible with its ideals of freedom and justice. It is significant in this regard that Abraham Lincoln responded to the conflict that brought slavery to an end with imagery very similar to that used by Niebuhr in his justification of selective violence. In his Second Inaugural Address, Lincoln spoke of the need for an armed conflict to end the issue but immediately turned to the greater need for a healing process to begin:

> [L]et us strive on to finish the work we are in, to bind up the nation's wounds, to care for him who shall have borne the battle and for his widow and his orphan, to do all which may achieve and cherish a just and a lasting peace among ourselves and with all nations.

There is no way for a dissenter to know at the outset of dissent what forms it might take during the struggle. But as long as there is injustice being done to persons by legally constituted authorities, as long as rights are being violated, there will be a need for dissent. No one should become complacent enough to assume that dissent is never necessary or always disloyal. As long as values remain imperfectly realized, there must always be morally sensitive people to remind us of our highest vision and best ideals. We must even be prepared to see dissent escalate from public proclamation to radical revolution. Unless we can enter into the values and ideals of even those who resort to violent revolution in the name of equity, freedom, or justice, we cannot know what the full depth of being moral can entail. The greatest tribute active dissent pays to the moral quest is to take it so seriously as to give it life in the fullest social and political terms. Although there must be room in our moral equipment for the swift blade of violence, the greatest tribute moral persons can make to dissent is to provide the kind of open, rational, and just society in which the body politic maintains its health without recourse to the surgeon.

CHAPTER REVIEW

A. The foundations of dissent

1. The Declaration of Independence refers to the right of a people to throw off a government that has become destructive of liberty; this indicates that dissent has a long American heritage.
2. Because dissent is more revolutionary than freedom of expression, it needs strong justification.
3. Dissent begins when someone senses a discrepancy between a set of ideals and current practice in a society.
4. The potential dissenter will feel a conflict between loyalty to country or to values that transcend the country.

5. Dissent esclates through a series of stages, the first of which is to seek redress against an unjust law or practice through the congress or the courts.
6. Passive disobedience, i.e., passively disobeying a law regarded as unjust sometimes follows if legal or legislative remedies are not successful.
7. Dissenters have to face the question of whether to accept punishment for breaking a law regarded as unjust.

B. The dilemmas of dissent

1. When a law is regarded as part of an unjust legal system, dissenters sometimes feel justified in refusing punishment for breaking a law.
2. Those who refuse punishment must carefully consider the effect of their refusal on the stability of the social order as a whole.
3. Dissent sometimes involves the violation of other persons' rights.
4. Dissent within a democratic society permits many more options than does dissent within a totalitarian regime.

C. Revolution and violence

1. The final stage in dissent is reached when revolution is proposed.
2. If revolution is contemplated, the justification of violence must be considered.
3. Those opposed to violence argue that it simply breeds more violence and is ultimately dehumanizing. Those who support the use of violence point out that unjust regimes often use violence under the guise of law.

D. The option of dissent

1. Dissent is always an option for those who believe injustice is being done by legally constituted authorities. An open, rational, and just society will reduce the need to resort to this form of moral protest.

SUGGESTED READINGS

Barnes, Gilbert Hobbs. *The Anti-Slavery Impulse 1830–1844*. New York: Harcourt, 1964.

A detailed narrative of the events and issues surrounding the anti-slavery and abolitionist dissent in the antebellum period.

Cohen, Carl. *Civil Disobedience: Conscience, Tactics, and the Law*. New York: Columbia Univ. Press, 1971.

Arguments for and against civil disobedience, illustrated by case studies.

Fortas, Abe. *Concerning Dissent and Civil Disobedience.* New York: New American Library, 1968.

A powerful but succinct analysis of dissent in America by one of its leading jurists.

Hall, Robert T. *The Morality of Civil Disobedience.* New York: Harper, 1971.

A systematic study of civil disobedience including theoretical and practical considerations.

King, Martin Luther, Jr. *Why We Can't Wait.* New York: New American Library, 1964.

The classic statement of civil protest (including "Letter from Birmingham Jail") by the famous American civil rights leader.

Rasmussen, Larry L. *Dietrich Bonhoeffer: Reality and Resistance.* Nashville: Abingdon, 1972.

A study of the moral dilemmas involved in Bonhoeffer's decision to abandon pacifism and engage in the plot to assassinate Hitler.

15

Social Justice

Society . . . makes justice rather than unselfishness its highest moral ideal. Its aim must be to seek equality of opportunity for all life.*

WHAT IS JUSTICE?

In this chapter we will be concerned with how a society handles issues of justice as they involve the treatment of persons based on their race, sex, or age and with respect to their right to education, housing, and employment. Justice, according to Morris Ginsberg,

> consists in the ordering of human relations in accordance with general principles impartially applied. . . . The central core of the idea of justice is . . . the exclusion of arbitrariness and more particularly the exclusion of arbitrary power.[1]

The key to the problem of social justice, as Ginsberg's definition implies, is how to treat people's differences (race, sex, or age, among others) in a nonarbitrary way with respect to their claims for, among other things, equal housing, learning, and working in a society that assumes that well-being requires security and adequacy in all three areas.

It would be impossible to act morally without any consideration being given to the differences between persons. Credit given on an examination or rewards granted for a successful contest must be based on a demonstrated difference between those who come out on top and those who do not. It would be manifestly unjust to license every third person whose name appears in the phone book as a surgeon.

The exercise of justice is not based on the ignoring of differences but rather on the application of general principles to differences that are *relevant* and *justified* in the particular area of concern. In his elaborated defini-

---

*Reinhold Niebuhr, *Moral Man and Immoral Society* (New York: Scribners, 1932), p. 258.
[1]Morris Ginsberg, *On Justice in Society* (Baltimore: Penguin, 1965), pp. 56, 63.

tion of justice, Ginsberg stresses the importance of avoiding arbitrariness. He says that justice is

> opposed to (a) lawlessness, anomie, to *capricious* uncertain, *unpredict-able* decisions, not bound by rules; (b) partiality in the application of rules, and (c) rules which are themselves partial or *arbitrary*, involving *ungrounded* discrimination; that is discrimination based on *irrelevant* differences.[2] (emphasis added)

Ginsberg also makes a strong case for viewing the problem of justice as the problem of *power*. Injustice becomes a problem when someone is deprived by someone else's power of that to which the former has a legitimate right. In a society based on law, power primarily means the gaining of a legal right and, secondarily, the power to enforce that right. What we will examine are those issues that surround the struggle of people to gain the legal right (and the power to secure its implementation) to equal housing, education, and employment opportunities.

Since Aristotle, it has been common to distinguish between *retributive* and *distributive* justice. Retributive justice tries to punish the violation of someone's rights or to restore the enjoyment of a right. *Distributive* justice seeks to ensure the *fair* distribution of rights and privileges to all members of the society, taking into account only *relevant* differences. Distributive justice tries not only to provide for the equitable distribution of the means to basic human well-being but also to redress or compensate for past inequities suffered by those who have been unjustly discriminated against. As we shall see, some of the most volatile issues of justice in contemporary America occur in this latter area.

Rights

The problem of justice would not arise unless persons had some essential rights that it is the obligation of any social order to provide. In 1948 the United Nations Commission on Human Rights drew up a declaration of human rights that was adopted by the U.N. General Assembly. Among the rights it declared to be "a common standard of achievement for all peoples and all nations" were

> the right to social security . . . and . . . the economic, social and cultural rights indispensable for . . . dignity and the free development of . . . personality. . . .
> the right to work, to free choice of employment, to just and favourable conditions of work and to protect against unemployment . . . the right to equal pay for equal work. . . .

[2]Ginsberg, pp. 56–57.

the right to education... directed to the full development of the human personality and to the strengthening of respect for human rights and fundamental freedom....

the right to a standard of living adequate for the health and well-being of himself and of his family, including food, clothing, housing and medical care and necessary social services, and the right to security in the event of unemployment, sickness, disability, widowhood, old age or other lack of livelihood in circumstances beyond his control.[3]

RACIAL JUSTICE

Racism

The aim of social justice is to ensure that these rights are not denied to persons or groups of persons for unjustifiable reasons, or where they have been denied, to redress the injuries suffered. In the United States the most glaring example of such denial has been the treatment of persons on the basis of color. There has certainly been no more long-term, festering social issue in this country since its founding than racism directed primarily against black people but also against American Indians and, more recently, people of Hispanic origin.

The cancer that produces injustice toward those of another race is racism. It is

the belief that certain racial groups are, by nature and heredity, superior to the rest of mankind and therefore justified in dominating and discriminating against inferior groups. While prejudice may be merely an attitude (conscious or unconscious), racism is a dogma, deliberately cultivated and transmitted. It purports to describe factual or even metaphysical differences within mankind. It consigns some human races to an inherent inferiority at the core of their being.[4]

Fundamentally, racism is a form of faith, a search for meaning. As George Kelsey has put it, racism is

an affirmation concerning the fundamental nature of human beings. It is a declaration of faith that is neither supported nor weakened by any objective body of fact.... The devotee of the racist faith is as certainly seeking self-identity in his acts of self-exaltation and his self-deifying pronouncements as he is seeking to nullify the selfhood of members of out-races by acts of deprivation and words of villification.[5]

[3]Department of State, *Selected Documents,* No. 5.
[4]Roger L. Shinn, "Racism," in *Dictionary of Christian Ethics,* ed. John Macquarrie (Philadelphia: Westminster, 1967), p. 287.
[5]George D. Kelsey, *Racism and the Christian Understanding of Man* (New York: Scribners, 1965), pp. 24, 23.

Racism is much harder to eradicate than prejudice because it is so oblivious to fact. Nevertheless, the defense of racism relies heavily on what the racist *alleges* to be fact. To justify discrimination on the basis of race, the racist claims (a) that there are significant differences between races and (b) that these differences are relevant in treating one race differently from another.

Part of the moral dilemma of dealing with racism is that the racist is not open to being shown that his "factual" beliefs are erroneous. Racism, as a faith, has the ability to interpret all examples that contradict its faith as *exceptions* to its unquestioned assumptions. When a racist encounters a black person who has achieved success (contrary to the racist's expectations), the racist is often heard to explain this fact as "unnatural" or as the black person's "transcending" his race or as the inculcation of "white" traits by the black person. Only the most massive exposure to contrary fact will be likely to jar the racist's deep-seated principles and fears.

The American Dilemma

America is peculiarly attuned to the dilemma of racial bias, as the Swedish sociologist Gunnar Myrdal pointed out many years ago in his book *An American Dilemma*. Americans have a strong creed, amounting to a national conscience, claiming belief in freedom of opportunity and the equality of all persons before the law. Because of this creed, Americans cannot and have not been able to dismiss as groundless the claims of black persons for equal treatment. That precisely is the dilemma peculiar to Americans. They recognize the rightfulness of redressing the injustices whites have dealt blacks and at the same time they resist paying the price such recompense demands.

Nevertheless, the persistence of the dilemma, the lingering commitment to justice for all, opens a chink in the armor of racism through which moral reflection can introduce alternative interpretations of "alleged" fact and suggestions for social change that can meet the demands of justice. But it must not be supposed that the question of justice depends entirely on a factual determination of similarities between races (or sexes) that the racist denies in his desire to be superior.

Schooling

Many racists insist that segregated schools are justified by the inferior intelligence of black persons. Although there is certainly no compelling evidence for that claim, the justice of equal and integrated schooling would not depend on the claim being either true *or* false. The overwhelming evidence seems to indicate that when black children score lower on standardized educational tests, it is because of a combination of factors, none of which relate significantly to hereditary intelligence. Malnutrition and the crowded, stressful, impoverished, and hostile environments in which some black children grow up account primarily for their failure to perform up to educational standards to which most white children are oriented and nurtured almost from birth. But even *if* one could show that black children will learn more slowly (for whatever reasons) than white children, that fact should not affect the equity of schooling opportunities. It might, in fact, be argued that *more* attention should be given to the education of black children simply because of their environmental "handicap" (just as is the case with children handicapped by other things such as disease, birth defects, etc.). The point is that the morality of treating people equally and justly should not be made to depend solely on a factual analysis of irrelevant differences. As long as we are dealing with *persons,* differences of color, sex, or age are, according to the American creed, unimportant.

Anthropological and Historical Foundations

This is not to say that exposing people who are biased against color to factual studies setting forth the similarities of the races in all things essentially human is not important. This kind of information, once passed through the chink in the armor, may pave the way for other, more compelling forms of persuasion away from bias.

SCIENTIFIC OBJECTIVITY AND SOCIAL RESPONSIBILITY

The dilemma of the social scientists in employing the techniques and objectivity of science here is highlighted by the fact that complex social problems have historically been resolved not so much through the application of facts or principles of right or justice [as] through the effective use of economic, social, political, or military power.... The knowledge and advice of social scientists is sought and accepted in inverse relationship to the degree of controversy, intensity of feelings and emotions, and complexity of political, economic, and other power considerations and vested interest competitions which are involved in the particular social problem.... A most troublesome dilemma is faced then by those social scientists who persist in an attempt at objective study of crucial and controversial social problems. Their findings may be used as effectively by those who seek to maintain the *status quo* and to block progress ... as by those who seek to facilitate democratic social change.... But the responsibility of the scientist to test and retest his hypotheses, to seek his facts, and to check on the accuracy of his predictions remain in spite of—and because of—the many obstacles which he is required to face and surmount. Only through maintaining his role as an objective searcher after truth can he hope to make any contribution toward a positive resolution of the survival problems of man.

Kenneth B. Clark, *Prejudice and Your Child* (Boston: Beacon, 1955), pp. 208–209.

Kenneth B. Clark is Professor of Psychology at New York City College. His research work on the effects of segregation and prejudice on personality development in children played a major role in determining the Supreme Court's 1954 decision outlawing desegregated schools.

Statements from leading anthropologists such as Stanley Diamond can give the lie to the "factual" claims of racism.

All of the historical and psychological evidence scrutinized by anthropologists lead to one conclusion: there is no differential capacity for the creation and maintenance of culture on the part of any population large enough to be sensibly called a race. . . . Nor has any genetically based differential capacity in intelligence among these major populations ever been established. On the contrary, the doctrine of racial equality is fully supported by scientific and historical inquiry.[6]

Historical information is also essential to the breaking down of racial bias. When people who wish to use race to defend discrimination point to the slum conditions, the poor educational performance, and the high unemployment among large segments of minority populations, it is necessary to explain how those conditions were brought about. One would need to explain how Africans were captured in their own homeland, shipped across the Atlantic like cattle, and sold through two centuries as slaves: how the will and spirit of a proud people were almost destroyed by the brutal, inhumane, degrading conditions of slavery in which slaves were treated as animals, sold as things, their families separated by callous, business-based decisions of slave owners. Even following legal emancipation, former slaves and their descendants encountered the bitter legacy of slavery from former slave owners and their descendants. For decades

[6]Stanley Diamond, "A Statement on Racism," *Current Anthropology* 4 (June 1963), p. 323.

segregation in large segments of the country was legally enforced. Even the pretense of "separate but equal" masked the reality of unequal and separate schools, churches, lunch counters, and other "public" facilities. Employment practices were a direct reflection of the same racial bias. Black persons continually suffered low wages, infrequent job promotion, and were traditionally victims of the "last hired, first fired" syndrome.

It took years of struggle, both in and beyond the courtroom and legislative assemblies, to secure passage not only of laws prohibiting racial discrimination but also enforcement power to make those laws effective. Perhaps the Civil Rights Act of 1964 is the high-water mark of that struggle. Today there would be few, save hard core racists, who would argue publicly for a repeal of such laws or for a return to the days in which public segregation was the norm.

Housing

The struggle for social justice has not ended, however. It has shifted into more difficult areas—legally less simple and psychologically more complicated. Other values and rights, such as freedom of choice, the sanctity of the neighborhood, and recognition only on merit are being opposed to or are supplanting the values and rights connected with removing racial bias and the discrimination to which it gives rise. Although few would defend the principle that black persons, simply because they are black, should be denied jobs or schooling or homes, many persons are defending the principle that people should be free to live where and with whom they wish. It follows, they claim, that if a traditionally white neighborhood wants to preserve its "unique" character and traditions, it should not be "forced" to accept persons who, in its opinion, would counteract that character and those traditions. Claims are made that "cultural comfort" is an important ingredient in any neighborhood and that black people are more culturally comfortable in a black community and whites in a white community. Thus, any attempt to foster integrated housing is looked on as a violation of the freedom of choice of those both within the neighborhood and of those being encouraged to move in. Real estate agents have been known to "steer" black clients away from white neighborhoods on the grounds that they wouldn't be comfortable living there.

The moral flaw in the cultural comfort argument is, of course, that while it respects the desires of a biased community to perpetuate its bias, it does not respect the free choice of a family that wishes to exercise its right to live where it wants. It also overlooks the necessity of working to achieve the kind of interracial experiences that alone can lead to genuine respect of one race for another. As long as neighborhoods do not actively work for racial integration, those in the neighborhood wind up being deprived of the excitement and joy of relationships with people of another race.

It is interesting to note that those neighborhoods that have experienced racial integration successfully have done so, at least in large measure, because the residents share other, more important things in common than race. They discover that hobbies, jobs, and other interests provide stronger bonds of friendship than racial commonalty.

Economic Factors: Busing

In this regard it is impossible to avoid the problem of economic disparity. Wealthier, more economically secure neighborhoods have less difficulty accepting a minority family if it has the same economic status as the neighborhood in general. The communities most antagonized by residential integration are those that are economically marginal or those into which minority families of low income are moving and are being subsidized to do so. White families in such neighborhoods are generally more fearful of declining property values than are similar families in wealthier communities who know that their minority neighbors can afford to "maintain" their property. The result is that much of the public conflict in racial housing occurs at the margins of the white society. (Some of the economic realities that underlie this fact are spelled out in Chapter 12.)

It could be argued that the brunt of the integration struggle is being borne by members of the black community as a whole and by the least economically secure members of the white community. This can be seen dramatically in the confrontations over integrated schooling and its attendant busing. In 1954 the Supreme Court declared separate but equal schools illegal because it turned out to be not only unequal but also a formidable obstacle to the kind of interracial contact believed by the Court to be essential to a well-rounded education. Since that decision, communities have struggled to integrate (or resist integrating) their schools.

Apart from communities that simply resist the whole idea of integrated schools, the controversy has shifted to the question of how far, and by what means, shall black and white children be brought together in the same schools. Courts generally have recognized only town or municipal boundaries as those within which such integration must occur. In order to achieve "racial balance," it has been determined by many courts that some busing of white and black children is necessary. (This is due in large measure, of course, to the segregated housing that prevails in these communities.) Many white, and some black, parents have opposed such integrationist plans not on the grounds of race, but in opposition to destroying neighborhood schools. Similar to and associated with the argument of cultural comfort in residential housing, the opposition to busing argument holds that people have a right to maintain schools in their own neighborhood. To bus a child past the closest school to one on the far side of town to achieve racial balance is, for some parents, to override a more important right and, indirectly, to heighten racial tension and antagonism. In addition, to bus a child solely for integration purposes is, they argue, to confuse the goals of education with other, unrelated social goals.

Once again, the moral issue is related to what efforts a *de facto* (in fact) segregated society should take to bring about *de facto* integration. The moral issue is how to rank values. Those who choose to reject busing as a means toward integration must recognize that they place a higher value on convenience of travel to and from school than they do on overcoming the racial antagonism and mistrust that has infected the social order for three centuries. (It could be argued, on their behalf, that as long as the courts do not require suburban towns to integrate their schools with urban areas in which most of the minority population lives, the burden of school integration will be shouldered disproportionately by the less affluent and therefore less powerful white communities.)

PSYCHOLOGICAL EFFECTS OF RACISM

In any assessment of the moral ranking given to racial integration and the steps necessary to implement it, space must be given to the effects of prolonged racial prejudice, not only on those on whom it is imposed but also on those who impose it. The victims of prejudice include the discriminators and the discriminated against. The effects on the discriminated against are obvious, including the most pernicious and long-lasting: the inculcation of a negative self-image. If people are discriminated against long enough, they will eventually come to think of themselves as being what their tormentors allege they are. Any parent who has seen the effects of continual belittlement of a child knows the horrible self-hate that the child develops and that may take years to remove. As long as the overcoming of racial prejudice is not at the top of the moral agenda, the subtle but insidious destruction of bias will remain virtually unchecked.

Many people in our society do not stop to realize the injustice and cruelty they needlessly and perhaps thoughtlessly inflict by going along with, or failing to protest against, an entrenched power structure that prevents the members of various minority groups from developing their capabilities as persons. If the public schools, libraries, hospitals, and churches in a community were destroyed by fire, tornado, or other disaster, such people would say that they had suffered a great misfortune, perhaps even a calamity. Yet these same people sometimes deprive a section of the community of the use of these facilities because of race alone. And that deprivation represents an even greater destruction of one of the most valuable assets the community has: the minds and lives of some of its own members.

By their prejudice, members of a community shut themselves off in fear from the riches of encountering and learning from different persons within the human family. The effects of such self-enclosure can be devastating on biased persons. They live in fear of difference, they constrict their behavior to avoid others, they turn inward on their own narrow view of the world. Their minds and lives become just as atrophied and sterile as the lives of those whom they segregate and oppress. The single most horrible effect of racial prejudice is that it keeps persons from encountering each other's humanity. When that happens, we touch others' lives only in the most superficial, mechanical way. If, as many philosophers and psychologists have argued, we grow as persons only when we develop open, trusting, and enriching relationships with a wide variety of other persons, then racial prejudice is both a sign and a cause of our dehumanization.

"Reverse Discrimination"

Although agreeing that racial prejudice is an evil that ultimately destroys the vitality of any community, many people are reluctant to adopt what has come to be known as "affirmative action," or what some call "reverse discrimination."

Recognizing that racial injustice can be transmitted more devastatingly by institutions than by individuals, many social agencies, including legislative bodies, have insisted that social institutions consciously and actively seek out minority employees or applicants. If, for example, admission to college is subject to scoring high on tests that give an advantage to people of suburban schooling and affluent families, an advantage denied to some by virtue of circumstances arising out of earlier or continuing racial bias, then the institutional patterns of college admission are racist. If advancement in the building trades rests on seniority, and the history of the building trades is one of craft unionism that mirrors the racial biases of earlier decades, then job opportunity in that field is colored by a racist system.

Some of the racist structures of our society are inadvertent. The relatively low percentage of minority members in the professions of law and medicine reflects the discriminatory patterns that began at the earliest levels—housing and schooling. The moral issue is how to break this stranglehold a racist, interlocking chain of institutions has on opportunities for minority persons to achieve equal access to jobs, housing, and education.

Affirmative action requires that firms, businesses, and other institutions ensure that they solicit minority applicants and that, if all other credentials are equal, minority applicants be favored for admission or employment. In other words, it is a conscious attempt to seek out and secure members of those minority groups traditionally discriminated against by employers and educational agencies.

The reaction to affirmative action has based itself on the claim that it is unjust to treat people according to anything other than their demonstrated merit. Therefore, singling people out for "preferential" treatment on the basis of color is a denial of the very principle being used to justify the reverse discrimination in the first place. Opponents also point out that the "victims" of reverse discrimination are persons who may not individually be guilty of discrimination. White persons living in the present are being punished, in effect, for the injustices of white persons in the past. Such retributive justice is not fair because it does not seek retribution from those who were the most responsible for the crimes of injustice.

Supporters of reverse discrimination point out that members of a majority race do not, in fact, succeed in a racist society simply because of individual merit. Being white, they have a real, if implicit, advantage in securing the best housing, employment, and education. It is necessary, therefore, to undergo a period of compensation to bring blacks, as a race, up to the starting point from which the contest can be won or lost on individual merit. Unless such compensatory action is taken, the effects of racism and discrimination will persist, dooming present and future minority generations to perpetual disadvantages and injustice.

The moral dilemma is that *individual* black persons have been denied consideration on the basis of merit because of the treatment of blacks as a *group.* To undo the effects of that individual-blind discrimination, remedial or compensatory action must be equally individual-blind, at least until such time as people of all groups can be treated as individuals who are not handicapped by the effects of past group prejudice. Thus, proponents of affirmative action insist that a white person who refuses to take into account, in the name of individual merit, the bigotry suffered by black persons in the past is playing a form of moral blackmail, or perhaps moral Catch-22.

A related objection to affirmative action is that it tries to "legislate morality." It is argued by some that no legal action can change attitudes. Unless there is a genuine heartfelt desire to enter into loving relationships with members of another race, no amount of legal coercion can produce the love necessary to sustain those relationships.

Morally, such a position, according to its critics, confuses love with justice. The enactment of justice does not require or depend on a loving relationship between those from whom justice is demanded and those to whom it is due. If love is demanded before justice is done, it might never be done because the human heart cannot be manipulated or fully trusted. Many black persons, during the civil rights struggle, said to those white persons who resisted the implementation of justice because their hearts had not yet been moved: "We don't want your love or sympathy, we simply want your heels off our necks so that we can rise and stand alongside you. *Then,* we can talk about love!" If love is made a condition of justice by those who preside over injustice, it usually is masquerading as paternalism or resistance. In fact, many black groups insist that it is more important for them to appreciate their own traditions and "peoplehood" before they can enter into interracial dialogue with integrity. Only justice can provide the necessary foundation for building the mansions of love. Otherwise, love is built on the sand of exploitation and control of one group by another.

Summary

In the final analysis, the case for equal and just treatment of members of different races, in all areas of public life, but most especially in housing, education, and employment is not morally problematic. The real difficulty lies not in arguing the justice of the case but in getting individual and institutional behavior to *be* more just. It is not even primarily a problem of creating more laws against racial discrimination; the problem is enforcing the laws that now exist more stringently and consistently. Perhaps the greatest tribute to America's moral conscience that the American dilemma reveals is that Americans discriminate against minority racial groups either with a guilty conscience or with elaborate, obviously self-serving rationalizations that mask explicit bigotry or racism.

SEXUAL JUSTICE: THE RIGHTS OF WOMEN AND SEXUAL MINORITIES

There is a much less guilty conscience and fewer attempts to fabricate rationalizations to disguise deep-seated prejudice in the case of discrimination directed against women and people whose sexual preferences are not, statistically, normal. As the racist argument about the alleged inferiority of black persons fades slowly away, arguments about the alleged inferiority of women and homosexual people are beginning to be heard more openly, claiming that women, and homosexual people, in particular, are to be treated differently from males and heterosexual people because they *are* different in *relevant* ways. Part of the recent public discussion about these areas of injustice is due to the heightened awareness by women and homosexual people of being its victims. Because of the courageous and persistent struggle of black persons for their rights, other groups have become conscious about ways in which they believe they have been historically and systematically denied rights. We might almost say that the decade of the 1970s was the decade of "rights consciousness."

The Liberation of Women

Many women, particularly in America, are claiming that they have been just as much victims of unjust discrimination as black persons. In support of their claim they point to laws in the various states that have the cumulative effect of denying women the same rights as men in securing and keeping jobs, establishing bank accounts, purchasing homes, and being paid equally for similar jobs. As Kate Millett puts it:

> Oppressed groups are denied education, economic independence, the power of office, representation, an image of dignity and self-respect, equality of status, and recognition as human beings. Throughout history, women have been consistently denied all this, and their denial today, while attenuated and partial, is nevertheless consistent.[7]

Feminists like Millett point to such statistics as the difference between the median incomes of full-time working men and women (in 1973: men—$7,664; women—$4,457); their status in the civil service (women comprise 86 percent of the lowest grades and only one-tenth of 1 percent of the highest grade); and their representation in the more prestigious professions (women make up only 9 percent of all professors, 3.5 percent of lawyers, 7 percent of medical doctors, and 1 percent of engineers).[8]

Of even more importance than statistics to many women is the subtle but insidious and pervasive atmosphere of male domination in which women live and in which young girls and boys are brought up. They point to the nurturing of girls toward certain kinds of behavior and vocations from the earliest days of infancy. Girls are taught to play with dolls and to be submissive, while boys are encouraged to play with trucks and to be aggressive. Sex "roles" are, from very early on, part of the assimilated expectations children develop and live by. (See Chapters 5 and 10 for a fuller discussion of the nature of sex roles and human identity.)

The Relevance of Sexual Differences

The basic moral issue at stake here is the *relevance* of sexual differences between men and women. Racist claims about black persons aside, the appeal to *nature* is more frequently made to justify discriminatory treatment of women and homosexuals than is any other kind of appeal. It is argued that women, for example, are by nature more capable of raising children and maintaining the tranquillity and order of a home than are men. They are more tender, sensitive, passive, peaceful, and emotional than men and should, therefore, be encouraged to restrict their activities to those areas in which their virtues can be applied. Traditionally, the areas into which men should go and dominate are those that require the application of the "natural" male

---

[7]Kate Millett, "Sexual Politics: A Manifesto for Revolution," in *Radical Feminism*, eds. Anne Koedt, Ellen Levine, and Anita Rapone (New York: Quadrangle, 1973), p. 365.
[8]Quoted in Thomas Mappes and Jane Zembaty, eds. *Social Ethics: Morality and Social Policy* (New York: McGraw-Hill, 1977), p. 116.

virtues: aggressiveness, initiative, hard-headed rationality, and a desire for competition. In a classic statement of the complementary roles and traits of men and women, Horace Bushnell (a nineteenth century Protestant-American clergyman) put it this way:

> [T]he sexes have a complementary relation.... The male is the force principle, the female the beauty principle ... one is the forward, pioneering mastery, the out-door battle-ax of public war and family providence; the other is the indoor faculty, *covert*, ... complementary, mistress and dispenser of the enjoyabilities. Enterprise and high counsel belong to one, also to batter the severities of fortune, conquer the raw material of supply; ornamentation, order, comfortable use, all flavors, and garnishes, and charms to the other.... Happily, it is just as natural to women to maintain this beautiful allegiance to the masterhood and governing sway-force of men, both in the family and the state, as we could wish it to be.[9]

Although many people might not use Bushnell's quaint form of expression, the sentiments he reveals are shared by large segments of contemporary society. Morally, one must begin by asking whether the differences between men and women he enumerates are really there. It is interesting to note that he ends his comments by acknowledging his (the male) wish that women be subject to the masterhood of men. Whenever self-interest is called on to support a claim of moral supremacy, the observer is warned to look out for a less than objective moral argument.

Second, even if the differences can be substantiated, one would have to ask whether they are natural or artificial. We all know that what one generation or culture sometimes calls natural is experienced by another generation or culture as quite alterable by human choice. It was once considered natural to walk and unnatural to fly or natural to marry at the age of twelve or thirteen and to die before the age of forty. Many so-called natural traits and expectations are the result of social and cultural conditioning rather than innate, biological restrictions. We should be particularly suspicious of defending "natural" inferiorities in others when it is to our own advantage to do so.

Third, when natural differences can be sustained, such as the ability of women to conceive and bear children, one must ask whether those differences justify the kinds of discrimination directed against women in areas of employment, housing, self-support, and so on. How does a woman's child-bearing capacity relate to her qualifications for admission to law school or for equal pay for work similar to that being done by a man? It is in this area that we find some of the most articulate arguments supporting discrimination based on sex differences. One such argument holds that biologically men are more aggressive than women. Given this fact, women

---

[9]Horace Bushnell, *Women's Suffrage: The Reform Against Nature* (New York: Scribners, 1869), pp. 14, 51–54.

would be subjected to failure and frustration if they are prepared equally with men for jobs that place a premium on aggressive behavior.

> [M]ost women would lose in such competitive struggles with men (because men have the aggression advantage), and so most women would be forced to live adult lives as failures in areas in which the society had *wanted them to succeed....* The biological element will manifest itself in any economic system ... the possible varieties of political-economic systems are limited by, and must conform to, the nature of man.[10]

In other words, because sex role distinctions are biologically grounded, it would be immoral to encourage women to go "against the grain." The result of such encouragement would be not only frustration at tilting against biological windmills, but also a diminution in women's sense of well-being. In addition, since a society works best when all its functions are performed at peak efficiency, women would do society a disservice by striving for jobs for which they are not naturally best suited.

To all these arguments it can, of course, be replied that they beg the question of which traits are inherited and which are culturally conditioned. In addition, they confuse the status of biological generalizations (*if* true) about an entire sex with the moral justification of denying to every individual within that group the right to attempt, by merit, what the group as a whole is believed incapable of doing. It may be true, for example, that students who study for a test are more capable of succeeding on it, but this generalization should not be used to justify denying someone who has not studied the right to take the examination. In responding to the argument that some sex roles are inevitable, Joyce Trebilcot argues that:

> What is inevitable is presumably not, for example, that every woman will perform a certain role and no man will perform it, but rather that most women will perform the role and most men will not. For any individual, then, a particular role may not be inevitable. Now suppose it is a value in the society in question that people should be free to choose roles according to their individual needs and interests. But then there should not be sanctions enforcing correlations between roles and sex.... Indeed, if individual freedom is valued, those who vary from the statistical norm should not be required to conform to it.[11]

In any attempt to justify sexual discrimination, the burden of proof should lie with those who benefit from such discrimination. Their task should be to show how sexual differences make a practical difference to the

---

[10]Steven Goldberg, "The Inevitability of Patriarchy," in Mappes and Zembaty, pp. 140–141.
[11]Joyce Trebilcot, "Sex Roles: The Argument from Nature," *Ethics* 85, no. 3 (April 1975), pp. 249–255 (Chicago: Univ. of Chicago Press, 1975), as found in Thomas A. Mappes and Jane S. Zembaty, eds., *Social Ethics: Morality and Social Policy* (New York: McGraw-Hill, 1977), p. 146.

area in which the discrimination occurs. And even if some arguments can be made persuasively in general, room should always be left for the singular individual who shows by deed that he or she is not impeded by the sexual trait in question.

> It is the business of reason, though always involved in prejudice and subject to partial perspectives, to aspire to the impartiality by which such claims and pretensions could be analyzed and assessed. Though it will fail in instances where disputes are involved and complex, it is not impossible to discover at least the most obvious cases of social disinheritance. Wherever a social group is obviously defrauded of its rights, it is natural to give the assertion of its rights a special measure of moral approbation. [12]

The Rights of Sexual Minorities

In addition to the rights of black persons and women, the rights of "sexual minorities" are receiving a great deal of attention today. Persons who wish to relate exclusively or primarily to members of their own gender are claiming that the laws and mores of the larger society frustrate their right to fair employment, housing, and acceptance into many social organizations.

Of all the three areas considered under the rubric of social justice, the issue of the rights of homosexual people is one that elicits the greatest degree of passion. It is certainly the area about which there is the greatest hesitancy in speaking. A majority of Americans probably regard homosexual relations as "perverse," "disgusting," dangerous for their children, "promiscuous," and "unnatural." It is this last charge, of being unnatural, that is the foundation on which the most powerful arguments against homosexuality have been built. Implicit in and central to the argument is the assumed link between an act's being unnatural and therefore immoral.

The "Natural"

The most common of such arguments, natural law, is summarized in Thomism (deriving from the thought of Thomas Aquinas; see Chapter 4). It claims that the created order has built into it certain purposes for its various parts. The purpose of the eye is to see, of the mind to think, of the stomach to digest. When a thing does not perform its primary function, it is unnatural or perverse.

It is not always clear in this kind of argument whether it is the damage done by the unnatural functioning of something that is the cause of its being immoral or whether there is something immoral as such about an

---

[12]Niebuhr, p. 236.

"unnatural" functioning. Within a Thomist framework, the unnatural is a sign of disorder, a violation or perversion of the natural order as it was intended by God to function. As such, the unnatural is defective. Inasmuch as sin is regarded as a defect, a rupture of the natural purposes built into the created order, the unnatural, being defective, is therefore sinful.

One essential assumption on which this argument is built is that each thing has *a primary* function. Another essential assumption is that it is possible, by reason, to discover this primary function. Thus, it is claimed, reason knows that the primary function of the sex organs is to procreate. Any alternative use of the sex organs, if it frustrates or subordinates their primary purpose, is sinful and consequently falls under moral censure (and therefore under moral and civil laws). Thus, masturbation, homosexuality, or any kind of heterosexual intercourse that *deliberately avoids* procreation (such as that which employs contraceptives) is unnatural and morally wrong.

Those who reply to this argument usually do so by questioning its fundamental assumptions. They argue that the unnatural may be nothing more than a statistical abnormality. It may be unnatural to run the mile in under four minutes or to play the violin at three years of age. Although in comparison to the normal functioning of the created order these acts may be surprising or upsetting, one would hardly call them immoral. It might also be pointed out that many medical devices used to sustain life are unnatural inasmuch as they are unusual interventions into the natural processes of the human body. Nevertheless, they are by all standards declared to the morally praiseworthy. Thus, it is not unnaturalness as such that is problematic, but rather an unnaturalness that has certain consequences.

This pushes the opponent on to the next assumption in the argument based on unnaturalness: that each thing has a primary function and that obstruction of that function frustrates the thing's essential nature. The first reply is to ask whether it is self-evident or rational to assume a single overriding function for something. Hands can be used to grasp (perhaps their original, biological function), but also to clap, to stroke, to paint with, to make fists out of, and so on. Is stroking an unnatural use of the hands? Applying that argument to the sex organs, opponents of the unnaturalness argument point out that sex organs can certainly be used for procreation (and are uniquely suited for that), but they can also be used for giving pleasure and for showing affection. Why would one of these functions be declared primary and the others unnatural when not subordinated to it?

MORALITY AND THE PERVERSION OF NATURAL ENDS

If a man "perverts" himself by wiggling his ears for the entertainment of his neighbors instead of using them exclusively for their "natural" function of hearing, no thinks of consigning him to prison. If he abuses his teeth by using them to pull staples from memos—a function for which teeth were clearly not designed—he is not accused of being immoral, degraded, and degenerate. The fact that people *are* condemned for using their sex organs for their own pleasure or profit, or for that of others, may be more revealing about the prejudices and taboos of our society than it is about perceptions of the true nature or purpose or "end" (whatever that might be) of our bodies.

Burton Leiser, "Homosexuality and the Unnaturalness Argument," from *Liberty, Justice, and Morals,* Burton Leiser (New York: Macmillan, 1973), as found in *Social Ethics: Morality and Social Policy,* eds. Thomas A. Mappes and Jane S. Zembaty (New York: McGraw-Hill, 1977), p. 219.

Burton Leiser (b. 1930) is a philosopher whose works include Custom, Law, and Morality *and* Liberty, Justice and Morals. *He has taught at State University College at Buffalo and at Sir George Williams College in Montreal.*

Opponents of the unnaturalness argument claim that certain acts have been declared "unnatural" because of the *effects* of the alternative uses of a thing, not because these uses are unnatural as such. But once the argument has shifted to a consideration of the effects of an act, the charge of unnaturalness is not sufficient to condemn the act as immoral. At this point, those who wish to avoid condemning homosexuality as evil look to the affection, trust, and fulfillment they claim exists between homosexual people. The trauma or pain felt by homosexual people they attribute not to the sexual relationship but to social attitudes of hostility and rejection.

The Effects of Homosexuality

If homosexuality is to be condemned and its practitioners discriminated against justifiably, its effects must be shown to be harmful either to others or, in some peculiarly significant way, to the homosexual him- or herself. At this level of debate, there is a great deal of contradictory evidence. Some claim that, psychologically, homosexuality is damaging to the personality; others claim it is and could be even more fulfilling if the larger society accepted it as a legitimate form of love and affection. (But it is not our purpose to treat these arguments here.)

The debate also considers the effects of homosexuality on those who are not homosexual people. Parents fear that their children will be attracted to a homosexual life style if it is permitted to be advocated or practiced publicly. Does a homosexual have a right, in the name of social justice, to hold any job for which he or she has the qualifications, regardless of sexual orientation? Perhaps the most sensitive of such jobs, in the eyes of many, is the school teacher. Does a society, out of fear or dislike of an unnatural or, to many, a morally repugnant sexual preference, have a right to restrict the opportunities of those who have such a preference? To defend such discrimination, one would have to show that a belief in and practice of homosexuality outside the classroom is more damaging than a teacher's belief in and practice of political opinions that are not statistically normal. As long as the teacher is not using the classroom to propagandize or proselytize, it is not clear why his or her personal beliefs and life style should be of any concern to his or her students or their parents.

Even if a majority of persons believed that the unnatural is immoral because it perverts God's intended primary purpose, it would be hard to justify civil action taken on the basis of that belief. The assumption in question is not universally held and involves some distinctive theological principles. In a democratic society, the use of such principles to justify a form of discrimination against practices that have not been *self-evidently* shown to be harmful is inappropriate and indefensible.

It would certainly be appropriate for the society to restrict the degree to which persons, no matter what their sexual orientation, can solicit or attract others to their position. While heterosexuality is approved by most Americans, even ardent heterosexuals are prohibited from rape, public displays of heterosexual intimacy, prostitution, or propositioning minors. The same restrictions should be placed on homosexual activity without making the further move to restrict the legal, social, and employment opportunities of homosexuals.

A TRIBUTE TO JUSTICE

In this chapter we have looked at injustice as the denial of basic civil rights to black persons, women, and homosexuals. A common thread that runs through the various arguments used to justify discriminatory treatment of the three groups has been the belief that all three suffer from some "natural" inadequacies. It is a tribute to the power of the ideal of justice that those who wish to exclude blacks, women, and homosexuals from equal treatment by the law in significant areas of social life feel that they have to do so by appealing to something as fundamental and nonarbitrary as nature. Whether nature displays the exact kind of inadequacy they claim, and whether a natural difference (when it exists) is sufficient to justify different social and legal treatment is another matter. We have seen alternative arguments presented by both sides.

A society may never agree completely on what is just in each and every situation in which injustice is perceived. But it is far better to debate the issue with both sides committed to the notion that justice should be "the exclusion of arbitrariness and, more particularly, the exclusion of arbitrary power." When the need for debate ends, the commitment to the search for justice also dies, and in its place is born the monster of prejudice, caprice, and self-interest, unchecked by the restraint of countervailing power manned by the forces of fairness, equity, and right.

CHAPTER REVIEW

A. What is justice?

1. Justice is the ordering of human relations in accordance with general principles impartially applied. It excludes arbitrariness.
2. Justice seeks to secure rights. Basic human rights have been identified by the U.N. Commission on Human Rights.

B. Racial justice

1. Racism is the denial of rights based on skin color. It affirms the inferiority of a racial group.
2. The American dilemma is that Americans have a creed that forbids racial discrimination and a history of racism.
3. Factual information about racism can be helpful in overcoming it.
4. Segregated housing reveals some of the moral dilemmas of combatting racism. Freedom to choose where to live is a right that sometimes conflicts with the need for integrated housing as a step toward racial harmony.
5. Busing to achieve racial integration in the schools has generated great controversy and revealed some economic disparities that affect which white communities bear the greatest burden of busing.

C. Psychological effects of racism

1. Racial prejudice harms not just those discriminated against but also the prejudiced person who lives in fear of the other. The single most horrible effect of racial prejudice is that it keeps persons from encountering each other's humanity.
2. One remedy designed to counter the effects of prolonged discrimination is "reverse discrimination" in which the racial group discriminated against is given special attention in order to allow it to catch up with the majority.

D. Sexual justice: the rights of women and sexual minorities

1. Women in this country have been the victims of unjust discrimination in education, employment, and status.
2. Sexual differences between men and women as grounds for different treatment have been advocated by some. Opponents of this position have denied that sexual differences are relevant and have insisted that individuals be treated on their merits.
3. Sexual minorities have suffered discrimination as well as provoked much public concern.
4. The significance of what is "natural" in relation to what is moral underlies much of the discussion about homosexuality and its treatment under law.
5. The effects of homosexuality on others and on homosexuals themselves must be considered in the debate on social justice for homosexuals.

E. A tribute to justice

1. The use of differences and "unnaturalness" pervades the arena of social injustice. But through the principle of excluding arbitrariness, a society can check the danger of prejudice, caprice and self-interest prevailing over social justice.

SUGGESTED READINGS

Atkinson, Ronald. *Sexual Morality*. New York: Harcourt, 1965.

A treatment of the different and opposing arguments on many dimensions of sexual morality, including the arguments from nature.

Bianchi, Eugene C., and Rosemary R. Ruether. *From Machismo to Mutuality: Essays on Sexism and Woman-Man Liberation*. New York: Paulist, 1976.

Alternate essays on ways in which traditional stereotypes of men and women can be overcome.

Blackstone, William T., and Robert Heslep, eds. *Social Justice and Preferential Treatment*. Athens: Univ. of Georgia Press, 1976.

A good collection of essays by philosophers and lawyers and government officials on the issues involved in preferential treatment of minorities.

Kosnik, Anthony. *Human Sexuality: New Directions in American Catholic Thought*. New York: Paulist, 1977.

A study of some of the most recent thinking by Catholic moral theologians on issues of sexuality.

Rawls, John. *A Theory of Justice*. Cambridge: Harvard Univ. Press, 1971.

A philosophical investigation of the meaning of justice based on individual rights. A major study that has evoked heated response.

Silberman, Charles E. *Crisis in Black and White.* New York: Random House, 1964.

A somewhat dated but still powerful analysis of racism and race relations in America.

16

Ecology and the Moral Use of Energy

It is the top of the ninth inning. Man, always a threat at the plate, has been hitting Nature hard. It is important to remember, however, that NATURE BATS LAST.*

ENERGY AND ECOLOGY

Without energy, nothing would happen. Energy is the power to do things. But every use of energy has consequences far wider and more long-range than its immediate application. As we move toward the end of the twentieth century, we are discovering some of the unsettling aspects of the use of energy, whether to heat our homes, drive our cars, produce our conveniences, or kill our enemies. These discoveries bring us face to face with the moral responsibility we have for using energy resources without causing unintended consequences for our environment, the ecological balance, and our "enemies." There are limits to life on a small planet. How we understand those limits and act accordingly has become a central moral concern for many millions of people today.

As people struggle to pay rising fuel costs and higher taxes for social services for increasing populations and to combat the effects on their health of chronic pollution, they come to see the consequences of not observing the limits of nature and ecology. An "ecological conscience" is now forming in many people. Ecology comes from the Greek word for house and means literally "the study of houses or environments." Recently it has come to mean a study of the web of life in which all living things are related to each other. In commenting on the work by the biologist Eugene Odom, William Blackstone asks us to think of ecology as involving a "biological spectrum which includes the following: protoplasm, cells, tissues, organs, organ systems, organisms, populations, communities, ecosystems, and the biosphere." The biosphere is

---

*Paul R. Ehrlich, "Eco-Catastrophe!" in *The Environment Handbook*, ed. Garrett De Bell (New York: Ballantine, 1970), p. 176.

the biologically inhabitable soil, air and water constituting that part of the earth in which ecosystems can operate, and an ecosystem or ecological system is viewed as the population of a community, whether human or nonhuman, and the nonliving environment with which it functions.[1]

Central to the ecological concern are those mechanisms that regulate the relations in nature. These regulatory mechanisms keep the organism in balance with itself and its environment. If you alter one part of the organism, the regulatory mechanisms will insure that other parts make suitable compensation; the heart pumps faster when the legs run more quickly. What ecology is most sensitive to are those man-made changes in the environment that bypass or override the ability of nature to make appropriate adjustments. When pesticides were introduced, they had the immediate effect of controlling undesirable bugs and the long-range effect of poisoning food supplies and creating conditions (which the regulatory mechanisms of nature couldn't combat) for the development of even more pesticide-resistant insects.

The moral issues involved in ecological awareness are among the most original and challenging moral dilemmas of our time: original because they require us to think about the possibility of granting rights to animals, trees, and other nonhuman organisms; challenging because they might require us to set aside long-cherished expectations about our standard of living and the economic practices used to sustain it.

FOUR POSSIBLE AREAS OF DANGER

There are four basic areas in which we experience the ecological problem most severely today. First, the population of the world is increasing at such a rate that food supplies, resources for daily existence, and space for living are being threatened. Second, the pollution and by-products of our industrial growth are threatening the ecological balance around the world. Third, due to profligate consumption there is a dangerous depletion of many of the natural resources needed for a healthy life (e.g., the oil crisis of recent years). Fourth, there is the danger of widespread sickness and death due to nuclear radiation, either in the form of improper containment of nuclear waste or, more catastrophically, in the form of nuclear war. Each of these problems is a warning signal that the regulatory mechanisms of nature are in danger of being overloaded or short circuited. Before turning to the nature of today's ecological problems, it is necessary to see briefly why they seem to have emerged at this time in history and what values have aided and abetted their development.

---

[1]William T. Blackstone, "Ethics and Ecology," in *Philosophy and Environmental Crisis*, ed. William T. Blackstone (Athens: Univ. of Georgia Press, 1974), p. 18.

Historical Roots of the Crisis

James C. Logan in his article "Ecological Considerations" traces much of the current ecological crisis to "the inherited value system" of Western thinking. Specifically, the values he identifies as contributors to the crisis are (1) that the human race is to be lord and master over the Earth. Relying upon the Biblical story in which Adam is given "dominion" over the Earth by God, this value isolates man from the rest of nature, leading him to believe that he can do what he wants with nature without regard for the consequences. (2) This led human beings to regard nature as without value, and thus subject to exploitation in the name of human need. From the investigation and utilization of nature came a third value: (3) that self-worth for individuals and nations was to be measured by their degree of consumption or possession of the world's resources. An ever rising standard of living has come to be regarded as a "right," and is defined as the ability to purchase the latest, most technologically sophisticated goods, without regard for the "need" for such goods or for the depletion of resources this need creates. Finally, (4) there is the value, expressed by John Locke (see Chapter 4 in this book) that every person "is absolute lord of his own person and possessions ... and subject of nobody." If individuals insist upon their right to own as much property as they can secure and to use it as they see fit, it will become virtually impossible to accord any place to the right of the ecological system as a whole, or the right of future generations to a liveable environment. Under the domination of such a value it would be very difficult for nations to work together in programs of mutual restraint to preserve ecological balance and the dwindling resources of the Earth.[2]

Few would deny that the human race faces grave ecological problems. As we shall see, however, there are some who would claim that the above values do not lead inevitably into ecological disaster and can, in fact, serve as the basis for extricating ourselves from danger. In any event, they argue, these values are superior to any alternative ones being suggested as their replacement. Other people argue strenuously that an entirely different set of values is necessary if we are to continue living in harmony with nature and in peace with ourselves.

Population

What are the conditions that now prevail or threaten us in the near future as far as our relation with nature is concerned? One of the most serious,

---

[2]James C. Logan, "Ecological Considerations," in *The Population Crisis and Moral Responsibility*, ed. J. Philip Wogaman (Washington, D.C.: Public Affairs Press, 1973), pp. 95–108.

and factually documented, perils is that of increasing population. "The world's population is increasing at a rate which renders distress, famine, and disintegration inevitable unless we learn to hold our numbers within reason."[3] Currently the world population (now around three billion) is expected to double in thirty-seven years. The doubling time has dropped from one million years, when world population first reached about five million (around 6000 B.C.), to one thousand to two hundred to eighty and now to thirty-seven.[4] One consequence of this increase in population is sheerly physical. According to Paul B. Sears, it will be less than 700 years until there is standing room only in the United States, with each space of 3 by 2 feet occupied. On this basis there is room for exactly 4,646,400 people in each square mile.[5]

The obvious problem that ever-increasing population poses is how to feed, clothe, shelter, and provide for millions more people from a finite, limited resource: Earth. Starvation will occur on a massive scale. The balance of nature could be so radically altered as to make life impossible for humanity in anything like its present numbers. Not only must the feeding cycle be maintained, but also the cycle that regenerates the air. This whole network of relationships is at risk. Even those who believe that technology can provide ways of sustaining such an increase in population admit that to make human beings adjust to the increased urbanization and industrialization "the individual must be specifically processed. . . . The more complicated and productive the synthetic habitat becomes through technological development, the more complicated becomes the acculturation process."[6]

A particularly troubling aspect of the population problem to some critics is the unequal consumption of the limited resources that remain. The most technologically developed country, the United States, with only about one-fifteenth of the world's population uses *well over half* the world's raw materials each year.[7] If there is to be a just and equitable solution to the population crisis on a worldwide basis, it is clear that Americans are going to suffer a greater decline in their level of consumption than the peoples of other countries.

In addition to the problems of feeding and providing for the basic survival, with dignity, of a ballooning population, there are the elemental problems of feeling crowded, almost suffocated, by the billions of people

[3]Vannevar Bush, quoted in Philip Appleman, "What the Population Explosion Means to You," *Ladies Home Journal* 80 (June 1963), p. 59.

[4]Paul Ehrlich, "The Population Bomb," in De Bell, p. 220.

[5]Paul B. Sears, "The Inexorable Problem of Space," in *The Subversive Science: Essays Toward an Ecology of Man*, eds. Paul Shepard and Daniel McKinley (Boston: Houghton-Mifflin, 1969), p. 82.

[6]Edward Higbee, *A Question of Priorities*, (New York: Morrow, 1970). Quoted by Edward Abbey, "How to Live on This Planet Earth," *New York Times Book Review*, April 19, 1970, p. 3.

[7]Ehrlich, in De Bell, p. 220.

one will bump up against (or live above or below in gigantic apartment complexes); of feeling bombarded by the increasing noise such a crowded environment creates; of feeling anxious about whether tomorrow will bring a further curtailment in provisions or a temporary reprieve; of feeling hopeless about the future for oneself and for one's children. The whole question of whether there should be any more children and if so, whose, is one that confronts those wrestling with the population aspect of the ecological crisis. These and other moral dilemmas will be discussed in the section on proposed solutions.

Ecological Disasters and the Pollution Problem

A few short years ago Lake Erie was considered to be virtually dead as far as life forms within it are concerned, due to the dumping and leakage of polluting materials from industrial firms along its shores. In Los Angeles the smog is so bad that 10,000 people a year are advised by their doctors to move elsewhere. The death rate in America from bronchitis and emphysema is nine times as high as it was twenty years ago, and the cause can be found almost totally in the pollution of our air by automobiles and factories. It has been estimated that the United States emits 188.8 million tons of pollutants into the air yearly.[8]

It is apparent that to produce many of the goods we want, we also produce, as a by-product, polluting, poisonous waste material that endangers the air we breathe, kills the soil in which we grow our food, and poisons the water we drink. In the late 1970s, the human tragedy of pollution was revealed in the case of a small community in Buffalo, New York, known as Love Canal. A chemical plant there had been dumping its chemical wastes into an area surrounded by residential homes for years. When a much higher than normal rate of still-births, cancers, and other medical illnesses struck the residents of Love Canal, they and the nation became aware of the stark dimensions of the pollution problem.

Many communities around the world, some stretching for miles along exposed beach areas, are also aware of the pollution problem through the presence on their shores of tons and tons of spilled oil. The ecological damage done to the shores of northern France by the crack-up of the oil tanker Torrey Canyon in 1967 has been said by some to be inestimable. Not only are beaches ruined for years, but the long-range effects on bird and sea life are devastating.

Efforts have been started in many communities to clean the air of its poisonous fumes. Manufacturers have been encouraged and in some cases

[8]William Steif, "Why the Birds Cough," in *The Ecology Controversy*, eds. Gary E. McCuen and David L. Bender (Anoka, Minn.: Greenhaven, 1970), pp. 56–61.

compelled to "scrub" the gases and exhausts emitted from their factories. Automobile makers have been required to produce devices that will burn gasoline more cleanly and efficiently. In some areas, dirty burning fuels such as coal have been replaced by cleaner fuels such as natural gas, oil, or nuclear power. But each of these efforts has consequences that are not palatable to everyone. The more money invested in cleaning the air emitted by a factory, the more the items it produces will cost the consumer. Switching to cleaner fuels means, in many cases, switching to resources dangerously near depletion or that have their own ecological dangers, especially nuclear-based energy.

Some ecologists even look beyond the immediate danger of individual pollutants to the potential disaster of "heat death." In the first half of the twentieth century, the earth underwent a marked rise in temperature compared to preceding decades. According to different estimates, human activity currently accounts for a net heating-up of between 1/2500 and 1/25 of the proportion of energy reflected back into outer space from the earth's surface. A 10 percent increase would turn the North and South Poles into tropical areas and would render the present tropics uninhabitable except for lizards and insects. On the other hand, some people argue that polluted air creates a cover through which the sun's heat will have a hard time penetrating, thus foreshadowing a new ice age. In our ignorance, we could be triggering an ice age or a heat death well before we are aware of the clues that would permit a forecast in time to reverse the fatal trend.

Nuclear Radiation

Of all of the man-made dangers that face our planet, one of the most frightening is that of nuclear radiation. One of the great discoveries of the twentieth century was how to get energy from the atom. Once the secret of the nucleus of the atom was unlocked, a bold and exciting future seemed ahead of us. From a relatively small source, enormous amounts of energy could be developed to run virtually all the engines of our society. But rapidly, the horrible side effects of atomic energy also became known. As one of the most eminent scientists involved in the development and production of the first atomic bomb said on watching its first test in the deserts of the southwest: "We have now known sin." The agonizingly brutal deaths of civilians in Hiroshima and Nagasaki emblazoned the sinful dimensions of atomic power on the conscience of the modern world.

When attention was turned to the peaceful uses of atomic energy, its destructive effects were masked behind the invisible radiation being emitted from the nuclear core of the atomic reactors supplying cheap energy. But the hazards were and are still there. These hazards have been described as falling into two broad categories: "The threat of violent, massive releases of radioactivity or that of slow, but deadly, seepage of harmful products into the environment."[9]

There is, of course, much debate about the relative and absolute safety of nuclear power plants. In defense of their plans to build a nuclear power plant in Minnesota, the Northern States Power Company claimed that their nuclear plant would add only 5 millirems a year, about the same amount as watching TV 1 hour each day for a year.[10]

Critics in reply to NSP's arguments state that radiation biologists "regard all radioactivity as harmful."[11] In particular, critics argue that even a very low level of continual radiation from waste material results in leukemia. In nine counties downstream from the Hanford, Washington, atomic energy plant, cancer increased 53.2 percent since the atomic reactor went into operation. Counties away from the river had no change in their cancer incidence.[12] Many of the organisms living in the waters into which the radioactive wastes are dumped soak up large amounts of radioactive isotopes in their tissues. Because of the ecological web, these organisms may eventually find their way into food supplies for animals and ultimately human beings.

Much more dramatic in the arsenal of arguments against the safety of nuclear reactors have been the actual incidents in which safety barriers have broken down. In 1979 America, and the world, was mesmerized for weeks by the threatened "melt-down" of the nuclear core at the Three Mile Island plant near Harrisburg, Pennsylvania. Although supporters of nuclear power point out that the melt-down did not, in fact, occur, critics say that adequate safety standards were not enough to keep it from almost occurring. They also point to a long list of safeguard failures at nuclear plants around the world. Most frightening to many people who live in the vicinity of large nuclear reactors is that the effects of their exposure to radiation are long-term and will not be fully known until it is too late to remedy or counter them.

Disposing of the radioactive waste material is one of the crucial problems of nuclear power. In some cases, the natural decay of harmful waste may take up to 1,000 years. It would take five cubic miles of water to dilute the waste from just one ton of fuel to a safe concentration. And the techniques of disposal fill many with apprehension. As two writers described it:

---

[9]Richard Curtis and Elizabeth Hogan, "The Myth of the Peaceful Atom," in McCuen and Bender, p. 24.
[10]Northern States Power Company, "Perspective on Safety at NSP's Monticello Nuclear Plant," in McCuen and Bender, p. 48–49.
[11]Grace and Andrew Gibas, "Radioactive Wastes in Drinking Water," in McCuen and Bender, p. 39.
[12]Gibas, in McCuen and Bender, p. 39.

These huge quantities of radioactive wastes must somehow be removed from the reactors, must—without mishap—be put into containers that will never rupture; then these vast quantities of poisonous stuff must be moved either to a burial ground or to reprocessing and concentration plants, handled again, and disposed of, by burial or otherwise, with a risk of human error at every step.[13]

The Depletion of Natural Resources

Although the list of ecological disasters could be extended indefinitely, one potential disaster that has directly affected most people in the Western world, and indirectly the international community, has been the imminent depletion of major energy resources. Anyone who remembers the oil embargo of 1973, the recurrent shortages of oil and natural gas, and the rapidly escalating cost of these fuels is fully aware of how precariously most modern nations are balanced on the edge of major fuel shortages. The energy crisis, as it has come to be called, was so serious that a president of the United States called its solution the moral equivalent of war.

Predictions vary widely on when the world will run out of oil and natural gas, two of the major fuels used for industry and personal needs. Some say the end of the 1980s, other say we can hold on with new discoveries until the beginning of the next century.[14] But nearly every responsible person agrees that there is only a finite amount of oil and gas and that if we continue to deplete it at current rates it must someday run out. Oil and gas are nonrenewable energy resources: they do not recreate themselves nor can they be recreated simply by human effort. Once they are gone, they are gone.

Other sources of energy (as we shall see shortly) have been suggested, but the transition time needed to enable society to utilize them will be lengthy and costly. Even if new pools of oil and gas are discovered, they are likely to be both very expensive to tap and, at best, a temporary solution. It has become clear to many energy experts that although investigating new energy resources, especially solar power, is essential, conservation is also mandatory. But conservation is costly as well, at least in terms of current and anticipated life styles for many in the Western world.

Increasing population, chronic pollution, the threat of nuclear radiation from peaceful as well as hostile uses, and rapid energy resource depletion are all warning signals to a crowded planet that it must take care of its ecological requirements if it wishes to survive beyond the next few generations. As frightening as these signals are, the ingenuity of human invention and the deep resources of moral reflection are responding to the chal-

---

[13]Curtis and Hogan, in McCuen and Bender, p. 29.
[14]See Richard Barnet, *The Lean Years: Politics in the Age of Scarcity* (New York: Simon and Schuster, 1980).

lenge in exciting and hopeful ways. It is to some of these proposals that we now must turn.

ECOLOGY, POLITICS, AND ECONOMICS: MORAL ALTERNATIVES

One of the first things to strike someone wading through the various moral alternatives to the present state of ecological danger is the interweaving of concern for the environment, with reflections on and suggestions for change in the political and economic structures of society. This should occasion no surprise since so much of our ecological problem has political and economic roots and consequences, though it is not necessarily easy to lay the blame at the doorstep of a *single* political or economic system.

A social order that encourages, or at least does not discourage, individuals who support a transportation system that relies on heavy consumption of fuel for private automobiles has clearly made a political and economic decision that has consequences for how fast oil is consumed. This is only one example of the way ecological considerations are entwined with political and economic realities. The intervention into one area will therefore have deep effects on the other areas as well.

Reliance on Free Enterprise

One proposed solution to the ecological crisis is to encourage the political and economic systems that, through free enterprise, have brought technology to its present sophisticated state. If technology has helped create the crisis, then it can be used to extricate us from it. More ingenious ways of extracting fuel from the ground, air, sun, or field can be devised if we will permit the scientific and business interests to pursue their self-interests without control or regulation from governmental bureaucracies. "Actually," claims Gary Allen,

> "our technology is the best hope for ending pollution and continuing to expand the food supply. Great strides are already being made toward solving these problems.... Our free technology can easily meet the demands of population growth!... It is true that some businesses ... polluted air and water in their search for the cheapest way to dispose of wastes, but the answer to this problem is to use our technology to turn those wastes into profit.... The biggest pollution problem we face is the pollution by the collectivist Establishment and Marxist revolutionaries of the minds of a once thoroughly independent and free people."[15]

---

[15]Gary Allen, "Government Control of the Environment," in McCuen and Bender, pp. 89–90.

In a sense this solution to the ecological crisis simply bypasses the moral dilemmas assumed by the other solutions. It rejects the assumptions that resources are finite, that choices must be made between alternative life styles, that we have more than enough time to undo the deleterious effects of current pollution, overpopulation, nuclear radiation, and resource depletion, and that those who control the consumption and pollution patterns of one part of the world are morally accountable for their effects on other parts of the world. This solution implicitly asks those who adopt it to take a basic risk: if the solution turns out to be wrong, not only will the human race pollute, populate, or nuclearly proliferate itself to death, it may well do so by first exacerbating the unjust distribution of resources and their control and consumption around the world. The moral justification for taking such a risk is that "competent" nations (as demonstrated by their technological superiority and the affluence of their standard of living) have shown their worthiness in being trusted to use the same instruments that brought them success to bring an end to the current ecological imbalance.

Acceptance of No Resolution

Another solution that does not take a particular stand regarding the merits or demerits of the systems that contributed to the ecological problem focuses attention on its possible irresolvability. Because of three basic forces (high population densities, high levels of personal consumption, and a messy technology of production), Nicholas Rescher believes that

> we may simply be unable to solve the environmental crisis as a whole: that once this or that form of noxiousness is expelled from one door, some other equally bad version comes in by another . . . the environmental crisis may well be incurable. It just may be something that we cannot solve but have to learn to live with.[16]

The moral consequences of Rescher's position will be, as he puts it, "a large dose of cool realism tempered with stoic resignation." This is "gloom without doom." But it is not a denigration of human beings. "Let us not sell man short. We have been in some unpleasant circumstances before and have managed to cope."[17] Concretely, of course, coping will involve a lower standard of living than we now have or expected for ourselves in the future.

Rescher's position does not speak directly to what responsibilities those who now have the lion's share of the world's resources and who consume them most conspicuously have toward the rest of the world. It is possible to accept the inevitability of ecological suicide and decide to live as if there

---

[16]Nicholas Rescher, "The Environmental Crisis and the Quality of Life," in Blackstone, p. 92.
[17]Rescher, in Blackstone, p. 104.

is no tomorrow. If we are all going to go under eventually anyway, why not live today without concern for solutions that will only affect future generations?

Survival as a Relative Value

This position raises the important moral consideration of survival, especially the survival of unborn generations. One of the persistent themes in much ecological discussion is our generation's obligations to our posterity, most of whom have not yet even been conceived. The survival of individuals, and even of groups, is not a self-evidently, overriding moral virtue. We can easily imagine situations in which other virtues may compel someone to choose not to survive (a soldier in war who heroically offers his life for another, or a pacifist community that chooses to be massacred by an oppressor rather than resist with violence).

Is it as easy to imagine the human race as a whole (through some kind of international forum) deciding that the limitations and degradations that would be the lot of those who inherit the present (irreversible) ecological disaster would be so dehumanizing that it is now its moral obligation to stop reproducing entirely or at least to reproduce at such a rate that race extinction would be a certainty sometime in the future? Such a decision would be unprecedented and could be justified, in part, only on the assumption that the limits of human ingenuity in solving its environmental problems had already been reached. Of course, those moral philosophies that rely in part on the guidance and intervention of superhuman powers could never assume that solutions to problems were absolutely beyond reach. This is particularly true of the Roman Catholic Church's official interpretation of the ethical principles of Thomism (see Chapter 4). Believing that natural law forbids the obstruction of the reproductive organs and believing that God has so ordained the natural law that it can never be obeyed to the ultimate disadvantage of the human race, the Roman Catholic Church has insisted that neither abortion nor birth control is a solution to the population crisis. Because of its faith in the supremacy of a divine being, this moral position is not overly troubled by its nonacceptance by those outside the Church who, in its opinion, leap to expedient and short-range solutions. In a sense, the Church has chosen to view survival as a relative moral value subordinate to the will of God as embodied in the dictates of natural law.

SURVIVAL AS A FUNDAMENTAL MORAL DILEMMA

We come here to the fundamental moral dilemma. If, both biologically and psychologically, the need for survival is basic to man, and if survival is the precondition for any and all human achievements, and if no other rights make sense without the premise of a right to life—then how will it be possible to honor and act upon the need for survival without, in the process, destroying everything in human beings which makes them worthy of survival? To put it more strongly, if the price of survival is human degradation, then there is no moral reason why an effort should be made to ensure that survival. It would be the pyrrhic victory to end all pyrrhic victories. Yet it would be the defeat of all defeats if, because human beings could not properly manage their need to survive, they succeeded in not doing so. Either way, then, would represent a failure, and one can take one's pick about which failure would be worse, that of survival at the cost of everything decent in man or outright extinction.

Daniel Callahan, "Population and Human Survival," in *The Population Crisis and Moral Responsibility*, ed. J. Philip Wogaman (Washington, D.C.: Public Affairs Press, 1973), pp. 50-51.

Daniel Callahan is director of the Institute of Society, Ethics and the Life Sciences. A Roman Catholic layman and philosopher, he was editor of Commonweal *during 1961-1968 and has written extensively on ethics in the fields of population, contraception, and abortion.*

Even contemplating the possibility of choosing against survival is an extreme moral position. Most of the dominant moral positions related to ecology assume some sort of responsibility not only for the present generation but for future generations as well.[18] *How* we plan for our posterity by husbanding present resources and their production and consumption is the heart of the present moral debate.

LIFEBOAT ETHICS

One of the best known, and to some most troubling, of the stands taken in the debate has been set forth by the eminent microbiologist and geneticist, Garrett Hardin. His moral position, known as "lifeboat ethics" has been set forth compellingly in two major pieces, "The Tragedy of the Commons,"

[18]Joel Feinberg, "The Rights of Animals and Unborn Generations," in Blackstone, pp. 64-67.

and "Living on a Lifeboat." Working from the premise that an unchecked increase in population is not desirable, Hardin claims that the human race must make choices about what qualities of surviving populations it wishes to nurture. Not all qualities are compatible with each other. In particular, free enterprise and the absolute right of free choice are not compatible with a healthy environment. As his telling example, Hardin asks us to picture a pasture open to everyone. If each person is seeking to maximize self-interest, each herdsman will try to place as many of his cattle in the pasture (or commons) as possible. Since his income depends upon the animals he has, it is of direct and immediate benefit to each person to keep adding animals to the commons. The negative effects on the commons, of the overgrazing that is a cumulative consequence of the previous decisions, are shared by all and thus are not felt as directly and immediately by each one.

> The rational herdsman concludes that the only sensible course for him to pursue is to add another animal to his herd. And another; and another. . . . But this is the conclusion reached by each and every rational herdsman sharing a commons. Therein is the tragedy. Each man is locked into a system that compels him to increase his herd without limit—in a world that is limited. Ruin is the destination toward which all men rush, each pursuing his own best interest in a society that believes in the freedom of the commons. *Freedom in a commons brings ruin to all.* [19]

Hardin concludes that "so long as we behave only as independent, rational, free-enterprisers," we will be locked into a system of "fouling our own nest."[20]

Having shown that unqualified insistence on the right to graze without limits on the commons leads to disaster for all, Hardin then turns to the question of what responsibility those who presently enjoy the benefits of the commons have toward those who stand outside it or who have not shown responsibility in their use of it. To do so, he switches to the metaphor of a lifeboat.

> Each rich nation amounts to a lifeboat full of comparatively rich people. The poor of the world are in other, much more crowded lifeboats. Continuously, so to speak, the poor fall out of their lifeboats and swim for a while in the water outside, hoping to be admitted to a rich lifeboat, or in some other way to benefit from the "goodies" on board. What should the passengers on a rich lifeboat do? This is the central problem of "the ethics of a lifeboat."[21]

[19]Garrett Hardin, "The Tragedy of the Commons," *Science* 168, (Dec. 13, 1968), pp. 1243–1248, as found in *The Environmental Handbook,* ed. Garrett De Bell (New York: Baltimore, 1970), pp. 36–37.
[20]Hardin in De Bell, p. 39.
[21]Garrett Hardin, "Living on a Lifeboat," in *Religion for a New Generation,* 2nd ed., eds. Jacob Needleman, A. K. Bierman, and James A. Gould (New York: Macmillan, 1977), p. 241.

It is assumed that each rich lifeboat has a "safety factor," a gap between what it now holds and what it could conceivably hold but which, unfilled, permits some flexibility to respond to ecological alteration. What Hardin wants to argue for is an ethic opposed to sharing the "goodies" of the lifeboat with anyone not presently on board.

He is clearly aware that his moral position is "abhorrent" and "unjust" to many people. But the alternatives, he argues, are suicidal. He is particularly critical of the ethic of sharing, which he identifies as Christian or Marxist ("from each according to his abilities to each according to his needs").

The problem of the rich lifeboat is essentially its population. If those on board represent nations whose population doubles every eighty-seven years and those on poorer lifeboats represent nations whose doubling time is twenty-one years, sharing would soon require each original person on the rich lifeboat to share with eight new persons added from the poorer boats. "How could the lifeboat possibly keep afloat?"[22]

Each person born into the poorer nations "constitutes a draft on all aspects of the environment." It is one more person taking up valuable space in the rich lifeboat and narrowing dangerously the safety factor as well as diminishing the goods available to its original inhabitants. "Every life saved this year in a poor country diminishes the quality of life for subsequent generations."[23] Thus, to keep alive people in poor countries who are taking no responsibility to curtail their population growth or to grow their own food will produce ruination in the commons. To admit these people as immigrants into the richer nations would place an "unacceptable burden" on the minority of people who conscientiously want to plan for their children's and grandchildren's futures. "We cannot safely divide the wealth equitably among all present peoples, so long as people reproduce at different rates, because to do so would guarantee that our grandchildren—everyone's grandchildren—would have only a ruined world to inhabit."[24]

To those who feel guilty about having been born into a rich lifeboat and who feel qualms about not sharing with those outside it, Hardin says simply:

> *Get out and yield your place to others.* Such a selfless action might satisfy the conscience of those who are addicted to guilt but it would not change the ethics of the lifeboat.... The net result of conscience-stricken people relinquishing their unjustly held position is the elimination of their kind of conscience from the lifeboat. The lifeboat, as it were, purifies itself of guilt.[25]

[22]Hardin, in Needleman et al., p. 243.
[23]Hardin, in Needleman et al., p. 249.
[24]Hardin, in Needleman et al., p. 252.
[25]Hardin, in Needleman et al. p. 242.

It is important to note that Hardin's argument relies heavily on the desire of individuals not only to survive but to survive as far as possible in the style to which they have become accustomed. Having assumed the supremacy of that value, his position falls into place as a reflection on the consequences of trying to act on some other basis. Ultimately, to avoid the the worst aspects of a lifeboat existence, Hardin believes that we must accept some kind of coerced behavior. "Freedom to breed will bring ruin to all."[26] If the rich nations are to control the population of the poorer countries, to instill in them, as it were, a responsible form of behavior, they must infringe on the freedom of these less well-off people around the world. This may well be unfair and unjust, but "the alternative of the commons is too horrifying to contemplate. Injustice is preferable to total ruin."[27]

The Right to a Livable Environment

Placing limits on the right of free choice is echoed by William Blackstone in his discussion of how to balance that right against what he calls the "right to a livable environment." If a human right is one that is essential in permitting persons to live a human life, to "fulfill [their] capacities as rational and free beings,"[28] then the right to a livable environment could be conceived as a right "which has emerged as a result of changing environmental conditions and the impact of those conditions on the very possibility of human life and on the possibility of the realization of other rights such as liberty and equality."[29] If pursuing unrestricted individual freedom will result in the tragedy of the commons, then some priority of rights must be made. Blackstone believes strongly that "both public welfare and equality of rights now require that natural resources not be used simply according to the whim and caprice of individuals or simply for personal profit."[30]

Spaceship Earth

One model for understanding how such limits on individual freedom might work and still provide a tolerable world community is that set forth by Kenneth Boulding in his image of "spaceship earth."[31] On the one

---

[26]Hardin, in De Bell, p. 49.
[27]Hardin, in De Bell, p. 47.
[28]Blackstone, in Blackstone, p. 31.
[29]Blackstone, in Blackstone, p. 31.
[30]Blackstone, in Blackstone, p. 32.
[31]Kenneth Boulding, "The Wisdom of Man and the Wisdom of God," *Human Values on the Spaceship Earth* (New York: National Council of the Churches of Christ in the U.S.A., 1966).

hand, Boulding claims, "there seems good reason to suppose that human life will be lived in a comfortable and need-satisfying environment, in which everyone will have enough to eat, agreeable surroundings, and a rich variety of experience." On the other hand, in order to achieve this kind of life

> we have to visualize the earth as a small, rather crowded spaceship, destination unknown, in which man has to find a slender thread of a way of life in the midst of a continually repeatable cycle of material transformations. In a spaceship, there can be no inputs or outputs. The water must circulate through the kidneys and the algae, the food likewise, the air likewise, and even though there must be inputs of energy . . . there can be no inputs or outputs of material, short of the transfer of energy into matter. . . . [This means that] there must be extreme parsimony in all matters pertaining to irreversible change.[32]

The ethic that such parsimony requires is one that will demand poverty of spirit, even in the midst of material affluence; purity of heart, "or the corruption of affluence will engulf us."[33] How we can acquire such an ethic, Boulding believes, will demand attention to sources outside the traditional ethics of the biblical religions of the West. As we explore what this new ethic might look like, we will be moving into the most original, challenging aspects of the ecological moral debate because we will be encountering assumptions and conclusions that strike at the very heart of what Western society has taken for granted about what it values.

DEEP ECOLOGY AND ASIAN WISDOM

Boulding, and many others, are now looking to Eastern or Asian religions to find an alternative attitude toward nature that may help us to restore ecological sanity. Believing that "what we do about ecology depends on our ideas of the man-nature relationship,"[34] many contemporary ecology-minded moral philosophers are finding in Asian religions a reverence for nature that restricts man's exploitation of it. The dualism that separates man from nature has always been suspect in Asian thinking. To set one thing off against other things is to violate the oneness that ultimately permeates everything. The Asian tradition can point to the accumulated frustrations of always trying to place the ego above or in opposition to other forces in the universe. Separation from something leads to a desire to conquer it so that it will not pose a threat. Only if we can understand our fundamental unity with all things can we exist in peaceful harmony with them.

[32]Boulding, pp. 6–7.
[33]Boulding, p. 13.
[34]Lynn White, Jr., "The Historical Roots of Our Ecological Crisis," in Needleman et al., p. 238.

This sense of oneness with nature has led to the development of what one writer has called "the deep ecology movement."[35] It is based on a vision of the person-in-nature.

> The person is not above or outside of nature. The person is part of creation on-going. The person cares for and about nature, shows reverence toward and respect for nonhuman nature, loves and lives with nonhuman nature, is a person in the "earth household" and "lets being be," lets nonhuman nature follow separate evolutionary destinies.[36]

Devall identifies the sources of this movement as the Eastern spiritual traditions associated in the West with the writings of Alan Watts and D. T. Suzuki, the rediscovery of native American religion and philosophy, and some of the mystical and "minority" philosophical traditions of the West. These sources combine to produce not just a new set of values about the earth but, according to the proponents of deep ecology, a whole new consciousness about existence. What is needed, says Paul Shepard, is "a scope or a way of seeing [that] must take a long view of human life and nature as they form a mesh or pattern going beyond historical time and beyond the conceptual bounds of other humane studies."[37]

The result of such a new viewing is to begin thinking not exclusively from a human point of view but trying to "think like a mountain." From such new thinking Devall believes that a number of principles essential to deep ecology will emerge. Lynn White refers to St. Francis' notion of "a democracy of all God's creatures" in which man is deposed from his monarchy over creation and can say "brother" or "sister" to ants, rocks, wind, and rain without having to control their destinies.[38] As Devall puts it, "Man does not perfect nature, nor is man's primary duty to make nature more efficient."[39] The principles Devall believes will emerge are the following:

1. A new cosmic/ecological metaphysics that stresses the identity (I/ Thou) of humans with nonhuman nature, a form of "biological egalitarianism."

2. An objective approach to nature in which nature is treated not simply as an extension of human needs.

3. A rejection of subject/object, man/nature dualisms and their replacement by a new awareness of the "total intermingling of the planet earth."

[35]Bill Devall, "The Deep Ecology Movement," *Natural Resources Journal* (Albuquerque: Univ. of New Mexico School of Law, n.d.).

[36]Devall, p. 303.

[37]Paul Shepard, "Introduction: Ecology and Man—a Viewpoint," in Shepard and McKinley, pp. 1-2.

[38]White, in Needleman et al., p. 238.

[39]Devall, p. 303.

4. Science should become a *contemplation* of the cosmos and not an instrument for its exploitation.

5. There is wisdom in the stability of natural processes unchanged by human intervention.

6. The quality of human existence should not be measured only by the quantity of products.

7. Hunting and gathering societies can provide principles for healthy, ecologically viable societies.

8. Diversity is desirable both culturally and as a principle of health and stability of ecosystems.

9. Life styles should strive for spiritual development and community rather than for consumerism.

To be relevant to moral thinking, of course, these principles must have consequences for our behavior in the world. Many of those in the deep ecology movement see the economic and political implications, in particular, of adopting a new ecological consciousness. Devall enjoins us to scrap most of our heavy reliance on industrial technology for an "appropriate technology" that will reduce consumption, use less energy, encourage diversified, organic, labor-intensive production. To accomplish this, he argues, we need to decentralize power politically and nurture local autonomy in our political and economic systems.[40]

Buddhist Economics

A trained economist who also sees the economic implications of some of the deep ecology movement is E. F. Schumacher (see Chapter 14 regarding his contribution to some of the moral problems in the economic arena). Drawing explicitly on the principles of Buddhist economics, Schumacher develops a conception of work that is not guided by ever-increasing production. Instead, from a Buddhist point of view, the purpose of work is "to give man a chance to utilize and develop his faculties; to enable him to overcome his egocenteredness by joining with other people in a common task; and to bring forth the goods and services needed for a becoming existence."[41]

The ecological implications of this understanding of economics are striking. Material consumption (which requires depletion of so much of the earth's resources and, in production, often pollutes and endangers public health) would not be the goal of economics. "Since consumption is merely a means to human well-being, the aim should be to obtain the maximum of well-being with the minimum of consumption."[42] This means a modest

---

[40]Devall, pp. 310–313.
[41]E. F. Schumacher, "Buddhist Economics," in Needleman et al., p. 218.
[42]Schumacher, in Needleman et al., p. 219.

use of resources. One side benefit of this reduced level of consumption would be a decrease in violence between persons and nations since they would have no reason to fight to accumulate resources. "Equally, people who live in highly self-sufficient local communities are less likely to get involved in large-scale violence than people whose existence depends on worldwide systems of trade."[43] A Buddhist economics would also insist that "a population basing its economic life on nonrenewable fuels is living parasitically, on capital instead of income."[44]

A DISSENTING OPINION

But "reverence" for the natural and "skepticism" about modern technology [reveal] the least noticed yet most fundamental fault in the renewed interest in ecology, namely, a romanticism that distorts the issues, needlessly arouses opposition, and is positively inimical to wise, deliberate control of the environment. . . . I should want to argue that nature is neutral with respect to ultimate wisdom or rationality, and also neutral with respect to virtue or goodness. . . . Nature is a realm of struggle, often savage, brutal struggle, where the big fish eat the little ones. . . . When people lose their capacity for surmounting nature, we say they "vegetate." . . . The problem is not to roll back the ages to the state of nature, but to exercise more careful human control over technology so that it does really serve as liberator. . . . Perhaps we may say that man evolves along with the nature of which he is a part, yet ever more as himself the controlling factor in that evolutionary process, so that the story becomes one mainly of the evolution of *man.* Man is part of nature, and yet he is not; and in that tension he finds his existence.

Thomas Derr, "Man Against Nature," *Cross Currents* (Summer 1970), as found in *Religion for a New Generation,* eds. Jacob Needleman, A. K. Bierman and James A. Gould (New York: Macmillan, 1973), pp. 182–184.

Thomas S. Derr (b. 1931) is a member of the faculty at Smith College and author of The Political Thought of the Ecumenical Movement, 1900–1939. *He has written many articles in the area of social ethics.*

---

[43]Schumacher, in Needleman et al., p. 220.
[44]Schumacher, in Needleman et al., p. 221.

WHAT CAN BE DONE?

Even those who do not fully accept the Eastern foundations of deep ecology or all of the latter's principles feel that some changes are inevitable and desirable in the economic practices of Western nations. Americans consume far more than their share of the world's resources. If they are to contribute to the solution of our ecological problems, their economic practices will have to be modified in some serious way. At the very least, argues Robert G. Burton, "it is in the general interest for us to modify our economic practices so as to include the cost of waste disposal and the recycling of such resources as air and water in the total cost of production. This would amount to the tempering of the profit motive by the principle of equal rights for all."[45] The effects on the environment must be just as much a concern of the economic process as its ability to satisfy individual consumer demand.

Keith Murray has proposed an "ecological platform" that would, among other things, alter political and economic practice to include public provision of birth control information and devices, foreign aid only to countries with programs of birth control, a guaranteed annual income (thus breaking the "compulsory link between jobs and income that has been a principal stimulus to growthmanship" in the economy), government purchase of control of land for the purpose of preservation, massive investment in environmental and ecological education, economic incentives and punishments to discourage the dumping of waste material and the polluting of air and water, and the return of farm land to the small farmer away from gigantic agri-businesses.[46]

Biologist and political activist Barry Commoner has been in the forefront of those arguing for massive federal transition from private corporate reliance on nuclear and nonrenewable fuel resources to democratically controlled use of solar power.

> If the heavy burden of the energy crisis on consumers is to be relieved, the present energy system must be replaced by one based on a source that is renewable (so that its price is stable), thrifty in its demand for economic resources (so that consumers can have access to their share), and benign in its effect on the environment (so that people can live in it without fearing for their health and safety).[47]

A solar-based system could deliver energy in a variety of forms: in forests, from wood; in agricultural areas, as alcohol made from grain or methane made from manure or plant residues; in rainy, mountainous areas, as hydroelectric power; in moderately or intensely sunny places, as photovol-

---

[45]Robert G. Burton, "A Philosopher Looks at the Population Bomb," in Blackstone, p. 115.
[46]Keith Murray, "Suggestions Toward an Ecological Platform," in DeBell, pp. 317–323.
[47]Barry Commoner, *The Politics of Energy* (New York: Knopf, 1979), p. 68.

taic electricity; in windy places, as wind-generated electricity; almost everywhere as direct heat.[48]

In the area of food production, some are now calling for an end to its dominance by multi-national corporations that have discouraged the growing of food by local producers for local needs. Food scarcity, argue Frances Lappe and Joseph Collins, is really due to economic decisions to use arable land around the world to grow things at a profit that ultimately only the rich can afford and that are not necessary to a basic diet. They argue for a return of arable land to local, democratically organized units that can grow the necessary basic foods for local consumption. The economic consequences of their proposals obviously hit hardest at systems based on unlimited corporate decisions to produce only on the basis of what will secure the highest profit, regardless of consequences to the soil and to the poor who have only the soil on which to rely.[49]

FOOD SELF-RELIANCE

As one writer summed up the tragic reality of so many underdeveloped countries, "the small farmer sells the nitrogen, phosphorus, potassium, and trace minerals from his soil in the form of tobacco or cotton and in return buys polished rice or noodles from the little . . . store down the road, thus selling the lifeblood of his soil to buy starch and carbohydrates. . . . Basic food self-reliance—and by this we mean adequate local supplies to prevent famine if imports of food were abruptly cut off—is the *sine qua non* of a people's security. Moreover, no country can bargain successfully in international trade so long as it is desperate to sell its products in order to import food to stave off famine.

Frances Moore Lappe and Joseph Collins, *Food First: Beyond the Myth of Scarcity*, with Cary Fowler, rev. and updated. (New York: Ballantine, 1978), pp. 224, 232.

Both Ms. Lappe and Mr. Collins are associated with the Institute for Food and Development Policy and have worked extensively in the field of world hunger, underdevelopment, and economics.

---

[48]Commoner, p. 54.

[49]Frances Lappe and Joseph Collins, *Food First: Beyond the Myth of Scarcity*, rev., updated. (New York: Ballantine, 1978).

The Automobile

Perhaps for Americans and western Europeans the most tangible part of our lives to be directly affected by moral thinking about ecology is that which relies on the use of the automobile. The automobile alone accounts for a major portion of the pollution spewed into the atmosphere and of the nonrenewable oil depleted to provide it fuel and run the industries that produce it. It is for many people the ultimate symbol of ecological danger, indifference, and wastefulness.

Those who adopt a moral position akin to Hardin's lifeboat ethics might choose to curtail their use of the automobile simply to make their lifeboat more livable once it becomes clear that unlimited freedom to drive a car will result in the asphyxiation of the lifeboat's residents. Those who are attracted more to the deep ecology movement may give up their reliance on automobiles not only because of their catastrophic effect on the environment but also because the car represents or provides nothing of particular value to a simple, nonmaterialistic life style. Transportation could easily be provided by public conveyance while at the same time a simplified life style would not lead to the building of enormous centers for the distribution of goods at great distances from where people live.

Cars use one-half of all oil consumed in the United States. If Americans owned cars that got 60 miles per gallon, the United States would cut in half its net oil imports and save four million barrels of oil per day.[50] Even those who have not adopted a fully developed moral position as comprehensive as deep ecology or lifeboat ethics can recognize that in a spaceship earth, such consumption and potential savings of the nonrenewable fuels cars demand would be in the self-interest of everyone aboard.

Once one comes to this conclusion, the moral question necessarily emerges: Is it the obligation of the political order to restrict the free choices of some to use as much oil as they can afford in order to save the environment for everybody so that room is left for other free choices to be exercised humanely? If some restrictions are necessary, can they be enacted without wholesale replacement of the values that undergird the present economic system? If wholesale replacement is necessary, can it be accomplished peacefully and gradually? If only adjustments in the present system are necessary, can the environment wait for them to occur?

The ecological situation reveals clearly that individual decisions alone will not be enough to eliminate the potential dangers from pollution, population, nuclear proliferation, and resource depletion. Each person can make choices about what and how much to consume, but private choice by itself will not have a major effect on the decisions of large corporations or governments. At some point, ecological concern will lead individuals to deci-

[50]Amory B. Lovins, L. Hunter Lovins, and Leonard Ross, "Nuclear Power and Nuclear Bombs," *Foreign Affairs* (Summer 1980), p. 1162.

sions about political and economic structures. At that point, the concerns of this chapter, in combination with the reflections of Chapters 13 and 14 on politics and economics as fields for moral activity will necessarily lead the student of morality to weigh the various rights and obligations affected by political and economic practice.

It is certainly possible, though by no means inevitable, that some will come to the conclusion that only a thoroughgoing reformation, not only of personal life style but also of the way in which nations produce and consume, is the moral and realistic solution to our problems. But no matter what the degree of reformation in personal and social choices about the world in which we live, we must all confront the question at some point "Is all this glut of power to be used for only bread-and-butter ends? Man cannot live by bread, or Fords, alone. Are we too poor in purse or spirit to apply some of it to keep the land pleasant to see, and good to live in?"[51] If we can consider this question seriously, then we might, in the words of George Macinko,

> contemplate the human condition in which the marriage of science and technology little more than a century ago gave man enormous powers, [the condition] which . . . has seen these powers exercised in ways increasingly destructive of the natural order. Perhaps this contemplation might see a controlled and humane use of power replace power used merely for the sake of control. If this comes to pass, then one might even answer affirmatively that not at all frivolous question recently posed by an astronomer, "Is there life on earth?"[52]

CHAPTER REVIEW

A. Energy and ecology

1. Ecology is the study of the interrelationships of all living things. The moral issues within this area have to do with taking responsibility for actions that will have short- and long-term effects on the ecosystem and the quality of human life around the globe.

B. Four possible areas of danger

1. The present crisis in ecology has been brought about in part by a traditional belief that human beings have the right to exploit an intrinsically valueless nature and to do so in the quest of ever rising standards of living.
2. The population explosion threatens the living space of the world as

---

[51]Aldo Leopold, *Game Management* (New York: Scribners, 1933), p. vii.
[52]George Macinko, "Land Use and Urban Development," in Shepard and McKinley, p. 382.

well as its capacity to house and feed the billions of persons predicted for the future.

3. Ecological disasters and pollution threaten the health and safety of lakes, rivers, arable land, air, and ultimately human life itself.
4. Nuclear energy poses the danger of increased radiation and the consequent long-term damage to human beings in the form of cancer, leukemia, and genetic damage.
5. The rapid depletion of nonrenewable natural resources, such as gas and oil, threatens the life styles of most of the developed world, which depends on these resources for energy.

C. Energy, politics, and economics

1. Political and economic systems can either encourage or retard the wasteful use of resources and responsible planning with respect to population, pollution, and radiation.
2. Some argue that the free enterprise system will resolve the ecological crisis; others argue that there is no solution and that we must learn to live with the inevitable.
3. Survival at what price becomes a major moral issue in the midst of the crisis.

D. Lifeboat ethics

1. Garrett Hardin has proposed a moral position known as "lifeboat ethics" in which he argues that limitations must be placed on individual freedom of choice if we wish to avoid disaster for all.
2. Hardin also argues that the survival of the richer, more responsible nations may require refusing to share with those nations that have not shown responsibility for ecological planning.
3. Other moralists argue for a right to a livable environment and for an understanding of the world community as a spaceship in which a balance of resources and use must be maintained.

E. Deep ecology and Asian wisdom

1. Asian religious traditons offer to some an understanding of the unity between the human person and nature that may provide a way out of the crisis.
2. In such an understanding, there is a democracy of all God's creatures. Exploitation of nature is replaced by contemplation of it. Life styles should be spiritual, not oriented to accumulation of goods.
3. The "Buddhist economics" of E. F. Schumacher suggests a reduced level of consumption as a means to an increased sense of well-being.

F. What can be done?

1. There are many planks in an "ecological platform" suggesting practical courses of action that can be taken, such as provision of more birth control information, support for public transportation, more reliance on solar power, and encouragement for local, self-sufficient farming.
2. Use of the automobile poses the most immediate and practical problem for most Americans. Reducing reliance on the family car can make a significant impact on the ecological situation.
3. Individuals as well as social systems must respond to the crisis. If human beings cannot live by bread alone, what kind of life styles will be appropriate for persons attempting to be ecologically responsible?

SUGGESTED READINGS

Barbour, Ian G., ed. *Earth Might Be Fair.* Englewood Cliffs, N.J.: Prentice-Hall, 1972.

Essays by a number of theologians, scientists, and philosophers on the relation between ethics, religion, and ecology.

Blackstone, William T., ed. *Philosophy and Environmental Crisis.* Athens: Univ. of Georgia Press, 1974.

Philosophical essays on ethics and ecology.

De Bell, Garrett, ed. *The Environmental Handbook.* New York: Ballantine, 1970.

A collection of some of the seminal articles on environmental problems.

Ophuls, William. *Ecology and the Politics of Scarcity.* San Francisco: Freeman, 1977.

An exploration of the political problems of coping with scarcity of resources. A plea for a steady-state economy.

Shepard, Paul, and McKinley, Daniel, eds. *The Subversive Science: Essays Toward an Ecology of Man.* Boston: Houghton-Mifflin, 1969.

A collection of essays from quite diverse sources on a multitude of aspects of the ecology question.

Wogaman, J. Philip, ed. *The Population Crisis and Moral Responsibility.* Washington, D.C.: Public Affairs Press, 1973.

A collection of philosophical and religious essays dealing specifically with the problem of population explosion.

17

War
and the Quest
for Peace

The world was divided into two parties which were trying to destroy each other because they both wanted the same thing, the liberation of the oppressed, the abolition of violence, and the establishment of a lasting peace. *

THERMONUCLEAR POWER

The problem of war in the thermonuclear age is one of the most urgent of the moral questions facing modern persons. The problem is incredibly complicated, and persons of intelligence and understanding hold different positions in part because of our inability to predict the future with any certainty. As we saw in the last chapter, the control and use of energy is much more than a scientific issue. When we have the power to use energy, particularly nuclear energy, deliberately against those we call our enemies, we face a moral and human problem of the first order. Decisions regarding its use will affect social, political, and economic relationships and may well determine the course of history and the fate of all mankind.

Weapons of Destruction

A single twenty-megaton H-bomb is said to deliver "more explosive power than that of all the weapons used by all nations for all purposes during all the years of World War II."[1] We are told that one of the thermonuclear or hydrogen bombs could destroy any city in existence. In addition to complete destruction over something like a hundred square miles, the radioactive fallout might settle on an area of many thousands of square miles and make it uninhabitable for a considerable time. We have moved in a few

---

*Hermann Hesse, "If the War Goes On Another Two Years," in *Little Victories, Big Defeats,* compiled by Georgess McHargue (New York: Dell, 1974), p. 4.
[1]David Rittenhouse Inglis, "The Nature of Nuclear War," in *Nuclear Weapons and the Conflict of Conscience,* ed. John C. Bennett (New York: Scribners, 1962), p. 43.

decades from a condition of power scarcity to a condition of power surplus and potential overkill. The United States and the Soviet Union have between them 14,000 strategic nuclear warheads, enough to destroy every city in the world seven times over.[2] Weapons of destruction have piled up so fast that the balance-of-power principle of the last century has been replaced by a balance-of-terror strategy, in which the threat of massive retaliation and total annihilation is stressed as a deterrence to enemy attack. The United States could currently destroy the Soviet Union many times over with its present arsenal of weapons, even if it were attacked first.

In addition to the armaments in the two superpowers, there has been a massive buildup of weapons of destruction among the smaller nations, each of which wants its own nuclear stockpile as a defense against the nuclear weaponry of other countries. Among these smaller states it is estimated that there are 500 additional nuclear weapons.[3] The spread of weapons to many different nations increases the risk that one or more of them will accidentally or purposely set off a chain-reaction war. A limited conflict between nonsuper powers might easily get out of hand: one nation, fearing for its very survival, might unleash a nuclear attack. A superpower might feel compelled, should its client state suffer severely on a conventional battlefield, to use nuclear weapons to save the situation.

Beyond even the dangers of escalating a limited war into all-out nuclear confrontation, there are the equally terrifying dangers of a nuclear war breaking out by (1) accident, through failure or mistake of some official or mechanism, or even by a strategically placed official who becomes nervous and loses his head; (2) by miscalculation, when one side in a dispute misjudges the point at which the other side would take a stand, refuses to be pushed further, and uses any and every means to defend national interests; and (3) by blackmail or terrorism, in which a fanatical group holds the world hostage to nuclear detonation to gain a political end. (A recent bestseller created a fictional story of the placing of a thermonuclear bomb in New York City by a leader of a small nation to force the United States to recognize a Palestinian state.)

WAR AS AN ANACHRONISM

The underpinnings of logic that have served historically to justify resort to war as the lesser of several evils have shifted or, in their traditional form, quite disappeared. Victory has been deprived of its historical meaning in total war with the new weapons, for the "victor" is likely to sustain such devastation as to lack the means of imposing his will upon the "vanquished."

---

[2]Ruth Leger Sivard, "Social Costs and the Arms Race," *The Nation* (June 17, 1978), p. 731.
[3]Sivard, p. 731.

And yet to accomplish this end . . . is the rational motive of war. Democratic participation or consent in a war decision is rendered most unmeaningful at the very time popular involvement in the devastation of war has reached an unprecedented maximum.

The history of war and man's attitudes about it should be reexamined in the light of these developments. . . . Such investigation might reveal how military planning became divorced from political planning and war became an end in itself rather than a means of achieving more or less rational political ends. . . .

That mankind should have carried the values and precepts of the age of firearms into the thermonuclear age represents a far greater anachronism than the one represented by his carrying the values and precepts of the age of chivalry into the age of firearms. Anachronisms are preeminently the business of historians. . . . Lacking a Cervantes, historians might with their own methods help to expose what may well be the most perilous anachronism in history.

C. Vann Woodward, "The Age of Reinterpretation," in *The Debate Over Thermonuclear Strategy,* ed. Arthur I. Waskow (Boston: Heath, 1965), p. 9.

C. Vann Woodward is Sterling Professor History at Yale University. Best known for his historical studies of the South, he is the author of The Strange Career of Jim Crow.

"JUST WAR" THEORY

The horrors of nuclear war, with its potential for unlimited destruction around the globe, must be set against the background of war as a traditional way of resolving disputes between groups of people, from kinship groups to nations. Wars have been fought using stones, clubs, spears, and bows as well as with swords, rifles, tanks, and conventional bombs.

Moral Criteria

War has been such a common recourse throughout human history that even the religious traditions of the West have produced sophisticated arguments on its behalf. The most important of these defenses of war invoke a crucial distinction between a just and an unjust war. Certain moral criteria must be met if a war is to be regarded as just and an individual regarded as obligated to fight if called. In the medieval period, for a war to be just, three general conditions had to be met: (1) a legitimate authority must declare the war, (2) it must be fought for a just cause, and (3) the means must be proportional to the end, that is, the good the war will achieve must outweigh the evil it will also produce.

More recently, these three points have been expanded into seven by Joseph McKenna.[4] He believes a just war must meet the following conditions: (1) it must be declared by recognized authority, (2) the seriousness of the injury suffered by the enemy must be proportional to the damage suffered by the other side, (3) the harm inflicted on the aggressor must be real and immediate, (4) there must be a reasonable chance of winning the conflict, (5) war must be a last resort to resolving the dispute, (6) the participants must have morally laudable intentions, and (7) the means employed to wage the war must be moral.

A crucial assumption made by just war theories is that each nation or sovereign state is justified in defending itself from attack against its borders or vital interests. It has also been traditionally assumed that wars between nation-states will affect only the entities directly involved and only those who are officially designated as and prepared to be combatants.

Does the "Just War" Justify Too Much?

Some moral philosophers are now arguing that these assumptions are no longer valid and that it is now virtually impossible to meet the seven conditions for a just war listed above. Donald A. Wells in particular has examined each of the seven conditions in the light of modern nuclear war and found them wanting.[5] With respect to the war being declared by a duly constituted authority, he points out that this criterion does not distinguish morally between one authority and the next. Hitler was a duly constituted authority as were Idi Amin and Josef Stalin. Is any war they declare therefore just? Was the United States' participation in the Vietnam War unjust inasmuch as it was never officially declared by the president? Why should the decision to wage war be left to an individual about whose wisdom or moral values we are not required to make a judgment?

With respect to the proportionality of violence used by the enemy determining the degree of violence used by the other side, Wells argues that

[4]Joseph McKenna, "Ethics and War: A Catholic View," *American Political Science Review* (September 1960), pp. 647–658.
[5]Donald A. Wells, "The 'Just War' Justifies Too Much," in *Religion for a New Generation*, 2nd ed., eds. Jacob Needleman, A. K. Bierman, and James A. Gould (New York: Macmillan, 1977), pp. 346–358.

in modern war it is impossible to determine what is a just proportion of violence. Is the bombing of civilians (at Hiroshima and Nagasaki) justified in proportion to the potential loss of soldiery if the war was prolonged or in proportion to the American lives already lost? Is the threat to the American way of life so great that it would justify the annihilation of all its communistic opponents? Ernest W. Lefever has claimed that genetic damage from a nuclear war, which might affect 20 percent of the world's population, "is well within the range of what a civilized society is prepared to tolerate." To refrain from using nuclear war when the alternative is communist enslavement is morally unacceptable and thus justifies resort to war. "A policy designed to save ten thousand persons from possible future death by radioactivity, which had the actual effect of inviting the death of ten million persons or the enslavement of a hundred million persons today, could hardly be called morally responsible or politically wise."[6]

Wells' rebuttal to Lefever would be that if the proportionality criterion is so flexible that it does not exclude a Hiroshima or nuclear mega-death, then it fails to differentiate justifiable use of violence from unjustifiable. It begs the question of whether any conceivable scale of violence would be unacceptable as long as the offended party feels its values and interests are of paramount importance and will be seriously undermined by a victory by the enemy. "Unless some case could be made that the modern values are infinitely more worthy than medieval values, the immense increase in human destruction that our wars now involve makes proportionality absolutely inapplicable."[7]

With respect to war as a last resort, Wells points out that "to permit war as a last resort is not the same as requiring that the last resort be taken."[8] If modern war necessarily means the death of millions of persons, most of whom will be noncombatants, why is it justified to resort to it at all? Are there any causes so inherently virtuous that their defence would justify the kind of massive annihilation or long-term genetic damage modern nuclear war would create? If war of this kind could be justified, would it also be possible to talk about justifiable genocide or justifiable murder of children? In other words, given the massive destruction of modern war, what values are so supreme and important that they justify resort to war in any case?

This question is directly related to the condition that a just war must be fought with the right intentions. Certainly the preservation of a nation-state could not, in and of itself, justify resort to war. Are all nation-states equally virtuous? Wells asks, "Is the preservation of the state so incontrovertibly significant that the resort to war to save it is always an act of

[6]Ernest W. Lefever, "Facts, Calculation, and Political Ethics," *The Moral Dilemma of Nuclear Weapons: Essays from Worldview* (New York: Council on Religion and International Affairs, 1961), pp. 41–43.
[7]Wells, in Needleman, et al., p. 351.
[8]Wells, in Needleman, et al., p. 352.

right intention?"[9] In a modern nuclear war, one might not directly intend to kill noncombatants, but the weaponry used is known ahead of time to be such that it cannot but help kill them. A soldier whose arrow kills an innocent bystander could be excused because he didn't know or intend what would happen. The decision to employ nuclear destruction on an enemy city is made in full knowledge and therefore with the intention of destroying all its inhabitants.

Wells concludes his analysis by arguing that the theory of the just war justifies too much. As long as nation-states have an unqualified right to survival, "given that the state is more important than the individual, indeed, that the state is more important than an infinite number of individuals, mere human death will never be a significant argument against war."[10] Those who wish to oppose the resort to war, especially nuclear war, will have to establish the superiority of values other than national interest or preservation of a particular way of life.

Surrender as a Moral Option?

If the value of life itself or the preservation of human beings who can still struggle to make life meaningful is a more important value than annihilating millions to preserve national interest, then it becomes possible to consider surrender to a foreign power as a moral alternative to war. Although surrender has been traditionally unthinkable for many persons, those who advocate it in the nuclear age point out that it would not only avoid nuclear destruction but would permit the humanizing or tempering of an oppressor's system of control. Even totalitarian dictatorships have changed over time, especially as they have extended their power over many diverse countries. Although no one would want to minimize the short-run effects of living under a brutal dictatorship, the long-run possibilities for change could still justify surrender rather than resort to all-out nuclear war.

OBSTACLES TO PEACE

Innate Aggression

These considerations, according to some, overlook basic facts of human nature as well as the interests that are served by a military posture that depends on the threat of war. One such fact, it is claimed, is that war is naturally caused by an innate, aggressive instinct in humans and that it will

---

[9]Wells, in Needleman, et al., p. 354.
[10]Wells, in Needleman, et al., p. 358.

continue unless the instinct is redirected or sublimated. This view has been developed recently by Robert Ardrey and Konrad Lorenz.[11] Although both men recognize the elements of learning and adjustment to conditions, they believe that the instinctive drive is the most important factor. This thesis has been vigorously challenged and refuted by various anthropologists, zoologists, and other scientists[12] who point out that human beings adapt to their group's traditional way of life and that warlike behavior is the product of the institutions and the history to which the individuals have been conditioned.

The Necessity of Deterrence

Even if one were to discount the claim that war is inevitable because human beings are innately aggressive, it would be harder to reject the insistence that aggressors, nevertheless, must be deterred. While disclaiming any intention to initiate an armed conflict, proponents of some kind of minimal deterrence capability point out that in the absence of deterrence conquest through arms becomes too tempting to resist. They argue that each nation must have enough arms to convince a potential aggressor that, should it initiate conflict, it would suffer more damage than would be acceptable. Disarmament should never be carried so far that deterrence is undermined. As Thomas C. Schelling puts it, "If disarmament is to work, it has got to improve deterrence and to stabilize deterrence. Until a much greater community of interest exists in the world than is likely in this generation, war will have to be made unprofitable. It cannot be made impossible."[13] If Schelling is correct, then peace should not be sought necessarily through arms reduction. It might even be prudent to build up one's arsenal with increasingly deadlier weapons so as to maximize one's deterrent force. "If the consequences of transgression are plainly bad—bad for all parties, and little dependent on who transgresses first—we can take the consequences for granted and call it a 'balance of prudence.'"[14]

Successful deterrence depends, of course, on each side being able to maintain unswerving commitment to peace on the one hand while conceiving deadlier and more effective weapons of destruction on the other. It also assumes that each nation will know when it has reached the minimal level of deterrence necessary for security and will be committed to stopping at just that point. The calculus of deterrence cannot allow too much room for the possibility that energetically pursuing deterrent capability might trigger an accidental release of arms.

[11]Robert Ardrey, *The Territorial Imperative* (New York: Atheneum, 1966); Konrad Lorenz, *On Aggression* (New York: Harcourt, 1966).
[12]See M. F. Ashley Montagu, ed. *Man and Aggression* (New York: Oxford Univ. Press, 1968).
[13]Thomas C. Schelling, "The Role of Deterrence in Total Disarmament," in *The Debate Over Thermonuclear Strategy*, ed. Arthur I. Waskow (Boston: Heath, 1965), p. 99.
[14]Schelling, in Waskow, p. 99.

The Military-Industrial Complex

One factor often overlooked in moral consideration of obstacles to peace is the enormous investment in war and war preparation of many thousands of persons and businesses. Large sections of the population have a vested interest in a military economy—the big corporations with billion dollar contracts for weapons, the big unions with large numbers of workers in defense plants, and the great number of persons trained in the arts of war. More than two hundred retired officers, including more than a score of generals and admirals, are reported to be on the payroll of one large aircraft corporation. Military men sit on the highest councils of state and have a powerful influence on Congress and on foreign policy.

In his farewell address to the nation when leaving the presidency, Dwight D. Eisenhower, a former general, warned the nation about the dangers of the military-industrial complex. (Some would now add the academic community since many of its researchers are doing work with military implications and are funded by the federal government.) Eisenhower pointed out that in a state of military insecurity, "there is a recurring temptation to feel that some spectacular and costly action could become the miraculous solution to all current difficulties."[15] When that action directly contributes to the profits of major industrial firms and en- hances the prestige and employment of people in the military, there is the danger, Eisenhower warned, of abuse of power.

Given the enormous complexity of much military equipment and the secrecy that must surround its details in the name of national security, it becomes difficult for someone in Congress, let alone a citizen without specialized knowledge, to know how to raise critical questions about the need for what the military requests. The propriety of asking such questions is further suspect when the request carries with it overtones of military defense against our enemies as well as economic benefit to thousands of persons. The result, as Eisenhower anticipated, has often been the pur- chase of weapons systems that are obsolete almost as soon as they are off the assembly line and are often incapable of meeting the standards set for them. Senator William Proxmire has argued before the United States Sen- ate that:

> [W]e are paying far too much for the military hardware we buy . . .
> and perhaps even more shocking, we often do not get the weapons
> and products we pay the excessive prices for. . . . Of eleven major
> weapons systems begun during the 1960s, only two of the eleven
> electronic components of them performed up to standard. [Proxmire
> added that these systems] typically cost 200 to 300 percent more than
> the Pentagon estimated. They were and are delivered two years later

---

[15]Dwight D. Eisenhower, "Farewell Radio and Television Address to the American People, January 17, 1961," Parts III–IV, in *Arms, Industry and America,* ed. Kenneth Davis (The Refer- ence Shelf, vol. 43, no. 1). (New York: Wilson, 1971), p. 77.

than expected. The after-tax profits of the aerospace industry, of which these contractors were the major companies, were 12.5 percent higher than for American industry as a whole. Those firms with the worst records appeared to receive the highest profits. . . . This is what I mean when I refer to the "unwarranted influence by the military-industrial complex.[16]

EFFORTS TO ACHIEVE PEACE

Religious Objections to War

Like warfare itself, criticism of war and efforts to achieve peace reach far back in history. The founders of the great world religions have been opposed to war, and pacifism has been found among adherents of Buddhism, Hinduism, Confucianism, and Christianity. Some prophets among the Hebrews looked forward to a time when people would mold their spears into pruning hooks and their swords into plowshares and would no longer know war. Among the early Greeks, opposition to war was found mainly among the Stoics. The early Christians stressed nonviolence and refused to bear arms, but this stand, along with that of the Stoics, was abandoned when certain emperors embraced Stoicism (Marcus Aurelius) or Christianity (Constantine). As we have seen, Christians in the medieval period sought to apply principles of justice to the conduct of war and to set limits to it in practice. Various religious sects or groups of Christians, such as the Anabaptists, Mennonites, and Quakers, have refused to bear arms. In the twentieth century, sentiment against war has been growing among Protestant denominations as well as among Roman Catholics.

A recent example of the religious communities' response to war and disarmament is a statement of the Vatican to the United Nations in 1976. It

absolutely condemns the use of weapons of mass destruction [and the armaments race is] to be condemned unreservedly. [It is a danger in terms of the use of these weapons, an injustice,] for it constitutes a violation of law by asserting the primacy of force and a form of theft, [a mistake since other forms of employment are possible and a folly since a system of international relations based on fear] is a kind of collective hysteria . . . which does not achieve its end [i.e., security].[17]

[16]William Proxmire, "Blank Check for the Military," address delivered before United States Senate, March 10, 1969, in Davis, pp. 82–83.

[17]"The Catholic Church and Disarmament," Statement of the Holy See on Disarmament from "Strengthening of the Role of the United Nations in the Field of Disarmament," in *The Nuclear Challenge to Christian Conscience,* ed. James Wallis (Washington, D.C.: Sojourners, 1978), p. 5.

The document concludes its condemnation of the armaments race as being against humanity and God on two fundamental moral grounds:

> When the damage caused is disproportionate to the values we are seeking to safeguard, "it is better to suffer injustice than to defend ourselves" (Pius XII) [and] it constitutes a provocation which explains— psychologically, economically, and politically—the emergence and growth of another kind of competition: the small armaments race. Terrorism, in fact, often appears to be the last means of defense against this abuse of power by the large nations and a violent protest against the injustice created or perpetuated by the use or threat thereof on the part of better-armed states.[18]

MARK TWAIN'S "WAR PRAYER"

O Lord our God, help us to tear their soldiers to bloody
shreds with our shells;
help us to cover their smiling fields with the pale forms
of their patriot dead;
help us to drown the thunder of the guns with the shrieks of
their wounded, writhing in pain;
help us to lay waste their humble homes with a hurricane of fire;
help us to wring the hearts of their unoffending widows with
unavailing grief;
help us to turn them out roofless with their little children to
wander unfriended the wastes of their desolated land in rags and,
hunger and thirst, sports of the sunflames of summer
and the icy
winds of winter, broken in spirit, worn with travail, imploring
Thee for the refuge of the grave and denied it—
for our sakes who adore Thee, Lord,
blast their hopes, blight their lives, protract their bitter
pilgrimage, make heavy their steps, water their way
with their tears, stain the white snow with the blood of
their wounded feet!
We ask it, in the spirit of love, of Him Who is the Source of Love,
and Who is the ever-faithful refuge and friend of all that are
sore beset and seek His aid with humble and contrite hearts.
AMEN.

Mark Twain, *The War Prayer* (New York: Harper, 1970).

---

[18]Wallis, p. 5.

Mark Twain (Samuel Clemens, 1835–1910) was one of America's most renowned writers. He was an essayist, novelist, and humorist best known for The Adventures of Tom Sawyer *and the* Adventures of Huckleberry Finn. The War Prayer, *a bitter attack on war, was not published until after his death.*

National Sovereignty Reexamined

Even apart from religious opposition, the revulsion against war is spreading rapidly among some young people but is by no means confined to the young (although it might be argued that some opposition to the military is motivated by a personal desire to avoid military service for selfish reasons). Opposition to the Vietnam War made it possible for many Americans to uncouple the traditional bond between patriotism and support for any war in which American forces were engaged.

Nevertheless, the tough moral questions concern the possibility of achieving peace while maintaining active responsibility for freedom and justice in the world. One of the most important, if not *the* most important moral and social issue of our time, has to do with the relationship of states or nations to one another. Are we destined in the near future to move into an era of peace, international understanding, and goodwill, or will more terrible wars threaten the future of our civilization and perhaps of humanity? For the first time in human history, humanity has the power to change its own nature and even to destroy all life.

The dropping of two atomic bombs on Japan in 1945 not only brought World War II to a sudden and decisive end but changed the nature of warfare itself, as we have seen. Unless we can revise our old-fashioned ways of thinking and acting, overcome our cultural lag, bring our morals up to date, and apply them to the new conditions that we face, the new power may destroy us.

Some would maintain that war is a phenomenon that can be eliminated. It is a social phenomenon like dueling and slavery. Just as these have been eliminated from most of the earth's surface, so war can be eliminated. In fact war already has been eliminated from considerable areas—in the fifty states in the United States and among the nations within the British Commonwealth, for example. Disputes arise between political units, but no longer do the peoples even dream of settling these disputes by warfare. People, however, do tend to become belligerent when threatened and especially when their emotions are stirred by aggressive leaders.

An especially obstinate fallacy is the view that the nation-state is the last stage of social evolution and that nothing must be done to impair the sovereignty of the nation. In fact, the nation may *not* be the last and highest expression of social progress. The times in which we live call for some form of world community and government since a world of competing and unrestrained national sovereignties is a world of conflict and periodic wars. The world is too interdependent for any nation to be the exclusive judge of policies and actions, especially when its national interests are involved. While nationalism and patriotism can be good, they can also be perverted and overemphasized. They can lead to the belief that the state can do no wrong or that its interests are superior to the interests of the world community.

Demilitarizing the Power Struggle

A dangerous practice, one that tends to lead directly to war, is the old game of power politics. It is closely related to the concept of national sovereignty, and it frequently takes the form of economic imperialism. Either economic or political considerations may be dominant, but the result is much the same. The drives for power and strategic position, for prestige, for sources of raw material, and for markets have been major causes of war. During the last few decades, ideological factors or wide differences in social philosophies have added to world tension.

Given these factors, the modern game of power politics is played with military might. The balance of power has been identified with the balance of terror. Any diminution in the capacity to terrorize a potential enemy might be taken, according to some, as a sign of weakness

> and an invitation to a Communist threat. . . . If all nuclear weapons suddenly ceased to exist, much of the world would immediately be laid open to conquest by the masses of Russian and Chinese men under conventional arms. [The logical conclusion of this line of thinking is clear.] We are against [disarmament] because we *need* our armaments—all of those we presently have, and more. We need weapons for both the limited and the unlimited war. . . . [19]

The only way to avoid reaching this logical conclusion, according to critics, is to demilitarize the power struggle. Recognizing the need for an international police force and the need for each nation to have enough force to secure obedience to its laws, Walter Millis, among others, has asked whether the international organization of power on a police force

[19]Barry M. Goldwater, "Why Not Victory?" in Waskow, pp. 68–69.

basis rather than on a military basis can develop to the point where it becomes generally "recognized as both practicable and desirable?"[20]

To achieve such a goal, Millis concedes, would presuppose a system of internally sovereign governments each with sufficient power to enforce domestic order. But such force could be kept within the bounds necessary to ensure that it could not be a military threat to its neighbors. The arms race would no longer be necessary, and thus the world would be spared the ever-present threat of nuclear catastrophe.

Millis admits that the appeal to a police force has serious drawbacks, among them its rigidity and its vulnerability to subversion and police-state tactics internal to each nation. He concedes that "nobody would think twice about it except for the appalling nature of the only apparent alternative—a thermonuclear 'balance of terror' and a resultant arms race likely to break down into a catastrophe worse than anything that even the police-form type of organization might invite."[21] Nevertheless, he argues, in practice, permitting only a police-force type of organization has worked. He points to the arrangements in Latin America. Most Latin American countries arm primarily for internal purposes. While external political interests have produced rebellions and subversion in other countries, this has been done for the most part without resort to war as such. Millis concludes that

> one may cite this as a case in which a considerable group of sovereign nation-states, varying widely in size, wealth, ethnic and linguistic backgrounds, social organization, and economic need, with an extensive tradition of organized warfare among themselves, has reached a tacit conclusion that organized war is no longer a necessary or useful institution in ordering their power relationships, and has in effect abandoned it.[22]

Although such a demilitarization of the power struggle does not solve the problems of economic or political injustice or the problems of freedom under dictatorships, it at least makes their solutions depend on something less than nuclear annihilation.

Psychological Strategies

Another way of avoiding the nuclear consequences of power politics played with military force is to approach the problem from a psychological angle. When people prepare for war and think of war, they tend to create

[20]Walter Millis, "Permanent Peace," in Walter Millis, Reinhold Niebuhr, Harrison Brown, James Real, and William O. Douglas, *A World Without War* (New York: Washington Square Press, 1961), pp. 133–134.

[21]Millis, et al., pp. 133–134.

[22]Millis, et al., p. 139.

war. That is the danger in what is known as "the military mind." When people live in a warlike atmosphere, the tinder is always there and a small spark may easily ignite it. Two persons may quarrel over a trivial thing; under ordinary circumstances the matter will blow over or be settled in some peaceful way. But let these same persons quarrel while each holds a loaded gun, and the chance for a peaceful settlement is much less.

Applied to nations, can we expect one nation to be secure by being stronger than any other nation without expecting the other nation to think the same way? If one nation becomes the strongest for a time, must not some other nation overtake it if it is to become secure in its turn? When other nations fear, they too begin to arm to the teeth and to combine against those whom they fear. This creates a vicious circle that has led to war in the past and is likely to do so in the future. Fear and the desire to be strong lead to national rivalry, then to power politics and imperialism, and finally to war.

In an age in which scientific discoveries are taking place so rapidly, how can we have any assurance that we can always be the strongest nation? Types of warfare become obsolete almost overnight. The atomic scientists tell us that any advantage we may possess today is likely to be temporary.

Given the psychological nature of much of the arms race, it is not surprising to find some psychologists bringing to bear on the problem findings from their field of study. One such scientist is Charles E. Osgood.

> Most Americans [he argues] are filled with the basically irrational conviction that the only way to avoid military conflict with the Communist world is to prepare for it. . . . Unconsciously projecting our own norms and values, we feel threatened when they are not adhered to and attribute it to the essential boorishness and deceit of others. By encouraging self-delusion and condoning a double standard of national morality, our psycho-logic has created an oversimplified world inhabited by angels and bogy men.[23]

Osgood asks us to picture two husky men on a long and rigid seesaw balanced above an abyss. As each man makes a move, the other must counter it. As they move progressively outward, the unbalancing effect of each step becomes greater and the more agile each man must be to maintain the precarious equilibrium. Both men become increasingly fearful but neither is willing to admit it for fear that the other will then take advantage of him.

On the assumption that both men (or nations) would like to get out of this increasingly untenable and dangerous situation, Osgood suggests some psychologically realistic steps they can take. They need to engage in a "peace offensive" whose goal is the reduction of tensions and the creation of an atmosphere in which an end to nuclear terror can be achieved. A

---

[23]Charles E. Osgood, "Reciprocal Initiative," in Waskow, pp. 69–70.

unilateral act by one side must be seen by the other side as reducing his external threat. It must be accompanied by an explicit invitation to reciprocate. In addition, a unilateral act of disarmament must be carried through with or without a prior commitment by the other side to reciprocate (thus disarming the opponent's claim that you are not seriously interested in pursuing peace). To be successful, unilateral acts must also be planned in phases and must be widely publicized in advance. Nevertheless, Osgood concedes, unilateral acts cannot be carried to the point, without reciprocation, where no deterrent capability exists nor any defense of a nation's "heartland."

The strongest objection to this effort to achieve peace is that it is not realistic enough, that it weakens a nation and prepares it to be overrun by its enemies. Osgood responds to the charge that his suggestion is idealistic by claiming that "the real idealists today, as Marc Raskin put it to me so well, are those who actually believe that the arms race can be continued indefinitely without something going wrong, who actually believe that the men behind the nuclear weapons are suprarational and will behave like so many computers."[24] Only by taking carefully calculated, unilateral steps toward disarmament can nations get off the dangerously teetering board that threatens to dump them all into the abyss of a thermonuclear holocaust. One such step might be the commitment to a series of strategic arms limitation treaties, which have traveled a rocky road in recent years. These treaties must be perceived as being in the best interest of all nations, not as ways of weakening one nation as another builds up its arsenal.

Conversion to a Peacetime Economy

Domestically, as we have seen, the military-industrial establishment accounts for a large sector of the economy. Demilitarizing the nation will have significant consequences for the economy unless the consequences are carefully prepared for. Recently, many analysts are turning to the issue of converting industries now tied to military production into peacetime or domestically useful production. Presently, it is estimated, the Pentagon has 3.4 million members in the armed services and 1.3 million civilian workers in seventy countries. There are 3.8 million industrial workers whose work is wholly tied to war production; millions more are indirectly dependent on the defense budget. Half of all scientists and engineers in private industry work in the aerospace and defense fields.[25] Military production managed by the Department of Defense is the largest planned economy outside the Soviet Union: its property amounts to 10 percent of the

---

[24]Osgood, in Waskow, p. 79.
[25]Richard J. Barnet, from *The Economy of Death,* as cited in Davis, p. 219.

assets of the entire American economy (it owns 39 million acres of land) and it is richer than any small nation in the world.[26]

One crucial result of this degree of military production is increasing inflation.

> Heavy military spending generates buying power without producing an equivalent supply of economically useful goods for the market. The excess of disposable income adds to pressure on prices and in time becomes a prescription for intractable inflation. A disproportionate number of its many victims are among the weakest members of society: the old suffer more than jobholders, the poor with marginal incomes more than the rich.[27]

In addition, productive capacity is shifted away from domestically and socially necessary goods to arms production.

By converting military production into other forms of production, many social ills can be cured at the same time that nuclear terror is eased. One analyst has argued that there are four areas of the civilian economy that desperately need the capital and skills now employed by the military: railroads, mass transit, resource recovery, and solar energy. With such conversion, he argues, they will generate far more jobs per $1 billion invested than the money now used by the Pentagon. Such conversion must be carefully planned; there will be necessary financial cushions to ease the change-over. But if conversion becomes a priority for the nation, the economic "blackmail" now used by some to dampen criticism of the military-industrial complex would be eradicated.[28]

International Organizations

Among the paths to peace are the growth of transnational or international organizations to promote cooperation among the nations, the general reduction of armaments, a growing sentiment in opposition to war, the growth of democracy, and the maintenance of full employment and a sense of security and well-being on the domestic scene. The twentieth century seems to be demanding some form of world community and order. Probably the nation-state is not destined to pass away soon. Just as it was superimposed on the family, tribe, or clan, thereby eliminating tribal warfare, transnational or international institutions need to be established as a step toward the elimination of wars between nations. The United Nations

---

[26]Robert J. Heilbroner, "Military America," a review of Seymour Melman's *Pentagon Capitalism: The Political Economy of War,* as cited in Davis, p. 143.

[27]Sivard, p. 731.

[28]William Winpisinger, "A Union Converts," in *Economic Conversion: From Military to Civilian Industry. Grapevine* 11, no. 7 (February 1980) (New York: Joint Strategy and Action Committee).

is a step in this direction. The world is so interdependent that acts in any one part of it affect the peoples in the rest of it.

World organizations will be necessary to give attention to issues that concern men and women everywhere or that are too far-reaching and important to be handled even by regional groups. The United Nations' Charter includes these words: "We the people of the United Nations, determined to save succeeding generations from the scourge of war, which twice in our lifetime has brought untold sorrow to mankind, and to reaffirm faith in fundamental human rights... have resolved to combine our efforts to accomplish these aims." If peace is to be secure, a strong world public opinion and a strengthening of the peace-keeping machinery of the world, including United Nations police forces, would appear to be necessary.

Although such organizations are important, of course, the spirit, the attitude, and the living faith that persons hold are of even greater importance. While the accident of birth makes a person a member of a nation, he or she is also a member of humanity. Persons can be loyal to humankind without being disloyal to their own state or kindred. When they feel that the rights of other groups are as sacred as those of their own, they are approaching moral maturity.

A former assistant Secretary of State has said, "Moral force does not move mountains, but it moves men to action, and by their action mountains can be moved—and civilizations built or destroyed."[29] There is a moral obligation facing persons of intelligence and goodwill to make a strenuous effort to transform the present international system into one that will be more effective in maintaining peace with freedom and justice for all without resorting to nuclear confrontation that might destroy all persons and values forever.

CHAPTER REVIEW

A. Thermonuclear power

1. Weapons of destruction: When we have the power to destroy every city in the world seven times over, we face a moral problem of the first order.

B. "Just war" theory

1. There have been historic attempts to develop moral criteria for distinguishing between just and unjust wars.
2. Some argue that in an age of nuclear weapons these criteria may justify too much.

[29]Ernest A. Gross, *The United Nations: Structure for Peace* (New York: Harper, 1962), p. 125.

3. It is even possible to consider surrender as a moral alternative to nuclear war.

C. Obstacles to peace

1. Innate aggression in the human species has been cited as a reason to believe wars can never be eliminated.
2. Others argue that every nation has a right and duty to maintain a minimal level of deterrent capability.
3. The military-industrial complex has a vested interest in maintaining an economy and attitude of war preparation.

D. Efforts to achieve peace

1. There have historically been many objections to war on religious grounds.
2. The supremacy of national sovereignty may need to be reexamined in the light of international implications of nuclear war.
3. Demilitarizing the power struggle may be one solution to war.
4. There are also psychological strategies that might help to defuse and de-escalate the arms race and the balance of terror on which it is based.
5. The economic interests of industries geared for war can be met by careful conversion to peacetime economies.
6. Finally, more attention must be given to international organizations like the United Nations if war with global consequences is to be avoided.

SUGGESTED READINGS

Barnet, Richard J. *The Economy of Death.* New York: Atheneum, 1969.

A study of the economic implications of war preparation.

Bennett, John C., ed. *Nuclear Weapons and the Conflict of Conscience.* New York: Scribners, 1962.

Ethical and religious problems raised by nuclear war.

Cousins, Norman. *In Place of Folly.* Rev. ed. New York: Washington Square Press, 1962.

An articulate plea for an end to nuclear weaponry by the former editor of the *Saturday Review.*

Kahn, Herman. *On Thermonuclear War.* Princeton: Princeton Univ. Press, 1960.

A physicist's defense of controlled thermonuclear war.

Ramsey, Paul. *The Just War: Force and Political Responsibility.* New York: Scribners, 1968.

A Protestant theologian's careful assessment and qualified defense of the "just war" theory.

Waskow, Arthur I., ed. *The Debate Over Thermonuclear Strategy.* Boston: Heath, 1965.

An excellent collection of essays on nuclear war covering a wide range of opinion and topics.

Epilogue

One choice persons can rarely make is the choice to refrain from making further choices. Life forces choices, from the trivial to the traumatic. It has always done so. A false nostalgia pervades the belief that in earlier times choices were easier because they were fewer or less complicated. Any time we are faced with alternative courses of action, only one of which can be chosen at that moment, the dilemma can be difficult, whether it involves deciding to leap from a cliff or stand and fight an onrushing mastodon, or to vote for or against a candidate who promises to end a war quickly by resort to nuclear weapons.

In this text we have invited you, as it were, to climb a tree, the ever-branching tree of moral reflection. We began at its roots, unearthing the sources from which moral thinking emerges—the life situation of each person which provides the conditions and produces the dilemmas of moral decision making. Each self is part of a unique tree with its own particular roots, patch of soil, and possibilities. But like other trees it only grows within the boundaries of certain common kinds of nourishment, soil conditions, temperature, and climate. These conditions place limits on the possibilities open to each individual tree and its parts. We discussed some of these issues under the rubric of freedom-determinism. We also noted that most people who read this text will have been brought up within the patch of soil we call the Jewish-Christian-Hellenistic tradition. While it is certainly possible to transplant oneself to new soil, a successful transplant, as well as continued growth in the same spot, will involve a solid understanding of the soil from which one's roots draw sustenance. For this reason we spent some time exploring the roots of Western moral teaching as it emerged from the confluence of Jewish, Christian, and Hellenistic sources.

As the tree grows, it produces buds on multiple and multiplying branches. Each bud, each individual, while drawing on a common heritage and linked to it historically, represents a new and unique expression of that heritage. Some branches and buds grow out from the trunk at bizarre angles, appearing almost to desire to separate from the tree entirely. In

383

moral thinking we can compare these buds to self-conscious, individual articulations of the meaning of morality, complete with the essential notions of the goal of moral action, its source and authority, and the criteria of its evaluation. Some of these buds flower into marvelously complex, coherent wholes, revealing, even while departing from, the principles of moral thought at the root and trunk of the tree. Although they are often more fully explicit and self-consciously worked out than are most of the flowers or buds nearer the trunk, these somewhat further-out flowers do not always feed back into the tree as directly as do their closer in kindred. We argued that while the moral philosophies of Kant, Hobbes, or Aquinas are invaluable in enabling us to reflect on morality with greater clarity, insight, and rigor, they do not always form the self-conscious foundation for everyday moral choice of the vast majority of people.

As the trunk of the tree grows, it must of course attend to its own nourishment if it is to be a strong and effective support for the branches it will send out from itself. As we grow as moral beings we must become conscious of our own selves, of who we are, how we define ourselves as healthy persons—sexually, biologically, medically, spiritually, rationally, and emotionally. Without that strong sense of self we cannot contribute to or be fed by relationships with others. We concentrated in our next section, therefore, on the moral problems involved in a growing consciousness of selfhood.

But selfhood cannot be achieved without a dialectical relation to other selves. The self is not self-sufficient. To become whole it must reach out to nurture and be nurtured in turn by other people. A trunk without branches may grow tall but it would be bare, spare, and desolate. It needs to feed itself into branches and be fed by their decoration and protection. We traced, therefore, the interrelationships which people have with those closest to them, concentrating on the tensions involved in maintaining a sense of individual integrity while remaining sensitive to the needs and demands of others with their own claims to individual integrity. The dilemmas of loving others sexually, familially, and in friendship were explored.

As the trunk branches out, branches themselves split and multiply. The healthier the tree the more profuse and diverse become the branchings, both opening upward and outward in a network of extraordinarily complex interconnections. While each twig is ultimately linked with the trunk, it becomes harder and harder to keep the links visible. Just so with the flowering of the person into a myriad of relations with other selves. There is a certain beauty, even utility, in being an integral part of a complex whole, but it becomes harder and harder to see how everyday decision making bears on or is affected by the multitudinous branches of one's social, political, economic, and ecological web. We have tried to discern and map out some of the linkages among people and the effect of their moral decisions on social, political, and economic structures.

Nevertheless the linkages remain and the tug of moral obligation can be felt as strongly in an economic decision about federal budget cutting as it can be in a decision to break off a relationship with someone to whom one has made previous binding commitments.

One of the most pressing and controversial areas of moral discussion today is the relation between moral certainty and tolerance for moral differences. Another area of heated discussion centers around the relation between "private" morality and public morality. When the two areas intersect passions are stirred which promise to affect not only personal life styles but also public policy. We hear much in the press about the decline of morality in western societies that were ostensibly once profoundly religious and whose moral norms flowed from a Judeo-Christian framework. The alleged decline of "family" values, of "rugged individualism," pride in craftmanship, self-reliance, respect for sexual restraint, and the virtue of hard work is decried. Much of this decline is traced to the rise of so-called "secular humanism," a set of values and beliefs *supposedly* rooted in a relativism which permits anything to be done as long as the individual desires it. The values of secular humanism, its critics claim, are a tolerance for diversity and a smug rejection of anything old-fashioned or traditional.

The clash between the defenders of the "traditional" values and their opponents (whatever the merits of each side) represents an age-old controversy between relativists and absolutists, some historical and contemporary examples of which we have mentioned in the text. The debate clearly has more than academic interest because many people see the values of their way of life and the life of their society caught up in the outcome of the controversy. Without denying that values must be grounded in some set of assumptions about the "absolute" nature of reality, we have maintained that a pluralism of perspectives on that reality is probably inevitable. This means in practical terms a tolerance for diverse moral choices within the general boundaries of rational discourse and humane consideration for others, as well as an ongoing exploration of the boundaries. To be more specific, to defend the dominance of particular values within sectors of private and public life requires the kind of moral awareness to which this text intends to contribute. As a thousand branches of the tree of moral development flourish, it becomes imperative, if one wishes to set forth a case for the relatively greater appropriateness of one branch, to understand not only its roots but its relation to the other branches with which, at some deeper level, it shares a common heritage. It may be the case, as the absolutists claim, that some branches are more firmly grounded, more directly linked to the roots, more capable of supporting life, than are other branches. But this claim can only be made persuasively from *within* the network of intertwining, tangled diversity. No branch can claim *without argument* or as self-evident a privileged, transcendent, or absolutist standpoint. It must make its claims heard by its power to appeal to other standpoints on the basis of coherence, reasonableness, consistency, viability, and "wisdom" about the human condition. We hope that one result of this text will be a greater sensitivity to and awareness of a multitude of moral standpoints and the pluralism of perspectives. The essential moral task is to understand the "logic" of each perspective, to grasp its assumptions and convictions about the source, purpose, and evaluation of moral behavior. Without this understanding, no defense of one's own moral stance is possible, let alone a critical evaluation of others. Simply appealing to "traditional" values or raising the spectre of moral collapse if absolute moral standards are not invoked bypasses the primary elements in moral responsibility. No moral system is so self-evidently true that it can dispense with the task of articulating its presuppositions and arguing for their logical consequences in moral decisions.

Simply talking about "values" or even "traditional values" is no solution to social or personal "decline." It is necessary to understand how moral philosophies develop, how they are informed and nourished, and how they guide a multitude of choices in many different areas of life. No one is excused from the obligation of moral reflection since life forces choices. But the people who have immersed themselves in the history of moral thought and have explored the many complicating and complex dimensions of moral choice in personal and social life will make a far more important contribution to the discussion of values than those who act simply upon reflex, instinct, or uninformed faith.

In addition to the debate between absolutists and relativists, traditionalists and secularists, there is the problem, unperceived by many, of the growing split between personal and social morality. It is quite common for many of us, upon hearing the word morality, to think almost exclusively of individual responsibilities to ourselves or to those persons with whom we are in direct contact. I know it is moral to tell the truth to my children and immoral to abuse the trust my boss has placed in me by cheating. Morality in this sense means individual uprightness and integrity. It is far more difficult for many people to see morality as reflected in the work of social systems and institutions. Consequently, it is difficult for many people to see their own responsibility for the decisions such institutions and systems make.

It has been argued by some that, for example, in dealing with poverty it is moral if I can bestow a gift upon a poor person but outside the scope of morality for an institution to channel money or aid from a richer segment of society to a poorer. In fact, some argue that morality is not being served when problems like poverty, injustice, unemployment, medical care, and the like are handled by institutions and structures rather than by individuals solely on a one-to-one basis. Their objection seems to be based on the belief that morality is a direct personal responsibility of one person for another. This means, to belabor our image of the tree once more, that each branch should touch every other branch directly if it is to bear moral responsibility for it.

In the latter part of the text we have clearly taken exception to this view. We have regarded the institutions and structures of a social order as vehicles through which individuals in community address the needs of people not in immediate contact with each member individually. Our underlying assumption has been that we as individuals are morally responsible in various degrees for all people whom our actions can affect even indirectly. Clearly the creation and maintenance of an institution is the result of human action. If an institution, such as the Congress of the United States, in turn acts in ways that have a direct effect on people, we as individuals bear a moral responsibility for the Congress, through electing representatives to it, lobbying for or against bills before it, and so forth.

It is obvious, of course, that in taking responsibility for institutional or social morality we find it difficult to trace the effects of our action through to their ultimate consequences. Personal choices are taken up along with hundreds of other choices and factors in determining the final outcome of a policy. As a result, many people become frustrated at not being able to control directly the practical effects of their intentions. An example often cited is that of the American welfare system, in which, many argue, good intentions have led to disastrous results because of the many layers of institutional bureaucracy necessary to carry out welfare policy. Whether their arguments for its ineffectiveness are accurate or not, many people feel that both donor and recipient of welfare are morally compromised because the system is impersonal and institutional. It is not uncommon for someone to respond generously to a single individual in need and to withhold support to many in need if that support is mandated by law and transmitted through social agencies.

We have taken the position that if one is to reject the moral rightness of using institutions and social structures to carry out moral goals, one must do so not only on the acknowledged assumption that only individual to individual morality is appropriate but also only after a thorough evaluation of the actual consequences of individual versus social morality. There *are* forceful arguments that can be made in defense of employing structures and institutions as the *most* effective way of implementing moral policy for large numbers of persons. To meet the moral challenges of the 1980s will require a thorough knowledge of the ways in which social institutions *have* been used as agents of social change and instruments of social policy. It will require an unprejudiced evaluation of the effects of social ethics on concrete groups of people and problems. Moral simplisms, unexamined, will not suffice. Only someone trained in the fundamentals of moral reflection will be able to penetrate behind the slogans and rhetoric likely to fill the political arena on this issue.

We have identified in our closing words just two of the living issues in ethics likely to be on the public agenda in the immediate future. There will be more such issues hardly anticipated at present. The purpose of this text will have been realized if you move out into the world of moral choice, private and public, with a deeper understanding of the need for roots in the moral wisdom of rational reflection and the experiences of others and a sensitivity for and appreciation of the variety of moral philosophies growing out of those common roots.

Index